The Cambridge Companion to the *Eroica* Symphony

This Companion provides orientation for those embarking on the study of Beethoven's much-discussed *Eroica* Symphony, as well as providing fresh insights that will appeal to scholars, performers and listeners more generally. The book addresses the symphony in three thematic sections, on genesis, analysis and reception history, and covers key topics including political context, dedication, sources of the symphony's inspiration, 'heroism' and the idea of a 'watershed' work. Critical studies of writings and analyses from Beethoven's day to ours are included, as well as a range of other relevant responses to the work, including compositions, recordings, images and film. The Companion draws on previous literature but also illuminates the work from new angles, based on new evidence and a range of approaches by twelve leading scholars in Beethoven research.

NANCY NOVEMBER is Associate Professor in Musicology at the University of Auckland. Recent publications include *Beethoven's Theatrical Quartets: Opp. 59, 74, and 95* (2013); a three-volume edition of fifteen string quartets by Beethoven's contemporary Emmanuel Aloys Förster (2016); and *Cultivating String Quartets in Beethoven's Vienna* (2017). She is the recipient of an Alexander von Humboldt Foundation Fellowship; and two Marsden Grants from the New Zealand Royal Society.

Cambridge Companions to Music

Topics

The Cambridge Companion to Ballet
Edited by Marion Kant

The Cambridge Companion to Blues and Gospel Music
Edited by Allan Moore

The Cambridge Companion to Choral Music
Edited by André de Quadros

The Cambridge Companion to the Concerto
Edited by Simon P. Keefe

The Cambridge Companion to Conducting
Edited by José Antonio Bowen

The Cambridge Companion to Eighteenth-Century Music
Edited by Anthony R. DelDonna and Pierpaolo Polzonetti

The Cambridge Companion to Electronic Music
Edited by Nick Collins and Julio D'Escriván

The Cambridge Companion to Film Music
Edited by Mervyn Cooke and Fiona Ford

The Cambridge Companion to French Music
Edited by Simon Trezise

The Cambridge Companion to Grand Opera
Edited by David Charlton

The Cambridge Companion to Hip-Hop
Edited by Justin A. Williams

The Cambridge Companion to Jazz
Edited by Mervyn Cooke and David Horn

The Cambridge Companion to Jewish Music
Edited by Joshua S. Walden

The Cambridge Companion to the Lied
Edited by James Parsons

The Cambridge Companion to Medieval Music
Edited by Mark Everist

The Cambridge Companion to Music in Digital Culture
Edited by Nicholas Cook, Monique Ingalls and David Trippett

The Cambridge Companion to the Musical, third edition
Edited by William Everett and Paul Laird

The Cambridge Companion to Opera Studies
Edited by Nicholas Till

The Cambridge Companion to Operetta
Edited by Anastasia Belina and Derek B. Scott

The Cambridge Companion to the Orchestra
Edited by Colin Lawson

The Cambridge Companion to Percussion
Edited by Russell Hartenberger

The Cambridge Companion to Pop and Rock
Edited by Simon Frith, Will Straw and John Street

The Cambridge Companion to Recorded Music
Edited by Eric Clarke, Nicholas Cook, Daniel Leech-Wilkinson and John Rink

The Cambridge Companion to the Singer-Songwriter
Edited by Katherine Williams and Justin A. Williams

The Cambridge Companion to the String Quartet
Edited by Robin Stowell

The Cambridge Companion to Twentieth-Century Opera
Edited by Mervyn Cooke

Composers

The Cambridge Companion to Bach
Edited by John Butt

The Cambridge Companion to Bartók
Edited by Amanda Bayley

The Cambridge Companion to the Beatles
Edited by Kenneth Womack

The Cambridge Companion to Beethoven
Edited by Glenn Stanley

The Cambridge Companion to Berg
Edited by Anthony Pople

The Cambridge Companion to Berlioz
Edited by Peter Bloom

The Cambridge Companion to Brahms
Edited by Michael Musgrave

The Cambridge Companion to Benjamin Britten
Edited by Mervyn Cooke

The Cambridge Companion to Bruckner
Edited by John Williamson

The Cambridge Companion to John Cage
Edited by David Nicholls

The Cambridge Companion to Chopin
Edited by Jim Samson

The Cambridge Companion to Debussy
Edited by Simon Trezise

The Cambridge Companion to Elgar
Edited by Daniel M. Grimley and Julian Rushton

The Cambridge Companion to Duke Ellington
Edited by Edward Green

The Cambridge Companion to Gershwin
Edited by Anna Celenza

The Cambridge Companion to Gilbert and Sullivan
Edited by David Eden and Meinhard Saremba

The Cambridge Companion to Handel
Edited by Donald Burrows

The Cambridge Companion to Haydn
Edited by Caryl Clark

The Cambridge Companion to Liszt
Edited by Kenneth Hamilton

The Cambridge Companion to Mahler
Edited by Jeremy Barham

The Cambridge Companion to Mendelssohn
Edited by Peter Mercer-Taylor

The Cambridge Companion to Monteverdi
Edited by John Whenham and Richard Wistreich

The Cambridge Companion to Mozart
Edited by Simon P. Keefe

The Cambridge Companion to Arvo Pärt
Edited by Andrew Shenton

The Cambridge Companion to Ravel
Edited by Deborah Mawer

The Cambridge Companion to the Rolling Stones
Edited by Victor Coelho and John Covach

The Cambridge Companion to Rossini
Edited by Emanuele Senici

The Cambridge Companion to Schoenberg
Edited by Jennifer Shaw and Joseph Auner

The Cambridge Companion to Schubert
Edited by Christopher Gibbs

The Cambridge Companion to Schumann
Edited by Beate Perrey

The Cambridge Companion to Shostakovich
Edited by Pauline Fairclough and David Fanning

The Cambridge Companion to Sibelius
Edited by Daniel M. Grimley

The Cambridge Companion to Richard Strauss
Edited by Charles Youmans

The Cambridge Companion to Michael Tippett
Edited by Kenneth Gloag and Nicholas Jones

The Cambridge Companion to Vaughan Williams
Edited by Alain Frogley and Aiden J. Thomson

The Cambridge Companion to Verdi
Edited by Scott L. Balthazar

Instruments

The Cambridge Companion to Brass Instruments
Edited by Trevor Herbert and John Wallace

The Cambridge Companion to the Cello
Edited by Robin Stowell

The Cambridge Companion to the Clarinet
Edited by Colin Lawson

The Cambridge Companion to the Guitar
Edited by Victor Coelho

The Cambridge Companion to the Harpsichord
Edited by Mark Kroll

The Cambridge Companion to the Organ
Edited by Nicholas Thistlethwaite and Geoffrey Webber

The Cambridge Companion to the Piano
Edited by David Rowland

The Cambridge Companion to the Recorder
Edited by John Mansfield Thomson

The Cambridge Companion to the Saxophone
Edited by Richard Ingham

The Cambridge Companion to Singing
Edited by John Potter

The Cambridge Companion to the Violin
Edited by Robin Stowell

The Cambridge Companion to

THE *EROICA* SYMPHONY

....

EDITED BY

Nancy November
The University of Auckland

CAMBRIDGE
UNIVERSITY PRESS

University Printing House, Cambridge CB2 8BS, United Kingdom

One Liberty Plaza, 20th Floor, New York, NY 10006, USA

477 Williamstown Road, Port Melbourne, VIC 3207, Australia

314–321, 3rd Floor, Plot 3, Splendor Forum, Jasola District Centre,
New Delhi – 110025, India

79 Anson Road, #06–04/06, Singapore 079906

Cambridge University Press is part of the University of Cambridge.

It furthers the University's mission by disseminating knowledge in the pursuit of
education, learning, and research at the highest international levels of excellence.

www.cambridge.org
Information on this title: www.cambridge.org/9781108422581
DOI: 10.1017/9781108524995

© Cambridge University Press 2020

First published 2020

Printed in the United Kingdom by TJ International Ltd. Padstow Cornwall

A catalogue record for this publication is available from the British Library.

Library of Congress Cataloging-in-Publication Data
Names: November, Nancy, editor.
Title: The Cambridge companion to the 'Eroica' symphony / edited by Nancy November.
Description: [1] | New York : Cambridge University Press, 2020. | Series: Cambridge compa-
nions to music | Includes bibliographical references.
Identifiers: LCCN 2019050812 (print) | LCCN 2019050813 (ebook) | ISBN 9781108422581
(hardback) | ISBN 9781108524995 (ebook)
Subjects: LCSH: Beethoven, Ludwig van, 1770–1827. Symphonies, no. 3, op. 55, E♭ major.
Classification: LCC ML410.B42 C12 2020 (print) | LCC ML410.B42 (ebook) | DDC 784.2/
184–dc23
LC record available at https://lccn.loc.gov/2019050812
LC ebook record available at https://lccn.loc.gov/2019050813

ISBN 978-1-108-42258-1 Hardback
ISBN 978-1-108-43557-4 Paperback

Contents

List of Illustrations   *page* xi
List of Musical Examples   xii
Notes on Contributors   xiv
Eroica *Chronology, 1770–2020*   xvii
Acknowledgements   xxii

Introduction
Nancy November   1

Part I Context and Genesis   5

1   Beethoven and Heroism in the Age of Revolutions
    Scott Burnham   7
2   Beethoven's 'Watershed'? *Eroica*'s Contexts and Periodisation
    Mark Ferraguto   24
3   The Symphony in Vienna and Abroad around 1800
    Erica Buurman   43
4   Genesis and Publication of the *Eroica*
    Federica Rovelli   61

Part II Analytical Approaches   79

5   Twentieth-Century Analytical Approaches
    to the First Movement
    William Drabkin   81
6   The Hero Who Practices Resignation: Beethoven's
    Eroica as 'Late' Work
    Vasili Byros   105
7   Registering the *Eroica*
    Nicholas Marston   139
8   After Invention: Traces and Materials in the *Eroica* Finale
    Elaine Sisman   157

Part III Reception   181

9   Who is the Hero? The Early Reception of the *Eroica*
    Beate Angelika Kraus   183
10 The *Eroica* in the Nineteenth and Twentieth Centuries
    Leon Botstein   198

x Contents

11 Performing, Arranging and Rearranging the _Eroica_: Then
   and Now
   Nancy November   221
12 The _Eroica_ Endures: Beethoven's Third Symphony
   in the Twenty-First Century
   Melanie Lowe   239

   Further Reading   256
   General Index   264

Illustrations

4.1   Kaspar Karl van Beethoven: letter to Breitkopf & Härtel,
       12 February 1805. D-BNba, Sammlung H. C. Bodmer,
       HCB Br 312   *page* 70

4.2   Wenzel Schlemmer: copyist's score of Beethoven's
       Incidental Music to Goethe's *Egmont*, Op. 84,
       supervised by the author, p. 125. D-BNba, NE 64   73

8.1   Beethoven: sketchbook Landsberg 6, p. 70.
       Notierungsbuch E 90, PL-Kj, Mus. ms. autogr.
       Beethoven Landsberg 6   167

Musical Examples

5.1 Beethoven, *Eroica* Symphony, Op. 55, outline of main motive in the cello part of the 'new theme' (after Halm, 'Der Fremdkörper', p. 481)   *page* 88

5.2 Beethoven, *Eroica* Symphony, Op. 55, bars 390–8, without second horn part   90

5.3 Beethoven, *Eroica* Symphony, Op. 55, bars 390–8, with implied dominant pedal and violin II conforming with horn II   90

5.4 Beethoven, *Eroica* Symphony, Op. 55, second-group themes related to principal motive   93

5.5 Beethoven, *Eroica* Symphony, Op. 55, comparison of bars 280–3 with bars 83–6 (after Cassirer, *Beethoven und die Gestalt*, p. 21)   94

5.6 Beethoven, *Eroica* Symphony, Op. 55, some passages built on vigorously repeated chords   96

5.7 Beethoven, *Eroica* Symphony, Op. 55, the different continuations, in the recapitulation and coda, of the theme from bars 57ff.   98

5.8 Heinrich Schenker, 'Beethoven's Third Symphony', Fig. 1: first movement, first middleground layer   100

5.9 Schenker, 'Beethoven's Third Symphony', Fig. 6: first movement, fourth middleground layer   101

5.10 Schenker 'Beethoven's Third Symphony', Fig. 10b and Fig. 13b: voice-leading details in the antecedent and consequent phrases of the theme at bars 83ff.   102

6.1 Beethoven, *Christus am Ölberge*, Op. 85, No. 5, recitativo, bars 18–30   107

6.2 Beethoven, *Eroica* Symphony, Op. 55, Allegro con brio, bars 1–11   107

6.3 *le–sol–fi–sol* schema-topic: 113

   a) Wolfgang Amadeus Mozart, Requiem in D minor, K. 626, 'Introit: Et lux perpetua', bars 43–6   113

   b) Joseph Haydn, String Quartet in D major, Op. 50, No. 6, 'The Frog', movement 1, bars 138–49   113

c) Haydn, Symphony No. 101 in D major, 'Clock', movement 1, bars 240–6   113

d) Mozart, *Grabmusik*, K. 42, aria: 'Felsen, spaltet euren Rachen', bars 142–51   113

e) Mozart, Mass in C minor, K. 139, 'Credo', bars 126–7   113

f) Johann Sebastian Bach, *Jesus nahm zu sich die Zwölfe*, BWV 22, aria: 'Mein Jesu, ziehe mich nach dir', bars 29–33   113

g) Beethoven, *Eroica* Symphony, Op. 55, Allegro con brio, bars 1–11   113

6.4 *le–sol–fi–sol*: abstract representation   116

6.5 Beethoven, *Eroica* Symphony, Op. 55, Marcia funebre, bars 145–72   121

6.6 Beethoven, *Eroica* Symphony, Op. 55, finale, bars 1–6   124

6.7 Beethoven, *Eroica* Symphony, Op. 55, finale, bars 408–40   127

6.8 Haydn, 'Theresa' Mass in B♭ major, 'Crucifixus', bars 79–82   129

7.1 Beethoven, *Eroica* Symphony, Op. 55, fourth movement, cf. bars 94–9   146

7.2 Beethoven, *Eroica* Symphony, Op. 55, fourth movement, cf. bars 29–348   150

7.3 Beethoven, *Eroica* Symphony, Op. 55, fourth movement, cf. bars 369–72   151

8.1 Beethoven, *Die Geschöpfe des Prometheus*, Op. 43, No. 16, finale. Allegretto, theme   159

8.2 Beethoven, Variations in E♭ major, Op. 35, finale. Alla Fuga: a) bars 1–9; b) bars 51–7; c) bars 89–94   163

8.3 Beethoven, Variations in E♭ major, Op. 35, Introduzione col Basso del Tema, bars 1–8   165

8.4 Beethoven, Variations in E♭ major, Op. 35, finale. Andante, final variation, bars 164–8   171

8.5 Beethoven, *Eroica* Symphony, Op. 55, finale, bars, 1–15   173

8.6 Beethoven, *Eroica* Symphony, Op. 55, finale, bars 292–6   175

11.1 a) Anonymous arrangement of Beethoven's *Eroica* Symphony for piano quartet (Vienna: Bureau des Arts et d'Industrie, 1807), movement two, bars 1–5   228

b) Ferdinand Ries's piano quartet arrangement (Bonn: Simrock, 1857), movement two, bars 1–5   228

c) Johann Nepomuk Hummel's flute quartet arrangement (Mainz: Schott, *c.*1830), movement two, bars 1–5   228

Notes on Contributors

Leon Botstein is President and Leon Levy Professor in the Arts of Bard College, author of several books, and editor of *The Compleat Brahms* (1999) and *The Musical Quarterly*. The music director of the American Symphony Orchestra and The Orchestra Now and conductor laureate of the Jerusalem Symphony Orchestra, he has recorded works by, among others, Szymanowski, Hartmann, Bruch, Dukas, Foulds, Toch, Dohnányi, Ferdinand Ries, Chausson, Richard Strauss, Schoeck, Popov, Reger and Liszt. In 2018 he assumed the position of artistic director of the Grafenegg Academy in Austria.

Scott Burnham is Distinguished Professor of Music at the Graduate Center, City University of New York and Scheide Professor of Music History Emeritus at Princeton University, where he taught from 1989 to 2016. He is the author of *Beethoven Hero* (1995), a study of the values and reception of Beethoven's heroic-style music, and *Mozart's Grace* (2013), an exploration of beauty in the music of Mozart.

Erica Buurman is Director of the Ira F. Brilliant Center for Beethoven Studies at San José State University. Her most recent publications include articles in *Ad parnassum* and *Bonner Beethoven-Studien*, and a chapter in *Beethoven in Context* (forthcoming). She is currently working on a monograph on social dance music in Beethoven's Vienna.

Vasili Byros (PhD, Yale University, 2009) is Associate Professor of Music Theory and Cognition at Northwestern University. He researches the compositional, listening and pedagogical practices of the long eighteenth century, with an emphasis on the music of Beethoven, J. S. Bach and Mozart. In 2017 he was awarded the Outstanding Publication Award from the Society for Music Theory, and the Charles Deering McCormick Professorship, Northwestern University's highest recognition of teaching excellence and curricular innovation. He is currently writing a monograph on late Beethoven.

William Drabkin is Emeritus Professor of Music at the University of Southampton. He is the author of the Cambridge handbook on Beethoven's *Missa solemnis* and the editor and transcriber of one of the composer's sketchbook of 1822. He is the general editor of two series of Heinrich Schenker's writings in English translation, *Das Meisterwerk in der Musik* (1994–7) and *Der Tonwille* (2004–5), and has served as Editor of the journal *Music Analysis* (2011–19). He continues to edit and translate the diaries and much of the correspondence for the *Schenker Documents Online* project.

Mark Ferraguto is Associate Professor of Musicology at the Pennsylvania State University. The author of *Beethoven 1806* (2019), he has published numerous

articles and reviews on the music, culture and politics of eighteenth- and early nineteenth-century Europe. He is co-editor of the multidisciplinary volume *Music and Diplomacy from the Early Modern Era to the Present* (2014) and an active performer on organ and harpsichord.

Beate Angelika Kraus studied Musicology as well as French and Italian literature and languages at the University of Hamburg (Germany) and at the Université de Paris-Sorbonne (Paris IV). Her dissertation on the reception of Beethoven in France from the beginning until the fall of the Second Empire was published in 2001. Currently she is a musicologist at the Beethoven-Archiv (Beethoven-Haus, Bonn) and is Editor of the Ninth Symphony as part of the new critical edition of Beethoven's works (Munich: Henle, 2020).

Melanie Lowe is Associate Professor of Musicology at Vanderbilt University's Blair School of Music. Author of *Pleasure and Meaning in the Classical Symphony* (2007) and co-editor of *Rethinking Difference in Music Scholarship* (2014), she is widely published on eighteenth-century music, topic theory and music in American media. Also deeply committed to the Scholarship of Teaching and Learning, she is the author of several articles on music history pedagogy and curriculum design.

Nicholas Marston is Professor of Music Theory and Analysis at the University of Cambridge, where he is also a Fellow (and currently Vice-Provost) of King's College. His research interests span Beethoven analysis and source studies, Schenkerian studies and the music of Schumann. He is a former Editor-in-Chief of *Beethoven Forum*, and has served as Chair of the Editorial Board of *Music Analysis*, now sitting on its Advisory Panel. Recent work includes the article "'. . . nur ein Gleichnis': Heinrich Schenker and the Path to "Likeness"', which won the *Music & Letters* Centenary Prize competition in 2019.

Nancy November is Associate Professor in Musicology at the University of Auckland. Recent publications include *Beethoven's Theatrical Quartets: Opp. 59, 74, and 95* (2013); a three-volume set of fifteen string quartets by Beethoven's contemporary Emmanuel Aloys Förster (2016); and *Cultivating String Quartets in Beethoven's Vienna* (2017). She is the recipient of an Alexander von Humboldt Fellowship and two Marsden Grants from the New Zealand Royal Society.

Federica Rovelli received her PhD in 2009. In 2012 she received a Humboldt Fellowship to study Beethoven's 'Scheide' Sketchbook. She has served as a research scholar in the *Beethovens Werkstatt* project and since 2018 has been an Assistant Professor at the Dipartimento di Musicologia at Cremona (Pavia). She is Editor of *Ein Skizzenbuch aus den Jahren 1815 bis 1816* and *Klaviersonaten*, vol. 3 (Beethoven-Haus, Bonn).

Elaine Sisman is the Anne Parsons Bender Professor of Music at Columbia University. She received her PhD from Princeton University. Her numerous

publications on Haydn, Mozart and Beethoven include *Haydn and the Classical Variation*, *Mozart: The Jupiter Symphony* and 'Music and the Labyrinth of Melancholy'. An Honorary Member of the American Musicological Society, she was elected a Fellow of the American Academy of Arts and Sciences in 2014.

Eroica Chronology, 1770–2020

1770	Beethoven born in Bonn, baptised 17 December
1773	Goethe's drama *Götz von Berlichingen* published
1781	Schiller's drama *The Robbers* published
1787	Schiller's drama *Don Carlos* published
1788	Goethe's drama *Egmont* published
1791	Death of Mozart (5 December)
1792	Travelled to Vienna hoping to study with Haydn (November)
1789–99	French Revolution
1792–1802	French Revolutionary Wars lead to Napoleonic Wars (1803–15)
1796	Napoleon's first victory as army commander (Battle of Montenotte)
1798	General Bernadotte spends time in Vienna as French ambassador; Anton Schindler reported (probably falsely) that it was Bernadotte who suggested to Beethoven that he should compose a symphony to honour Napoleon
1799	First troubling symptoms of Beethoven's deafness; begins systematic use of sketchbooks. Napoleon becomes First Consul of France
1799–1800	Symphony No. 1 in C minor, Op. 21 (first performed April, 1800)
1800–1	Piano Sonata in A♭, Op. 26 with slow movement 'Marcia funèbre sulla morte d'un eroe'; ballet music *Creatures of Prometheus*, Op. 43 (performed and published 1801)
1801–2	Contradance WoO 14 No. 7 (drawing on the theme from Op. 43 also used in *Eroica*). Beethoven commissioned by Countess von Kielmansegge (Dessau) to write a 'Revolutionary Sonata' (November 1801), but he is reluctant to take this on (April 1802) and the Countess withdraws her offer on hearing that his proposed fee was very high. Around 1802, Beethoven to Krumpenholz (according to his former student Carl Czerny): 'I am only a little satisfied with my previous works. From today I will take a new path'
1802	'Heiligenstadt Testament'. Piano Variations (two sets): Op. 34 in F major; Op. 35 in E♭ major (on the *Eroica* finale

theme). Beethoven to his publisher, Oct. 1802: 'Both [of these sets] are written in a really entirely new style'. Symphony No. 2 in D major, Op. 36 (first performed 1803; published 1804). Beethoven begins sketching *Eroica* after work on Op. 35 in the 'Wielhorsky' Sketchbook (Autumn)

1802–3	Haydn ceases active composition. Sketching *Eroica* in 'Landsberg 6' (end October 1802 or May/June 1803); main work in 1803, final revisions at the beginning of 1804
1803	Symphony No. 3 in E♭ major, Op. 55 (performed 1804, published 1806). Kaspar Karl van Beethoven offers the *Eroica* to Simrock, Breitkopf & Härtel (May), which are later withdrawn (December), probably due to Lobkowitz's six-month performing rights. Simrock reports that 'Beethoven has now composed two symphonies, of which one is already finished' (August), probably referring to *Eroica*'s completion Beethoven plays the *Eroica* on the piano for (and according to) Ries, who reports that Beethoven wants to dedicate the symphony to Napoleon and name it 'Bonaparte' (October) Oratorio, Christ on the Mount of Olives, Op. 85
1804	Austrian Empire founded by Francis I. Napoleon crowns himself Emperor of the French. Beethoven is disillusioned with Napoleon (Ries reports in May), and at some point crosses out 'intitolata Buonaparte' on the autograph score's title page energetically, causing a hole; but his views of Napoleon continue to vary (e.g., writing to Breitkopf, in August: 'the symphony is actually entitled 'Ponaparte', and at some stage writing 'geschrieben auf Bonaparte' in pencil on the autograph score's title page, under the erasure). Starts sketching Symphony No. 5 in C minor, Op. 67. First performances of *Eroica* in two 'rehearsals' in Lobkowitz's palace in Vienna; private performance in Raudnitz, Lobkowitz's palace in Czechoslovakia (August); re-offers *Eroica* to Brietkopf (August) but they decline (May/June 1805) after delays; receives payment from Prince Lobkowitz for the dedication of *Eroica* and the Triple Concerto, Op. 56 (November)
1805	Semi-public performances of *Eroica* in Vienna (January); mixed reviews. Napoleon defeats the Austro-Russian army at the Battle of Austerlitz
1806	Symphony No. 4 in B♭ major, Op. 60 (first performed March 1807). *Eroica* is finally published in orchestral parts by Kunst- und Industrie-Comptoir, Vienna; the title 'Eroica' first

appears with the publication of these parts. Holy Roman Empire dissolved as a consequence of the Treaty of Pressburg. Prince Louis Ferdinand of Prussia, whom Beethoven knew through Lobkowitz, loses his life to the Napoleonic troops in battle

1806–7   Publication of list of the most significant errors in the original edition of *Eroica* (*Allgemeine musikalische Zeitung*). Arrangement of *Eroica* for septet, by Girolamo Masi (London: Monzani and Co., *c.*1807)

1807   Arrangement of *Eroica* for four-hand piano (Leipzig: Kühnel). Friedrich Rochlitz publishes the first technical/analytical review of *Eroica* (*Allgemeine musikalische Zeitung*, 9, cols. 321–33)

1807–8   Final work on Symphony No. 5, Op. 67, and Symphony No. 6 in F ('Pastoral'), Op. 68 (both first performed in the same concert, December 1808)

1809   War is declared against France (April); French troops occupy Vienna (May). Death of Haydn (31 May). *Eroica* is published in orchestral score by Cianchettini & Sperati in London, with the title ('Sinfonia Eroica composta per celebrare la morte d'un Eroe', later 'per festeggiare il sovvenire di un grand'uomo')

1810   Beethoven makes a note on a sketch leaf about possibly dedicating his Mass in C to Napoleon (eventually dedicated to his patron Prince Kinsky)

1811–12   Symphony No. 7 in A major, Op. 92 (first performed December 1813)

1812   Symphony No. 8 in F major, Op. 93 (first performed February 1814). French invasion of Russia marks a turning point in the Napoleonic Wars

1813   *Wellington's Victory*, Op. 91, to commemorate the Duke of Wellington's victory over Napoleon at the Battle of Vitoria on 21 June 1813 (first performed December 1813)

1815   Congress of Vienna; Napoleon escapes exile and begins the Hundred Days before being defeated at the Battle of Waterloo

1817   Arrangement of *Eroica* for nonet, Carl Friedrich Ebers (Leipzig: Hofmeister). Authentic metronome markings for *Eroica* are published by Steiner, Vienna

1818   Near total deafness; begins use of 'conversation books'

1819   Starts work on Symphony No. 9 in D minor, Op. 125

1821   Napoleon dies in exile on the island of Saint Helena

1822   *Eroica* is published in orchestral score by Simrock in Bonn

1823	Symphony No. 9 (primary work)
1824	Symphony No. 9 (first performance May 1824; publication 1826)
1826	Beethoven becomes ill, ceases composition (December)
1827	Beethoven dies (March 27). Arrangement of *Eroica* for two pianos by C. Czerny
1832	Arrangement of *Eroica* for Piano, Flute, Vn, Vc (ad lib.) by Johann Nepomuk Hummel (London: Chappell & Co.; includes arrangement for piano solo)
1837–65	Liszt transcribes the entire cycle of Beethoven's symphonies for solo piano
1847	Marcia funebre played at the funeral of Felix Mendelssohn
1862–5	First collected edition of Beethoven's works (Leipzig: Breitkopf & Härtel)
1880	Gustav Nottebohm's monograph on the 'Eroica Sketchbook', with selective transcriptions and commentary
1892	Hans von Bülow re-dedicates the *Eroica* to Otto von Bismark
1926	First recordings of *Eroica*, with Henry Wood and Albert Coates conducting
1937	Arturo Toscanini rehearses *Eroica* with the BBC SO, declaring 'Is-a not Napoleon! Is-not 'Itler! Is-a not Mussolini! Is-a *Allegro con brio*!'
1945	Marcia funebre played to commemorate Franklin D. Roosevelt
1948	Wilhelm Furtwängler records *Eroica* – one of the slowest versions on record
1957	*Eroica* performed under Bruno Walter at the memorial concert for Arturo Toscanini
1963	Marcia funebre played to commemorate John F. Kennedy
1972	Marcia funebre performed at public memorial following the terrorist attacks at the summer Olympics, Munich
1980s	The earliest recordings on period instruments (Hogwood, 1983; Brügen, 1987; Goodman, 1988; Schröder, 1989; Norrington, 1989)
2001	Bärenreiter Urtext edition of *Eroica*, edited by Jonathan del Mar
2003	Release of *Eroica*, BBC television film, dir. Simon Celland Jones. Ensemble 28 records a reconstruction of the first performance in the Lobkowitz Palace (CD released 2004)
2009	Premiere of Tan Dun's Internet Symphony No. 1 ('Eroica') by the YouTube Symphony Orchestra

2013   Entire '*Eroica* Sketchbook' published in facsimile, with transcription and commentary by Lewis Lockwood and Alan Gosman; *Beethoven Werke* (Gesamtausgabe, Beethoven-Haus Bonn) edition of *Eroica*, edited by Bathia Churgin (Henle)

Acknowledgements

It has been a great pleasure to watch the interconnecting themes of this book emerge and to have had the privilege of discussing the chapters with its enthusiastic team of authors. Over the two years of this book's evolution, life's serious challenges have intervened for just about every person represented in the list of authors: I deeply appreciate the dedication and perseverance of each author. Sincere gratitude to Kate Brett for her guidance at every step, and to Eilidh Burrett for expert advice on the book's completion. For the timely completion of this volume I am indebted to Janet Hughes, for assistance with editorial suggestions and proofreading; and to Aleisha Ward for her help with proofreading. Grateful thanks to the librarians at Beethoven-Haus for their ever-generous time with bibliographic questions, in particular Stephanie Kuban and Dorothea Geffert; and to Christine Siegert for her kind hospitality on my research trips to Beethoven-Haus.

This book is dedicated to the memory of family members of two contributors to this volume, who died while it was in preparation. Andrea Reiter (wife of William Drabkin) was an Austrian literary scholar who took a special interest in the writings of Heinrich Schenker from historical and cultural viewpoints, and acted for many years as language consultant to the Schenker Documents Online project. Margot Sisman (mother of Elaine Sisman) was a refugee from Nazi Germany who was determined that her daughters should study at the Juilliard pre-college division because she could not afford to attend the Juilliard School of Music when she was admitted during the war.

Introduction

NANCY NOVEMBER

Eroica endures. This fact, discussed at some length in the final chapter of this book, was brought home strongly to me as I edited this volume. Escaping briefly from *Eroica*, or so I thought, after a day of proofreading, I turned to YouTube. Using a Google search with keyword 'Agatha Christie', I chanced upon a 1984 TV drama, *Second Sight – A Love Story*, starring Elizabeth Montgomery. The similarities to Beethoven's biography can be seen in the main character's stubborn and somewhat difficult temperament, and the painful irony that the sense that she most prizes and needs (sight) should be taken away from her. With hindsight – and with the help of this book's chapters on reception – it was clear that the choice of the *Eroica* finale for this movie's opening credits (fading in at bar 449) is overdetermined.

That the *Eroica* Symphony crops up frequently in popular culture is no surprise. It is one of the most discussed, performed and reinterpreted of Beethoven's symphonies, indeed of symphonies altogether. It is also one of the most controversial of his works in terms of interpretation. There is general consensus among past and present commentators that the *Eroica* is a 'watershed' work (there is a film about that, too: *Eroica,* 2003), but little agreement on why or how. Rather, there are continued efforts to locate the 'heroic' element or pin down the 'hero' of (or in) the work; this has resulted in a great deal of discussion of contextual elements – especially Beethoven's views of Napoleon, of revolution and of his conception and representation of heroism – but few detailed analyses. The work has attracted, and continues to attract, major analysts and thinkers, including Heinrich Schenker and Carl Dahlhaus. Lewis Lockwood explains: 'Its special status remains essential in modern discussions of his artistic career, despite inevitable reappraisals.'[1] The multivalent nature of the work makes for reappraisal, especially of its connections to biography, politics and society in the 'Age of Revolutions': *Eroica* lends itself to new and varied approaches, both cultural and musical. It is consistently invoked not only as a compositional model but also as a testing ground for music theory.

This *Cambridge Companion* functions, in part, to fulfil a need for a guide to the wealth of literature the work has spawned. The guiding takes place not so much through literature surveys or summaries as by addressing the main topics associated with the symphony – among them

political context, dedication, sources of the symphony's inspiration, 'heroism' and the idea of a 'watershed' work. These topics cut across the book's three sections, on genesis, analysis and reception history respectively. The *Companion* includes critical study of writings and analyses from Beethoven's day to ours, and a range of other relevant discourses relating to the work, especially compositions, recordings, images and film. The reader will find many fresh insights here, with consideration of little-studied analytical avenues (register in Chapter 7, for instance) and source material (arrangements and film in Chapters 11 and 12 for example). Thus the *Companion* alerts students and scholars to a range of evidence relating to *Eroica*, and suggests new lines of enquiry.

Above all, this book answers to a need to understand and critique the mythology surrounding the work, and to consider where it comes from and what it has to tell us. The first four chapters are important in laying out the groundwork here, starting from a broad consideration of heroism and moving towards a detailed discussion of the genesis of *Eroica*. Scott Burnham writes: 'the narrative urge associated with critical interpretations of this music may tell us more about ourselves than simply the way we hear the *Eroica* symphony'.[2] In evaluating previous viewpoints, this book attends to influential listeners and performers of the past, considering how their perspectives have influenced their interpretations, and ours. The final four chapters are key in this respect. This *Companion* is less Germanocentric than previous *Eroica* studies, while it still acknowledges important German scholarship and reception of the work. There is, for example, discussion of the special character of French reception of the work, including that of Hector Berlioz (Chapters 9 and 10); and consideration of how the symphony gets reinterpreted in light of shifting cultural and political aspirations and fears, including those in Europe and the United States (Chapters 10–12).

Two *Cambridge Companion* volumes of particular importance in this area are those on Beethoven and the symphony.[3] There are relevant articles on Beethoven's large-scale orchestral works in the former, and on structural principles and narrative strategies in the latter. The present volume departs from these with its focus squarely on *Eroica*. There are several books devoted to *Eroica*, but none that offers such a breadth of topic coverage and approaches. Martin Geck and Peter Schleuning's *'Geschrieben auf Bonaparte.' Beethoven's 'Eroica': Revolution, Reaktion, Rezeption* (1989) and Thomas Sipe's 1998 Cambridge Music Handbook devoted to *Eroica* are typical of *Eroica* studies in their emphasis on reception, and lesser attention to analysis.[4] Fabrizio Della Seta's *Beethoven. Sinfonia Eroica: Una guida* (2004) contains a wealth of analytical detail, albeit from one perspective.[5] The present volume places analyses in the

centre, with four chapters (5–8) that offer a synthesis of previous analytical discourse as well as new approaches. In this respect, the *Companion* helps fill some important gaps, including discussion of Schenker's approach to the work (Chapter 7), and detailed analysis of the finale (Chapter 8), which has been neglected in favour of the first two movements in previous studies.

Two other recent studies of the *Eroica* are comprehensive, but tend to adopt single approaches. Christoph Hohlfeld's *Beethovens Weg: Eroica op. 55* (2003) sets out to show the symphony's 'watershed' position in Beethoven's oeuvre by exploring a supposed 'evolution' in his works in C minor and E♭ major.[6] The compositional trajectory that he traces is based on a theory of proportions. Constantin Floros explores the close relationship between the *Eroica* and *Die Geschöpfe des Prometheus*, Op. 43, in his *Beethoven's Eroica: Thematic Studies* (2012).[7] His book is based on his theory about Beethoven's planned dedication of the *Eroica* to Bonaparte. The *Companion* steps back for a broader, more critical look at the *Eroica*'s context, including but not dwelling on dedication. It encompasses discussion of factors that might demystify and de-emphasise the 'turning point' theory, including periodisation as it pertains to the work (Chapter 2), and a careful look at the context of symphonic writing around 1800 (Chapter 3).

Each chapter stands alone as well as illuminating a part of a contextual area. The reader will find loose chronological ordering within each of the book's three sections. Certain chapters naturally pick up closely related topics. So Chapters 4 and 9, respectively on genesis and early reception, both deal with the topic of dedication but from different angles. Chapters 2 and 11 both consider the symphony within the culture of nineteenth-century musical arrangements. And Chapters 11 and 12 both consider modern-day *Eroica* reception, one from the angle of performance, the other through film. Chapters 2 and 12 can usefully be read together with Chapter 7; Chapters 2 and 12 (and several others) consider the prevalence of teleological and 'triumph' narratives in *Eroica*'s reception; while Chapter 7 suggests an alternative reading, developing a narrative of 'failure' in the finale that runs contrary to the typical 'heroic' readings of *Eroica*.

Notes

1. L. Lockwood, *Beethoven's Symphonies: An Artistic Vision* (New York, NY: Norton, 2015), p. 52.
2. S. Burnham, 'On the Programmatic Reception of Beethoven's "Eroica" Symphony', *Beethoven Forum*, 1 (1992), p. 24.

3. *The Cambridge Companion to Beethoven*, ed. Glenn Stanley (Cambridge: Cambridge University Press, 1999); and *The Cambridge Companion to the Symphony*, ed. Julian Horton (Cambridge: Cambridge University Press, 2013).

4. Martin Geck and Peter Schleuning, *'Geschrieben auf Bonaparte.' Beethoven's 'Eroica': Revolution, Reaktion, Rezeption* (Berlin: Rowohlt, 1989) and T. Sipe, *Beethoven, Eroica Symphony* (Cambridge: Cambridge University Press, 1998).

5. F. Della Seta, *Beethoven. Sinfonia Eroica: Una guida* (Rome: Carocci, 2004).

6. C. Hohlfeld, *Beethovens Weg: Eroica op. 55* (Wilhelmshaven: Noetzel, 2003).

7. C. Floros, *Beethovens Eroica und Prometheus-Musik* (Wilhelmshaven: Noetzel, 1978); and C. Floros, *Beethoven's Eroica: Thematic Studies*, trans. Ernest Bernhardt-Kabisch (Frankfurt: Peter Lang, 2012).

Context and Genesis

1 Beethoven and Heroism in the Age of Revolutions

SCOTT BURNHAM

This chapter seeks to contextualise Beethoven's *Eroica* Symphony by survey-ing powerful elements of the cultural *Zeitgeist* that appeared in the dramatic literature Beethoven cherished. For it was an age of renewed interest in epic heroes and heroic dramas. The literary products of ancient Greece figured heavily in this enthusiasm. In Germany and Austria, Johann Heinrich Voss's artfully powerful translations of the *Iliad* and the *Odyssey* brought the epic heroic types of Homer to vivid life, while the Attic dramatists Aeschylus, Sophocles and Euripides were increasingly studied, revered and emulated. Plutarch's *Parallel Lives*, conceived around the second century AD, brought a profusion of real-life Greek and Roman heroes into the general cultural consciousness of late eighteenth-century Europe.[1] This modern passion for the ancients helped inspire a new age of German dramatic art. Novel heroic types emerged from the dramas of Goethe and Schiller, possessed of 'great-ness of soul' and offering compelling models of self-sacrifice and of speaking truth to power. The revolutions in America and France provided a tumultuous world-historical confirmation of the anti-tyrannical heroic impulse at work in these dramas, while the complex aftermath of the French Revolution, including the campaigns of Napoleon, provided a nearly con-stant fascination and fear, as well as new arrays of heroic role models.

The general impact of the French Revolution on European culture can hardly be overestimated. By enforcing such a radical break with the past, the Revolution helped bring about a new aesthetic consciousness and a corresponding new sense of time.[2] Karol Berger has observed that the French Revolution galvanised an Enlightenment trend already present in Western modernity away from an older, cyclical sense of time and eternity into a one-way, future-oriented sense of time. Accompanying this transition was a pervasive sense of acceleration: 'Time's cycle had been straightened into an arrow, and the arrow was traveling ever faster.'[3] The continual presence of war in post-revolution Europe was also a ready source of the sublime, provided of course that one was at a safe distance. In the words of James Winn: 'Like the ocean, great fires, and destructive storms, war is attractive to poets as an instance of the sublime, an experience bringing together awe, terror, power, and reverence on a grand scale.'[4] Beethoven

lived in tumultuous and unsettling times, and the *élan vital* of his heroic-style music expresses among other things the accelerating pace of the portentous events happening around him.

The figure of Napoleon in particular meant much to Beethoven as a consummate model of 'self-made greatness', despite his ambivalence about dedicating the Third Symphony to Napoleon after he crowned himself Emperor in 1804. Never before or subsequently did Beethoven consider naming one of his major compositions after an historical figure,[5] so it seems clear that he at least once judged Napoleon to be a real-life hero worthy of such a creative tribute. And while aspects of Napoleon's career epitomised the heroic rise of the autonomous individual, many other varieties of heroism were in play, including those that Beethoven would have encountered in literature. They involve upholding the necessity of rebellion in the face of tyranny, asserting the overriding importance of free thought and freedom in general, the rise of the autonomous individual, the ability to endure fated hardships, and the triumph of the free will in overcoming adversity and even overcoming one's own self, culminating in the moral commitment to sacrifice oneself for a higher ideal.[6]

The French Revolution and Napoleon arguably provided real-life cata-lysts to Beethoven's sense of human heroism. But perhaps even more crucial to his broader sense of heroic potential were cultural forces that emanated from distinctively different places. At the time of Beethoven's birth, Germanic writers and thinkers were completing a momentous turn away from French Enlightenment models to those of England and ancient Greece. Encouraged by the polemics of Gotthold Lessing, and by Swiss critics Johann Bodmer and Johann Breitinger, German writers of the later eighteenth century rejected the rules-based poetics of Enlightenment France (quintes-sentially instantiated in the dramas of French classicism) in favour of a more directly expressive aesthetics.[7] This shift had many ramifications, chiefly including a celebration (and emulation) of Shakespeare as the single greatest modern literary artist, and of Homer as the *fons et origo* of Western literature as well as a potent source of transhistorical resonance with modern German letters. The modern reverence for the Greeks was also connected to a perceived similarity of language between German and Greek; both lan-guages are root-based 'agglutinative' tongues, and German writers took great pride in this special connection.

Homer

Homeric epic counts as a hugely influential force in German culture of the *Goethezeit*. Goethe himself credited the reading of Homer (as well as

Ossian and Shakespeare) as crucial to his literary awakening. He also emulated Homeric epic in the creation of his bourgeois epic *Hermann und Dorothea*.[8] Schiller counted Homer as chief among the 'naïve' poets celebrated in his 1795 essay 'Über naïve und sentimentalische Dichtung'.

Beethoven was fond of citing Homer, as in this instance from his *Tagebuch*: 'But now Fate catches me! Let me not sink into the dust unresisting and inglorious, but first accomplish great things, of which future generations too shall hear.'[9] There follows one of the great scenes in the *Iliad*, the climax of Hector's heroism: the very moment when he realises he will die at the hands of Achilles, but resolves not to go down without a fight. It is easy to imagine Beethoven thrilling to passages like this, finding courage to push through in the midst of his own travails.

Although Beethoven expressed regret at not being able to read Homer in the original, the 1793 translation of the *Iliad* by Voss that Beethoven quoted deploys an accentual version of Homer's dactylic hexameter and thus transmits something close to the rhythm of the original.[10] Voss's translation reflects the values of his age, in that it strives to emulate Homer's achievement as closely as possible, while acting on the perceived affinity between the German and Greek languages. In turn, Voss's translation was deeply respected by Goethe and others.

What does Voss preserve of Homer's hexameter? Each line of Voss's accentual dactylic hexameter contains six stresses (marking the six feet), as well as the obligatory caesura in the third foot (often marked by a word ending that falls on the first syllable of the third foot). He also takes advantage of the occasional flexibility between dactyls and spondees characteristic of heroic hexameter (the two-syllable spondee sometimes substitutes for the three-syllable dactyl), while preserving the invariant dactyl–spondee combination of the last two feet (long–short–short/long–long, or in Voss, strong–weak–weak/strong–weak).[11] Compared with the rhymed couplets in iambic pentameter of English translators such as Pope and Chapman, Voss is thus much closer to the rhythmic life of Homer.[12] In addition, Voss's translation is often quite literal. A comparison of the two and a half lines from Book 22 of the *Iliad* cited in Beethoven's *Tagebuch* with the Homeric original will show both the rhythmic similarity and the closely literal tendency of Voss's translation (the obligatory caesura in the third foot is marked by a space):

νῦν αὖτέ με μοῖρα κιχάνει.
μὴ μὰν ἀσπουδί   γε καὶ ἀκλειῶς ἀπολοίμην,
ἀλλὰ μέγα ῥέξας   τι καὶ ἐσσομένοισι πυθέσθαι.
Nun aber erhascht mich das Schicksal,
Dass nicht arbeitslos   in den Staub ich sinke noch ruhmlos,
Nein, erst Grosses vollende,   von dem auch Künftige hören.

Not only is Voss almost completely literal (the only exception here is that he deploys the figurative 'in den Staub sinken' for Homer's 'perish'), but his rhythms are almost exactly those of Homer (the first two lines are exact in the number of syllables and placement of accents, the last is very slightly altered). Beethoven himself paid attention to the scansion of Voss's lines, for he entered scansion marks in his diary, perhaps with a mind towards setting these lines to music.[13]

These lines are not the only Homeric citations in Beethoven's *Tagebuch*. Others echo the theme of Fate, as in entry No. 26: 'For Fate gave Man the courage to endure', which is from the *Iliad* Book 24, line 49.[14] The words are those of Apollo, who is decrying Achilles' desecration of Hector's corpse by comparing Achilles unfavourably to other men who grieve the loss of even a closer relation than was Patroclus to Achilles, namely the loss of a brother or a son, and yet can ultimately endure such a loss with dignity (rather than engage in acts of vengeful desecration).[15] 'The courage to endure' is thematised in Beethoven's opera *Fidelio* by the unjust imprisonment of Florestan.[16] In another diary entry (No. 169), Beethoven quotes from Penelope's lamenting prayer to Artemis (*Odyssey* Book 20, lines 75–6): 'Sacrifice once and for all the trivialities of social life to your art, O God above all! For eternal Providence in its omniscience and wisdom directs the happiness and unhappiness of mortal men.' The injunction to sacrifice social trivialities to art is Beethoven speaking to himself, while the reference to 'eternal Providence' is from Penelope's prayer (she is referring to Zeus' 'ewige Vorsicht').[17] Thus we see Beethoven reinforcing his own urge for self-sacrifice by invoking a God-given, God-driven destiny that mortals cannot control but can only resign themselves to. What Beethoven takes from Homer, then, is the injunction to endure, to sacrifice, and to attempt big things in spite of fated handicaps. The power of Fate is acknowledged and reckoned with, to be sure, but what remains is the countervailing power of the autonomous individual to achieve what it can in the face of fated adversity.

Dramas of the *Sturm und Drang*

Joining Homer as the other great 'naïve' poet in Schiller's reckoning is Shakespeare. Both Schiller and Goethe sought to emulate Shakespeare in their early dramas. Part of shedding the influence of the French was the urge to partake in a new freedom of expression, manifest in a teeming variety of language and character as well as a sublime disregard for the classic unities of time and place observed in the dramas of Racine and Corneille. Moreover, the French requirement of *bienséance* (decorousness)

was also regularly violated, both in luridly dramatic scenes and in down-right vulgarity. German dramatists also embraced Shakespeare's potent mix of tragic and comic elements, which would have been anathema in French drama and its cherished *vraisemblance* (verisimilitude). Shakespeare was a natural model for writers who sought to heed Lessing's call for German authors to put less description and more drama into their writing.[18] The rhapsodic odes of Pindar and the excla-matory poetic style of Klopstock also served as powerful models for the younger generation of German writers. These proclivities and directives made the 'Sturm und Drang' ('Storm and Stress') movement all but inevitable.

Although the designation *Sturm und Drang* arose from the title of a play by Friedrich Maximilian Klinger, the two most famous dramas in this manner were Goethe's 1773 *Götz von Berlichingen* and Schiller's 1781 *Die Räuber*. The heroes of these dramas, Götz von Berlichingen and Karl Moor respectively, represented a new type of hero, the 'erhabene Verbrecher' or 'sublime outlaw'. Götz was based on a real historical figure from the sixteenth century who was involved in the German Peasants' War. The plot of Goethe's play is complicated, and the fate of its real-life hero is altered, such that he now suffers an early death. As a heroic figure, Goethe's von Berlichingen is a man of action and instinct who finds himself opposed by schemers of a more modern age. He dies in prison while exclaiming the word 'Freedom'.

Goethe's *Götz von Berlichingen* was explicitly intended to emulate Shakespeare's dramatic range. Moreover, Goethe composed the drama in prose, which in itself represents a decided turn away from more traditional dramas. *Götz von Berlichingen* was written less than ten years after the death of an earlier literary giant, Johann Christoph Gottsched, who championed French literary models and the ideals of the Enlightenment. Gottsched, like other writers of his era, composed his dramas in rhyming Alexandrine couplets, in direct imitation of the French classical dramatists. An Alexandrine line has twelve or thirteen syllables (depending on whether the last syllable of the line is accented or unaccented), with invariant accents on the sixth and twelfth syllables. Here is an excerpt from Gottsched's drama *Der sterbende Cato*, which was premiered in 1731 (the extra space in the middle of the line indicates the caesura):

Wie sanft, wie süsse schläft   ein tugendhafter Mann,
Den sein Gewissen nicht   im Schlummer stören kann!
Ich kam und habe selbst   den Cato liegen sehen,
Es ist ihm zweifelsfrei   ein harter Fall geschehen,
Da er den Sohn verlor;   doch bleibt er tugendhaft!

Vermutlich stärket ihn   der Götter eigne Kraft,
Dass er nicht zaghaft wird   und gleiche Grösse zeiget:
Obgleich die ganze Welt   sich schon vor Cäsarn beuget.

Act 5, Scene 5

(How gently, how sweetly a virtuous man sleeps,
Whose conscience cannot disturb him in his slumber!
I came upon Cato and saw him lying there,
Doubting not that he suffered a hard turn
In losing his son; yet he remains virtuous!
He is presumably strengthened by the native power of the gods,
Such that he shows the same greatness and does not become timid:
Even though the entire world already bows to Caesar.)[19]

As a distinct contrast to the regularity of these Alexandrine lines, consider this charged speech from Act 3, Scene 17 of Goethe's *Götz von Berlichingen*, shouted out the window by Götz when he is asked to surrender: 'Mich ergeben! Auf Gnad und Ungnad! Mit wem redet Ihr! Bin ich ein Räuber! Sag deinem Hauptmann: Vor Ihro Kaiserliche Majestät hab ich, wie immer, schuldigen Respekt. Er aber, sag's ihm, er kann mich im Arsche lecken!' ('Surrender myself! To be at his mercy! Who do you think you're talking to? I'm a robber! Tell your captain: I have, as always, due respect for His Imperial Majesty [the emperor]. But your captain – and tell him this – he can lick my ass!')

That last utterance instantly became the most famous line of the play. Such a sentiment is clearly more *malséance* than *bienséance*, while the impassioned and colloquial prose of the entire speech is the furthest thing from the elevated elegance of classical French Alexandrines or their German equivalents. On another front, the staggering number of scenes in Goethe's drama (act by act there are 5, 10, 22, 5 and 14 scenes, in total 56) is a fulsome repudiation of the unity of place required in French Enlightenment drama.

While Götz von Berlichingen was not natively disposed to rebellion (he was only reluctantly involved in the peasants' revolt), the hero of Goethe's popular poem from the same time, *Prometheus*, is emphatically unequivocal in sounding the anti-tyrannical note that would become crucial to German heroic drama of the age:

Ich kenne nichts Ärmeres
unter der Sonn' als euch Götter!
Ihr nähert kümmerlich
Von Opfersteuern
Und Gebetshauch
Eure Majestät
Und darbtet, wären

Nicht Kinder und Bettler
Hoffnungsvolle Toren.

(I know nothing more impoverished under the sun as you gods! You miserably nourish your majesty with sacrifices and the breath of prayers, and you would starve if children and beggars weren't such hopeful fools.)

Goethe's Prometheus also prides himself on his self-reliance, answering his rhetorical questions 'Who helped me fight the wanton Titans?' and 'Who saved me from death and slavery?' with these words: 'Hast du's nicht alles selbst vollendet, / Heilig glühend Herz?'(Didn't you do all this yourself, my sacredly glowing heart?). A few lines later, Goethe asserts the role of Fate in the formation of the heroic self: 'Hat mich nicht zum Manne geschmiedet / Die allmächtige Zeit / Und das ewige Schicksal, / Meine Herrn und deine?' ('Did not all-powerful Time and eternal Fate, my masters and your own, forge me into a man?'). Even the gods themselves must answer to Fate and to Time. The striking vehemence of Prometheus' dramatic monologue may have contributed to Beethoven's surprise and dismay at Goethe's personal deference to the nobility, which Beethoven observed in Teplitz in 1812.

The heady language and attitude of Goethe's literary productions of the 1770s were shared by Schiller, whose 1781 drama *Die Räuber* is also composed in prose and features a similar hero, Karl Moor, an 'erhabene Verbrecher', as the head of the robber band. Shakespearean features abound, including the variety of social classes portrayed in the drama, and the main character's brooding soliloquy in Act 4, Scene 5, an obvious reference to Hamlet's famous monologue, spoken as Karl Moor holds a pistol to his head: 'Time and Eternity – linked together in a single moment! Horrid key that closes the prison door of life behind me and unlocks night's eternal lodging in front of me. Tell me, oh tell me, where, where will you lead me? To a foreign land, never circumnavigated'. Toward the end of the soliloquy, Moor suddenly puts the pistol down: 'So I'm going to die for fear of a life of anguish? Should I concede victory over myself to misery? No – I will endure this! Let torment be weakened by my pride! I will complete this.' Unlike Hamlet, who casts his inability to kill himself (or to kill Claudius, his usurping uncle) as a lack of decisiveness, suggesting that the 'native hue of resolution is sicklied o'er with the pale cast of thought', Karl Moor consciously decides to endure his fate, to live through to the end. This decisive act of self-overcoming resonated with Beethoven and is arguably echoed in his 1802 Heiligenstadt Testament.

The Robbers created quite a stir at its 1782 premiere in Mannheim. As a witness reported: 'The theater was like a madhouse, with rolling eyes,

clenched fists, and hoarse cries among the audience! Strangers fell sobbing into one another's arms, women stumbled to the exit, close to fainting. There was general dissolution, like a chaos from whose mists a new creation broke forth.'[20] Why the uproar? The play features lurid portrayals of evil and of violence that must have been shocking. Based on the premise of a 1775 story by Daniel Christian Schubart, Schiller's drama revolves around two brothers, Karl and Franz Moor. Karl, the 'sublime criminal', possesses a noble soul, and is consequently beloved as a son, leader and lover. Franz is the very epitome of evil, a hypocrite who poses as the good son in the family and attempts to poison his father's view of Karl. Franz's evil doings even extend to making his father believe that Karl has been killed, exiling the old man while pretending to the world that he has died, and then later trying to convince an older servant to kill Karl, who has returned home in disguise.[21] When the otherwise loyal servant refuses to do a deed that goes against his God and his conscience, Franz exclaims 'Aren't you ashamed? An old man, and you still believe in that Christmastime fable? … I'm the master here. I'm the one who will be punished by God and by conscience, if there even is a God and a conscience.' Thus the audience was treated to blasphemy, along with the violence of several onstage suicides, and the spectacle of seeing the older Moor drop dead when his son Karl confesses that he is indeed the leader of the robbers. Towards the very end of the play there is a shocking killing: when Karl must finally leave Amalia, in order to honour his vow to remain the leader of the robber band, she demands that he kill her, to put her out of her misery. He staunchly refuses, but when one of the other robbers takes aim at her, he cries out: 'Stop! Don't you dare – Moor's beloved should only die at the hands of Moor.' And then he kills her on stage, to the shock of his fellow robbers, not to mention the audience.[22]

Many found the outré action of Schiller's play unacceptable (including the Habsburg censors, who succeeded in banning Schiller's works from 1793 to 1808), but the younger generation thrilled to its provocations – great numbers of students attended performances of this and other *Sturm und Drang* dramas.[23] This may be due in part to the way that *The Robbers* captures a brewing spirit of rebellion in the years running up to the French Revolution. Germanist Walter Hinderer observes in his study of Schiller: 'Both Schiller's theoretical utterances as well as his youthful dramas up to *Don Carlos* demonstrate that the problematic of rebellion and insurrection and the character analysis of political leaders belonged to his loftiest concerns even before the French Revolution.'[24]

Among the 'theoretical utterances' Hinderer refers to is Schiller's essay 'The Theatre Considered as a Moral Institution', which he first

delivered as a talk in 1784, while he was working on his drama *Don Carlos*. Schiller felt the theatre was an institution that could model moral behaviour; as he puts it, 'the theatre makes us aware of [various] fates and teaches us the great art of enduring them'.[25] With such an agenda in mind, one begins to understand the theatrical necessity for Schiller not only of the native goodness of some of his characters, such as the loyal servant Daniel, or the loving devotion unto death of Amalia, but also of the self-consciously nihilistic machinations of Franz and the overriding greatness of personality exuded by Karl Moor himself, who is ultimately destroyed by the ways of the world but takes full responsibility for his own role in that world. Such strongly drawn characters, each of whom expresses his or her innermost motivations, profile Schiller's intent to model moral character in his dramas.

In addition to Schiller's 'An die Freude', the closing sentences of his essay on the theatre would have inspired the Beethoven of the Ninth Symphony. For Schiller imagines the theatre creating an ideal state of moral enlightenment:

> where men from all circles, zones and classes, every constraint of artificiality and fashion discarded, torn from every pressure of fate, made into brothers through *one* all-encompassing sympathy, resolved again into one family, forget themselves and the world, and approach their heavenly origin. Every individual enjoys the rapture of all the others, which falls back on him amplified and beautified from a hundred other eyes, and his breast has room for one feeling only, and it is this: to be human.[26]

Dramas of the *Deutsche Klassik*

Schiller's drama of the Spanish Inquisition, *Don Carlos*, brought heroic nobility to its most dignified level, in the figure of the Marquis von Posa. Posa is admired by the Spanish King for his candour and revered by the King's vacillating son Carlos. By the end of the play, Posa will have sacrificed his very life for Carlos and for the dream of a better future for the King's subjects. In *Don Carlos*, Schiller abandons the prose of *The Robbers* and adopts an elevated pentameter line, known as *Blankvers* (blank verse) and brought to prominence in the German *Klassik*. Far from precluding the use of highly charged dramatic language, Schiller's verse form in fact profiles such language by staging it in bursts of dramatic intensity. The culminating moment of the drama may well be Posa's personal injunction to the King to grant freedom of thought to his subjects (Act 3, Scene 10):[27]

Gehn Sie Europens Könige voran.
Ein Federzug von diesem Hand, und neu
Erschaffen wird die Erde. Geben Sie
Gedankenfreiheit –

(Put yourself at the head of Europe's kings.
A stroke of the pen from this your hand, and the earth
Is made anew. Grant freedom of thought –)

'Geben Sie Gedankenfreiheit.' With these words, Posa throws himself at the King's feet. The directness of his plea, in the very face of the King, makes memorable drama out of speaking truth to power. The King greatly admires Posa's candour, though he will not act on it.

In the final act, Posa consummates his heroism, by contriving to sacrifice himself in order to rescue Carlos from imprisonment. The moment when Posa reveals this to Carlos is again marked by a concentrated power of dramatic expression, now in the form of halting interjections followed by triumphant effusion, marked throughout by telling word repetitions:

POSA (*ergreift seine Hand*): Du bist
 Gerettet, Karl – bist frei – und ich – (*Er halt inne*).
CARLOS: Und du?
POSA: Und ich – ich drücke dich an meine Brust
 Zum erstenmal mit vollem, ganzem Rechte;
 Ich hab es gar mit allem, allem was
 Mir teuer ist, erkauft – O Karl, wie süss,
 Wie gross ist dieser Augenblick! Ich bin
 Mit mir zufrieden.

(POSA (*seizes his hand*): You are
 Saved, Karl – you're free – and I (*He pauses*).
CARLOS: And you?
POSA: And I – I hold you to my breast
 For the first time with full and total right;
 I have purchased this right with all, all that
 Is dear to me – O Karl, how sweet,
 How grand is this moment! I am
 Satisfied with myself.)

Act 5, Scene 3

The repetitions first enact a kind of apprehensive shadow play between Posa and Carlos (Und ich – und du? – und ich – ich drücke dich) and then serve to accentuate Posa's emotionally elevated sense of the moment (mit allem, allem; wie süss, wie gross). Thus Posa brings about both the culminating political moment ('Geben Sie Gedankenfreiheit') and the culminating personal moment ('wie gross

ist dieser Augenblick!'), and he does so with a directness of expression that stands out all the more because it dramatically animates the underlying rhythm of blank verse.

Goethe's own drama of the Spanish Inquisition, *Egmont*, was completed around the same time that Schiller's *Don Carlos* was premiered (1787). Though Schiller shifted from prose to pentameter verse between *The Robbers* and *Don Carlos*, Goethe retained the prose of *Götz von Berlichingen* for his *Egmont*.[28] Both *Don Carlos* and *Egmont* feature complex plots with intrigues and love interests at various levels. Most important for our present concerns is the similarity in heroic action: like the Marquis von Posa, Egmont sacrifices himself for a better future.

While he is waiting in a prison cell for his execution to take place, Egmont's heroic resolve is strengthened by a vision as he slumbers, in which his beloved Klara appears as the figure of Freedom. She indicates to him that his death will rouse the provinces to free themselves, hails him as a victor, and holds a crown of laurels over his head.[29] Egmont wakes to the sounds of the troops approaching to take him to his execution. As the drums roll, he is seized with the exaltation of the moment:

> Hark! Hark! How often this sound called me to step freely onto the field of struggle and victory! How cheerfully my companions strode along the dangerous path of glory! I too am striding from this prison toward an honourable death; I die for freedom, for which I lived and fought, and to which I now offer myself as a suffering sacrifice.[30]

Egmont's final words (and the final words of the entire drama) seem to speak directly to Schiller's view of the theatre as a place of moral exemplification: 'And to save what is dearest to you, die joyfully, as I do in setting you an example.'

In addition to the theme of self-sacrifice, Goethe explores the individual's relation to Fate in Egmont's oft-quoted speech of Act 2:

> As if whipped on by invisible spirits, the sun-steeds of time pull the light chariot of our destiny along; and the most we can do is to maintain courage and calm, hold the reins tight, and steer the wheels to right or to left, here avoiding a stone and there avoiding a plunging crash. Where we are headed, who knows? We hardly recall whence we came.[31]

And again, in the last scene of the last act, while saying farewell to Ferdinand, Egmont draws the moral even more succinctly: 'Man believes that he directs his own life, is his own leader; and yet his innermost being is drawn along irresistibly toward his fate.'

Beethoven's esteem for Goethe's *Egmont* extended to the composition of incidental music for the drama in 1809/10, including an overture whose

soaring conclusion is heard again at the end of the drama as the Victory Symphony required by Goethe himself to portray Egmont's posthumous triumph. At least one contemporaneous witness, Goethe's friend and fellow poet Marianne von Willemer, felt that Beethoven's music fully captured the spirit of the drama. Writing to Goethe in 1821, she observed that '[Beethoven] has understood you completely; one could almost say that the same spirit that animates your words enlivens his tones'.[32]

Beethoven's long-standing admiration for Schiller's *Don Carlos* would seem to be indicated by the fact that he quoted from *Don Carlos* on several occasions.[33] In 1793, he inscribed the following lines from Act 2, Scene 2 in the *Stammbuch* of a female friend, Theodora Johanna Vocke, perhaps to explain some of his own untoward behaviour:

> Ich bin nicht schlimm, . . . – heisses Blut
> Ist meine Bosheit – mein Verbrechen Jugend.
> Schlimm bin ich nicht, schlimm wahrlich nicht – wenn auch
> Oft wilde Wallungen mein Herz verklagen,
> Mein Herz ist gut –

> (I am not evil, . . . – hot blood
> Is my wickedness – youth, my crime,
> Evil I am not, truly not evil – even if
> Wild agitations often testify against my heart,
> My heart is good –)

And after this seemingly personal protestation, borrowed from Carlos's plea to his father to entrust him with important affairs of state, Beethoven adds three precepts: 'To do good wherever one can; to love freedom above all else; never to deny the truth, even before the throne.'[34] This declaration outlines a way of life and a code of conduct, and it stands as a distillation of the ideals embodied by Götz von Berlichingen, Karl Moor, the Marquis von Posa and Egmont. These figures and their heroic actions clearly resonated with Beethoven's own urges and ideals.[35]

Heroines

Matthew Head has usefully encouraged us to consider the role of the heroine in Beethoven's dramatic music.[36] His injunction is well considered, especially when one acknowledges that Beethoven's most definitive portrayal of heroism involves not a hero but a heroine. Unlike the generalised heroic trajectory often heard in some of Beethoven's symphonies, there is a concrete heroic act that we actually see and hear in his opera *Fidelio*: the moment in the dungeon when Leonora (disguised up to now as

the young man Fidelio) thrusts herself between the murderer Pizarro and her unjustly imprisoned husband Florestan, exclaiming 'you must first kill his wife' with a piercing interval of a fifth from E♭ to high B♭. The moment is shocking in several ways, because not only does Leonore dramatically stand up to Pizarro and begin the process that will result in the freeing of Florestan, she also reveals herself as a woman and as the wife of Florestan.

To speak in the terminology of Aristotle's aesthetics, the extraordinary moment of Leonore's high B♭ is both a *peripeteia* and an *anagnorisis*, both a reversal of fortune and a recognition. For Aristotle, these two categories of dramatic event were crucial to the cathartic effect of many Greek tragedies. To combine them in one moment is overwhelmingly powerful.

The context of Leonora's heroism is the prison, and specifically the dungeon, that lowest and darkest depth, a powerful modern-day symbol of the underworld. The great Western epics (Homer's *Odyssey*, Vergil's *Aeneid*) each involve a journey to the underworld. This visit to Hades functions like a symbolic death, or a 'night of the soul', and an important feature of the epic hero is that he or she *can go to the underworld and return*. It's not so easy to return – remember the famous words of the sibyl when Aeneas consults her about going to Hades:

> facilis descensus Averno;
> noctes atque dies patet atri ianua Ditis;
> sed revocare gradum superasque evadere ad auras,
> hoc opus, hic labor est.

> (the road to hell is smooth;
> the gates of darkest Hades stand open night and day;
> but to retrace your steps and escape back to the upper air:
> there's the rub, there's the work).   Virgil, *Aeneid*, Book 6, lines 126–9

Leonora travels to the symbolic underworld of the dungeon and comes out alive – in this respect she is like an epic hero. In fact, both Florestan and Leonora share this epic heroic feature. He is confined to the dark place for the sake of the Truth, and he gets out alive; she goes there for the sake of his Liberty, and her heroism gets them both out. In this sense, she is a different kind of epic hero, since her heroism consists in what she must do in the underworld: whereas the epic heroes Odysseus and Aeneas travel to the underworld to *find out* about their destiny, Leonore travels there to *fulfil* her destiny. This adds another dimension to an already powerful dramatic conjunction: her destiny is fulfilled in the same moment that serves as both the anagnorisis and the peripeteia of the dramatic plot.

Female heroines were rare in Western culture during the centuries leading up to Beethoven's era. Among the ancients, one thinks of the defiant bravery of Antigone, who put common humanity above the decrees

of a tyrant, and suffered mightily for it. Various Greek goddesses have been revered as heroines, such as Athena, who defied the other gods by assisting mortal heroes such as Odysseus; or Artemis, the virginal goddess of the hunt, who rescued Atalanta and Iphigeneia in some accounts of these myths. Other Western traditions boast their own heroines, such as the Norse warrior goddess Freia. A more contemporaneous model for Leonora may well have been Joan of Arc in Schiller's 1801 drama *The Maid of Orleans*, from which Beethoven was fond of quoting.[37] Like Leonora, Schiller's Johanna functions as a liberating angel who dresses in male garb, and while Leonora literally unchains Florestan in the most moving scene of the opera, Johanna, hearing a blow-by-blow account of the decisive battle raging outside her English prison cell, breaks her own chains in a burst of preternatural strength and hurries out to the battlefield to turn the tide. She too must be counted as a potent model of heroism for Beethoven, one who may have had more influence than any other single heroic figure in terms of actual influence upon his music.

Beethoven and the *Eroica*

Beethoven clearly found much to inspire him as a creative artist in the new dramatic art of Goethe and Schiller. He may well have felt the urge to create music of similar power and urgency, music that would not only strive to represent the transcendent impact of heroic action but also convey the forceful, even shocking, intensity of the *Sturm und Drang*. Eleanor Selfridge-Field, in her 1972 article 'Beethoven and Greek Classicism', argued in a similar way for the influence of Greek tragedy on Beethoven's style. The Dionysian thrust of those tragedies, their shattering and cathartic events – for Selfridge-Field, these dynamic features are reflected in Beethoven's use of 'fate' motives, stormy openings and other moments of extreme drama.[38] While we can never hope to measure exactly the influence of the various eras of Western literature on Beethoven's art, I would point out that there are many literary works closer to home that may have worked on him with more immediate impact: not only the dramas of Goethe and Schiller, but also the exclamatory poetic rhapsodies of Klopstock. And yet, it will not do to separate the Greeks from the Germans, for Klopstock, Goethe, Schiller and many other German writers and thinkers were deeply affected by their new appreciation for Homer, for the Attic tragedians Aeschylus, Sophocles and Euripides, the rhapsodic poetry of Pindar and the biographical accounts of exemplary Greeks (and Romans) in Plutarch.

All these influences surely played a part in forming Beethoven's musical ambitions. The single most potent product of this urge to match the dramatic impact of the literature he loved may well be the *Eroica* Symphony. The recognition of the unprecedented intensity and power of this symphony has often been entangled in attempts to identify specific literary sources, or actual heroes whose doings are somehow represented by the music.[39] Lewis Lockwood's response to this tendency is to characterise the *Eroica* as portraying a composite kind of heroism: 'The "hero" of the *Eroica* is not a single figure but a composite of heroes of different types and different situations.' And he goes on to delimit this group of heroes, by calling the *Eroica* 'a work devoted to the "heroic" as a partly classical idea, in which the protagonists are the Greek or Roman heroes. These are exactly the figures who had been described by Plutarch in his *Parallel Lives*.'[40] Richard Wagner, in a short story he wrote in Paris in 1840, recognised the extraordinary dramatic power of the *Eroica*, but declined to name any specific hero or heroes it might be portraying. Instead he characterised the symphony as itself constituting a heroic act:

> He [Beethoven], too, must have felt *his* powers aroused to an extraordinary pitch, his valiant courage spurred on to a grand and unheard of deed! He was no general – he was a musician; and thus in *his* realm he saw before him the territory within which he could accomplish the same thing that Bonaparte had achieved in the fields of Italy.[41]

The unheard of deeds begin with the symphony's very first sounds and continue from the hyper-dramatised sonata-form first movement through the stunning tableaux of the Funeral March, the energised rebirth of the Scherzo, and the heady interplay of dance and counterpoint in the finale. With the *Eroica* Symphony, Beethoven created a symphonic work comparable in its impact to the dramas of Schiller and Goethe. For just as they remade the genre of the drama, so Beethoven remade the genre of the symphony, infusing it with the often shocking energy of the *Sturm und Drang*, as well as the greatness of soul mustered by the idealised heroic figures of the time, both men and women. Heard as a musical representation of ideal heroism and also as a world-historical heroic act in itself, Beethoven's *Eroica* Symphony stands as both a creation of its age and an achievement for the ages.

Notes

1. Beethoven in particular had a well-documented enthusiasm for Plutarch, as did Goethe and Schiller.
2. I thank Barbara Milewski for artfully stressing this point in a special presentation to my graduate seminar on Chopin at the Graduate Center, City University of New York, 16 April 2019.

3. K. Berger, *Bach's Cycle, Mozart's Arrow: An Essay on the Origins of Musical Modernity* (Berkeley, CA: University of California Press, 2007), p. 176.

4. J. Winn, *The Poetry of War* (Cambridge: Cambridge University Press, 2008), pp. 4–5.

5. L. Lockwood, *Beethoven: The Music and the Life* (New York, NY: W. W. Norton, 2003), p. 186.

6. For additional discussions of these and other kinds of heroism relevant to Beethoven, see M. Head, 'Beethoven Heroine: A Female Allegory of Music and Authorship in Egmont', *19th-Century Music*, 30 (2006), pp. 97–132, and L. Lockwood, 'Beethoven, Florestan, and the Varieties of Heroism', in S. Burnham and M. P. Steinberg (eds.), *Beethoven and His World* (Princeton, NJ: Princeton University Press, 2000), pp. 27–47.

7. The classic treatment of this paradigm shift remains M. H. Abrams, *The Mirror and the Lamp: Romantic Theory and the Critical Tradition* (Oxford: Oxford University Press, 1953).

8. For more on Homer's impact on German writers and thinkers of this era, see J. Wohlleben, 'Homer in German Classicism: Goethe, Friedrich Schlegel, Hölderlin and Schelling', *Illinois Classical Studies*, 15 (1990), pp. 197–211.

9. Entry 49 of the *Tagebuch*, quoting from *Iliad* Book 22, lines 303–5. Cited by Maynard Solomon, in 'Beethoven's Tagebuch', from M. Solomon, *Beethoven Essays* (Cambridge, MA: Harvard University Press, 1988), p. 259.

10. Klopstock deployed hexameter earlier, and influentially, in his epic poem *Messias*, published serially between 1748 and 1773. My thanks to Kristina Muxfeldt for making me aware of this in a personal communication.

11. On rare occasions, Homer will substitute a spondee in the fifth foot, always for expressive reasons (as in *Odyssey* Book 5, line 32, a line whose heavy spondaic tread marks the dread impact of Zeus' command to Hermes that Odysseus' journey homeward shall not be made in the convoy of the gods or of mortal men: οὔτε θεῶν πομπῇ οὔτε θνητῶν ἀνθρώπων. After the opening dactyl, every foot of this line is a spondee).

12. While Chapman's *Odyssey* is in iambic pentameter, his *Iliad* is in iambic heptameter. He published them both together in 1616, having published the *Iliad* in installments in 1598. Alexander Pope's *Iliad* was published a century later, in 1715.

13. As noted by Solomon, 'Beethoven's Tagebuch', p. 259.

14. Voss: 'Denn ausduldenden Muth verlieh den Menschen das Schicksal.' Homer used the word *thumos* (heart, soul, life), and the original line literally reads 'The Fates placed enduring hearts in men.'

15. Remember that Hector had killed Achilles' friend Patroclus, thus rousing Achilles' vengeance.

16. See Lockwood, 'Beethoven, Florestan, and the Varieties of Heroism'. According to Solomon, 'Beethoven's Tagebuch', p. 246, this diary entry (No. 26) most likely was written in 1814, the very year of the premiere of *Fidelio* in Vienna.

17. In Voss, as in Homer, this sentence is a parenthetical qualification referring to Zeus: '(denn dessen ewige Vorsicht / Lenkt allwissend das Glück und Unglück sterblicher Menschen)'. In this instance Voss is not terribly literal. What Homer says, more or less, is '(for he knows well all that is fated [what shall happen] and not fated [what shall not happen] of mortal men)'. Voss alters 'knows well all that is fated and not fated of mortal men' to 'directs the happiness and unhappiness of mortal men'. Voss may have been responding to another meaning of Homer's term for 'not fated' (*ammoria*, a word which literally means 'without a share' and can mean luckless or unhappy). But his verb 'lenken' is stronger than Homer's, who simply says that Zeus knows what will happen rather than directs it.

18. E. Selfridge-Field, 'Beethoven and Greek Classicism', *Journal of the History of Ideas*, 33 (1972), p. 581.

19. All translations mine unless otherwise noted.

20. Cited in the Afterword to F. Schiller, *Die Räuber* (Stuttgart: Reclam, 1969), p. 143.

21. Karl's disguised return allows Schiller to include the Homeric touch of a faithful old servant recognising the master, as when Eurycleia recognises Odysseus by his scar in Book 19 of the *Odyssey*.

22. A similarly lurid killing takes place in Schiller's next *Sturm und Drang* drama, *The Conspiracy of Fiesko*. The title character unwittingly slays his own wife, who is disguised as a man in order to attain safe passage through an embattled town.

23. As noted by M. Solomon, 'Beethoven and Schiller', in *Beethoven Essays* (Cambridge, MA: Harvard University Press, 1988), p. 208.

24. W. Hinderer, *Schiller und kein Ende: Metamorphosen und creative Aneignungen* (Würzburg: Königshausen & Neumann, 2009), p. 210.

25. F. Schiller, 'Was kann eine gute stehende Schaubühne eigentlich wirken?', in Benno von Wiese (ed.), *Schillers Werke: Nationalausgabe, Band 20: Philosophische Schriften, 1. Teil* (Weimar: Hermann Bohlaus Nachfolger, 1962), p. 96.

26. Ibid., p. 100.

27. To place such a dramatic confrontation in the middle of the play is part of Schiller's dramatic architecture, as when he stages a climactic dialogue between Queen Elizabeth and Mary Queen of Scots at the very centre of his 1800 verse drama *Maria Stuart*.

28. Goethe composed another drama from this period, *Iphigenie auf Tauris*, first in prose, but then rewrote it in blank verse during his famous Italian journey (1786–8). Another drama he composed while in Italy, *Torquato Tasso*, was also in blank verse.

29. Egmont's vision makes for an interesting parallel to Florestan's similar prison-cell vision, in which his beloved Leonore appears to him as a savior. On the importance of Klara as a heroic figure, see Head, 'Beethoven Heroine'.

30. *Egmont*, Act 5, Scene 4.

31. The translation is from J. W. Goethe, *Egmont: A Tragedy in Five Acts*, trans. Charles E. Passage (New York, NY: Frederick Ungar, 1980), p. 49. Goethe used these same lines again at the close of his autobiography *Dichtung und Wahrheit*.

32. Cited by L. Blumenthal, in her *Nachwort* to J. W. Goethe, *Weimarer Dramen I: Egmont, Iphigenie auf Tauris, Torquato Tasso* (Munich: Deutscher Taschenbuch, 1963), p. 234.

33. For more about Beethoven's relation to the dramas, poems and aesthetic theories of Schiller, see Solomon, 'Beethoven and Schiller', pp. 205–15. See also Thomas Sipe, *Beethoven: Eroica Symphony* (Cambridge: Cambridge University Press, 1998), pp. 92–3; and William Kinderman, *Beethoven* (Berkeley, CA: University of California Press, 1995), pp. 7–10.

34. The wording of these precepts is from Lockwood, *Beethoven: The Music and the Life*, p. 72.

35. For a succinct summary of the influence of Goethe's and Schiller's plays on the young Beethoven, see Lockwood, *Beethoven: The Music and the Life*, pp. 36–7.

36. See Head, 'Beethoven Heroine'.

37. My thanks to William Kinderman for making me aware of this possibility in his talk 'Leonore as Political Symbol in Beethoven's *Fidelio*', presented at a Mini-Conference on Beethoven's Fidelio, Boston University Center for Beethoven Research, 24 October 2018.

38. See Selfridge-Field, 'Beethoven and Greek Classicism', *passim*. In her remarkably wide-ranging account, Selfridge-Field also finds evidence in Beethoven's music of the 'edle Einfalt und stille Grösse' ('noble simplicity and quiet grandeur') that Winckelmann famously touted in 1755 as the special quality of Greek art.

39. I described some of the attempts to assign programmatic accounts to the first movement of the *Eroica* in the opening chapter of *Beethoven Hero* (Princeton, NJ: Princeton University Press, 1995), pp. 3–28.

40. Lockwood, *Beethoven: The Music and the Life*, p. 213.

41. R. Wagner, 'Ein Glücklicher Abend', in *Gesammelte Schriften und Dichtungen* (Leipzig: E. W. Fritzsch, 1871–3), vol. 1, p. 182.

2 Beethoven's 'Watershed'? *Eroica*'s Contexts and Periodisation

MARK FERRAGUTO

Few works of art have enjoyed so remarkable a reputation as Beethoven's *Eroica* Symphony. All at once, it is said to define Beethoven's 'middle period' and 'heroic decade', to epitomise his 'new path', 'symphonic ideal' and 'heroic style', and to signal the birth of the Romantic symphony, perhaps of musical Romanticism in general. An 'authentic "watershed work"', writes Joseph Kerman, the *Eroica* 'marks a turning-point in the history of modern music'.[1] It is, according to Mark Evan Bonds, 'a work of singular historical significance, both for its emotional content and technical innovations'.[2] Nor have claims about the symphony's importance been restricted to its aesthetic value: in the words of biographer Jan Swafford, the *Eroica* is 'one of the monumental humanistic documents of its time, and of all time'.[3] The *Eroica* has hence been seen as a 'watershed work' on at least three levels: within Beethoven's career and oeuvre, within the histories of music and art, and within the history of ideas.

Upon what basis are these extraordinary claims founded? To what extent are they justifiable? In order to begin to answer these questions, it seems important to consider not only what critics and listeners have traditionally valued about this symphony, but also the ways in which it has been made to tell a particular set of stories – about Beethoven's life, about his compositional and 'spiritual' development, and about music and art more generally. As Tia DeNora has observed (in dialogue with the work of the sociologist Norman Denzin), 'lives are produced through words', and concepts such as '[p]eriods, turning points, stages, phases, crises, advances, setbacks, tragedy, comedy, and farce are all to be considered as examples of the convenient molds for shaping a life'.[4] This is the case with biographical subjects no less than with abstract ones such as 'the symphony', 'the Classical style' or 'music'. The concept of the 'watershed work', in this context, needs to be understood both as an aesthetic construct and as a literary device that helps to shape a certain type of narrative.

Seeking to provide a more nuanced assessment of the *Eroica* as a watershed work (both for Beethoven and more broadly speaking), this chapter pursues three interrelated lines of inquiry. First, what have critics typically viewed as the most distinctive features of the *Eroica*, and to what

extent are these features truly unique or unprecedented? Second, why has this symphony, more than any other work by Beethoven, been viewed as a turning point in his career, and what are the critical foundations (and implications) of this notion? Lastly, might recent scholarship on Beethoven's 'middle' or 'heroic' period change the way we think about the *Eroica*?

The *Eroica* as a Musical Watershed

In his entry on the nineteenth-century symphony for *The New Grove Dictionary of Music and Musicians*, Mark Evan Bonds summarises many of the features that critics have found most remarkable about the *Eroica*. They include the unprecedented size and 'emotional scope' of the first movement, the presence of the 'functional' genre of the Funeral March in lieu of a typical slow movement, the 'novel length and speed' of the 'through-composed' Scherzo, the 'proportionately substantial finale' with its complex integration of forms and styles (and the related sense of end-orientation), and 'an overarching emotional trajectory' that approximates 'a process of growth or development' and has often been 'associated with the idea of struggle followed by death and culminating in rebirth or rejuvenation'.[5] Bonds assesses the *Eroica* in terms of genre history: against the backdrop of earlier symphonies, the *Eroica* stands out for its expanded dimensions, its novel use of forms and the impression it creates of a dramatic trajectory or narrative arc.

While this list helps to articulate what makes the *Eroica* unusual, it does not account for the symphony's extraordinary impact on listeners and critics. Other commentators have attempted to explain this impact as a function of Beethoven's stylistic development. Carl Dahlhaus, for instance, argued that the *Eroica* represents the culmination of a new compositional direction that Beethoven pursued beginning in 1802, the so-called 'new path' or 'wholly new style' of which the composer spoke (in largely unrelated contexts) around this time:

> [I]n works written in and after 1802, Beethoven expressed the processual character of form in a way that justified his speaking of a 'new path' or a 'wholly new style' . . . [O]ne way of describing the compositional problem that Beethoven was trying to solve around 1802 – in combination with other problems – is as the difficulty of designing musical forms that create an impression of processuality in an emphatic sense by being simultaneously thematic and non-thematic: thematic to the extent that a thematic substance is the prerequisite of a formal process; non-thematic in so far as the composer avoids setting down a fixed, pregnantly

delineated formulation at the beginning of the work to provide the 'text' for a commentary. In brief, the 'thematic material' is no longer a 'theme'.[6]

For Dahlhaus, the idea of musical form as process – first expressed in such works as Beethoven's Op. 31 piano sonatas and the Opp. 34 and 35 piano variations – is the 'outstanding characteristic' of the *Eroica*'s first movement. Basing this movement not on a theme but on an inherently dialectical 'thematic configuration' (the E♭ major arpeggio followed by the chromatic descent to C♯), Dahlhaus suggests, allows Beethoven to create this movement's characteristic impression of 'urgent, unstoppable forward motion'. This technique, he argues, is among the main reasons that Beethoven's Third Symphony 'represents a "qualitative leap" beside the two earlier ones'.[7]

Joseph Kerman similarly maintained that the *Eroica* displays the first fruits of Beethoven's 'symphonic ideal', an unprecedented fusion of technical and expressive mastery.[8] While the notion of 'musical form as process' certainly plays a role in this formulation, Kerman placed more emphasis on the integration of the multi-movement cycle. However, his attempt to claim the 'symphonic ideal' as unique to Beethoven has raised questions, and James Webster argues that its core elements were already apparent in Haydn's symphonies of the 1770s. Webster's summary of Kerman's thesis bears repeating:

> Kerman assumes not only the relevance of cyclic integration for Beethoven's music, but its status as a criterion of value – as unquestioningly as he assumes it had no role to play in earlier sonata-style music. It will be worth rehearsing in systematic order the features he claims Beethoven 'perfected at a stroke' in the Eroica: (1) radical intent; (2) moral and rhetorical characteristics (the impression of a psychological journey towards triumph or transcendence; extramusical ideas; an ethical aura); (3) techniques designed to bring this about, comprising (a) evolving themes and thematic connections between movements; (b) run-on movements, functional and gestural parallels between movements; and (c) the mutual dependence of contrasted parts, the projection of the underlying principles of sonata style over an entire work, integration ('a perfect mutual trajectory'), and the function of the finale as a culmination.[9]

As Webster argues, '[Haydn's] Farewell Symphony incorporates every one of these features, and it integrates them in a through-composed, end-oriented work, as radical as any from Beethoven's middle period.'[10] After a substantial discussion, he concludes that 'It was not "Beethoven's achievement" to "conceive the symphonic ideal," let alone to "perfect it at a stroke" or "develop the technical means to achieve it." It was Haydn's, and it was from Haydn (and to a lesser extent Mozart) that he learned it.'[11] Webster's point is well taken – in writings on Haydn (and Mozart), these features have been viewed merely as aspects of 'Classical style'; in writings

on Beethoven, however, they have been made the basis of the 'symphonic ideal'. One could make an equally compelling case that it was Haydn, not Beethoven, who pioneered the techniques of 'thematic configuration' and 'musical form as process'. Consider, as one of many possible examples, the first movement of Haydn's String Quartet Op. 33, No. 1 in B minor, in which the tonally ambiguous 'theme' (first presented in D major/B minor) undergoes multiple transformations as it is placed in new harmonic and syntactical contexts.

It is not difficult to think of other pieces by Mozart, Haydn or their contemporaries with many of the characteristics often claimed to be exclusive to Beethoven at this moment in his career (or to the *Eroica* in particular). Both Paul Wranitzky's *Grande sinfonie caractéristique pour la paix avec la Republique française* (1797) and Anton Eberl's Symphony in E♭ major, Op. 33 (1804), for instance, contain funeral marches in C minor. Eberl's funeral march, though not so titled, is clearly an example of the type – rife with militaristic rhythms and pathetic outbursts, it shares several distinctive gestures with the funeral march of the *Eroica*. (Eberl's symphony, it should be noted, was premiered several months before the *Eroica* on 6 January 1804, was later performed alongside it in the Palais Lobkowitz and was also dedicated to Prince Lobkowitz.) Other works, such as Mozart's 'Jupiter' Symphony No. 41 in C major, offer more evidence that the idea of 'a proportionately substantial finale' (and related end-orientation) was by no means exclusive to Beethoven: both the topicalisation of fugal writing in this movement and the function of the coda as a kind of sublime peroration anticipate Beethoven's practice. Even some of the most quintessentially 'Beethovenian' moments in the *Eroica*'s first movement – the dissonant sonority on which the movement seems to grind to a halt, the 'new theme' in the development section, the early entry of the solo horn before the recapitulation – have precedents in the oeuvre.[12] The question remains: what, if anything, truly separates the *Eroica* from the other symphonies of this period? What makes it a 'watershed work'?

For Scott Burnham, the *Eroica* conjures an unmistakable sense of 'presence' which separates it from the music of Haydn, Mozart and early Beethoven, and which lies at the heart of Beethoven's 'heroic style'. This sense of presence foreshadows Wagner's conception of an 'ever-present fundamental line' and manifests itself in a new set of 'musical values':

> These include thematic development as a way of making ever-greater stretches of music coherent and plastic (often resulting in action-reaction cycles), the captivating presence of nonregular period structures, monolithic treatment of harmony, overall teleological motion, extreme and underdetermined closure, and the monumentalisation of underlying formal articulations. The resultant line is

of course not melodic in the everyday sense of a prominent and foregrounded voice set against a background accompaniment. Instead, the entire texture is heard to participate in the fundamental illusion of melody, that of motion through time, and thus to partake of melody's sense of unfolding presence. This type of presence is one of the primary metaphors ascribed to the heroic style, and it attracts other, nonmusical metaphors as well, notably including protagonist, Will, and Self.[13]

Burnham suggests that this sense of 'presence' and the new musical values it is said to embody distinguish the *Eroica* from other symphonies and help to explain the many metaphorical and programmatic interpretations of it that have been proffered throughout its reception history. In response to Webster's claims about Haydn, moreover, Burnham maintains:

> The precedence of some of the material features of Beethoven's heroic style in the works of Haydn permits us to give a more defined shape to what is truly unprecedented in Beethoven: the sense of an earnest and fundamental presence burdened with some great weight yet coursing forth ineluctably, moving the listener along as does earth itself. Broadly speaking, Beethoven's music is thus heard to reach us primarily at an ethical level, Haydn's primarily at an aesthetic level.[14]

In Burnham's view, the Beethovenian 'presence' is not merely (or even primarily) a technical phenomenon; it is also an 'ethical' one. Precisely because of this ethical aspect, he suggests, Beethoven's music is not to be confused with that of other composers.

Burnham is by no means the only commentator who has heard the *Eroica* as the harbinger of a new 'ethical' orientation in Beethoven's output. For Kerman, the ethical is a central aspect of the 'symphonic ideal':

> The combination of [Beethoven's] musical dynamic, now extremely powerful, and extra-musical suggestions invests his pieces with an unmistakable ethical aura. Even Tovey, the most zealous adherent of the 'pure music' position, was convinced that Beethoven's music was 'edifying'. J. W. N. Sullivan taught the readers of his influential little book to share in Beethoven's 'spiritual development'.[15]

Although Kerman mentions both a new 'musical dynamic' and 'extra-musical suggestions' as factors in this sense of an 'unmistakable ethical aura', precisely what this term signifies remains ambiguous.

What does it mean for instrumental music to be 'ethical'? The answer to this question is complex and may have less to do with the intrinsic quality of the music itself than it does with the external factors that have been seen as relevant to Beethoven at this moment in his life. Maynard Solomon, for instance, has suggested that Beethoven's participation in the musical and philosophical ideals of the French Revolution imbued his music with a newfound sense of the ethical:

> The Revolution sought to transform French music into a moral weapon in the service of a momentous historical mission. The frivolities and sensuousness of *galant* music were abjured, and the 'scholastic' contrivances of Baroque and Classical forms were done away with; music was assigned, in the words of the historian Jules Combarieu, 'a serious character which it had not had since antiquity outside of the Church'. In brief, the Revolution introduced an explicit ideological and ethical function into music, which was later to become one of the characteristics of Beethoven's 'public' compositions.[16]

Solomon's hypothesis is, of course, supported by Beethoven's identification with Revolutionary politics and thought in the years leading up to the first French occupation of late 1805 (and intermittently thereafter). Nonetheless, one must concede that the Revolutionary music of Gossec, Méhul and Cherubini did not earn them the title 'hero', nor did it generate the same kind of response to their music as an 'ethical' art that Beethoven's has attracted. What are we to make of this situation?

Solomon's notion is also problematic because 'ethical' qualities can be (and have often been) recognised in the music of other composers. If the Revolution is truly what imbued Beethoven's music with an 'ethical aura', then what explains the existence of moral or ethical qualities in the earlier music of Haydn or Mozart (or Bach or Monteverdi)? Webster, for example, argues:

> Haydn's influence on Beethoven . . . also encompassed the art of projecting strong rhetorical impulses and deep ethical concerns (which Beethoven had from the beginning) in musical works which simultaneously exhibit the greatest craft and the profoundest coherence – which generate their rhetoric and their morality precisely by means of that coherence.[17]

The 'rhetorical impulses and deep ethical concerns' that Webster hears in the music of Haydn and Beethoven derive not from Revolutionary impulses but rather from the sense of 'coherence' that he understands as a component of the 'Classical style'. Such coherence entails the integration of the multi-movement cycle; the teleological processes of thematic development, formal departure and return; and the overall sense of an end-oriented process. The coherence of cyclic works has, in this sense, itself been imbued with an ethical or moral significance. Indeed, music of the 'Classical style' encourages the notion of an 'ethical aura', especially where 'transcendent' finales, large-scale minor–major trajectories and, of course, titles or texts are concerned. There are many examples of works before Beethoven that express the optimism of the Enlightenment age through the dramatic opposition of moral or emotional states: while Mozart's *Die Zauberflöte* (1791) dramatises the shift from ignorance to knowledge, Haydn's *The Creation* (1798) musicalises the shift from chaos to divine

light, to take two well-known examples. Forgiveness, reconciliation and mutual understanding were also common themes in opera. (Is the climax of the *Eroica*'s finale, the Poco Andante during which the strings finally yield to the winds – and play the 'tune' for the first time – not a relative of that most sublime reconciliation in comic opera, 'Contessa, perdono' from Mozart's *Le Nozze di Figaro*?) In this sense, Beethoven was building upon a whole tradition of artworks grounded in an ethical or moral perspective. Although the notion of the 'ethical' has been subsumed by the paradigms of the 'symphonic ideal' and the 'heroic style' and has been transformed into a Beethovenian musical convention, it arguably serves to situate his music within this cultural context, rather than to help him transcend it.

The valorisation of these interrelated concepts – 'musical form as process', the 'symphonic ideal', 'presence', the 'ethical' and the 'heroic' – and the attempts to reserve them for Beethoven are, of course, products of later reception history. They are critical strategies by which the music of Beethoven has been made to emerge as somehow 'greater' than that of his contemporaries and predecessors. After all, how else could one justify the notion of Beethoven as the 'man who freed music'?[18] This is not to say that these concepts lacked relevance to Beethoven, but rather that their importance for his art (and for his art alone) has often been inflated. This has had the effect not only of creating an artificial divide between Beethoven and other composers but also of marginalising works within Beethoven's oeuvre that do not fit the privileged aesthetic paradigms. The 'heroic style' has posed a particular problem in this regard, leading many critics to adopt a one-sided view of Beethoven and to ignore or attempt to suppress the works that do not seem to reflect the heroic ideal.

That the *Eroica* has often been hailed as marking the emergence of the 'heroic' in Beethoven's oeuvre (both as a period and as a style) is unsurprising, given its musical character, its title, its suppressed Napoleonic paratexts and its references to Prometheus in the finale. But it is important to remember that, as with the 'ethical', in no sense did Beethoven create the 'heroic', or, for that matter, many of the musical features that later scholars have associated with his so-called heroic style. By titling his symphony 'heroic', Beethoven was relating it not only to an abstract philosophical ideal but also to a fashionable aesthetic trend and an extant cluster of works that relied on the imagery and metaphorical connotations of the heroic. The heroic had long been a genre designation in dramatic music, and the term *'heroische Oper'* (and its cognates) appeared on the title pages of numerous operas. It is in part by virtue of this convention that the original playbill for Beethoven's ballet *Die Geschöpfe des Prometheus* (1801) referred to the work as a 'heroic, allegorical ballet'. As Nicholas Mathew has observed, in the wake of the French Revolution, Haydn composed numerous 'heroic' vocal

and instrumental works in which he combined 'a martial and monumental tone with a broadly political function' and commanded a new sense of listener engagement.[19] The association of the heroic with the key of E♭ major, often credited to Beethoven, was also firmly rooted in contemporary practice. As John David Wilson has shown, this key was frequently chosen in dramatic works to represent the nobility of the hunt and the classically heroic sense of *Tugend* (virtue) it conjured up.[20]

Moreover, and crucially, there is evidence that Beethoven's contemporaries were already beginning to understand the symphony as an intrinsically 'heroic' genre, independently of the *Eroica*. Writing in 1805, the philosopher Christian Friedrich Michaelis noted that 'in many great symphonies by Haydn, Mozart, and Beethoven, among others, one finds an order, a spirit similar to the grand plan and character of a heroic epic [*eines Heldengedichts*]'. That he was not referring in particular – or at all – to the *Eroica* is suggested not only by the date of the article (prior to the *Eroica*'s publication) but also by the first feature he describes as a characteristic of these heroic-epic symphonies: a 'simple introduction' which 'prepares and builds up expectation, which only gradually is to be fulfilled or exceeded'. Beethoven's *Eroica* includes no such introduction. Nevertheless, other aspects of Michaelis's description resonate with elements that later commentators have thought unique or special to the *Eroica*:

> Then other sections are added in which a great rich theme is developed. Its content becomes clearer in all its depth and opulence [thematic unfolding, musical form as process]. This theme expresses a heroic character by asserting itself in a struggle with many opposing motions [theme as protagonist, the impression of drama or narrative]. Here contrasts are appropriate, here the accompaniment and the polyphonic, figured treatment of the music are allowed to appear powerfully and place the principal subject in a brilliant light [learned counterpoint as means of thematic development] . . . Its melody is flowing without being weak, often sublime without being bombastic [a sense of melodic presence]. The individual features of its musical portrait [the implication of extramusical or programmatic content] intermesh marvelously, make one another necessary, and form a large, effective, magnificently organised whole [cyclic integration or coherence].[21]

Michaelis's description of the 'heroic-epic' symphonies of Haydn, Mozart and early (!) Beethoven, 'among other [composers]', suggests that many of the allegedly new musical values that later critics have specifically associated with the *Eroica* were, in the early 1800s, already viewed as aspects of a pan-Viennese or perhaps pan-European style of symphonic composition. From this perspective, what has come to be

known as Beethoven's 'symphonic ideal' is congruent with at least one version of the 'ideal symphony' in the late eighteenth and early nineteenth centuries.

The *Eroica* and the Beethoven Myth

Now for a caveat. In laying out some of the ways in which Beethoven's *Eroica* reaffirms and reimagines – rather than rejects – late eighteenth- and early nineteenth-century notions about what a symphony should be, I do not mean to deny its originality or to question, to borrow Kerman's term, its 'radical intent'. The *Eroica* is almost certainly the longest, most complex and most demanding (both for audiences and for performers) symphony that had yet been written. But by drawing attention to the critical strategies by which the *Eroica* has been elevated above other works from the period (not least the ascription of value to such attributes as 'length', 'complexity' and 'difficulty'), it becomes possible to historicise Beethoven's achievement and to bring it into sharper relief. It also forces us to think more deeply about how and why the *Eroica* has attained such extraordinary significance over the course of the last two centuries.

A large part of the *Eroica*'s appeal has been its perceived role as not merely a musical watershed but also a biographical one. The *Eroica* has become symbolic of the 'revolutionary' breaking of artistic, personal and spiritual bonds that is central to what Dahlhaus called the 'Beethoven myth'. Bruno Nettl provides a keen summary of this myth and what it has meant:

> Beethoven, the master of serious music, had a hard life; his deafness dominates our idea of him. He worked hard, sketched his works for years before getting them right, is seen as a struggler against many kinds of bonds – musical, social, political, moral, personal. He is thought to have seen himself as a kind of high priest, giving up much for the spiritual aspects of his music. He was a genius, but he had to work hard to become and be one. It is perhaps no coincidence that he has been, to Americans, the quintessential great master of music – for this is, after all, the culture in which hard work was once prized above all, labor rewarded; the culture in which you weren't born to greatness but were supposed to struggle to achieve it.[22]

Undoubtedly, a series of events as unusual and difficult as those in Beethoven's life has the makings of a tragic story, but as Beethoven's shadow has loomed larger and larger, these events have been made into a kind of tragic history, one with all the conventions of a Romantic plot.[23] As K. M. Knittel has pointed out, the desire to read Beethoven's life in this way has been 'overpowering' – on the one hand, Beethoven's personal

'crises' and subsequent bursts of productivity have lent themselves to the Romantic narrative of 'struggle' and 'transcendence' towards which biographers have long gravitated; on the other hand, the music (or, more precisely, a carefully curated subset of Beethoven's works) has been seen as both reflecting and substantiating this narrative.[24] As a result, it is increasingly difficult to extract Beethoven from the complex of ideas associated with him, one effect of which is the tendency to misinterpret or overinterpret elements of both life and works to correspond with certain preconceived notions. The literary critic Michel Foucault famously described this problem as the 'author function', noting that the 'aspects of an individual which we designate as making him an author are only a projection, in more or less psychologising terms, of the operations that we force texts to undergo, the connections that we make, the traits we establish as pertinent, the continuities that we recognise, or the exclusions that we practice'; these are, in short, the means through which an author is 'constructed'.[25]

The particular ways in which Beethoven has been 'constructed' result from a complex and overdetermined merging of life and works. The *Eroica* has played a major role in this process, largely because it has been made to correspond with what has been interpreted as an especially profound experience in Beethoven's life: his 'overcoming' of the depression and suicidal impulses articulated in the so-called Heiligenstadt Testament of 1802. Here, for example, is J. W. N. Sullivan:

> The most profound experience that Beethoven had yet passed through was when his courage and defiance of his fate had been followed by despair. He was expressing what he knew when he made the courage and heroism of the first movement succeeded by the black night of the second. And he was again speaking of what he knew when he made this to be succeeded by the indomitable uprising of creative energy in the Scherzo. Beethoven was here speaking of what was perhaps the cardinal experience of his life, that when, with all his strength and courage, he had been reduced to despair, that when the conscious strong man had tasted very death, there came this turbulent, irrepressible, deathless creative energy surging up from the depths he had not suspected. The whole work is a miraculously realized expression of a supremely important experience, and is justly regarded as a turning-point in Beethoven's music. The last movement is based on what we know to have been Beethoven's 'Prometheus' theme. Having survived death and despair the artist turns to creation. By adopting the variation form Beethoven has been able to indicate the variety of achievement that is now open to his 'Promethean' energy. The whole work is a most close-knit psychological unit. Never before in music has so important, manifold, and completely coherent an experience been communicated.[26]

The idea that Beethoven 'was expressing what he knew', 'speaking of what he knew' or 'speaking of what was perhaps the cardinal experience of his life', and the conjecture that the *Eroica* is a 'miraculously realized expression of a supremely important experience', demonstrate the tendency to assume a dialectic between Beethoven's private experiences and their alleged musical expressions. Sullivan's complex allegory involving Beethoven, Prometheus and the four-movement form of the *Eroica* shows how tempting it can be to use the life to understand the music, and vice versa.

Maynard Solomon's biography, arguably the most insightful psychological portrait of Beethoven yet written, is also problematic in this regard. His discussion of the relationship between the Heiligenstadt Testament and the *Eroica*, though less extravagant than Sullivan's, is in some ways more radical:

> In a sense, [the Heiligenstadt Testament] is the literary prototype of the *Eroica* Symphony, a portrait of the artist as hero, stricken by deafness, withdrawn from mankind, conquering his impulses to suicide, struggling against fate, hoping to find 'but one day of pure joy'. It is a daydream compounded of heroism, death, and rebirth, a reaffirmation of Beethoven's adherence to virtue and to the categorical imperative.[27]

In Solomon's conjecture, the Heiligenstadt Testament is 'the literary prototype' of the *Eroica*: the elements of 'heroism, death, and rebirth' that he identifies as covert expressions in the document reappear as overt expressions in the music. The symphony thus represents a kind of catharsis for Beethoven in which he purges the fears and destructive impulses that he mentions in the letter. Solomon is, of course, right to point out similarities between the document and the *Eroica*; but however plausible the connection may seem, there is no evidence to support his thesis – a widely adopted one – that the symphony relates to Beethoven's experiences in October 1802. The title *Sinfonia eroica* does not imply that the symphony represents 'the artist as hero' (as Wagner once suggested) nor do the events in the symphony (including the implied tragedy of the Funeral March) suggest that it is in any way connected to Beethoven's being 'stricken by deafness', as Solomon implies. Additionally, neither titles nor any other markings relate to Beethoven's 'conquering his impulses to suicide' or 'struggling against fate' or 'hoping to find "but one day of pure joy"'. In his letters, Beethoven makes no connection between the Heiligenstadt Testament (or the experience it describes) and this piece. On the contrary, what we know about the extramusical content of the *Eroica* – besides what we glean from the titles and other programmatic references – is that Beethoven insisted that the piece was 'about' Napoleon, even well after

he had suppressed its original title and planned dedication.[28] The dominance of the heroic paradigm has hence led critics into drawing parallels between Beethoven's life and music, parallels that cannot be substantiated by fact and are often (as in this case) impossible to prove.

Underlying this trope in Beethoven reception is what Hans Heinrich Eggebrecht called *Leidensnotwendigkeit*, 'the requirement of suffering for the production of art', or more precisely, 'the requirement of suffering of Beethoven the man (or rather that of humanity, which is exposed in Beethoven), so that Beethoven's art can emerge as music of "experience," "suffering and joy," or "overcoming"'.[29] From this 'requirement' arises a powerful conflation of biographical subject and musical utterance – the notion that Beethoven the man is the subject of his own music, rather than merely its author – that has governed Beethoven reception since the nineteenth century. In Beethoven's music, wrote the influential nineteenth-century music historian August Wilhelm Ambros, 'The painting of the powerful spiritual life of a titanic nature is unravelled before us – we are no longer interested in the *tone painting* alone – we are also interested in the *tone painter*. As a result, we stand in almost the same position with Beethoven as we do with Goethe – we regard his works as the commentary on his life', and vice-versa.[30]

One can see how the notion of Beethoven as hero has been so fundamental a part of the construction of the 'heroic style' and the reception of the *Eroica* in particular. One also sees how inextricable the musical features thought of as 'heroic' have become from notions of the 'heroic' that drive Beethoven's biography. The extent of the influence of the Romantic plot on approaches to the music is considerable: both sonata form and the multi-movement cycle, for example (especially, but not exclusively, when accompanied by extra-musical suggestions), have often been made to correspond with the pattern of struggle and transcendence central to the Beethoven myth. In this respect, even many purportedly structuralist approaches to Beethoven's music have been influenced by the Romantic plot archetype.

The *Eroica* and Beethoven's 'Creative Periods'

In part because of these biographical considerations, the *Eroica* has long been viewed as a turning point – perhaps as *the* turning point – in Beethoven's creative development. Despite the contrary views of scholars such as Carl Dahlhaus (who viewed the *Eroica* as the culmination of the 'new path' begun in 1802) and Alan Tyson (who considered it the 'most characteristic product' of Beethoven's 'heroic phase', also said to have begun in 1802), the scholarly consensus has tended to converge around

the idea that the *Eroica* is the first unequivocal work of Beethoven's so-called middle or heroic period (*c*.1803–12).[31] Of course, periods, like authors, are constructions, and while convenient, they are also reductive. Periods or styles function in large part through synecdoche: select works are made to stand in for the period or style, while other works composed contemporaneously are marginalised or suppressed because they do not fit the aesthetic paradigm. Beethoven's Fourth (1806) and Eighth Symphonies (1812), for instance, have typically been thought not to be musically representative of the 'heroic style', causing critics either to ignore them or to attempt to explain them away as works of 'consolidation' or 'repose' during which Beethoven gathered steam for his next monumental (and truly Beethovenian) effort. Likewise, the String Quartet in F major, Op. 135, as Knittel has shown, has long been viewed as a retrogressive work because it is less outwardly radical than the other 'late' quartets.[32] Stylistic periods are often linked to events in an artist's biography; in the case of Beethoven, this link has been very powerful. For Solomon,

> the completion of each new musical problematic, that is, of each style period, is somehow connected to a shift in [Beethoven's] psychic equilibrium, simultaneously engaging both the past and the future. Archaic materials re-emerge at every such critical point in his biography, with attendant malaise and anxiety resulting from a deepening access to repressed memories and feelings. But Beethoven emerges from each crisis having momentarily mastered both his anxieties and his new structural and expressive issues.[33]

Solomon's notion of Beethoven's creative periods is hence teleological on multiple levels, with the struggle–transcendence paradigm being acted out both within each creative period and across the entire oeuvre.

The idea of Beethoven's three creative periods or styles has a long history, but the periodisation of his oeuvre has varied and did not assume a stable form until well after his death. In the first decade of the 1800s, critics were already hinting at the possibility of distinct creative periods in Beethoven's oeuvre, especially when they were confronted with his newest and most challenging works. One review of the *Eroica*'s first public performance outlined three different perspectives on Beethoven's art and noted that one group of listeners, situated between the staunch conservatives and the outright devotees, supported Beethoven but registered a dangerous break in his style with the *Eroica* (see also Chapters 9 and 12):

> They wish that Mr. v. B. would use his well-known great talent to give us works that resemble his first two Symphonies in C and D, his graceful Septet in E♭, the spirited Quintet in D Major [Op. 29 in C Major?], and others of his earlier compositions, which will place B. forever in the ranks of the foremost instrumental composers. They fear, however, that if Beethoven continues on this path, both he and the public will come off badly.[34]

For these critics, the *Eroica* signalled a shift in style, but an undesirable one. A similar response may be seen in an 1816 review of the Fourth Symphony, a work which, ironically, later critics would view as a regression in the wake of the *Eroica*:

> That this composer follows an individual path in his works can be seen again from [the Fourth Symphony]; just how far this path is a correct one, and not a deviation, may be decided by others. *To me* the great master seems here, as in several of his recent works, now and then excessively bizarre, and thus, even for knowledgeable friends of art, easily incomprehensible and forbidding.[35]

Here, one clearly perceives a divide between an 'early' Beethoven, the works of whom had been accepted and normalised, and a 'recent' Beethoven (albeit a decade-old one, in the case of this critic) whose works were thought 'bizarre', 'incomprehensible' and 'forbidding'.

Ernst Theodor Amadeus Hoffmann and later Adolf Bernhard Marx were primarily responsible for turning the critical tides and preparing the way for the valorisation of the 'middle' Beethoven. While Hoffmann saw in the Fifth Symphony and other works the essence of Romanticism and absolute music, Marx believed that these same works, and the *Eroica* perhaps above all, were programmatic in the highest degree, reflecting concrete ideas or images (what he called a *bestimmte Idee*). The late works, by contrast, were not fully embraced until well after Beethoven's death. Initially written off as the products of deafness or madness, these works came to higher recognition in the era of Wagner (who particularly championed the String Quartet in C♯ minor, Op. 131, and the Ninth Symphony) and Liszt (who brought the late piano sonatas into the limelight). Hence, while the earliest critics valorised what we would call Beethoven's early period, associating it with the 'high Viennese modernism' of Haydn and Mozart, later critics championed the middle period, viewing it as the epitome of the new aesthetic ideals of Romanticism; still later critics argued that both of these periods were in some sense preparatory and that Beethoven's most supreme, transcendent works were those of his late period. As Webster has shown in a revealing study, these different emphases within the prevailing ternary scheme have roots in various biological, historical and artistic models.[36]

The most familiar ternary periodisation of Beethoven's oeuvre – early–middle–late corresponding to imitation–individuality–transcendence (and/or illness) – is often credited to Wilhelm von Lenz, who maintained in an 1852 study that 'like Raphael and Rubens, Beethoven has a first, a second, and a third manner, all three perfectly characterized'.[37] Lenz, who viewed these styles as continuous and interpenetrating, was among the first to systematically base his model on stylistic rather than biographical concerns.

However, his was by no means the first attempt at a ternary periodisation of Beethoven's oeuvre, and the earliest efforts – undertaken in an era of incomplete work catalogues and limited source material on Beethoven's life – were often highly indebted to conventional models. Johann Aloys Schlosser's ternary periodisation (published as part of his – the first – Beethoven biography of 1827), for instance, has much in common with later approaches to Beethoven's oeuvre – but only in a superficial sense. For Schlosser, the first and second periods are reminiscent of Haydn and Mozart, with the second being 'transitional' but also 'looking back to earlier times'.[38] The second period, epitomised by the *Eroica*, is characterised by a 'serious' tone, which is 'interrupted at times by boisterous merriment'.[39] And in the third period, the works are 'shaped by inner necessity. Everything follows organically from what preceded, so that everything accidental, uncertain, or extraneous is excluded'.[40] But Schlosser's second period encompasses only Opp. 40 to 60 (*c*.1800–6), and, surprisingly, the 'watershed work' marking the emergence of the third and final period is the Fifth Symphony of 1807–8. In fact, Schlosser completely glosses over the tail end of Beethoven's career, not because he views the works of 1808 to 1827 as representative of a protracted 'late' style, but rather because his discussion reproduces, word for word, an anonymous article originally published in 1818 (in the short-lived Viennese journal *Janus*).[41] Nevertheless, one can easily map his description of the third period onto the works of Beethoven's final decade, showing how arbitrary these categories can be.

A decade after both Beethoven's death and the publication of Schlosser's biography, François-Joseph Fétis revisited and revised the ternary periodisation of Beethoven's oeuvre in his *Biographie universelle des musiciens*. According to Fétis, Beethoven's first period was characterised by a reverence for and progressive mastery of the style of Mozart. The second period, lasting 'about ten years', was characterised by stylistic independence, and the third period had elements of 'mysticism' and formal innovation but also a loss of 'spontaneity' and occasional bouts of 'incoherence'. Fétis viewed the second period as most representative of Beethoven's mastery, and his account is striking for the new emphasis it places on the *Eroica*:

> But it is particularly in the third (*heroic*) symphony, opus 55, that the genius of the artist manifests itself in the absolute character of the creation. There, all trace of earlier forms vanishes; the composer is himself; his individuality arises majestically; his oeuvre becomes the model of a period in art history.[42]

Fétis thus explicitly linked the *Eroica* with the advent of Beethoven's second creative period, a notion that would be echoed by many later critics. Richard Wagner similarly considered the *Eroica* to be

the first work in which Beethoven struck out in a 'personal' direction because it contained the 'poetic content' that he believed to be central to Beethoven's most groundbreaking works. Despite the fact that no 'clear-cut division of Beethoven's output into separate periods is to be found in Wagner's writings', in his view, the *Eroica*, along with a handful of other works, paved the way for the summa of Beethoven's art, the Ninth Symphony.[43]

To give a more recent example of the part the *Eroica* has played in narratives about Beethoven's creative development, consider Michael Broyles's account of the emergence of the 'heroic style'. For Broyles, the *Eroica* is a 'pivotal' work which 'marks the end of a phase in Beethoven's artistic life' and 'inaugurates a new one'.[44] Beethoven's tendency to maintain 'a rigid stylistic dualism' between sonata and symphony styles, he argues:

> reached a critical turning point with the *Eroica*, at which time a third factor, the music of revolutionary France, began to affect Beethoven's compositional direction. Grafted upon the stylistic tension already ensuing from the dichotomous tendencies of the sonata and symphony styles, the French revolutionary element provided the catalyst for a volatile situation which almost guaranteed significant change. The 'heroic' style of Beethoven, that is, the style that characterizes his music during the first decade of the nineteenth century, is essentially the result of the interaction and finally the synthesis of these three stylistic currents of the late eighteenth century.[45]

This is, on one level, an elegant attempt to weave together several aesthetic and philosophical trends and to explain the uniqueness of Beethoven's art. At the same time, it is a narrative of struggle and transcendence in which conflicting tendencies (the eighteenth-century sonata and symphony styles), spurred on by the intrusion of French Revolutionary elements, are not so much resolved as sublimated in the 'synthesis' of Beethoven's 'heroic style'. Familiar literary structures of this kind continue to shape much writing about Beethoven.

The three-period model and its associated constructions have come under scrutiny in recent years. The reasons for this are manifold and include 1) the tendency to collapse Beethoven's Bonn years and early Vienna years into a single period; 2) the tendency to undervalue or dismiss Beethoven's early music by virtue of its being 'early'; 3) the tendency to elevate the music of the canonically 'heroic' and 'late' Beethoven at the expense of 'other' works understood as not being in the mainstream of Beethoven's development; and 4) the desire to broach alternative and/or more integrative models of Beethoven's life, career and compositional development. One consequence of all this is that the *Eroica*'s status as a watershed work for Beethoven has become more ambiguous. Giorgio

Pestelli and Stephen Rumph, for instance, have advocated taking the year 1809 as the start of Beethoven's second creative period, thereby placing less emphasis on the *Eroica* as a benchmark of style. This scheme has several advantages in that it registers major changes in Beethoven's life and music *c.*1809, which the traditional ternary model papers over, such as the signing of the 'annuity contract' (guaranteeing Beethoven income as long as he remained in Vienna), the political upheaval of the second French occupation, the death of Haydn and the turns towards antiquarianism and lyricism in Beethoven's music. Nancy November has also advanced an alternate model, advocating for a 'theatrical epoch' spanning roughly 1800–1 (*Die Geschöpfe des Prometheus*, Op. 41) to 1815 (*Leonore Prohaska*, WoO 96) and marked by 'intensifications' in 1804–6 (*Leonore/ Fidelio*, Op. 72) and 1809–10 (*Egmont*, Op. 84). This model accounts for the *Eroica*'s significance in quite a different way by encouraging us to view the piece through the lens of Beethoven's theatrical experiences and professional tenure as a composer at the Theater an der Wien (instead of through the lens of his symphonic or compositional development). Ultimately, no single model will satisfy all needs, and there will always be varied opinions depending on which realm or realms one chooses to privilege (personal, professional, stylistic, aesthetic, philosophical, cultural, political, economic etc.). Rather than attempting to streamline our understanding of Beethoven's life and oeuvre, embracing multiple models offers us perhaps the best possibility of registering the *Eroica*'s continuities with earlier styles, trends and philosophies while still appreciating the discontinuities for which it has long been admired.

Notes

1. W. Drabkin, J. Kerman and A. Tyson, 'Beethoven, Ludwig van', *Grove Music Online*, www .oxfordmusiconline.com/grovemusic/view/10.1093/gmo/9781561592630.001.0001/omo-9781561592630-e-0000040026 (accessed 16 February 2019).
2. J. Larue, E. K. Wolf, M. E. Bonds, S. Walsh and C. Wilson, 'Symphony', *Grove Music Online*, www.oxfordmusiconline.com/grovemusic/view/10.1093/gmo/9781561592630.001.0001/omo-9781561592630-e-0000027254 (accessed 16 February 2019).
3. J. Swafford, *Beethoven: Anguish and Triumph* (Boston, MA: Houghton Mifflin Harcourt, 2014), p. 364.
4. T. DeNora, 'Deconstructing Periodization: Sociological Methods and Historical Ethnography in Late Eighteenth-Century Vienna', *Beethoven Forum*, 4 (1995), p. 4.
5. Larue et al., 'Symphony'.
6. C. Dahlhaus, *Ludwig van Beethoven: Approaches to his Music*, trans. M. Whitall (Oxford: Clarendon Press, 1993), pp. 166 and 167.
7. Ibid., p. 173.
8. W. Drabkin, J. Kerman and A. Tyson, 'Beethoven, Ludwig van', *Grove Music Online*, www .oxfordmusiconline.com/grovemusic/view/10.1093/gmo/9781561592630.001.0001/omo-9781561592630-e-0000040026 (accessed 16 February 2019).
9. J. Webster, *Haydn's 'Farewell' Symphony and the Idea of Classical Style* (Cambridge: Cambridge University Press, 1991), p. 368.

10. Ibid.

11. Ibid., p. 372.

12. The dissonant sonority is used prominently in the slow introduction of Mozart's Symphony No. 39 in E♭ major (on the notes F, A♭, C and D♭); many sonata-form movements included 'new themes' in their development sections (see B. Churgin, 'Beethoven and the New Development-Theme in Sonata-Form Movements', *The Journal of Musicology*, 16, (1998), pp. 323–43); a solo horn anticipates the recapitulation in the first movement of Haydn's Symphony No. 6 in D major ('Le matin').

13. S. Burnham, *Beethoven Hero* (Princeton, NJ: Princeton University Press, 1995), p. 61.

14. Ibid., p. 65; see also p. 151.

15. Drabkin et al., 'Beethoven, Ludwig van'.

16. M. Solomon, *Beethoven*, rev. edn (New York, NY: Schirmer, 1998), p. 71.

17. Webster, *Haydn's 'Farewell' Symphony*, p. 373.

18. See R. Haven Schauffler, *Beethoven: The Man Who Freed Music*, 2 vols. (Garden City, NY: Doubleday, Doran & Co., 1929).

19. N. Mathew, 'Heroic Haydn, the Occasional Work and "Modern" Political Music', *Eighteenth-Century Music*, 4 (2007), pp. 7–25 and 12.

20. J. D. Wilson, 'Of Hunting, Horns, and Heroes: A Brief History of E♭ Major before the *Eroica*', *Journal of Musicological Research*, 32 (2013), pp. 163–82.

21. C. F. Michaelis, 'A Few Remarks on the Sublime in Music', *Berlinische musikalische Zeitung*, 1 (1805), pp. 180–1, quoted and trans. in *The Critical Reception of Beethoven's Compositions by His German Contemporaries*, ed. W. M. Senner, W. Meredith and R. Wallace (Lincoln, NE: University of Nebraska Press, 2001), vol. 1, p. 34.

22. B. Nettl, 'Mozart and the Ethnomusicological Study of Western Culture', in *Disciplining Music: Musicology and its Canons*, ed. K. Bergeron and P. V. Bohlman (Chicago, IL: University of Chicago Press, 1992), p. 145.

23. On Romantic drama narrative, see H. White, *Metahistory: The Historical Imagination in Nineteenth-Century Europe* (Baltimore, MD: Johns Hopkins University Press, 1973), pp. 8–9.

24. K. M. Knittel, 'The Construction of Beethoven', in *The Cambridge History of Nineteenth-Century Music* ed. J. Samson (Cambridge: Cambridge University Press, 2001), pp. 118–50 and 121.

25. M. Foucault, 'What is an Author', in *The Foucault Reader*, ed. P. Rabinow (New York, NY: Pantheon Books, 1984), pp. 101–20, and 110.

26. J. W. N. Sullivan, *Beethoven: His Spiritual Development* (London: Unwin Books, 1964; originally published 1927 by J. Cape), p. 77.

27. Solomon, *Beethoven*, pp. 157–8.

28. When asked about composing funeral music to commemorate Napoleon's death in 1821, Beethoven reportedly responded, 'I have already composed the proper music for that catastrophe', presumably referring to the Marcia funebre (Solomon, *Beethoven*, p. 182).

29. H. Eggebrecht, *Zur Geschichte der Beethoven-Rezeption: Beethoven 1970* (Laaber: Laaber-Verlag, 1994), p. 34.

30. Quoted in ibid., p. 35.

31. A. Tyson, 'Beethoven's Heroic Phase', *Musical Times*, 110 (1969), pp. 139–41 and 141.

32. See K. M. Knittel, '"Late", Last, and Least: On Being Beethoven's Quartet in F Major, Op. 135', *Music and Letters*, 87 (2006), pp. 16–51.

33. M. Solomon, 'The Creative Periods of Beethoven', in *Beethoven Essays* (Boston, MA: Harvard University Press, 1988), pp. 116–25 and 122.

34. 'Vienna, 17 April 1805', *Der Freymüthige*, 3 (1805), p. 332, quoted and trans. in *The Critical Reception of Beethoven's Compositions*, ed. Senner et al., vol. 2, pp. 15–16.

35. 'News. Kassel', *Allgemeine musikalische Zeitung*, 18 (1816), pp. 758–9, quoted and trans. in *The Critical Reception of Beethoven's Compositions*, ed. Senner et al., pp. 59–60.

36. J. Webster, 'The Concept of Beethoven's "Early Period" in the Context of Periodization in General', *Beethoven Forum*, 3 (1994), 1–27.

37. W. von Lenz, *Beethoven et ses trois styles*, 2 vols. (St Petersburg: Bernard, 1852–3), vol. 1, p. 66.

38. J. A. Schlosser, *Beethoven: The First Biography*, ed. Barry Cooper and trans. Reinhard G. Pauly (Portland, OR: Amadeus Press, 1996), p. 139.

39. Ibid.

40. Ibid., p. 141.

41. 'Ludwig van Beethoven (Beschluß)', *Janus*, 2 (7 October 1818), pp. 9–12.

42. F.-J. Fétis, *Biographie universelle des musiciens et bibliographie générale de la musique*, 2 vols. (Brussels: Meline, Cans et Compagnie, 1837), vol. 2, p. 110.

43. K. Kropfinger, *Wagner and Beethoven: Richard Wagner's Reception of Beethoven*, trans. Peter Palmer (Cambridge: Cambridge University Press, 1991), p. 118.

44. M. Broyles, *Beethoven: The Emergence and Evolution of Beethoven's Heroic Style* (New York, NY: Excelsior Music Publishing, 1987), p. 97.

45. Ibid., 2.

3 The Symphony in Vienna and Abroad around 1800

ERICA BUURMAN

Changing Contexts for Symphonic Performance in the Late Eighteenth Century

By the time Beethoven began composing symphonies, the genre occupied a different position in contemporary musical life from that of a generation previously. The symphonies of Beethoven's predecessors performed various functions, some of which had become obsolete by the time his First Symphony was premiered in April 1800. Eighteenth-century symphonies could function not only as items on concert programmes, but also as overtures or entr'actes in plays and operas, as church music performed between sections of High Mass, as *Tafelmusik* (literally 'table music' performed during formal meals), or as outdoor serenades. A sub-genre of the symphony, sometimes known as the 'Sinfonia pastorella', was specifically associated with church performance. In Austria, symphonies had also played a prominent role in monasteries, which typically supported their own orchestras to perform symphonies in church services and as *Tafelmusik*. In any context, symphonies usually accompanied another entertainment or ceremonial event. Even on concert programmes, symphonies were not usually the main event; rather, they tended to act as 'curtain-raisers' to programmes that featured a range of vocal and instrumental genres.

Professional musical life in and around Vienna changed in several important ways towards the end of the eighteenth century, affecting the role of the symphony in everyday life. From 1782, Joseph II's religious reforms reduced the role of instrumental music in church services, which led to the disbanding of many church *Kapellen* and the gradual disappearance of the 'Sinfonia pastorella'. Even more significant was the general disbanding of *Kapellen* at aristocratic courts towards the end of the century, since many symphonic performances regularly took place in aristocratic households that maintained *Kapellen*. In his 1796 *Jahrbuch der Tonkunst von Wien und Prag*, Johann Ferdinand von Schönfeld lamented the current of state affairs:

> It was formerly the strong custom that our large princely houses maintained their own house *Kapellen*, among which the most splendid geniuses often developed (evidence of this is our great Haydn), though it is now due to a coldness for the love of art, or a lack of taste, or economy, or other further reasons, in short to the shame of art, that this laudable practice has been lost, and one *Kapelle* after another has been extinguished, so that apart from that of Prince Schwarzenberg hardly any more exist.[1]

Schönfeld was probably correct in citing 'economy' as a factor in the decline of courtly *Kapellen*. Economising became an increasing priority in the early decades of the nineteenth century, when Vienna experienced several periods of severe inflation caused by Austria's involvement in the Napoleonic Wars. Money concerns did not drive the disbanding of *Kapellen* in every case, however. What Schönfeld disparagingly referred to as a 'lack of taste' might be more fairly construed as a change in taste. The cultivation of lavish courtly entertainments characterised the *ancien régime* (as epitomised by the court of Louis XIV), and the French Revolution probably contributed to a shift in attitude among the aristocracy, who began to scale down their entertaining.

Furthermore, the *Harmonie,* a chamber ensemble of wind instruments, came into fashion around the time that orchestras were disappearing from aristocratic households. *Harmoniemusik* was an increasingly popular musical entertainment in late eighteenth-century Vienna, particularly after Emperor Joseph II established the imperial *Harmoniemusik* in 1782. The *Harmonie* came to replace the full orchestra in some private households; Prince Grassalkowitz, for instance, reduced his *Kapelle* to a *Harmonie*.[2] A *Harmonie* was cheaper to maintain than a full orchestra, but could still perform many of the same functions, such as providing *Tafelmusik* and performing at private concerts. *Harmonie* ensembles were also better suited than orchestras to outdoor performance. The *Harmonie* ensemble employed by Prince Alois Liechtenstein (1759–1805) performed outdoor public concerts in Vienna during the summer months, and *Harmonie* ensembles also performed in various outdoor spaces such as the Augarten, the Prater, the glacis (a green belt between the city walls and the suburbs) and even on the city walls themselves. The rise of the *Harmonie* hastened the decline of orchestral music in aristocratic households, and resulted in a shift in the musical repertoire cultivated among court musicians. Court composers were no longer required to produce a steady stream of new symphonies, since the orchestra was no longer the pre-eminent ensemble among private musical establishments. Towards the end of the century there was, by contrast, a marked increase in the composition of new repertoire

for *Harmonie*, especially divertimentos, cassations and arrangements from popular operas.

The symphony did not, however, disappear from private musical entertainments, even in households that had disbanded their *Kapelle*. Although many aristocrats ceased to maintain a full complement of string and wind players among their regular staff, musicians could still be hired on an ad hoc basis. In the 1780s the Viennese music dealers Johann Traeg and Lorenz Lausch placed newspaper advertisements indicating that they could secure musicians for private concerts or balls, as well as offering orchestral music for hire in manuscript form.[3] This service may have catered partly to aristocrats who no longer maintained *Kapellen* but still wished to organise concerts in their homes from time to time. Traeg's advertisement also states that 'There are, to wit, in this town ever more families who entertain weekly by means of large or small musical concerts', suggesting that private concerts by professional performers were on the rise even among non-aristocratic households.[4] Thus, while the number of private concerts may have been decreasing in the houses of the nobility, the practice of presenting such concerts was simultaneously extending to wealthier members of the bourgeoisie.

The practice of hiring music and musicians for one-off private concerts seems to have slowed down after the 1780s, to judge from contemporary newspaper advertisements. In January 1785 Lausch announced that he would no longer lend out performing parts to anyone except to regular subscribers, apparently as a result of 'previous disorderliness',[5] and Traeg eventually stopped offering manuscript music for hire. By 1796, newspaper adverts placed by the Lausch firm (which continued trading after Lorenz's death in 1794) stated that they could supply musicians for house balls, without mentioning private concerts, suggesting that there was a decline in demand for the latter.[6] Private concerts nevertheless continued to play an important role in Vienna's musical life, and numerous patrons are documented as presenting concerts in private households throughout the 1790s and 1800s.[7] The banker Joseph Würth sponsored two substantial concert series in his new palace on the Hoher Markt in 1803–4 and 1804–5, which focused on large-scale instrumental works and included performances of Beethoven's First and Third Symphonies. A third concert series at Würth's palace did not materialise, probably because of the disruption to Viennese life caused by the Napoleonic Wars and the French occupation of Vienna in 1805. Prince Lobkowitz, one of Beethoven's most important patrons, was also a leading figure in the culture of private concerts. Lobkowitz bucked the trend of declining

courtly *Kapellen* by founding a house ensemble in the 1790s. With a core string section of seven players, Lobkowitz could organise regular chamber music concerts, and extra instrumentalists were hired for orchestral performances.[8]

In the larger European cities, public performance emerged as the most frequent context for symphonic performance by the end of the eighteenth century. Vienna's public concert culture, whose origins can be traced back as far as the 1750s, developed sporadically, and will be discussed separately below. Paris and London were Europe's leading centres for concert life in the late eighteenth century, and concerts in these cities were a frequent platform for the performance of Austro-Germanic symphonies. Haydn's symphonies for the Esterházy court became popular in both of these cities, and led to important commissions in the 1780s and 1790s. His 'Paris' Symphonies (Nos. 82–7) and Nos. 90–2 were commissioned for Le Concert de la Loge Olympique, a Parisian concert society founded in 1780 as a rival to the long-running Concert Spirituel. Haydn's greatest symphonic success, however, came from his twelve 'London' Symphonies, composed for his two visits to England in the early 1790s. These visits were made possible by the reorganisation of musical life at the Esterházy court after the death of Prince Nikolaus Esterházy in 1790. Like many aristocrats of the time, Nikolaus's successor Prince Anton dismissed most of the court musicians, and Haydn thereafter had few duties at court (though he continued to receive a nominal salary and a pension). The London visits came at the invitation of the violinist and impresario Johann Peter Salomon, and Haydn's Symphonies Nos. 93–104 were composed for Salomon's concert series at the Hanover Square Rooms.

The changing context of symphonic performance at the end of the eighteenth century inevitably led to a decline in the production of new symphonies. There were fewer salaried *Kapellmeister* who were expected to compose new works for the court orchestra to perform at regular functions and concerts. However, the new emphasis on the symphony as a public concert genre resulted in a rise in its status. The extraordinary success of Haydn's 'London' Symphonies, which were composed on a grander scale than his previous symphonies and quickly became popular elsewhere in Europe, has also been seen as contributing to the shift in attitude towards the symphony at the end of the eighteenth century.[9] Whereas symphonies had traditionally functioned in concert programmes as a framework for vocal and virtuoso items, the 'London' Symphonies were the main attraction at the Salomon concerts.

Developments in Viennese Concert Life

Vienna lagged behind other European centres in the development of a regular and institutionalised public concert culture. There was no organisation regularly leading the city's musical life until the establishment of the Gesellschaft der Musikfreunde, whose official statutes were published in 1814. A major hurdle was that the city did not have a concert hall until 1831, when the Gesellschaft opened its purpose-built premises in the Tuchlauben. Before this, concert organisers could make use of large venues such as theatres, the ballrooms in the imperial palace and the university hall, but only when they were not otherwise in use. Since theatrical entertainments usually took place daily, the theatres were only available on church holidays (so-called *Spielfreie Tage*) when theatrical performances were forbidden by imperial decree. Initially *Spielfreie Tage* encompassed the whole of Lent, most of Advent, and the eve and anniversary of the death of the most recently deceased Habsburg ruler, though the rules were later relaxed so that the theatres could open on certain days during these periods.[10] Other venues used for public concerts included the Mehlgrube (a building in the Neuer Markt that housed a restaurant and a large room used for concerts and balls), Ignaz Jahn's restaurant in the Himmelpfortgasse, and the hall at the Augarten. A regular public concert culture of sorts was established for the duration of Lent and Advent, though this mostly centred on one-off events and the occasional concert series.

The only concerts that were permanent fixtures in the annual calendar were those of the Tonkünstler Societät, an organisation founded in 1771 to provide for musicians' widows and orphans. From 1772, the society usually held four annual benefit concerts in one of the imperial theatres (the Kärntnerthortheater or the Burgtheater), two taking place at Easter and two at Christmas. The programmes at these concerts followed contemporary practice in featuring a miscellany of instrumental and vocal music, though the centrepiece was usually a grand oratorio. All members of the society were expected to perform or else to pay a small fee, which resulted in very large performing forces. Mozart reported enthusiastically to his father that one of his symphonies had been performed at the society's concert of 3 April 1781 by an orchestra that included forty violins, ten violas, eight cellos, ten contrabasses and doubled wind instruments (including six bassoons).[11] It was by no means typical for Viennese concerts to feature such large orchestras, and performances on this scale were only possible at charitable events (including the Tonkünstler Societät benefit concerts) where the musicians supplied their services free of charge.

On *Spielfreie Tage* the theatres were also frequently hired out to musicians who wished to present their own concerts (known as academy concerts or *Akademien*). The musician, who was usually a virtuoso singer or instrumentalist, would cover the costs associated with presenting the concert, and receive all the profits. Smaller venues were also used for benefit concerts, but the theatres, particularly the prestigious court theatres, could attract and accommodate the largest audiences. Obtaining permission to use the court theatres was not easy, particularly between 1794 and 1806 when they were managed by Baron Peter von Braun (1764–1819), who was notoriously unsupportive of musicians wishing to present concerts. In a letter to Breitkopf & Härtel, Georg August Griesinger reported that Braun 'doesn't easily lend his orchestra for accompanying, or on the day when the concert is supposed to take place, he announces [for performance in the other theatre] a new or very popular piece and ballet, and thereby deprives the poor musician of his numerous public'.[12] The Theater an der Wien, the most prestigious theatre outside the city walls, was also managed by Baron von Braun between 1804 and 1806 (Braun having bought the theatre in 1804). Securing the best venue could be difficult for musicians wishing to present a concert for their own benefit, and those well connected with Baron von Braun and other members of the court organisation tended to fare better than outsiders.

A new addition to Viennese concert life in the 1780s was the subscription series. The pioneer in this realm was Philipp Jakob Martin, who first organised a series of concerts in the Mehlgrube in the winter of 1781–2, followed by several more over the next decade. From 1782, Martin also began organising Sunday morning concerts in the Augarten during the summer, for which a subscription to all twelve concerts could be purchased for two ducats.[13] Mozart participated as a soloist in Martin's subscription concerts in the Mehlgrube and the Augarten, and some of his symphonies were also performed on these occasions. In 1785 Mozart organised his own subscription series in the Mehlgrube during the Lenten season, for which several of his piano concertos were newly composed.

The subscription model of concert organisation was ideal for independent artists such as Mozart, providing regular performance opportunities and insurance against financial losses incurred through hiring the venue and other related expenses. By securing subscriptions in advance, Mozart was even able to hire the professional orchestra of the Burgtheater for his 1785 Mehlgrube concerts, which was unusual for the time; Martin generally engaged unpaid *dilettantes* rather than professional musicians for his subscription concerts. Nevertheless, public subscription concerts apparently declined after these promising ventures of the 1780s. The summer Augarten concerts continued to be a regular fixture in the Viennese

calendar, but concert series organised by independent musicians remained relatively rare. The violinist Ignaz Schuppanzigh (1776–1830) organised the city's first chamber music concerts as a subscription series in the winter of 1804–5, though he was an experienced impresario, having organised the Augarten concerts since 1799. A likely reason for this decline was the difficulty of persuading subscribers to commit to attending multiple concerts, particularly when the city offered so many other forms of entertainment that did not require similar commitment (including opera, theatre and balls).

The subscription series fared better when organised by aristocratic music societies. Beginning in the 1780s, the Gesellschaft der associierten Cavaliers, founded by the imperial librarian Gottfried van Swieten, organised regular performances of large-scale choral works, particularly those by Handel and Haydn. Performances typically took place first for an invited audience, either in the hall of the imperial library or in the palace of one of the society's members, and then for a public audience in one of the theatres. The society's members jointly covered the costs of organising these performances, in what was essentially a form of collective patronage. A similar aristocratic organisation, whose members included Prince Lobkowitz and other leading musical patrons, was established in 1807 with a view to organising orchestral concerts. The result was a highly successful concert series in 1807–8, known as the Liebhaber Concerte, whose programmes centred mostly on symphonies, overtures and concertos. Each of Beethoven's four completed symphonies was performed at least once over the course of the series, and works by Haydn and Mozart were also well represented.[14] The concerts were funded by subscriptions, which were sold among the aristocratic community, rather than sponsored exclusively by the organising committee. Tickets were not made available to the general public, however, and the concert series was also distinguished from regular concerts by its explicit aim to present great musical works, and 'to affirm the dignity of such art and to attain still higher perfection'.[15] Although the series was apparently a success, the disruptions to Viennese life caused by the return to war with France prevented a further season of concerts in 1808–9.

The subscription model of the Liebhaber Concerte differed from that of commercially driven concerts, since patrons bought tickets partly to support an elite and idealistic musical endeavour. Organisers of one-off benefit concerts generally could not afford this kind of musical idealism, since the success of such concerts depended on attracting a broad audience. Fully public concerts therefore continued to present mixed programmes that appealed to popular taste, particularly with favourite arias from the latest operas and virtuoso showpieces. The programmes of the semi-public

Liebhaber Concerte, on the other hand, explicitly focused on grand and serious musical works, and accordingly placed more emphasis on symphonies.

Although the public (or semi-public) concert emerged as the most important context for the symphony after the decline of courtly *Kapellen*, Vienna offered fewer opportunities for symphonic performance than cities with a more established commercial concert culture. Symphonies were of secondary importance on the programmes of the Tonkünstler-Societät concerts (whose emphasis was mostly on large-scale choral works) and in virtuoso benefit concerts (in which the main attraction was the solo performer). The decline of the subscription series after the 1780s also meant that independent musicians and composers wishing to organise concerts could hope, at best, for a one-off benefit in one of the theatres. Whereas Haydn composed six new symphonies for each of his London visits in the 1790s, it would be virtually impossible for a composer in Vienna to present six new symphonies in a single season under the commercial model of concert organising. Concerts supported by the aristocracy were more promising for regular symphony performances, especially with the emergence of an idealistic approach to concert programming exemplified by the Liebhaber Concerte. Nevertheless, aristocratic concert societies provided only intermittent additions to the city's concert life, and a regular public concert life that emphasised symphonies failed to materialise before the establishment of the Gesellschaft der Musikfreunde.

Symphonies as Sheet Music

Around 1800, music that circulated on the Viennese sheet music market did not consist exclusively of printed music, but also included manuscript copies. Music printing arrived relatively late on the Viennese publishing scene, compared with other European centres. The Artaria publishing firm was the first to run a successful music engraving workshop from the 1770s, printing music from engraved pewter or copper plates. Numerous rival companies were established soon afterwards and music printing quickly became a flourishing industry in the city. Printed music was also imported from other cities such as Amsterdam, Paris and London and sold by Viennese music dealers. Even after the arrival of printed music on the market, however, music copying continued to represent a significant portion of the Viennese music publishing industry. Copyists did a healthy trade in manuscript copies of published music, as well as copying on demand when multiple parts were needed for a performance.

Music engraving functioned most efficiently for works that required a small number of plates, and for which there was a high demand. Unsurprisingly, the catalogues of music publishers such as Artaria were dominated by chamber music and works for solo keyboard. Symphonies and other large-scale works were largely avoided by music engravers, since the effort and expense involved in engraving (and then storing) such a large number of plates for a single work did not make the process worthwhile. The limited opportunities for concert performance also meant there was a relatively small market for orchestral music, and publishers would be unlikely to recover the costs of the engraving process. In 1791 the Viennese publisher Hoffmeister began an ambitious three-year project of publishing a subscription series of all his forty-four completed symphonies, alongside twenty-eight new ones, printed on the finest quality paper.[16] Hoffmeister evidently aimed to lead the market for symphonies in a new direction, away from the practice of manuscript copying. Eventually, however, the project was abandoned after only seven symphonies had been printed, due to an apparent lack of demand. Symphonies continued to circulate on the Viennese market primarily as sets of parts in manuscript form throughout the 1790s. It was not yet customary for symphonies to be published in score, particularly as there was no real need for them in performance since orchestral concerts were usually directed by the concertmaster from the violin.

Most music copyists traded primarily as artisans, working whenever their services were required. However, the copyists Lorenz Lausch and Johann Traeg were also two of the city's most important music dealers in the 1780s and 1790s. Lausch dealt exclusively in manuscript music, whereas Traeg also imported printed music. The Lausch firm eventually came to specialise in transcriptions from popular opera, though Lausch initially also traded in symphonies, as indicated in a *Wiener Zeitung* advert of 1782:

> Lorenz Lausch, who has the honour of providing the symphonies for the current dilettante concerts [Martin's concert series in the Mehlgrube], informs all music lovers that beside the newest symphonies from Herr Haydn . . . other symphonies are also available, as well as cassations for violin and flute, quintets, quartets, trios and duets and keyboard music in manuscript.[17]

As a music dealer, Johann Traeg specialised in instrumental music, and by the 1790s he was undoubtedly Vienna's leading supplier of symphonies. In 1799 he published a catalogue of all the works in his stock, which included more than 500 symphonies by eighty-one different composers, including manuscript as well as imported prints.[18] But by then the market for symphonies had already shrunk significantly since

the 1780s, when Traeg began trading. The symphonies in the 1799 catalogue are priced much lower than in earlier advertisements in the *Wiener Zeitung*, suggesting that Traeg was selling off stock that was no longer as profitable. Traeg's supplementary catalogue of 1804 confirms that the symphony was of declining importance to his trading: whereas symphonies represented the largest category of instrumental music in the 1799 catalogue, in the 1804 supplement they represented one of the smallest. In the intervening five-year period Traeg had obtained only thirty-three new symphonies, compared with fifty-seven pieces for *Harmonie*. Works for string quartet and solo keyboard are also better represented in the 1804 supplement than the 1799 catalogue, indicating a growing market for works for the salon.

Viennese music dealers and publishers attempted to adapt to the changing market for symphonies in various ways at the end of the eighteenth century. In the early 1780s, Lausch and Traeg launched business ventures in which manuscript parts were offered for hire. Beginning in 1783, Lausch charged a yearly subscription of twelve gulden, payable semi-annually, for which he offered 'a work' every two weeks: this could either be six chamber pieces (i.e., quintets, quartets, trios, duets or sonatas) or three symphonies.[19] Should any customer wish to keep the music they had hired, Lausch could then provide a copy for an additional price. Traeg quickly followed suit with an almost identical subscription system, first advertised in the *Wiener Zeitung* in February 1784.[20] Like Lausch, Traeg offered three symphonies or six chamber works every two weeks for an annual price of twelve gulden, payable in three-monthly instalments. For a quarterly payment of five gulden, customers could also receive twice the number of works (six symphonies or twelve chamber works). The provision of hire materials had clear merits: customers could try out music before committing to buying their own copy, and music-lovers could have access to large quantities of music without having to build up an impractically large personal library. The system was particularly useful for anyone organising performances of symphonies and other large-scale works. Nevertheless, both dealers ceased to offer materials for hire by the end of the decade, indicating an apparent decline in demand for performance parts (evidently corresponding with a decline in private performances of symphonies).

Another way in which publishers adapted to the changing market was to offer symphonies in transcription for small chamber ensembles. In a newspaper advertisement of December 1792, Artaria announced the publication of symphonies by Pleyel arranged as string quartets:

> Of the many Pleyel symphonies, three of the best have been chosen and arranged by Herr Went for a quartet of two violins, viola and cello. This arrangement is so excellent that these symphonies also have the most beautiful and enjoyable effect as quartets, and we hope hereby to offer a treat for quartet-lovers.[21]

Artaria had previously avoided publishing symphonies, specialising instead in chamber music and works for solo keyboard. String quartet arrangements, which primarily targeted Vienna's many amateur musicians seeking to make music in the home, were much more likely to be commercially successful than symphonies in full scoring. Traeg's 1799 catalogue also includes symphonies in arrangements for chamber ensemble, suggesting that such arrangements came into fashion as orchestral performances were in decline. Traeg's stock included fifteen symphonies arranged as quintets (six each by Haydn and Mozart and three by Pleyel). In the string quartet category, Traeg's catalogue includes an entry under J. Haydn of '8 Quartett Sinfonien arrang.'[22] There are also thirty-one works labelled 'Quartet Sinfon.', all by older composers (C. P. E. Bach, Kobrich, Monn and Ignaz Jakob Holzbauer), which may be early symphonies originally composed for four-part string orchestra.[23] Traeg's categorisation suggests that these works were primarily marketable as string quartet music, even if they were technically classed as symphonies.

Around 1800, string quartets and quintets were the preferred medium for symphony arrangements. By 1803, for instance, Beethoven's First Symphony had been issued in string quintet arrangements by publishers in Vienna, Bonn and Paris.[24] Other combinations of instruments were also added to the repertoire of symphony arrangements in the early nineteenth century: Beethoven himself corrected and approved his Second Symphony as a piano trio, and the Offenbach publisher Johann André published a series titled 'Collection de Sinfonies de divers auteurs' that included Beethoven's First and Second Symphonies arranged as nonets.[25] Such arrangements allowed symphonies to have a second life beyond the concert environment (see also Chapter 11). By the middle of the century, piano duet arrangements of Classical symphonies were a core addition to the salon repertoire enjoyed by amateur pianists. Such duet arrangements became an important avenue by which music enthusiasts could become thoroughly acquainted with the symphonies of Haydn, Mozart and Beethoven, which by then were recognised as central to the canon of symphonic masterworks. In this way piano arrangements of symphonies approached the purpose of a study score, another later nineteenth-century development in music publishing, since they offered a means of learning the important works in the canon.

Beethoven's Seventh and Eighth Symphonies were an important landmark of music publishing when they first appeared in editions by the

Viennese publisher S. A. Steiner & Comp. in 1816–17. Both symphonies were published in several formats, including arrangements for nine-part *Harmonie*, string quartet, piano trio, piano solo, piano duet and two pianos. The Seventh and Eighth Symphonies were also published in full score, marking the first time that a symphony was published in score and parts simultaneously. The arrangements ensured that the publication of the score and parts would not be loss-making overall, as the sales of the more marketable chamber music could compensate for the expense of engraving the parts. Since it was not yet standard practice to conduct a symphony from the score, the publication was evidently underpinned by the emerging notion of the symphony as an object worthy of study, or a text that exists independently from the act of performance.[26]

Overall, nineteenth-century developments in the publishing of symphonies correspond with contemporary developments in concert life, particularly in aristocratic concert societies (especially the Liebhaber Concerte), which consciously sought to promote great and worthy works of art. Ultimately, these trends reflected the increase in the status of the symphony in nineteenth-century musical culture, though the genre's elevated status was by no means solidified by the time Beethoven began his career as a symphonist.

Contextualising Beethoven's Early Symphonies

When Beethoven moved to Vienna at the end of 1792, he found an environment which offered fewer opportunities for symphony performances than his native Bonn. One of his duties as a member of the *Kapelle* at the Bonn court had been to perform as a violist in the court orchestra. As is well known, Beethoven participated as a member of the orchestra in regular opera performances after 1789, when the theatre was re-opened following a five-year interruption. Recent research has also indicated that there was a thriving concert life at the Bonn court by the time of Beethoven's final departure, having been initiated by the music-loving Elector Maximilian Franz in the 1780s.[27] The court had its own dedicated concert venue, the *Grosser Akademiensaal*, located directly above the theatre. Concert life at the Bonn court appears to have been private, as there is little evidence of tickets being advertised or made available to the general public. From the surviving documentation, it is not possible to determine how frequently court concerts occurred. However, when the court ensemble (including the 20-year-old Beethoven) accompanied the Elector to Mergentheim for a six-week stay between September and October 1791, their performances reportedly

included six concerts of orchestral music, suggesting that such concerts were a regular part of the ensemble's activities. Symphonies were undoubtedly core to the orchestra's repertoire: an extensive inventory of Elector Maximilian Franz's music library lists over 650 items of orchestral music, including symphonies, divertimenti, serenades and overtures. The centrality of the symphony is confirmed by the only documented concert programme from the 1791 Mergentheim visit, which included three symphonies (by Mozart, Pleyel and Wineberger respectively) alongside two concertos and two arias. Regular concert performances that emphasised symphonies were evidently a routine aspect of Beethoven's early professional life.

On his first arrival in Vienna, Beethoven was still a salaried member of Maximilian Franz's *Kapelle*, and it was assumed that he would return to Bonn after a period of studying composition (initially with Haydn, later also with Albrechtsberger and Salieri). Had he continued his career as a court musician, his compositions would eventually have included symphonies for the court orchestra to perform. He had in fact already sketched ideas for at least two different symphonies while in Bonn: he sketched a first movement of a C minor 'Sinfonia' as early as 1788–9, and a C major 'Sinfonia' appears among his sketches from 1790.[28] When the Bonn court was disbanded in 1794, following the occupation of Bonn by French forces during the Revolutionary Wars, Beethoven suddenly found himself an independent musician without professional ties to any regular performing ensemble. There was now little reason to expect symphonies to become a core part of his compositional output, as they had been for a previous generation of *Kapellmeister* such as Haydn.

While there were undoubtedly fewer orchestral performance opportunities for an independent composer in Vienna than for a courtly *Kapellmeister*, the city nevertheless offered more opportunities for a composer to win widespread recognition and acclaim. Public concerts were held only infrequently, but one such concert in Vienna could reach a larger and broader audience than the regular private concerts at the Bonn court. Vienna was also home to a large concentration of wealthy music lovers who were willing to support serious music and musicians. Concert societies and series organised by Viennese aristocrats were increasingly underpinned by ideals concerning the promotion of great musical works (evidenced from the 1780s in the concerts of the Gesellschaft der associierten Cavaliers and its emphasis on grand choral works). In these circumstances, a composer working in Vienna might produce only a handful of symphonies, but these works could make a greater impact on the musical scene than they might in a private musical establishment, where symphonies formed part of regular in-house entertainment.

Beethoven began his first attempt at composing a symphony for Vienna in 1795. This was an important breakthrough year for the 24-year-old composer, which saw his public debut as a concerto soloist at one of the Tonkünstler Societät concerts in March, and the publication of his Piano Trios Op. 1. Beethoven sketched ideas for a symphony in C major intermittently until finally abandoning it in 1797, though some of the material was later recycled in his First Symphony. His first opportunity to present a benefit concert in one of the theatres came relatively late: by the time of his first concert in the Burgtheater in April 1800 he had already established himself as one of Vienna's leading musicians. He evidently hoped, though, that public concerts would become a regular feature of his working life. In a letter to his childhood friend Franz Wegeler of 29 June 1801, Beethoven wrote, 'if I stay here for good I shall arrange to reserve one day a year for my Akademie'.[29] This was overly optimistic: in the end, Beethoven only presented further public concerts for his own benefit in the years 1803, 1808, 1814 and 1824. Of these, 1814 was his most successful year of concert-giving, in which he arranged four benefit concerts and a further charity concert whose programmes included the recently completed Seventh and Eighth Symphonies and *Wellingtons Sieg*.

Symphonies composed for grand public concerts were evidently part of Beethoven's long-term compositional plans from an early stage. However, his ambition to compose a symphony as early as 1795 should be viewed in the context of his attempts to make his mark on the Viennese music scene, rather than as reflecting a particular desire to specialise in this genre. In July 1801 Beethoven wrote a long letter to his friend Amenda in which he revealed his despair about his deafness, and also reflected on his achievements so far: 'What is there that I might not accomplish? Since you left I have composed everything except opera and church music.'[30] He tackled these last two genres not long after his letter to Amenda, with his oratorio *Christus am Ölberge* in 1803 (technically a concert work, but nevertheless his first major essay in religious music) and the first version of *Leonore* in 1804. Beethoven evidently aimed to excel in all the major musical genres, as Mozart had done.

Composing symphonies and other large-scale concert works could nevertheless pose serious financial risks for a self-employed musician such as Beethoven. There was little guarantee that a concert venue would be available for its performance, so that composing a symphony might end up being a fruitless venture. Furthermore, whereas an opera might run for several months, a symphony might be performed only once at a public benefit concert, with no promise of future performances. Symphonies were also less attractive to Viennese music publishers than smaller genres that were cheaper to produce and easier to sell. While Beethoven clearly desired

to show himself to be a capable symphonist from early in his career, circumstances in Vienna meant that he could not afford to devote too much time and energy to the genre.

As an independent musician, however, Beethoven was in a more favourable position than most for gaining recognition as a symphonist. He received generous support from music-loving aristocrats from his early years in Vienna, particularly from Prince Lichnowsky, who provided him with accommodation and meals during the 1790s, and paid him an annual stipend of 600 gulden from 1800. This support allowed Beethoven to devote time to ambitious large-scale projects that did not necessarily offer immediate financial reward (symphonies being a prime example). Lichnowsky also actively promoted Beethoven's career, taking him on an extended concert tour in 1796 and introducing him to many of Vienna's leading aristocratic patrons of music. The prince may also have helped Beethoven to secure the Burgtheater and its orchestra for his first benefit concert, perhaps providing additional financial assistance with its organisation. (Beethoven's dedication of his two Piano Sonatas Op. 14 to Josephine von Braun, wife of the court theatre director Baron Peter von Braun, has also traditionally been viewed as an attempt to gain favour with the latter, and therefore to increase his chances of being granted permission to use one of the theatres.) Without the financial support and connections of Lichnowsky, it would have been more difficult for Beethoven to organise his first public concert, or to focus his energies on composing orchestral music.

Beethoven was also well placed for securing his second benefit concert, which included the premieres of his Second Symphony, Third Piano Concerto and *Christus am Ölberge*. In 1803 he was given a temporary appointment as composer at the Theater an der Wien, where he was engaged to compose an opera. One of the perks of this appointment was that he was allowed to use the theatre for a benefit concert, without having to apply through the gatekeeping Baron von Braun (who had in fact turned down Beethoven's request to use one of the court theatres for a concert in 1802). In April 1803 Beethoven was therefore able to present a second benefit concert in the Theater an der Wien, for which he engaged the theatre orchestra. He was furthermore able to raise ticket prices far above those for regular theatre performances (something he was not allowed to do for the premiere of the Ninth Symphony in the Kärntnerthor Theater in 1824), which made the 1803 concert especially profitable. He received further organisational support from Prince Lichnowsky, who attended the rehearsal from its 8 a.m. start on the day of the concert: when the musicians were flagging and tempers were beginning to fray, Lichnowsky

ordered baskets of food and wine for the players, and the rehearsal could resume with much improved general morale.

On the commercial sheet music market, Beethoven also received more support than could usually be expected for the publication of symphonies, particularly from the Second Symphony onwards. He had offered his First Symphony to the Leipzig-based Bureau de Musique for an unspectacular fee of 20 ducats (which was the same price he set for the Septet and the Piano Sonata Op. 22 respectively). That a work on the magnitude of a symphony was priced the same as a piano sonata reflects the relatively low market value of the symphony in music publishing, and highlights the fact that an independent composer wishing to make money would be better off focusing on smaller genres. For the Second Symphony, however, Beethoven was able to secure a much higher fee, receiving 700 gulden for the symphony together with the Third Piano Concerto from a newly established Viennese publishing firm, the Kunst- und Industrie-Comptoir (valuing the works around 77 ducats each).[31] This was a very generous fee for a symphony, given that there was little demand for such works on the market. Like other publishers at the time, the Kunst- und Industrie-Comptoir specialised in smaller genres such as piano and chamber music, and was likely to make a financial loss from the publication of a symphony. David Wyn Jones identifies the firm's publication of Beethoven's symphonies as 'a novel form of patronage', providing the composer with another avenue for earning money from his symphonies that was not available to most other musicians.[32] In 1806 Beethoven also published his own piano trio arrangement of the Second Symphony with the Kunst- und Industrie-Comptoir, enabling him to receive a second publication fee for this work.

By the time Beethoven began concentrated work on the *Eroica* in 1803, he had reasons to be optimistic about securing the performance and publication of a new symphony. He would presumably have assumed that he would be able to secure the Theater an der Wien for another benefit concert the following year, while he was still the in-house composer. (In the event, no such concert happened, as discussed in Chapter 4). Furthermore, he was now recognised as one of the foremost musicians of the day, and news that he was composing a new symphony on a grand scale would be likely to generate serious interest among the music lovers of the high aristocracy. He could therefore reasonably expect at least some kind of organisational or financial support from aristocratic patrons for future performances. These circumstances were fundamentally different from Beethoven's early career as a court musician, when he had first made tentative sketches for a symphony while still in his late teens. Had Bonn not

been overrun by French forces in 1794, Beethoven might have returned to his old post and gone on to compose many more symphonies than the nine he eventually completed. Yet various aspects of Viennese musical life around 1800, particularly the city's high concentration of wealthy patrons who cultivated a serious attitude towards music, both enabled and incentivised Beethoven to compose symphonies that were more monumental and individualistic than those of his eighteenth-century predecessors.

Notes

1. J. F. von Schönfeld, *Jahrbuch der Tonkunst von Wien und Prag* (Vienna: Schönfeld, 1796), p. 77. All translations are the author's own unless otherwise stated.
2. Ibid., pp. 77–8.
3. See advertisements in the *Wiener Zeitung*, 80 (1783), *Anhang* [p. 3] (Lausch) and *Wiener Zeitung*, 17 (1784), p. 421 (Traeg).
4. Cited in D. W. Jones, *The Symphony in Beethoven's Vienna* (Cambridge: Cambridge University Press, 2009), p. 12.
5. *Wiener Zeitung*, 5 (1785), p. 123.
6. *Wiener Zeitung*, 8 (1796), p. 229.
7. See M. S. Morrow, *Concert Life in Haydn's Vienna* (Stuyvesant, NY: Pendragon Press, 1989), pp. 16–17, and D. Edge, Review of Morrow, *Concert Life*, *Haydn Yearbook*, 16 (1992), pp. 139–66.
8. Jones, *The Symphony*, pp. 43–8.
9. See N. Zaslaw, *Mozart's Symphonies: Context, Performance Practice, Reception* (Oxford: Clarendon, 1989), pp. 520–1.
10. O. Biba, 'Concert Life in Beethoven's Vienna', in R. Winter and B. Carr (eds.), *Beethoven, Performers, and Critics* (Detroit, MI: Wayne State University Press, 1980), p. 77.
11. Letter of 11 April 1781, cited in D. Edge, 'Mozart's Viennese Orchestras', *Early Music*, 20 (1992), p. 79.
12. Letter of 6 November 1799, cited in J. A. Rice, *Empress Marie Therese and Music at the Viennese Court, 1792–1807* (Cambridge: Cambridge University Press, 2003), p. 170.
13. Letter from Mozart to his father, 8 May 1782, in *Mozart's Letters, Mozart's Life* ed. R. Spaethling (London: Faber & Faber, 2000), pp. 311–12.
14. The programmes of all twenty concerts are listed in Jones, *The Symphony*, pp. 126–8.
15. Cited in ibid., p. 124.
16. Ibid., pp. 29–31.
17. *Wiener Zeitung*, 28 (1782), *Anhang* [p. 3].
18. See Jones, *The Symphony*, pp. 13ff.
19. Advertised in *Wiener Zeitung*, 80 (1783), *Anhang* [p. 3].
20. *Wiener Zeitung*, 17 (1784), p. 421; cited in Jones, *The Symphony*, p. 12.
21. *Wiener Zeitung*, 98 (1792), p. 3318.
22. N. November, *Cultivating String Quartets in Beethoven's Vienna* (Woodbridge: Boydell Press, 2017), p. 72.
23. Ibid.
24. K. Dorfmüller, N. Gertsch and J. Ronge, eds., *Ludwig van Beethoven: Thematisch-bibliographische Werkverzeichnis*, 2 vols. (Munich: G. Henle, 2014), vol. 1, pp. 128–33.
25. Ibid.
26. See L. Goehr, *The Imaginary Museum of Musical Works: An Essay in the Philosophy of Music* (Oxford: Clarendon Press, 1992).
27. The details in this paragraph are taken from J. D. Wilson, 'From the Chapel to the Theatre to the *Akademiensaal*: Beethoven's Musical Apprenticeship at the Bonn Electoral Court, 1784–1782', in K. Chapin and D. W. Jones (eds.), *Beethoven Studies 4* (Cambridge: Cambridge University Press, 2020).

28. L. Lockwood, *Beethoven's Symphonies: An Artistic Vision* (New York, NY: W. W. Norton, 2015), p. 231.

29. S. Brandenburg, ed., *Ludwig van Beethoven. Briefwechsel: Gesamtausgabe*, 7 vols. (Munich, 1996–8), vol. 1, no. 65; translation in E. Forbes (ed.), *Thayer's Life of Beethoven* (Princeton, NJ: Princeton University Press, 1967), p. 283.

30. Brandenburg, *Briefwechsel*, vol. 1, no. 67; translation in Forbes (ed.), *Thayer's Life of Beethoven*, p. 281.

31. Jones, *The Symphony*, p. 163.

32. Ibid., p. 165.

4 Genesis and Publication of the *Eroica*

FEDERICA ROVELLI

Few subjects in the history of genetic criticism have received as much attention as that of the *Eroica*. The bibliography dedicated to it bears witness to the entire history of the discipline, from Gustav Nottebohm's research on the '*Eroica* Sketchbook' (1880) – a seminal publication and one of the first monographs on a Beethoven sketchbook – to Lewis Lockwood and Alan Gosman's 2013 edition of the same sketchbook, 'Landsberg 6', conceived on the model of modern historical-critical editions.[1] The 130-year period delimited by these two publications includes a phase of significant expansion in the study of Beethoven's sketchbooks, culminating in the comprehensive study by Alan Tyson, Douglas Johnson and Robert Winter.[2] This period also saw the rise of the study of the creative process in a broader sense. These studies took as their point of departure the concept that compositional activity continued well beyond the use of the sketchbooks – persisting throughout the writing of the autograph score, the creation of its copies and parts by copyists and the correction and editing of the first printed editions.[3] Thanks to an exemplary contribution by Michael C. Tusa (focused specifically on copies and parts), studies of the *Eroica*'s genesis have once again signalled a new direction.[4]

The sections of this chapter are conceived as discrete parts, each dedicated to a different phase of the creative process. The aim is to organise the knowledge acquired so far on this topic, in order to provide a complete overview, and to add new information wherever possible. This chapter also seeks to raise awareness of the variety of methodological approaches developed by musicologists during nearly two centuries of the discipline's existence. So the boundary between one section and another represents a substantial change of perspective, permitting the reader to develop multiple viewpoints on the topic.

The earliest evidence clearly connected to the *Eroica* dates from 1803, and consists of two letters written by Kaspar Karl van Beethoven. On 21 and 25 May of that year, the composer's brother wrote to the publishers

This article was written during my work on the collaborative project *Beethovens Werkstatt: Genetische Textkritik und Digitale Musikedition* at the Beethoven-Haus in Bonn and my first months at the Department of Musicology and Cultural Heritage of Cremona at the University of Pavia. I am very grateful to both institutions for their generous support for its realisation. I would like to thank Elizabeth Parker for her valuable help and passion in translating the Italian version of my text.

Breitkopf & Härtel in Leipzig and Simrock in Bonn, mentioning the availability of a new symphony, along with other new works, for publication.[5] Although the two letters cannot be considered proof of the existence of the completed work, they do testify to the existence of a project related to the Third Symphony, which must have reached a certain state of maturation given that Beethoven had publication in view. Three anecdotal accounts, although mutually contradictory, all suggest that the composer had begun to contemplate the symphony well before that date (around 1801 or even as early as 1798).[6] In the absence of direct evidence of precisely when Beethoven began working, an account by Ferdinand Ries provides decisive proof of approximate dating: on 22 October 1803 he mentions a performance of the work on the piano by the composer himself.[7] It should be noted that the performance described by Ries does not presuppose the existence of a complete orchestral score.[8]

In any case, from this time onwards the symphony certainly existed in a fairly complete state, even if not fully orchestrated: references to it appear more and more frequently in the letters of the composer and his circle. Negotiations with both Breitkopf & Härtel and Simrock were conducted in parallel until the end of November or beginning of December of that year, when they were abruptly broken off at the composer's behest.[9] The reasons for this interruption probably pertained to the relationship between Beethoven and the future dedicatee of the symphony, Prince Lobkowitz, who, shortly after October, acquired the exclusive right to perform the work for six months. After those six months, however, Beethoven returned to his original plan, offering the symphony to the English publisher George Thompson and resuming contact with Breitkopf & Härtel.[10] Negotiations with the latter, restarted in August 1805, continued until the end of June of the same year: various letters, which will be discussed below, show progress towards a successful conclusion of the negotiations (discussing the format of the edition, the fee, intermediaries responsible for transport of the manuscripts, with a separate page containing a new variant).[11] Later on the relationship between the composer and the publisher fell apart. Beethoven was unable to send Breitkopf & Härtel all of the works promised at the beginning, but still wanted the symphony to be published as soon as possible, along with some piano sonatas.[12] The publisher, worried about the danger of copies of the work becoming available to someone else,[13] pressed for a quick conclusion of the negotiations and proposed a reduction in the fee, which the composer was unwilling to accept. On 5 May Beethoven requested the return of his manuscripts, which he received with a final letter on the subject dated 21 June.[14]

Sketches and Folded Leaves

The genesis of the *Eroica* is marked by a well-known peculiarity. Beethoven used a theme in the finale that he had already employed on three other occasions: in the ballet *Die Geschöpfe des Prometheus*, Op. 43; in the Contredanses WoO 14, No. 7; and in the Piano Variations, Op. 35 (see also Chapter 8). Assuming that the composer had this theme in mind for the future Symphony Op. 55, the preparatory materials for its first occurrence are contained in the sketchbook Landsberg 7, now preserved in Berlin.[15]

The sketches directly linked to the genesis of the symphony have been discovered in two other sketchbooks, and in a miscellany. The Wielhorsky sketchbook, used between autumn 1802 and spring 1803, is traditionally cited first since it contains sketches that seem to have been written earliest: a movement plan (a condensation of the main features of the new projected work) and some other annotations in E♭ major (pp. 44–45).[16] Not only the tonality and the metre chosen for the first movement, but also the structure of the main theme ('a triadic turning-theme', to use Lockwood's words),[17] allow us to recognise a familial relationship with the *Eroica*.[18] The connection with the *Eroica* is very strong because the annotations in question, dating back to autumn 1802, are found immediately after the sketches for the Variations Op. 35; they are limited to the first three movements of the symphony, as if the thematic connection envisaged for the finale constituted a predetermined starting point. However, this correspondence is not obvious: the tonality and metre chosen for the second movement of this project ('Adagio in C dur' in 6/8), for example, are not those of the future Marcia funebre, just as the 'menuetto serioso' is very different from the Scherzo of the future *Eroica*. For this reason, the annotations in the Wielhorsky sketchbook have been the subject of a debate. On one side are scholars who recognise the beginnings of ideas for the *Eroica* and speak, not without reason, of an 'Ur-*Eroica*'. Their opponents certainly recognise a plan for a symphony in E♭ major with characteristics similar to those of the *Eroica*, but insist that this symphony, at that particular moment, did not exist; they refer to these annotations more cautiously in connection with a 'Wielhorsky Symphony'.[19] Other sketches for the *Eroica* have been identified in the sketchbook-miscellany Artaria 153,[20] containing counterpoint and instrumentation exercises collected by Beethoven beginning in 1801. These annotations (related to the coda of the third movement) are found on page 12, together with some sketches for the Leonore Overture No. 1 (Op. 138) to *Fidelio*, and can be dated alternatively between 1803–4 and 1806–7.

Nearly half of the Landsberg 6 sketchbook pages contain annotations that can be firmly connected to the *Eroica*; these were penned between

October 1802 and October 1803.[21] The advanced state of these musical ideas is very different to those in Wielhorsky, and for this reason it is assumed that there were other sketches for the *Eroica*, now lost.[22] Some scattered sketches, a 'cluster of ideas for the symphony' for the first three movements, are found on pages 4–9. By contrast, pages 11–91 show systematic work on all four movements. Thomas Sipe has noted: 'in general, the four movements appear consecutively, but the placement of blank or almost blank pages might imply that Beethoven may have set out space for the movements ... in advance'.[23] The order of the sketches, indeed distributed fairly uniformly in four groupings (beginning on pp. 10, 49, 60 and 70 respectively) and separated by the blank pages mentioned by Sipe, appears to be the result of Beethoven's preliminary organisation of the sketchbook before using it.

The most recent studies on Landsberg 6 bring to light another physical characteristic of the sketchbook that will require more systematic and deeper study in the future. A number of vertical creases are still visible on many pages of the sketchbook, which demonstrate how these leaves were folded by the composer.[24] But this feature is not exclusive to this sketchbook, and new research is gradually showing how Beethoven strategically employed this practice throughout his life.[25] Beethoven's reasons for folding these leaves are clear only in a few cases. Syer and Gosman hypothesise two categories: on the one hand, Beethoven would have used them as a signal (like a 'dog-ear') to help find annotations that were unfinished or important for some other reason; on the other, he made folds to take in the annotations he wanted to see at a single glance, without necessitating a page turn. These two categories, however, are insufficient to elucidate all the cases found in Landsberg 6. Moreover, both reduce the phenomenon to a single micro-chronological hypothesis that fails to account for all the existing possibilities in the reconstruction of the sequence of events that constitute every writing process.[26] These two hypotheses only apply to a sequence in which Beethoven first wrote his annotations and then folded the pages. In other words, the folds have only been seen as a response to the need to *re-read something written previously*.

The annotations on pages 82, 84 and 88, in which Beethoven set down three continuity drafts (starting from bar 396 of the fourth movement), seem to suggest a different solution.[27] When one considers excerpts from these pages, it is obvious that the first two bars, besides being almost identical in content, have strong similarities in the writing tool and the ink used.[28] In the second bar of page 84 the first quaver rest needed to complete the bar is missing.[29] Beethoven, in writing his sketches, typically observed very strict economy, often omitting rests this way. However, given the context in which this sketch is located – with all rests complete –

this omission must be attributed to momentary distraction, a classic 'copyist's error'. The leaves 83/84, 85/86, and 87/88 have been folded so as to leave the annotation on page 82 easily visible and only the left portion of pages 86 and 88 usable, as though the composer, while essaying multiple attempts to arrive at a satisfactory version of the passage, had recopied the incipit starting from his initial model each time.

The annotations on pages 42 and 48, through which the future bars 114–15 of the second movement were worked out, offer a similar example of Beethoven's use of the folded pages. Although the writing tool seems different from one annotation to the other (the second one seems much thinner or even defective), the pages between them were folded as in the first example, leaving the annotation on page 42 easily visible and only the left portion of page 48 usable.[30] The goal, in practical terms, could be the same: once again the leaves could be folded to remove a physical impediment, in order to *copy* a fragment of text from one point to another of the sketchbook.[31] The function of the folds discussed in the cases above thus does not seem merely limited to *rereading something already written*: if anything, it seems to be another way of materially organising the arrangement of the writing space in the pages of the sketchbook; and, on a purely micro-chronological level, it should be considered to be a constitutive part of the actual 'writing process'.

The Autograph Score: An Ideal-Typical Reconstruction

The link between the sketches and the copies used for the preparation of the first edition consists of a source which, ironically, remains unavailable: the autograph score in the composer's own hand. Despite this fact, in tracing the process that led to the publication of the symphony one should imagine that Beethoven must have dedicated the greater part of his time on this work to this document. To get an idea – however vague – of what unfortunately is no longer at our disposal, it is useful to outline some hypotheses and summarise the strategies by which the composer came to produce similar autographs. Obviously, a schematic description of such processes requires simplifying some aspects, so one can only propose a logical sequence of necessary steps. However, using the insights that Beethoven research has accumulated in the past, one can outline the typical progress of the composition of a symphony.

Beethoven collected his musical ideas in his sketchbooks and was usually able to construct a musical framework that allowed him to work out the full score. How he got from the sketches to the score remains largely a mystery and constitutes one of the great questions still open for

Beethoven research: not only is it unclear how and when the composer usually moved from his preliminary work to the preparation of the score, but also whether he had a regular practice in this regard. On an ideal-typical level one could imagine that once the preparatory phases of the sketches were completed – in which the various sections were conceived, fixed, elaborated and disposed in a more or less definitive order – the composer would have proceeded according to criteria specific to the genre of the work in question. Drawing a boundary line between the various phases is certainly risky: one cannot exclude the possibility that the sketches were made in parallel with the work on the score or even that the composer used sketches in his autographs.[32] Further, one can presume that Beethoven would have begun on the new manuscript when the time seemed right. His predictions were not always exact, though, and the preliminary sketches elaborated in his notebooks – however numerous and detailed – were not always sufficient to clarify all the textual particulars of his works. As obvious as this observation may seem, Beethoven's mis-calculations are evident in the state of the many extant autograph scores, which are full of corrections and even sometimes abandoned in a fragmentary and incomplete state.

In cases where he felt particularly sure of his preparatory work with the sketches, he probably moved immediately to score preparation, according to a practice discernible in the cases of certain works.[33] His composition strategy was strongly hierarchical: the continuity draft of the leading voice developed in the sketchbooks – which in the case of symphonic music usually corresponded to one of the string section parts or to one of the winds to which the melodic priority could be assigned – was copied from the sketchbooks into the score and filled out step by step. Working as his own copyist, Beethoven divided such a continuity draft among the various instruments; sometimes he acted as a 'creative copyist', allowing himself to make small changes, mainly regarding the pitches or the rhythmical structure of the melody. One does not know how he went on to develop the orchestration, whether bar-by-bar from top to bottom, or by instrument groups (in a gradual additive process). Lewis Lockwood has focused attention on a specific annotation typical of orchestral scores, the 'cue-staff' annotation (a guide notation sketched by the composer through the score-manuscript at the bottom of the page, below the full orchestral score), suggesting that such a strategy was reserved exclusively for the instrumentation stages.[34]

In other cases, Beethoven did not feel entirely satisfied when progressing from the sketches to the actual orchestral score. For this reason, he sometimes used a different method, beginning instead with the *Concept*, a highly detailed draft – almost a rough copy, similar to a short score – thus

adding an intermediate compositional stage between the sketches and the complete score. Beethoven certainly used this expedient during his last years of activity,[35] but it has not been demonstrated that he had developed such a practice by the time the *Eroica* was conceived. Whether or not there existed a *Concept* for the *Eroica* Symphony, there certainly was an autograph score, although the composer parted with it before his death: the auction catalogue of his scores contains no mention of this invaluable document.[36] One can assume that the manuscript was discarded by the composer himself immediately after the preparation of the principal copy (still preserved in Vienna and described below); according to Jonathan Del Mar, once the copying was completed, the composer would have considered it of little importance and may well have given it to Carl Czerny.[37] The geneses of Beethoven's subsequent symphonies suggest another solution: in these cases the composer retained the autograph scores and even used them to register the corrections and variants made over time on different documents.[38] But it has not been possible to establish whether something analogous happened in the case of the *Eroica*. Alternatively, it could be posited that the autograph was no longer useable due to an excessive number of corrections (and was discarded for this reason) or that it was really lost. A third possibility is that, having been sent in haste to one of the publishers in contention for the first edition (perhaps to Breitkopf & Härtel), it was returned to Vienna after the negotiations had failed, by which time a more up-to-date manuscript had already been prepared (e.g., the above-mentioned copy still preserved in Vienna, which will be discussed in the next section), with which Beethoven would continue working until completion.

In any case, at a certain point the completed score was in the hands of Beethoven, and given to the copyists. They prepared the full score and individual parts for performing purposes; a number of these same copies were also used as models for the engraving of the plates for the first edition.

Copying the Full Score

Fundamental to the reconstruction of the late stages of the genesis of the symphony are two groups of non-autograph documents, whose preparation was carefully supervised by the composer himself: the Vienna score copy, and copies of the instrumental parts, also preserved in Vienna.[39] These documents, although penned by copyists, arouse particular interest, not only because of the absence of an autograph score, but also because they reveal something noteworthy: that the genesis of the *Eroica* reflects

Beethoven's need to resolve some compositional problems at an advanced stage of composition, at a time when the copies had already been completed. In other words, these documents point the way to a deeper understanding of Beethoven's final phases of composition.[40]

The copied score, primarily the work of the copyist Benjamin Gebauer, was likely prepared from the lost autograph and was corrected by the composer in several stages.[41] Unlike the autograph, this copy remained in Beethoven's possession until the end, when it was acquired by Joseph Dessauer soon after the composer's death.[42] Its title page bears evidence of his reconsideration of the dedication to Napoleon Bonaparte.[43] By reconstructing the stages through which the page came to take on its current appearance, we can identify a total of four different hands. Gebauer wrote most of what is now legible: 'Sinfonia grande / intitolata <illegible> Bonaparte / del Sigr. / Louis van Beethoven' (Grand Symphony / entitled <illegible> Bonaparte / by Sigr. / Louis van Beethoven'). The second line of the title, immediately after the word 'intitolata',[44] was erased with such vehemence that the paper was torn. Then, in pencil, Beethoven himself inserted the words 'geschrieben / auf Bonaparte' (written / on Bonaparte), which are particularly difficult to read today, but deciphered in the past by many other scholars.[45] A third, unidentified hand then inserted the date '804 im August'. Finally, a fourth hand, also unidentified, added two annotations at the bottom: 'Sinfonie 3' and 'Op. 55'. On the same page Beethoven made further annotations: there are instructions for the preparation of orchestral parts (in all three mariginalia), along with other signs, letters and figures, whose meanings remain uncertain.[46] The date inserted by the third hand ('804 im August') apparently refers to a performance arranged for Prince Lobkowitz at Eisenberg or Raudnitz. However, we can reject the hypothesis that this date represents the completion of the entire score, since the documents concerning the payment of the copyists (hired by Prince Lobkowitz) demonstrate that these parts, extracted from the copy in question, had already been prepared before this date.[47]

Another much-debated proposition is that the title page of this document may be the one described in the famous anecdote by Ferdinand Ries about Napoleon's self-coronation, according to which the composer tore out the title page of the score bearing the dedication. Ries – describing Beethoven's adverse reaction – clearly speaks of a copy (the symphony, according to his account, was 'schon in Partitur abgeschrieben' – 'already copied in score'). But the actual title page of the surviving document does not correspond to his description, which reads: 'at the very top of the title page one reads the word "Buonaparte" and at the bottom "Luigi van Beethoven" ... but not

a word more' ('ganz oben auf dem Titelblatte das Wort "Buonaparte" und ganz unten "Luigi van Beethoven" . . . aber kein Wort mehr'). Moreover, the title page of the score copy in Vienna was certainly not torn from the manuscript.[48] We could conjecture that, over the years, Ries forgot the details, and amplified and dramatised an event that he himself had witnessed, without meaning to falsify his biographical account.[49] An alternative hypothesis has been proposed, in which Ries's anecdote refers to another copy, different from the one prepared by Gebauer, which, just like the autograph, has disappeared.[50]

Markings in Beethoven's hand are found on nearly every page of this copy of the score. Taking into account the writing tools and colours of ink employed, at least three different layers of writing are recognisable. In addition to the light brown ink associated with the hand of Gebauer, there are markings in pencil, red chalk and various different types of inks: for the second and fourth movements in particular there is a much darker ink associated with a different writing tool (a quill with a much broader nib than the others). Most of the composer's interventions are editorial: indications for articulations and dynamics. He probably made the corrections in red chalk, while revising the first edition (to be discussed below), making them so conspicuous as to allow the document's use as a model for corrections by the publisher.[51] In addition to the editorial interventions, the most obvious changes relate to the repeat signs in the Allegro con brio (fol. 19v–20r) and the Scherzo (fol. 149r–v).[52] Even if the revisions demonstrated here cannot be comprehensively reconstructed – in the first case up to five different textual stages have been identified[53] – and also leave several questions unanswered, one incontrovertible fact emerges: Beethoven needed to revisit the decisions already made about both sets of repeat signs after the score copy had been completed. These changes constitute proof of the continuation of the creative impulse throughout the final stages of the work, focusing on issues of macroformal balance. The problem in the first movement was mentioned by Kaspar Karl during the negotiation with Breitkopf & Härtel in connection with Beethoven's initial concerns about the length of the piece.[54] According to Kaspar Karl's account, these concerns were resolved during the first performances, leading the composer to reintroduce that previously deleted repeat sign for the exposition. Kaspar Karl indicated in the letter the exact point where the first repeat sign was to be reintroduced (Illustration 4.1) and inserted an additional leaf (a 'beyliegendes Blatt') with substitute bars to be inserted next to the second repeat sign in the score that was already in the publisher's hands. The additional leaf is unfortunately lost.

The Orchestral Parts (the Copyists's Workshop)

The other primary resource for clarifying various details of the genesis of the *Eroica* Symphony consists of copies of the orchestral parts, also preserved in Vienna and bearing evidence of Beethoven's revisions, like Gebauer's copy of the score.[55] Some of these parts were probably used for the premiere performance in Vienna at the palace of Prince Lobkowitz on 9 June 1804.[56] Alongside Beethoven's corrections are recognisable various interventions made by Ries in his capacity as the master's assistant in the editorial phase. The complete set contains parts corrected by both Beethoven and Ries (Fl I/II, Ob II, Clar I/II), parts corrected only by Ries (Ob I, Fg I/II, Cor I, Vl I, Va) and parts without any corrections, based directly on the first printed edition. The entire set of Vienna parts is the product of collective work: in total, twelve different copyists' hands have been identified.[57] This should not be surprising. Alan Tyson's focus on the relationship between Beethoven and his copyists has already elucidated their central role in collaborating with the composer.[58] Through examination of anecdotal reports and epistolary evidence, there emerges a picture resembling typical Renaissance workshops, in which the composer works closely with whole groups of copyists, dividing up the tasks and duties and assigning them specific parts of the work. One anecdote in particular from the biography by Wegeler and Ries offers illuminating details of Beethoven's procedure in this matter and explains how the composer could assign each copyist very small portions of the musical text to be copied.[59]

Returning now to the *Eroica* parts: Otto Biba maintains that the first sub-group of parts identified earlier (Fl I/II, Ob II, Clar I/II) coincides with the first to be copied.[60] In all these parts we can see corrections made by Beethoven and Ries. Within the set, the parts were not copied uniformly: in the first three movements, for example, one can identify the hands of different copyists (alternately, the so-called copyists '8' and '11'), while the fourth movement was entirely entrusted to 'copyist 9'.[61] In addition to showing different handwriting, the fourth movement of each of the parts is always preceded by a title page. On the basis of this fact one could even assume that the last movement of the symphony was copied and performed before the others.[62] The handwriting of 'copyist 9', responsible for this movement, is not found on any other occasion, almost as if this collaborator had been engaged only for this special task.[63] The second sub-group of parts (Ob I, Fg I/II, Cor I, Vl I, Va) contains those that were copied before the first edition was published. In this instance, the individual parts were entrusted to a single copyist. This set does not contain corrections in Beethoven's hand, but the bassoon parts have corrections by

Ries, who worked directly with the composer during the entire redaction phase. The second bassoon part also shows the plate number of the original edition (512) on its first page. This information led Bathia Churgin to assert that this part, together with the first horn part, was used as the *Stichvorlage* (the model for engraving the plates).[64]

A further observation can be made about the bassoon parts. The handwriting found here seems to belong to one of Beethoven's most important copyists, Wenzel Schlemmer, who was to collaborate with the composer until his death in 1823. Several factors contribute to this conclusion: the correspondence of the bass clef, the 3/4 metre and key signature of three flats over the two dots next to the clef, and the word 'Fagotto'.[65] The same bass clef, disposition of the dots and penmanship of the word 'Fagotto' are found in another manuscript confirmed as written by Schlemmer (Illustration 4.2) and all these features are comparable with characteristics Tyson reported as typical of this copyist's writing.[66] The presence of other bass clefs of different shapes (starting from the third staff), and certain directions for expression that are sometimes written differently (such as the 'p' of *piano*) do not constitute evidence against this assumption. These elements could have been integrated later, either by an apprentice copyist (who was therefore in charge of simpler tasks), or by one of the musicians who over the following years used the parts in question for the performance of the Symphony. In this regard, it is useful to point out that the pages of the two bassoon parts, not reproduced here, are written in different colours of ink, which tends to confirm this idea. The hypothesis that Schlemmer had already collaborated on the occasion of the preparation of the *Eroica* parts had been advanced by Tyson on the basis of some epistolary evidence from 1805, but the copyist's assignment still remained to be clarified. So the identification of Schlemmer's hand in this document could confirm and specify the intuition of the British scholar.[67]

Returning to the genesis of the entirety of the *Eroica*, we could envision how the different sub-groups of parts just specified might actually correspond to different stages in the creative process. In fact, in the third movement (at the end of the second part of the second repetition of the Scherzo) the first sub-group displays the rubric for a 'prima volta' that is cancelled by an erasure. This is the same variant present in fol. 149r–v of Gebauer's score copy. Prevailing opinion has it that the original set was produced before the printed edition was complete, and that certain parts have been replaced over the years. In particular, Tusa claims that the lack of coherence found in this set today is due to problems of wear and tear on the paper and can be further explained by the growth in orchestral forces over the years.[68] But one can also consider the hypothesis that the first copies of the parts were prepared for rehearsals with reduced forces, and that the

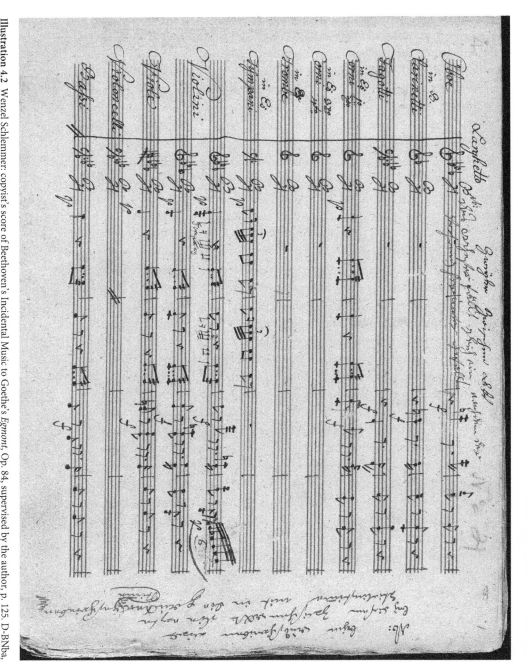

Illustration 4.2 Wenzel Schlemmer copyist's score of Beethoven's Incidental Music to Goethe's *Egmont*, Op. 84, supervised by the author, p. 125. D-BNba, NE 64 (reproduced with permission, Beethoven-Haus, Bonn)

first set produced was therefore incomplete. As for the possibility of the organisation of rehearsals of the symphonies with reduced forces, Beethoven himself wrote about this in a letter regarding the Ninth Symphony, Op. 125.[69] Other documents link the Eighth Symphony, Op. 93, to a similar practice.[70]

Marketing, Packaging and Editing: The First Printed Edition

From the correspondence with Breitkopf & Härtel emerges quite a clear idea of what Beethoven – acting now as his own agent – had in mind for this first edition. Such publications were aimed primarily at professional performers. But the composer, in contravention of the custom of the time, envisioned instead an orchestral score in pocket format. In his farsighted plan, every connoisseur would be able to procure a copy of the score in this format, leading to better sales and distribution of the work.[71] He also had clear ideas about the publication of the instrumental parts: in one of the last letters of Kaspar Karl to Breitkopf & Härtel before the collapse of the negotiations, we learn that the first violin parts were to contain many cues for other instruments during the bars of rest (*Stichnoten*).[72] These cues would certainly have simplified the work of the *Konzertmeister* charged with conducting the orchestra, clarifying his vision of the work as a whole. The Vienna copy, mentioned above, also bears a similar direction: 'N.B. in die erste Violinstimme werden gleich die anderen Instrumente zum Theil eingetragen' ('N.B. likewise in the first violin part cues from the other instruments should be entered'). So the composer's vision of his desired 'editorial product' was precise and well defined. The expedience of the *Stichnoten*, according to Beethoven, had already been tested with the first edition of the First Symphony, Op. 21.[73] But evidently this usage had not yet been consolidated in the typographical practice of the period.

Although Beethoven had wanted to publish his work in score format, the first edition of the *Eroica* was released only in parts at first; it was issued in October 1806 by the Kunst- und Industrie-Comptoir firm of Vienna.[74] None of the details of the negotiations through which the composer granted his work to the small Viennese publishing house have come down to us through correspondence. The first announcement of the publication of the symphony appeared in the *Wiener Zeitung* of 29 - October.[75] The parts, eighteen in all, contained many errors; within a few months of publication in 1807, two lists of *Errata* were made available – both were located after the end of the general comments on the symphony and published independently of the composer's wishes.[76] These lists are primarily concerned with corrections of wrong notes and

missing accidentals. One detail in particular has caught the attention of scholars: bars 150–51 of the first movement (the bars that precede the repeat sign corrected by Beethoven in Gebauer's copy and mentioned by Kaspar Karl during the negotiation with Breitkopf & Härtel) are repeated twice. It is very difficult to understand what might have caused this repetition: either it was a mistake caused by an engraver, confused by the signs of correction and restoration present in fol. 19v–20r of Gebauer's copy (as maintained by Del Mar),[77] or the composer had actually selected this option, introducing what he considered an improvement in one of the last phases of his work (as suggested by Biba and Churgin).[78]

In any case, Beethoven was not satisfied with the first edition, and continued to make corrections in his personal printed copy, later preserved in the archives of Prince Lobkowitz. His corrections were carried out with various writing implements (red chalk, ink and pencil) and seem to indicate again several distinct phases of corrections, dating back to the beginning of 1807.[79] While the cancellation of the repetition of bars 150–1 of the first movement, clearly visible and in Beethoven's hand, defines the composer's final textual choice, it fails to clarify whether, at that moment, the composer was emending an error or actually changing his mind about the passage. When the symphony was published again by the Kunst- und Industrie-Comptoir (1807–8), the repetition of the two bars had definitively disappeared. Two new editions were finally published in score – according to the composer's wish – by Cianchettini & Sperati of London (1809) and Simrock of Bonn (1822); however, there is no evidence that Beethoven had anything to do with them.

Notes

1. G. Nottebohm, *Ein Skizzenbuch von Beethoven aus dem Jahre 1803* (Leipzig: Breitkopf & Härtel, 1970); and *Beethoven's 'Eroica' Sketchbook: A Critical Edition*, 2 vols., ed. A. Gosman and L. Lockwood (Urbana, Chicago and Springfield, IL: University of Illinois Press, 2013). Nottebohm's essay was particularly popular owing to an English translation: *Two Beethoven Sketchbooks. A Description with Musical Extracts*, trans. J. Katz (London: Gollancz, 1979). The sketchbook is today identified as PL-Kj, Mus. ms. autogr. Beethoven, Landsberg 6.
2. D. Johnson, A. Tyson and R. Winter, *The Beethoven Sketchbooks* (Berkeley, CA: University of California Press, 1985).
3. Lewis Lockwood first insisted on the importance of studying materials other than sketches (in particular autographs) in order to reconstruct the creative process, observing: 'the vast mass of sketches, although still largely unknown, have attracted so much attention in the past that they have tended to overshadow the potential importance of the autographs as primary documents not only for text-critical and analytical problems but also for the compositional process as well'. L. Lockwood, 'On Beethoven's Sketches and Autographs: Some Problems of Definition and Interpretation', *Acta Musicologica*, 43 (1970), pp. 32–47; reprinted in L. Lockwood, *Beethoven: Studies in the Creative Process* (Cambridge, MA: Harvard University Press, 1992), pp. 5–16 and 6.
4. M. C. Tusa, 'Die authentischen Quellen der "Eroica"', *Archiv für Musikwissenschaft*, 42 (1985), pp. 121–50.

5. *Ludwig van Beethoven. Briefwechsel: Gesamtausgabe*, 7 vols., ed. S. Brandenburg (Munich: Henle, 1996–8) (BGA); respectively BGA 138, vol. 1, pp. 163–4; and BGA 139, vol. 1, p. 165–6.

6. Reports by A. Schindler, A. Bartolini and C. Czerny quoted in *Ludwig van Beethoven, Symphonie No. 3, Es-Dur, op. 55, 'Eroica'*, ed. O. Biba (Vienna: Gesellschaft der Musikfreunde in Wien, 1993), pp. 31–6. This is a facsimile of the score copy, with Beethoven's corrections and changes; together with hand-written orchestral parts for the first and early performances, also containing Beethoven's corrections and changes.

7. This is Ries's famous letter to Simrock, BGA 165, vol. 1, pp. 190–2, in which the composer's pupil describes the symphony as a work whose performance is to make 'heaven and earth' tremble.

8. As inferred for example by B. Churgin, 'Exploring the *Eroica*: Aspects of the New Critical Editions', in *Haydn, Mozart & Beethoven. Studies in the Music of the Classical Period*, ed. S. Brandenburg (Oxford: Clarendon Press, 1998), p. 185.

9. BGA 152, vol. 1, p. 175; 163, vol. 1, pp. 188–9; 165, vol. 1, pp. 190–2 and 173, vol. 1, pp. 199–201.

10. BGA 178, vol. 1, pp. 209–10 and 188, vol. 1, pp. 218–20.

11. BGA 188, vol. 1, pp. 218–20; 194, vol. 1, pp. 225–6; 199, vol. 1, pp. 229–30; 209, vol. 1, pp. 243–4; 212, vol. 1, pp. 245–6; 218, vol. 1, pp. 252–3; 223, vol. 1, pp. 257–8 and 226, vol. 1, pp. 259–60.

12. These are the Piano Sonatas Opp. 53 and 54.

13. Biba (ed.), *Symphonie No. 3*, p. 25.

14. BGA 226, vol. 1, pp. 259–60.

15. This sketchbook, identified as D-B, Mus. ms. autogr. Beethoven, Landsberg 7, is edited in *Ein Notierungsbuch von Beethoven aus dem Besitz der Preussischen Staatsbibliothek zu Berlin*, ed. K. L. Mikulicz (Leipzig: Breitkopf & Härtel, 1927).

16. The sketchbook (RUS-Mcm, F. 155 no. 1) is edited in *Kniga eskizov Betchovena za 1802–1803 gody* [Sketchbook from the years 1802–3 (Wielhorsky)] (Moscow: Russian State Edition, 1962). On its dating, see Johnson, Tyson and Winter, *Beethoven Sketchbooks*, pp. 130–6.

17. L. Lockwood, 'The Earliest Sketches for the *Eroica* Symphony', in *Beethoven: Studies in the Creative Process* (Cambridge, MA: Harvard University Press 1992), pp. 134–50.

18. A complete transcription of p. 44 is offered in Lockwood, 'The Earliest Sketches', pp. 138–9.

19. As representative of the two positions, see L. Lockwood, *Beethoven's Symphonies: An Artistic Vision* (New York, NY: Norton, 2015), pp. 59–63 and T. Sipe, *Beethoven: Eroica Symphony* (Cambridge: Cambridge University Press, 1998), p. 23.

20. Although a facsimile edition of 'Artaria 153' (D-B, Mus. ms. autogr. Beethoven, Artaria 153) has not been published, the digital reproduction of its pages can be found in the *Digitale Sammlung* of the *Staatsbibliothek* of Berlin at: https://digital.staatsbibliothek-berlin.de/werkansicht? PPN=PPN644450606&PHYSID=PHYS_0012&DMDID=DMDLOG_0001 (accessed 9 July 2019). About the mentioned sketches, see A. Tyson, 'The Problem of Beethoven's "First" Leonore Overture', *Journal of the American Musicological Society*, 28 (1975), pp. 292–334.

21. On the dating issues already raised by Nottebohm, Tyson and Syer, see Gosman and Lockwood (eds.), *'Eroica' Sketchbook*, vol. 1, pp. 6–8.

22. Gosman and Lockwood (eds.), *'Eroica' Sketchbook*, vol. 1, p. 30.

23. Sipe, *Beethoven: Eroica*, p. 26; and Biba (ed.), *Symphonie No. 3*, p. 123.

24. The main contributions on this subject, based on examples from Landsberg 6, are found in K. R. Syer, 'A Peculiar Hybrid: The Structure and Chronology of the "Eroica" Sketchbook (Landsberg 6)', *Bonner Beethoven Studien*, 5 (2006), pp. 167–8; and Gosman and Lockwood (eds.), *'Eroica' Sketchbook* (Chapter 5: 'Page Folds in Landsberg 6'), vol. 1, pp. 14–19.

25. The author recognised similar cases in the Scheide sketchbook (US-PRscheide, M. 130), reporting on a specific example: F. Rovelli, '"Laboratorium artificiosum". Un regard dans l'atelier de Beethoven', *Genesis. Revue internationale de critique génétique*, 42 (2016), especially pp. 174–6. S. Cox, whose PhD thesis is dedicated to the Engelmann sketchbook (D-BNba, Sammlung H. C. Bodmer, HCB Mh 60) and to whom I owe thanks for the information, also confirms the presence of similar folds in the sketchbook she studied.

26. The term 'micro-chronology' is used in the sense defined in the glossary of the project *Beethovens Werkstatt: Genetische Textkritik und Digitale Musikedition*, which can be consulted at https://beethovens-werkstatt.de/glossary/mikrochronologie/ (accessed 11 January, 2019).

27. Using the definition of Barry Cooper, *Beethoven and the Creative Process* (Oxford: Clarendon Press, 1990), p. 105, a 'continuity draft' is 'a fairly long sketch and tends to represent a relatively late stage of composition. It consists of a single-stave (occasionally two-stave) draft for an extended portion of a composition.'

28. See Ludwig van Beethoven, sketchbook Landsberg 6, Notierungsbuch E 90, PL-Kj, Mus. ms. autogr. Beethoven Landsberg 6, a) p. 82, staff 1; b) p. 84, staff 1; and c) p. 88, staff 1 (relating to fourth movement, bars 396–7): https://jbc.bj.uj.edu.pl/dlibra/publication/285/edition/265/content.

29. Ibid., p. 84, staff 1.

30. Gosman and Lockwood (eds.), *'Eroica' Sketchbook*, vol. 1, p. 30.

31. See Beethoven, sketchbook Landsberg 6, p. 42, staff 1 and p. 48, staff 1 (see n. 29).

32. This is the case of the so-called '"cue-staff" notations discussed below.

33. See, for example, the autographs of Op. 101 and Op. 59, No. 3.

34. His observations on the subject were developed in two publications from 1970: L. Lockwood, 'On Beethoven's Sketches' and 'Beethoven's Unfinished Piano Concerto of 1815: Sources and Problems', *The Musical Quarterly*, 56 (1970), pp. 624–46. On the topic see also B. R. Appel and J. Veit, 'Skizzierungsprozesse im Schaffen Beethovens: Probleme der Erschließung und der Digitalen Edition', *Die Tonkunst*, 2 (2015), pp. 122–30.

35. This is the case of the Piano Sonata in E major Op. 109: the *Concept* is mentioned in the letter BGA 1446, vol. 4, pp. 454–9. Part of the document in question is still preserved in Vienna (A-Wgm, A 47).

36. Biba (ed.), *Symphonie No. 3*, p. 37.

37. *Symphonie No. 3 in Es-dur, "Eroica", Op. 55* [Critical Commentary], ed. J. Del Mar (Kassel: Bärenreiter, 1997), p. 15.

38. J. Dufner, 'Beethoven and His Copyists: Written Conversation', *The Beethoven Journal*, 29 (2014), pp. 14–23.

39. Both document groups are edited in Biba (ed.), *Symphonie No. 3*.

40. Tusa, 'Die authentischen Quellen', pp. 121–2.

41. For the identification of the copyist, see T. Albrecht, 'Benjamin Gebauer, ca. 1758–1846. The Life and Death of Beethoven's "Copyist C". With Speculation Concerning Joseph Arthofer, ca. 1752–1807', *Bonner Beethoven Studien*, 3 (2003), pp. 7–22. The 'copyist C' was previously identified, but not recognised specifically as Gebauer, in A. Tyson, 'Notes on Five of Beethoven's Copyists', *Journal of the American Musicological Society*, 23 (1970), pp. 452–6.

42. The document was sold at the auction on 5 November 1827 as lot no. 144, see: Biba (ed.), *Symphonie No. 3*, p. 39.

43. A reproduction is found in Lockwood, *Beethoven's Symphonies*, p. 50.

44. On this reading, instead of the most commonly accepted 'intitulata', see F. Della Seta, *Beethoven. Sinfonia Eroica: Una guida* (Rome: Carocci, 2004), p. 41.

45. Most recently in *Beethoven: Symphonie Nr. 3 Es-Dur Opus 55, Sinfonia Eroica*, ed. B. Churgin (Munich: Henle, 2015), p. 198.

46. According to Biba (ed.), *Symphonie No. 3*, 38, the annotation on the top right could be deciphered as follows: 'd[en] 26 S.[eptember]'.

47. J. Fojtíková and T. Volek, 'Die Beethoveniana der Lobkowitz-Musiksammlung und ihre Kopisten', in S. Brandenburg and M. Gutiérrez-Denhoff (eds.), *Beethoven und Böhmen. Beiträge zu Biographie und Wirkungsgeschichte Beethovens* (Bonn: Beethoven-Haus, 1988), pp. 228 and 234. The payment was made in the period between April 1803 and June 1804.

48. Churgin (ed.), *Symphonie Nr. 3*, pp. 198–9.

49. Della Seta, *Sinfonia Eroica*, p. 42. More recently, Lockwood has again strongly supported the hypothesis that the manuscript seen by Ries should be identified with the Gebauer's copy. Lockwood, *Beethoven's Symphonies*, p. 53.

50. *Das Werk Beethovens. Thematisch-bibliographisches Verzeichnis seiner sämtlichen vollendeten Kompositionen*, ed. G. Kinsky and H. Halm (Munich: Henle, 1955), p.129.

51. Tusa, 'Die authentischen Quellen', pp. 125, 136–7.

52. Ibid., pp. 138–44 and 144–7.

53. Ibid., pp. 143–4.

54. BGA 212, vol. 1, pp. 245–6.

55. The set of sixteen parts (A-Wgm, XIII 6154) was also described in detail for the first time by Tusa, 'Die authentischen Quellen', pp. 126–32. Churgin (ed.), *Symphonie Nr. 3*, p. 185,

infers that the parts must have been eighteen in total, like those later published in the first edition.

56. Biba (ed.), *Symphonie No. 3*, p. 13.
57. Ibid., p. 46.
58. A. Tyson, 'Steps to Publication – and Beyond', in Denis Arnold and Nigel Fortune (eds.), *The Beethoven Companion* (London: Faber & Faber, 1971), pp. 469–73.
59. F. G. Wegeler and F. Ries, *Biographische Notizen über Ludwig van Beethoven* (Koblenz: Baedeker, 1838), p. 36: 'Four copyists sat in the room outside, and he gave them the pages one by one as they were finished' (English translation in Tyson, 'Steps to Publication', p. 470).
60. Biba (ed.), *Symphonie No. 3*, p. 43.
61. The designation of the individual copyists (Copyist 9 etc.) follows that proposed in ibid., p. 46.
62. Ibid., p. 43.
63. For an identification of this copyist, see Fojtíková and Volek, 'Lobkowitz-Musiksammlung', pp. 226–9.
64. Churgin (ed.), *Symphonie Nr. 3*, p. 201.
65. The complete reproduction of the bassoon part is available in: Biba (ed.), *Symphonie No. 3*, vol. 3, pp. 299–316. For the following comparison, see in particular p. 2 of the part, reproduced on p. 300.
66. Tyson, 'Notes', appendix, p. 468.
67. Tyson, 'Notes', pp. 441–2. Tyson based this hypothesis on two letters: BGA 209, vol. 1, pp. 243–4 and 222, vol. 1, p. 256.
68. Tusa, 'Die authentischen Quellen', p. 126.
69. BGA 1924, vol. 6, pp. 8–9. The letter refers to the Ninth Symphony, Op. 125, but illustrates a principle that can certainly be generalised.
70. F. Rovelli, 'Revisionsprozesse in Beethovens Niederschriften der achten Symphonie op. 93', *Editio. Internationales Jahrbuch für Editionswissenschaft*, 31 (2017), pp. 90–116.
71. BGA 188, vol. 1, pp. 218–20.
72. BGA 212, vol. 1, pp. 245–6.
73. Beethoven alluded to the first printed edition published in November 1801 by Hofmeister & Comp., which actually contains such indications.
74. On the title page: 'SINFONIA EROICA / à due Violini, Alto, due Flauti, due Oboi, due Clarinetti, / due Fagotti, tre Corni, due Clarini, Timpani e Basso. / composta / per festeggiare il sovvenire di un grand Uomo / e dedicate / A Sua Altezza Serenissima il Principe di Lobkowity / da / Luigi van Beethoven. / Op. 55. / N° III delle Sinfonie. / [l.:] 512. [r.:] f 9 / À Vienna / Nel Contor delle arti e d'Industria al Hohenmarkt N° 582'. A late copy of this edition, with some corrections of the original plates, is preserved at the Beethoven-Haus (D-BNba, Slg. H. C. Bodmer, Md 2) and can be consulted at: www.beethoven.de/sixcms/detail.php?id=15288&template=dokseite_digitales_archiv_en&_dokid=T00003094&_seite=1-1 (accessed 6 July, 2019).
75. The advertisement of the publication is quoted in Churgin (ed.), *Symphonie Nr. 3*, p. 203.
76. *Allgemeine musikalischen Zeitung*, 9 (1807) cols. 286–7 and 333–4. The second list is reproduced in Churgin, 'Exploring the *Eroica*', p. 189.
77. L. van Beethoven, *Symphony No. 3 in E-flat major*, ed. J. Del Mar (Kassel: Bärenreiter, 1997), pp. 16–17.
78. Biba (ed.), *Symphonie No. 3*, p. 26 and Churgin, 'Exploring the *Eroica*', p. 193. Biba also reproduces the two variants of the passage in the different versions of the first printed edition, but he erroneously numbers the bars as 151 and 152.
79. Described in detail by Churgin (ed.), *Symphonie Nr. 3*, p. 203. According to her numbering system, this is the source C_3 (CZ-Nlobkowitz, Roudnicky Archiv X.G.c.15), which Sieghard Brandenburg brought to the attention of specialists in 1987.

PART II

Analytical Approaches

5 Twentieth-Century Analytical Approaches to the First Movement

WILLIAM DRABKIN

It hardly needs to be stressed in these pages that the *Eroica* is a watershed work in Beethoven's output. It is widely regarded as the project with which Beethoven came to terms with his deafness, so poignantly described in letters of 1801 and in the unsent letter of October 1802 addressed to his brothers, the so-called Heiligenstadt Testament. If one concurs with Maynard Solomon, who wrote that Beethoven, with his Second Symphony, is 'settling his accounts – or making peace – with the high-Classic symphonic tradition',[1] then we can regard the composition of the *Eroica* as the musical embodiment of his determination to 'seize Fate by the throat', as he expressed it in 1801 in a letter to his friend from Bonn, Franz Georg Wegeler.[2]

The *Eroica* is also a work of unprecedentedly large proportions in the Austrian-German symphonic tradition: its first movement, though conceived in a design we can easily recognise as 'sonata form', is nearly 700 bars long. And the movements that follow are not only correspondingly long, but they all exceed their formal conventions. The second movement may be described as extended song form: an A–B–A funeral march with trio is expanded to A–B–A–C–A, with the final A-section not marked by weakness or relaxation but instead pushing inexorably towards a tragic end. The third movement is ostensibly a straightforward scherzo plus trio, but there is a mismatch between the tonal plan and the thematic unfolding at the outset, which creates a tension at odds with the quiet dynamic level: the beginning predictably takes us from the home key of E♭ major to its dominant, B♭; but the first statement of the melody (oboe and strings) is already in the dominant, and it is then repeated a fifth higher by the flute and strings in F major, the dominant of the dominant. This harmonic mismatch is not put right until the theme is recapitulated, *fortissimo*, by the full orchestra. And the finale of the *Eroica* is a movement *sui generis*: building upon a pre-existent work – a set of piano variations of 1802, itself based on a dance composed for a Viennese ball and recycled in the *Prometheus* ballet score – it is a hybrid of sonata, rondo and variation form, in which the theme emerges only after its bass line is itself initially subjected to a series of variations.

Part of the symphony's novelty – or novel circumstances – is the existence and survival of so much written documentation of its composition. Although the composing score went missing in Beethoven's lifetime, a fair copy of the work with corrections in Beethoven's hand survives, as does a large sketchbook of 1803–4 in which the symphony takes up the lion's share of the pages. This manuscript is known as Landsberg 6, one of nine Beethoven sketchbooks owned by the musician Ludwig Landsberg (1805–59), but it is often referred to simply as the '*Eroica* Sketchbook'. It was described in detail in a book published in 1880 by the pioneer of Beethoven sketch studies. The author, Gustav Nottebohm, included a considerable number of transcriptions from the sketchbook, and these have reinforced the notion that the symphony is the result of considerable labour on Beethoven's part, and that its groundbreaking qualities are largely due to an effort every bit as heroic as the symphony itself. A facsimile and complete transcription of the manuscript were published in 2015; they document the early genesis of the symphony in even greater detail – especially its first movement, in which there are four distinct preliminary phases of work. This written evidence of what we take to be Beethoven's grappling with the problems of composing on a large scale has only enhanced the attraction of the *Eroica* to those who analyse it, to understand what it is made of, and how it was put together.

One of the shortest publications on the *Eroica* enquires about 'the value of music analysis' and brings to the fore a dimension of engagement that is often forgotten. For most people, music is composed, performed and listened to; analysis suggests that it is also worthy of serious contemplation, and that it has value not merely for the pleasure it gives to those who hear it (and the gratitude of those who have taken trouble to learn and perform it), but also for those who have questions about it, whether they concern the specific work at hand or music more generally. What follows here is a series of analytical problems, or issues, associated with the first movement of the symphony, which go beyond the processes of composition, performance and listening. Whether the meaning of the *Eroica* is better understood as a result of airing these problems is something that will be debated endlessly; I merely offer a sample of the issues that have attracted attention over the last century.

Locating the Second Subject

There is nothing particularly unusual in the overall tonal plan of the first section – the exposition – of the Allegro con brio. It begins with a series of statements of the main theme in the home key of E♭, in bars 3, 15 and 37. This is followed by a transitional passage, bars 37–57, in which Beethoven

moves towards B♭, the dominant, and cadences in that key. The music remains in B♭ for 90 bars, until a short phrase (bars 148–53) returns the music to the home key for a repeat of the exposition.

In Beethoven's earlier works in sonata style, and in much of the music of his eighteenth-century predecessors, it is usually not difficult to find a theme that is not only set in the contrasting key but is sufficiently distinct in character from the main theme to be identified as the primary theme of that 90-bar section: its 'second subject', as it has usually been called since the earliest theoretical descriptions of sonata form.[3] But where does that theme begin? What is the 'second subject' of the *Eroica*? (What, indeed, is a second subject?)

These questions can be fraught with difficulties. Donald Tovey included a diatribe against the term 'second subject' in nearly every one of his writings on classical form. In the introduction to his book on the Beethoven piano sonatas, he complained that:

> Some students begin their analysis of a sonata by glancing through it to see 'where the Second Subject comes' and where other less unfortunately named sections begin. This is evidently not the way to read a story. The listener has no business even to know that there is such a thing as a 'Second Subject' until he hears it.[4]

The problem, as Tovey and others understood it, is not that second subjects do not exist, but rather that pieces of music show a wide range of ways of modulating to a contrasting key and articulating the new key. Sometimes the arrival is signalled by a revised repeat of the main theme (Haydn), sometimes by a rhetorical figure that could hardly be called a theme: Tovey cites the first movement of Beethoven's Sonata Op. 111. And there may possibly be a series of discrete ideas in the new key (or at least no longer in the home key). This is what we find in the *Eroica*: a series of themes which collectively introduce, embellish and confirm the key of B♭ (see Table 5.1).

It might be enough to say that all these ideas, being unambiguously in the key of B♭, are part of a group of subjects and leave things at that. But the ear differentiates between things that sound preparatory and those that sound confirming, between lyrical and vigorous, between irregular and regular in design. And in spite of Tovey's admonition about looking 'to see where the Second Subject comes', listeners who take stock of what they have heard may naturally want to prioritise some ideas over others. Virtually all performances nowadays respect Beethoven's instruction to give listeners the opportunity to hear the entire exposition for a second time. And since the same five elements listed above appear in their original form and their original order in the recapitulation – though transposed to

Table 5.1 *Thematic material in the transition to B♭ major and the second group*

Bar	Description of theme
45	A transitional idea, in the dominant key but not yet confirming the new key with a clear beginning in B♭
57	A lyrical theme, emerging from that cadence but digressing into an extended passage of harmonic instability (beginning with a diminished seventh harmony after eight bars) before coming to an even stronger full close
83	A slower idea (crotchet pulse), built from repeated chords and manifesting signs of antecedent-plus-consequent construction, i.e. a pair of complementary phrases
109	A vigorous idea based on a broken chord, extensively elaborated, which begins with a clear reference to the rhythm and melodic shape of the main theme
144	Another broken-chord idea which leads into a quotation of the main theme turns back to a repeat of the opening (i.e., the main theme in bar 3)

the home key – one has three opportunities to consider how the themes stand in relation to each other – more, of course, on repeated hearings.

When it comes to the winner of the second-subject-of-the-*Eroica* competition, opinion is divided. Tovey, in his all-too-concise 'essay in musical analysis', speaks of a 'vast "second subject"', 'which 'display[s] its procession of themes', of which the one beginning at bar 44 is 'of cardinal importance' though it has 'escaped the notice of analysts'.[5] He then quotes bars 44–51 but does not illustrate or speak about any of the other themes in B♭. This is consistent with Tovey's accounts of and remarks on the *Eroica* elsewhere: in a highly informative single-line reduction of the Allegro con brio in his *Encyclopaedia Britannica* article on sonata form, he marks this theme as the beginning of the 'second group', which he notes in passing that 'nine conductors out of ten overlook'.[6] The heading 'New Theme' above bar 84 and bar 109 reinforces Tovey's notion of a group as a succession of themes.

Walter Riezler was more prescriptive. Though he by no means ignored the theme at bar 57, he understood it to be part of the transition, on account of the unstable harmony and the agitation introduced by the semiquavers in the ninth bar of the passage. He began his account of bars 83ff. with a question: 'Is what now comes a true "second subject", such as we are acquainted with in the symphonies of Haydn and Mozart, and in those of Beethoven's first period?' And he answers it in the affirmative, partly because of the 'spiritual contrast' with what has gone before whereby 'the music seems for a time to be reposing'.[7] One wonders how well Riezler knew Haydn's later symphonies, many of which use a revised version of the main theme rather than a new idea with a clear 'spiritual contrast'. But what he says about Mozart and the early Beethoven is

accurate, and it is this repertory that most influenced theories of sonata form as developed in the nineteenth century.

In their magisterial *Elements of Sonata Theory*, James Hepokoski and Warren Darcy are in no doubt about where the second subject is to be found. They describe bars 45ff. as 'a new, questioning theme' that comes to a 'decisive tonic resolution' at bar 57, which 'launches a new theme ... S proper'.[8] They thus go further than Tovey, and in the opposite direction to Riezler, not only identifying bar 57 as the start of the second group but also assigning it as a point of focus: 'S proper', rather than simply 'S'.

Hepokoski and Darcy argue, further, that bar 109 is the main theme of a closing area, that section which rounds off the action by confirming the contrasting key as the goal of the exposition. This theme, they argue, is not preceded by a strong cadence in the dominant but behaves more like a continuation of the preceding theme and its elaboration; that earlier idea, beginning in bar 83, can thus only be understood as an 'introductory or preparatory module' to the closing theme, not a second theme in its own right. They are sensitive to what they call the 'reception history' of the *Eroica*, and they readily admit that the earlier theme 'has often been mistaken for a "second theme"'.[9] But they insist that the crucial confirmation of the contrasting key, the point which marks the movement's 'essential expositional closure' – the final phase of the exposition – begins not in bar 109 but as early as the downbeat of bar 83. In other words, the 'spiritual contrast' for which Riezler pleaded so earnestly is of little interest for sonata theory and, in the *Eroica*, leads (according to Hepokoski and Darcy) to a poor understanding of how the second-group themes work together.

Is there an answer to the question, a resolution of the problem, a way of reconciling more than one of these points of view? Heinrich Schenker, who published the most extensive analysis of the symphony (1930), with a thirty-five-page, two-stave reduction and a further forty-nine graphic examples, takes a surprisingly metaphorical angle on the problem. Dismissive though he claimed to be about the textbook account of sonata form, because of its tendency to carve up pieces of music into sections, he nonetheless observed that the underlying course of the melody 'expressed an initially careless impulse, a youthful insouciance and lack of inhibition' according to which one must assign bars 57–82 to the modulatory section and regard bars 83ff. as 'the so-called second subject'.[10]

There is certainly a cadence in B♭ in bar 57, but it seems rather abruptly appended to the interplay between the oboe, clarinet, flute and violin, slamming the door on this wonderful interplay of the melodic instruments – as if to say 'not yet'; perhaps this is what Schenker meant by 'lack of inhibition'. By contrast, the theme emerging in bar 57 expands to

provide a far more substantial cadential preparation, with fully two bars of predominant (ii^6) harmony, followed by a cadential $^6_4$ that makes the ensuing V–I resolution to B♭ far more emphatic than the one 26 bars earlier. After such a build-up, it was only natural for Beethoven to introduce a theme of greatly contrasting character, slower and more measured. What is crucial, however, is the antecedent–consequent construction of the later theme: an eight-bar phrase (83–90) to which bars 91ff. form a direct, if expanded, response. To listeners familiar with Beethoven's earlier instrumental works, and with Mozart and much of Haydn, bar 83 marks the start of something that, while not tonally new, is nonetheless thematically special.

The 'New Theme' in the Development Section

When Beethoven arrived in Vienna in 1792, he had some lessons from Haydn, who was then the most celebrated composer in the city. He had also come to know much of Mozart's music from his experience as a practising musician in the court orchestra of his native Bonn. His friend Count Ferdinand Waldstein's prophesy, that by hard work Beethoven would 'acquire Mozart's spirit from Haydn's hands', is the first written statement linking the three great Viennese 'classic' composers together. It is sometimes interpreted, in analytical terms, as Beethoven learning the art of motivic and thematic development from Haydn while adhering to the symmetry of Mozart's large forms, in which the recapitulation runs in close parallel to the exposition. However, there is a marked disparity in the proportions of the other sections. While Mozart's development sections are about half the length of the expositions they follow, those of Beethoven are longer; and with the younger composer, the coda sometimes expands to become a section in its own right, rather than merely giving emphasis to the final cadence. It may well be that the near-exactness of Beethoven's recapitulations helps to restore an overall balance in his forms between the qualities of likeness and difference.

In works written at the same time as and immediately after the *Eroica* – the composer's so-called 'heroic phase' – the development is almost as long as or even longer than the exposition. In the 'Waldstein' Sonata Op. 53, also composed in 1803–4, an 85-bar exposition is followed by a 70-bar development; in the next large-scale sonata, Op. 57 in F minor (the 'Appassionata', 1805) the development (70 bars) is longer than the exposition (65); and it may seem proportionally longer still, since the exposition is not marked to be repeated. A year later, in the first of the quartets Op. 59

dedicated to Count Razumovsky, the 102-bar exposition is again played only once; the development is 140 bars long.

In each of these three works, the development may be divided into two parts, or phases; doing so enables the listener to refocus attention on the ways in which Beethoven transforms his thematic materials. In the 'Waldstein', bars 90–111, he reduces the main theme to its end-motives, while in bars 112–41 he develops the arpeggios that emerge from the second-subject chorale. In the 'Appassionata' an elaboration of ideas from the main theme and transition (bars 68–108) leads to a literal quotation of the start of the second subject, which initiates the second phase of the development (bars 109–33). And in the first 'Razumovsky' quartet Beethoven makes a feature of the divided development by introducing a standing on the dominant after 49 bars, only to back away from an early return to the home key; the second part comprises a diversion to D♭ major, a lengthy fugato and a second, definitive (but relatively short) standing on the dominant.[11]

As extensive as they are, these development sections are dwarfed by that of the *Eroica* which, lasting 244 bars, contains many of the elements described above. After a lengthy introductory passage based on the transitional theme at bar 45, a substantial, far-reaching elaboration of the principal motive leads to a further airing of the transitional theme in the A♭ major before a fugato emerges in its relative key, F minor. However, throughout this passage Beethoven avoids anything that could be construed as an area of repose: the first true point of arrival in the development, a perfect cadence in the remote key of E minor, does not occur until after 130 bars: this cadence is heralded by off-beat $^{6\natural}_{5}$ pre-dominant chords far more menacing than anything heard previously, so that the arrival in E minor, however remote from the home key, comes as something of a relief.

This arrival is marked by what is commonly denoted as a 'new theme', and in this respect the *Eroica* differs from the development sections of the symphonies, sonatas and quartets that were composed in its wake. But is that theme entirely new, or is it somehow related to one – or more – themes heard previously? This is a question that has exercised writers for a long time; and it may imply that the status of the *Eroica* as a quintessentially middle-period work invited writers on music to look beyond the newness of the theme, to search for a way of integrating it into the whole.

The Austrian composer and theorist August Halm was the first to publish an essay specifically about this theme, in the year of his death (1929).[12] Halm may have also been the first to note that the tenor part (taken by the cellos, with reinforcement from the second violins) of what he called this 'foreign body' (*Fremdkörper*) outlines a broken chord in

Example 5.1 Beethoven, *Eroica* Symphony, Op. 55, outline of main motive in the cello part of the 'new theme' (after Halm, 'Der Fremdkörper', p. 481)

E minor, filled in with passing notes, and does so in a way that corresponds to the shape of the principal motive (Example 5.1).

In making this observation, Halm nonetheless questioned its value for our understanding, our appreciation, of the movement as a whole. If, after all, the Allegro con brio comprises 700 bars, the development section alone nearly 250, was it absolutely necessary to explain everything in the development as somehow thematically related to what had been set out in the exposition?

A year later, Heinrich Schenker completed the mammoth task of making a full voice-leading analysis of all four movements of the symphony. He included a graph that shows the shape of the main theme embedded in the bass of the 'new theme' (Schenker's Fig. 24), but he refrained from remarking on the relationship between the two themes in his accompanying text – until the final section, where he eulogises Halm for his insights into the problems of music analysis and his devotion to the study of the German masterworks. (Considering that Schenker found Halm's short essay and Nottebohm's monograph on Landsberg 6 the only pieces of secondary literature on the *Eroica* worth consulting, this was high praise indeed.)

Walter Riezler took issue with Halm and Schenker, insisting that 'the structure of the episode' is governed not by the cello line but by the first oboe's melody, and that it is a mistake to explain away the former as the main motive elaborated by passing-note motion.[13] Riezler had an altogether different idea: he regarded the theme as based upon one of those 'turning figures', as he called them, which pervade the symphony from beginning to end: the oboe e–d♯–e–f♯–g–f♯ in the 'new theme' is a variant of the violins' opening figure, g–a♭–g–f–g–a♭, and for that reason the theme need not be regarded as new.

In the absence of consensus about a work by Beethoven, twentieth-century scholars sometimes appealed to the composer's sketchbooks for clues to his intentions. It is worth having a look at the manuscript in which he worked out the plan of the symphony. The earliest sketch transcriptions, made by Nottebohm in 1880 when the manuscript was still in the possession of the Landsberg family, present a number of continuous drafts of the movement; these show not the oboe melody, which Riezler and

others have taken to be the 'new theme', but the cello line below it, which essentially mirrors its contour. That is, in Nottebohm's transcriptions it is always the lower line of the theme that Beethoven has written down, not the top line by which we normally identify melodic movement. (Nottebohm did not refer to this feature anywhere in his commentary.) This raises the question: Did Beethoven have the oboe melody in his head when he got to this point in the sketchbook, or did he conceive the cello part as the tune? In preparing their recent edition of the whole of the sketchbook, Lewis Lockwood and Alan Gosman came across further sketches in which the 'new theme' makes an appearance, and some of these do indeed show the incipit of the oboe melody.[14] But it is always the cello part that Beethoven continues in the sketch, as if it were the governing line. (Like Nottebohm, the editors did not discuss this theme in their commentary.)

Could it be argued, then, that the cello line is the underlying melody of the 'new theme', and that the first oboe sings above it to disguise the intention of what lies beneath? That would still leave open the question as to whether the cello line is really a version of the opening theme stretched from two bars to four and filled in by passing notes. I myself doubt that the new theme, played an octave above its original pitch and as the lower voice of a delicate contrapuntal setting, will be heard as a version of the main theme of the symphony. In any event, the introduction of new themes in development sections is by no means unprecedented – there are examples in Mozart's instrumental music, and occasionally in Haydn's – and the oboe is, after all, the highest and most prominent part. The real question that Halm may be asking is this: can listeners perceive a connection between the two themes once it has been pointed out to them in writing? Is that, ultimately, 'the value of music analysis'?

The Recapitulation: Just Before and Just After

As the point of recapitulation (bar 398) approaches, the second horn gives what sounds like a premature entry of the principal motive. And when the main theme does actually return at the appropriate time, its first six bars appear exactly as they had at the beginning of the movement; but the continuation is recomposed so that, instead of cadencing in the home key, it makes a surprise modulation to F major. How is each of these events to be understood? And, since they occur in such close proximity, are they related to one another?

It is worth recalling a famous anecdote transmitted by Ferdinand Ries, in which he recorded his outrage when, on hearing the first rehearsal of the

Example 5.2 Beethoven, *Eroica* Symphony, Op. 55, bars 390–8, without second horn part

Example 5.3 Beethoven, *Eroica* Symphony, Op. 55, bars 390–8, with implied dominant pedal and violin II conforming with horn II

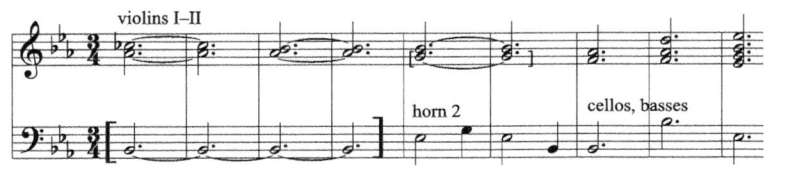

symphony, he was sure that the horn player had miscounted the bars of rest in his part and came in too early.[15] But the premature horn entry is not only intentional but, as the sketches show, was also planned from the outset.[16] And while it is meant to sound striking, it is not something that could be omitted without creating further problems. For if the second horn player, knowing that the recapitulation was to begin four bars later, had not entered where instructed the harmonic rhythm would be unbalanced, with two bars of pre-dominant harmony (represented by the violins' minor third ab/cb) followed by six bars of dominant seventh (represented by the major second ab/bb; Example 5.2). In other words, something is needed after four bars, even if the horn entry does not sound quite right, and even if it sounds wrong enough to be attributable to a counting mistake.

One possible explanation is that the notes played by the horn pull one of the violin lines down, and so they continue the trend initiated by the stepwise descent from cb to bb, with ab–g in an inner part, at the same time reinstating the dominant pedal that had dropped out a few bars before (Example 5.3).

Seen in this light, it is not the second horn player who enters four bars early but the second violins who linger too long on ab^1, when they should have moved to g^1, and so fail to contribute to the – perfectly normal – $\frac{6}{4}$ chord preceding the final dominant seventh.

If the horn entry is locally upsetting, what follows after the return of the opening, without in any way sounding like a performance mistake, introduces a more serious perceptual problem. For what should have been a repeat of the opening bars of the music (minus the two introductory

chords) veers in a new direction: the tonality is no longer the home key of
E♭ major but one that had been previously avoided: the only earlier use of
F major harmony had been in bar 45, as the dominant of the contrasting
key of B♭. In the recapitulation the cellos, having duly reproduced the start
of the main theme, continue as before with a chromatic line; but instead of
the c♯ being pulled back to d as a lower neighbour, Beethoven treats it as if
it were a d♭ which must resolve downwards, to c♮ supporting the dominant
of F, and in so doing force the violins to move down to f^2 instead of
reaching for the expected upper neighbour, a♭^{2}. What is more, the instrument that Beethoven uses to confirm and celebrate this unexpected twist is
one that has not yet been used, and indeed that one would least expect to
find in a symphony in the key of E♭ major: the horn in F. For listeners who
think of the Classical style as human comedy in musical terms, the passage
comprising bars 390–416 could be titled 'The Misbehaving Horn Players':
one brings in the main theme too early, another plays it in the wrong key.

The absence of a♭ in the violins eight bars into the recapitulation can,
moreover, be related to its presence four bars before it: the second violin
a♭^{1}, which had sounded against the g in the second horn part. In other
words, not only the main theme but also the neighbour note that is meant
to follow it are sounded together four bars before the expected point of
recapitulation: the primary note and its upper neighbour are heard simultaneously, rather than consecutively.[17]

Some restoration of A♭ is offered when the first flute, in taking up
the main theme in the key of D♭, copies the horn player's insistence
upon the fifth scale degree as the goal. That is, since the horn, when it
reaches c^2, stays on that note for a full five bars (411–15) before lipping
the pitch up to d♭^{2}, the flute also remains on the fifth of D♭ for the
same amount of time. But this note is the very a♭^{2} which had been
missed out some fifteen bars earlier when the violins were forced
downwards. The flute's a♭^{2} eventually resolves to g^2: implicitly in bar
430, when the main motive returns, and explicitly when it is repeated
fortissimo ten bars later, now with g^3 as the highest note in both the
wind and the strings. Beethoven, then, does not deny us the neighbour-note figure g^2–a♭^{2}–g^2 in the recapitulation, he actually gives it to
us twice: it just does not take the form in which we had been expecting
to hear it in this part of the composition.[18]

Thematic Development, Thematic Relationships

The discussion of the recapitulation, in which harmonic and thematic
matters may be said to intersect, is a fitting introduction to a larger field

of enquiry into the *Eroica*: the nature of its themes, and the interrelationships between them. True, not all music theorists set much store by motivic relationships in music, or 'thematic unity' as it is sometimes called. Schenker, whose interest lay in voice-leading connections between the surface of a work and its deeper underlying structure, often poked fun at those he dubbed *Reminiszenzenjäger* ('hunters of [thematic] reminiscences'), while Tovey, in his essay on Beethoven's art forms, pronounced that 'themes have no closer connexion with larger musical proportions than the colours of animals have with their skeletons', and that 'the notion that music can be logically connected by mere thematic links has done almost as much harm to composers as to theorists and teachers'.[19]

As sensible as these pronouncements may be, they do not help us to explain why a certain theme in a certain place in the music may be compelling. If the laws of musical structure suggest that a modulation from one key to another early in a composition (in the exposition) is strategically important, we are still keen to know why one theme, rather than some other, has been used to articulate the arrival in that key, and also which theme – or version of some earlier theme – is employed to get from the home key to the new key. (If this were not the case, we would then be able to invent any number of new Classical works merely by using the main theme of one sonata with the secondary themes of another, suitably transposed to a contrasting key.) Such questions have attracted writers for a long time, and the *Eroica* is certainly a work that has generated interest along these lines, partly because of its sheer length, and partly because of its position in Beethoven's oeuvre as a work that purportedly ushered in a new creative period.

Some thematic relationships can almost be forecast by the position they occupy in the design of a movement. In particular, the very end of a broadly conceived sonata exposition often includes an echo of the main theme: this technique helps to bridge the point at which the exposition is repeated. The closing subject, if such a theme precedes this bridging idea, often makes a reference to the main theme; and in the *Eroica* Beethoven does both these things, and even adds further references to the main theme as the closing theme is expanded (Example 5.4).

But while thematic relatedness across a work, or a movement of a work, can help us to hear it as hanging together (the German word *Zusammenhang* is often translated as 'coherence'), it can also run the risk of damping the listening experience as a result of lack of variety, lack of contrast. This is a problem that different composers have addressed in different ways, and sometimes in different compositions. One often associates Haydn with a technique that in the twentieth century became known as 'monothematicism', because the most prominent theme in the second group of his sonata forms is sometimes

Example 5.4 Beethoven, *Eroica* Symphony, Op. 55, second-group themes related to principal motive

(a) bars 3–6

(b) bars 109–112

(c) bars 132–135

(d) bars 148–153

a version of his opening theme. By contrast, Mozart's deployment of thematic material seems more diffuse, more varied on the surface, though there are exceptions in his mature works (especially those in minor keys). Beethoven's thematicism may be regarded as a synthesis of the two, though there is also an element of thematic transformation that looks ahead to techniques more commonly associated with the middle of the nineteenth century (Schumann, Liszt and Wagner); here the relationships between themes do not require special pleading on the part of analysts, and yet the contrast of character and mood are indisputable.[20]

For this reason, some writers of the past hundred years have rejected Tovey's dictum on theme and design and are instead keen to find thematic interrelationships commensurate with Beethoven's grand structural plans, and in particular to understand the entire first movement of the *Eroica* as growing out of its opening theme. This may not be as difficult as it sounds, since the theme is made up of two contrasting components from which all manner of material may be derived: (a) arpeggiation (broken chords); and (b) stepwise movement upwards and downwards, that is, passing and neighbour notes.

Riezler, whose Beethoven life-and-works study includes a thirty-five-page appendix devoted to 'an attempt at an analysis of the organic structure' of the first movement of the *Eroica*, described (b), as we have seen, as turning motion; he noted the importance of turning figures in both the bass line in bars 6–9 and the melody emerging from the violins' syncopated g^2.

Example 5.5 Beethoven, *Eroica* Symphony, Op. 55, comparison of bars 280–3 with bars 83–6 (after Cassirer, *Beethoven und die Gestalt*, p. 21)

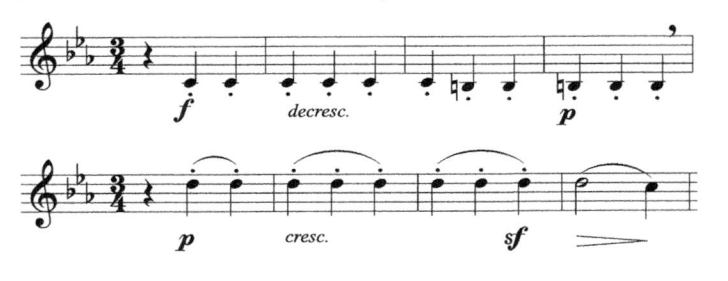

He also perceived the new theme in the development as based on a turning figure and thus could relate it to the violin line at the start of the movement.

Writing a decade earlier than Riezler, the German conductor Fritz Cassirer saw everything in Beethoven's work in terms of intimate thematic relatedness. His *Beethoven und die Gestalt*[21] packs close to a hundred unnumbered music examples from the first movement of the *Eroica* alone into the space of about twenty-five pages, and his account of the symphony – and of thirteen further works – reads like a chain of inter-related music examples accompanied by a brief, highly florid text. To give but one extreme example of thematic connection in the first movement, at the bottom of page 21 Cassirer juxtaposed the theme at bar 83 and the lead-in to the 'new theme' in the development (see Example 5.5), and some even more tenuous threads are drawn between first-movement material and themes from later movements in the symphony.

Of course, it is dangerous to criticise an isolated claim without con-sidering the whole of the author's argument; and Cassirer does make some trenchant observations about thematic relationships, especially between the first and third movements (both in E♭, and both in 3/4 time), which many will probably find convincing. But the arguments that fail to per-suade weaken the stronger ones, and this causes the foundations of his analysis to subside.

A more promising search for thematic connections in the first move-ment of the *Eroica* was made by the American composer, conductor and neuroscientist David Epstein. His wide-ranging *Beyond Orpheus* includes a substantial chapter on the *Eroica* in which he sought to find thematic interrelationships not only on but also somewhere below the surface of the music, in things that Schenker would have called 'middleground motives' and Carl Dahlhaus 'subthematicism'.[22] Like Cassirer and Riezler before him, Epstein was concerned with unity in music, and the first of his analytical chapters is entitled 'Unity in Beethoven's *Eroica* Symphony (First Movement)'; compared with the earlier authors, he

showed a more secure sense of the harmonic underpinning of thematic material.

Epstein made much of a bass progression which, while not meriting the status of theme in the conventional sense of the term, is nonetheless an important feature of the *Eroica*'s harmonic landscape and a major unifying feature: the stepwise progression from ♭VII to ♭VI to V, leading eventually to the local tonic. (Riezler had noted this, too, but did not deal with it systematically.) It makes its first appearance, as A♭–G♭–F → B♭, in the modulation to the dominant, enabling Beethoven to reach the contrasting key in the shortest possible time: A♭ major in bar 43 is the subdominant of the old key, F major in bar 45 the dominant of the new.

Elsewhere, Beethoven uses this progression more broadly and emphasises different features. At the beginning of the development, where it takes the form B♭–A♭–G → C, he broods at length – for twelve bars in all – on the semitone A♭–G. (Schenker heard this as a transformation of the neighbour-note figure g–a♭–g of the main theme.[23]) At the start of the recapitulation, the tonic itself (E♭) is reinterpreted as ♭VII and so leads to the unexpected entry of the horn in F. And in the first part of the coda the same progression is expanded to such an extent that it is easy to lose sight of the intended harmonic goal (see below).

The (Not Slow) Introduction

The two introductory chords (often called 'hammer blows'), whose initial functions are to state the key of the symphony and establish the tempo of the first movement, are sometimes thought of as acquiring a certain thematic status as the first movement unfolds. Insofar as they precede the exposition – that is, they are not repeated when the exposition is played for the second time, nor do they return in the recapitulation – they are not part of the sonata plan itself. The use of strong tonic chords, or a strong chord progression, as a call to attention was not a new idea, nor was it restricted to the symphonic genre: one finds it in several of Haydn's later string quartets. But while a single chord has no element of the time dimension – and one cannot easily regard two of them as a 'motive' in the conventional sense, since they lack harmonic contour – the idea of repeated chords gains in meaning as the first movement progresses, as the distance between similar hammer blows is shortened from three beats to two, and the space between them is filled in with broken chords that recall the opening motive. And when an entirely different, highly dissonant chord emerges in the development section – separated once more by three beats, but no longer played on the downbeat – it, too, can remind us of the opening in spite of a new

Example 5.6 Beethoven, *Eroica* Symphony, Op. 55, some passages built on vigorously repeated chords

texture, an altered metric position, a lengthening from crotchet to minim, and a function that is more climactic than introductory (Example 5.6).

The Extended Coda

From about 1803 onwards, the codas to the outer movements of Beethoven's instrumental works generally get longer. The first-movement codas of the 'Waldstein' Sonata and, to a greater extent, the *Eroica* do more than emphasise the ending: both contain harmonic progressions that could find a place in a sonata-form development section. This gives rise to the possibility of regarding some Beethovenian codas as

'secondary developments' or 'terminal developments', terms that may have been first used by the French composer Vincent d'Indy.[24]

In the *Eroica*, the music that follows the end of the recapitulation is 140 bars long, which is nearly as long as the exposition (or recapitulation) itself. Like these sections, the coda unfolds in several phases. The first begins with the above-mentioned ♭VII–♭VI–V progression, which had initially been presented in the space of just three bars (43–5) but is now stretched over fourteen (551–64). Because of its sheer length, and the increase in dynamic level (from *piano* to *forte* to *fortissimo*), the C major at bar 561 will be difficult to hear, initially, as the dominant of F, by contrast with F major in bar 45 (and especially G major at the start of the development). On the contrary: Beethoven's continuation in the coda marks C major as a tonic in its own right, crucially by framing its own dominant seventh, the $^6_5$ chord above B.

The return of the 'new theme' in bar 581 is another marker of the world of the development, in spite of the greater proximity of F minor to the home key, the E minor of bar 284. The theme is repeated in the tonic minor but with new orchestration. And the ensuing 36 bars of dominant preparation (bars 595–630) recapture the mood of the last 60 bars of the development, this time without the horn's early entry.

When the tonic returns, Beethoven is not simply content to allow the main theme to play itself out, reaching the high B♭ no fewer than eight times for 'heroic' effect, as Kerman would have it.[25] He also corrects the harmonic 'fault' in the second-group theme at bar 57, replacing its diminished seventh (bar 65) with a dominant seventh (Example 5.7). Once the damage has been repaired, the movement can be brought to a swift conclusion, with just three tonic chords. We may thus view this coda as part exploratory, part celebratory; but in the context of the coda as a whole, the celebration is somewhat underplayed.

The Overall Structure of the First Movement

The search for thematic unity, or coherence, is a feature of twentieth-century analytical writing. But the mere relatedness of lines, harmonic progressions or textures does not explain how a work unfolds in time. Sonata form is an important start in clarifying the first movement of the *Eroica* which, though unprecedentedly long, behaves in most respects according to the form most frequently used for first movements in the music of Haydn, Mozart and Beethoven. Even if a textbook definition of sonata form was not published until Beethoven's last years (in Anton Reicha's *Traité de haute composition musicale*, 1824–8) and the term

Example 5.7 Beethoven, *Eroica* Symphony, Op. 55, the different continuations, in the recapitulation and coda, of the theme from bars 57ff.

Sonatenform itself first appears more than a decade after his death (in Adolf Bernhard Marx's *Die Lehre von der musikalischen Komposition*, 1837–47), Beethoven was fully conscious of the basic elements of sonata form as practised by his contemporaries and immediate predecessors: his sketches are frequently annotated with markers for the start of the second subject, the development and the recapitulation.[26]

An important account of the form of the first movement is given as a single-stave precis of the movement, in Tovey's entry on Sonata Forms for the 14th edition of the *Encyclopaedia Britannica*. The technique is not unique to the *Eroica*: elsewhere in this essay, and in related entries on Rondo, Scherzo and Variation, he uses single-stave sketches. But that of the *Eroica* is not only the longest but also the most heavily annotated, with verbal notations showing formal elements – first group, transition, dominant preparation, second group, statements and counter-statements of themes – as well as themes, modulations, rhythmic figures, rhythmic diminutions, and large-scale exact or transposed repetitions of material previously heard. Spread over eight pages in small print, Tovey's precis is not unlike Beethoven's own single-stave drafts in the sketchbook, except that it represents the final version, contains more analytical and descriptive commentary, and is complete.

A more ambitious overview was undertaken around the same time by Schenker. His study comprised a fifty-six-page text: four *Bilder* ('pictures', or graphs) making up a thirty-five-page booklet in landscape

format, which offer a much fuller precis of the music (on two staves throughout) of each movement and include highly detailed analytical annotations; and a set of forty-nine further music illustrations printed on six large sheets of paper which, when unfolded, measure 75 x 50 centimetres (about 30 x 20 inches). The production costs were enormous. And given that much of the Western world was in recession at the time of its completion, it is hardly surprising that Schenker was unable to place the work with a major German music publishing house: both Breitkopf & Härtel and Peters of Leipzig turned it down. He resorted to issuing it, at his own cost, as the third volume of a series of yearbooks, *The Masterwork in Music*, of which he was the sole author and which the Munich publishers had discontinued a few years before on economic grounds. (We learn from Schenker's diary that his wife Jeanette was willing to finance the publication from her personal savings; but his pupil Hans Weisse succeeded in persuading the conductor Wilhelm Furtwängler, who admired Schenker's way of contemplating music, to raise three thousand marks and thus save the couple from financial difficulties.)

By the time of the *Eroica* study, which was his last written-out essay in music analysis, Schenker's concepts of musical coherence had coalesced into a theory of structural levels (or layers), the entire network of relationships within a musical work being controlled by a simple two-voice *Ursatz* and a series of 'voice-leading transformations' applied to it. From this framework he was able to trace the growth of the movement in stages, from a 'background' (represented by the *Ursatz*) through various 'middleground' levels to a 'foreground' reduction in which the essentials of the surface become clearly visible.

Of the theoretically possible forms of *Ursatz*, Schenker chose the simplest for the first movement of the symphony, in which the upper voice (called the *Urlinie*) descends by step through the interval of a third – a 'third-progression' (*Terzzug*), in Schenker's terminology – and is supported by the cadential movement of a bass line in note-against-note counterpoint: $\hat{3}-\hat{2}-\hat{1}$ above I–V–I. For a piece in E♭ major, the upper voice $g^2-f^2-e♭^2$ is supported by E♭–B♭–E♭.

But a musical form such as sonata form divides tonally into two broad parts: a harmonically open-ended exposition (here, E♭ modulating to its dominant, B♭), and a development and recapitulation, in which that harmonic progression must be closed up – the dominant *key* must be returned to its natural state as a dominant *chord* of the home key. In Schenkerian terms, the *Urlinie* is 'interrupted' at $\hat{2}$ and begins over again: $\hat{3}-\hat{2} \parallel \hat{3}-\hat{2}-\hat{1}$. In addition, there is a strong pull towards a return to the opening of the piece – the recapitulation – which is represented by the

Example 5.8 Heinrich Schenker, 'Beethoven's Third Symphony', Fig. 1: first movement, first middleground layer

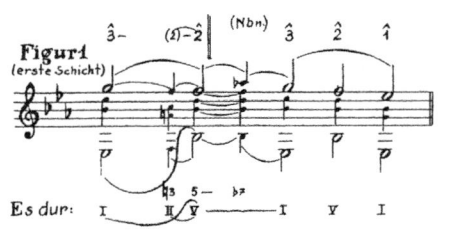

seventh above the dominant, a♭ supported by the continued B♭ in the bass, the seventh, a hovers, so to speak, over the entire development section. This elaboration of the *Urlinie* and its supporting bass is called the *erste Schicht*, the 'first layer' of the middleground (Example 5.8).

Since there is a temporary resting on the first of the dominant chords, that is, a strong sense of arriving at and remaining in the key of B♭ major, the f² in the upper voice must be shown to descend, by step, to the keynote of B♭ major, f²–e♭²–d²–c²–b♭¹. This stepwise descent of a fifth (*Quintzug*, or 'fifth-progression') represents the modulatory section and all the themes of the second group; it is first shown in Schenker's Fig. 2, the second middleground layer. In Fig. 3, the third layer of the middleground, he shows support for this descent with a bass-line progression, B♭–D–E♭–E♮–F–B♭, which outlines a I–V–I progression.

Schenker described the fourth and last of his middleground layers (his Fig. 6) as an 'illustration of the octave registers of the exposition', now showing the outlines of the first 152 bars in the actual registers in which they unfold. What had been given in his Fig. 3 as a single 'fifth-progression', the linear descent from f² to b♭¹, is now shown as a series of four *Quintzüge*, of which the first, second and fourth are set in a higher octave. These progressions correspond to the elements that make up the modulation to and subsequent music in the key of B♭: the modulation (bars 45–57), the theme at bar 57, the 'so-called second subject' at bar 83 and the entire passage from bar 109 to the end of the exposition. This last descent is the 'fourth, thoroughly elaborated fifth-progression' which, being set in the upper register, leads to the higher b♭² at bar 144, which can then descend by step (to a♭²) at bar 152; the a♭² now either leads directly to g² for a repeat of the exposition or it is stretched out over the course of the development and will resolve 246 bars later at the start of the recapitulation (Example 5.9). (This is marked in Schenker's Fig. 6 by the words *zur Wiederholung oder Durchführung*.)

The explanation of the first three middleground layers takes up less than a page of text; the next twenty-five pages clarify the details of *Bild 1*,

Example 5.9 Schenker, 'Beethoven's Third Symphony', Fig. 6: first movement, fourth middleground layer

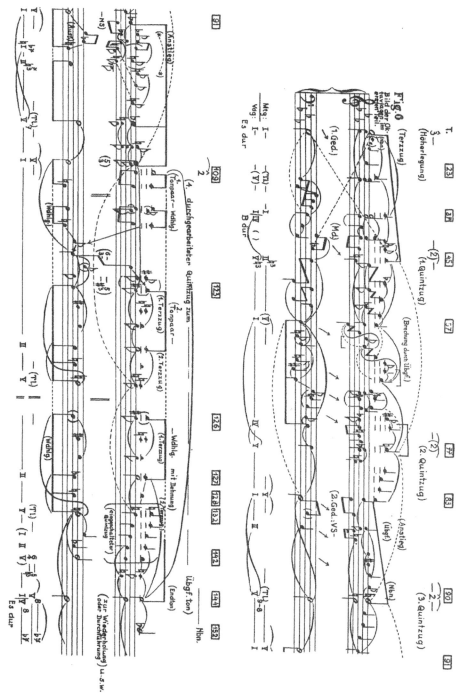

Example 5.10 Schenker 'Beethoven's Third Symphony', Fig. 10b and Fig. 13b: voice-leading details in the antecedent and consequent phrases of the theme at bars 83ff.

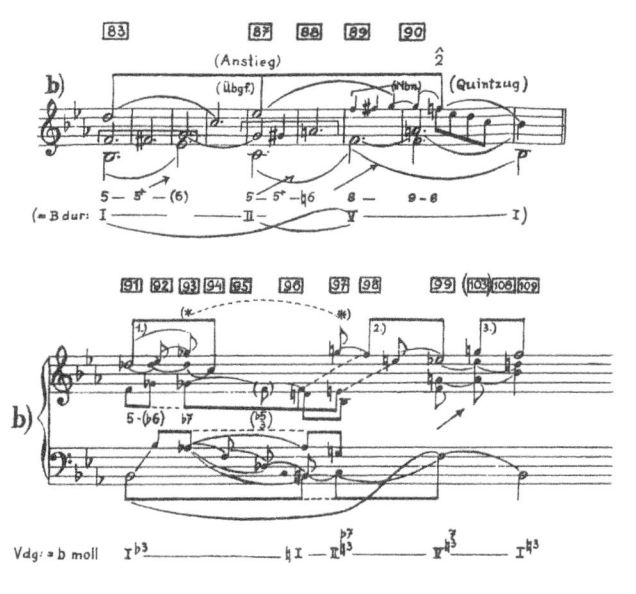

the foreground graph, in considerable detail. This text is set out section by section – bars 1–15, 15–37, 37–45, 45–57, 57–83 and so on – with great emphasis laid upon the underlying counterpoint.

Where an even closer examination is required, Schenker divides these sections into smaller units: thus, the antecedent of the second subject, bars 83–91, is explained separately, with further music examples used for clarification. His Fig. 10b shows the underlying sequence of five to six exchanges in the first part of the antecedent; Fig. 13b shows that this pattern is broken in the consequent phrase, and also that the ♭6–g♭ resulting from the change from major to minor is eventually converted into a g♮ when the consequent phrase is extended and eventually resolves to B♭ major (Example 5.10).

The foregoing commentary has been intended as an introduction to some of the issues faced by musicians who cared deeply about the materials, fabric and structure of the *Eroica* in the twentieth century and who committed their thoughts to pen and paper. It is unlikely that agreement will ever be reached on many of the issues these contemplations have addressed. Schenker's claim to have presented the *Eroica* 'in its true content for the first time', as he subtitled his 1930 study, is little more than wishful thinking if taken at face value. To opponents of his view of musical coherence, or 'synthesis' (as he commonly called it), these words

may be more self-aggrandisement, an expression of the author's conviction of having discovered the true path to understanding the great German tradition over the course of four decades.

If Riezler's 12,000 words on the analysis of the first movement alone, and Schenker's 30,000 on all four, leave much to be explained and so many viewpoints to be assessed objectively, it is hard to imagine that contemporary writers will rush to improve on these scholarly monuments, let alone write something that can be regarded as definitive, a 'standard work' in publishing parlance. What seems certain, however, is that Beethoven's *Eroica* will continue to exert its fascination upon those who wish to learn how music goes: to have a better understanding of what it means to be a second subject or a new theme, how the entry of an instrument or theme can both confound musical expectations and promote coherence at a higher level, and how one musical idea may be said to be in a relationship with another. If these goals are worth pursuing, then the symphony is more than an outstanding example of classical music: it represents a major contribution to Western civilisation itself.

Notes

1. M. Solomon, *Beethoven* (London: Cassel, 1977), p. 104.
2. E. Anderson, ed. and trans., *The Letters of Beethoven* (London: Macmillan, 1961), no. 54, vol. 1, p. 68.
3. What is often referred to as the 'textbook definition of sonata form' prevalent in the twentieth century was first set out by Anton Reicha in the second volume of his *Cour de composition musicale* (Paris, 1825); Reicha termed the main theme of a sonata movement its *idée mère* ('mother idea'), and the primary contrasting theme as the *seconde idée mère*; his diagram of the form is reproduced in I. Bent, *Analysis* (Basingstoke and London: Macmillan, 1987), p. 20.
4. D. Tovey, *A Companion to Beethoven's Pianoforte Sonatas* (London: Associated Board, 1931), p. 1.
5. D. F. Tovey, 'Beethoven: Third Symphony in E♭ Major (*Sinfonia eroica*)', in *Essays in Music Analysis*, vol. 3 (London: Oxford University Press, 1935), p. 30.
6. D. F. Tovey, *Musical Articles from the Encyclopaedia Britannica* (London: Oxford University Press, 1944), p. 220. In the musical illustration, the heading 'Second Group' appears one line lower than expected in the reduction, above bar 65 instead of bar 57. This is surely a mistake: Tovey cannot have imagined the second group to have begun on a diminished seventh chord.
7. W. Riezler, *Beethoven*, Eng. trans. G. D. H. Pidcock (London: M. C. Forrester, 1938), p. 255.
8. J. Hepokoski and W. Darcy, *Elements of Sonata Theory: Norms, Types, and Deformations in the Late-Eighteenth-Century Sonata* (New York, NY: Oxford University Press, 2006), p. 143.
9. Ibid., p. 187.
10. H. Schenker, 'Beethoven's Third Symphony: Its True Content Described for the First Time', trans. D. Puffett and A. Clayton, in *The Masterwork in Music*, vol. 3, ed. W. Drabkin (Cambridge: Cambridge University Press, 1997), p. 17.
11. When the tonality returns to F major, Beethoven first recapitulates an extension of the main theme at bar 242, but the main theme does not return in the home key until bar 254. Whichever of these points is chosen to mark its end-point, the development is still significantly longer than the exposition.
12. A. Halm, 'Über den Wert musikalischer Analysen, I: Der Fremdkörper im ersten Satz der Eroika', *Die Musik*, 21 (1929), pp. 481–4.
13. Riezler, *Beethoven*, p. 267.

14. L. Lockwood and A. Gosman, eds., *Beethoven's Eroica Sketchbook: A Critical Edition*, 2 vols. (Urbana, IL: University of Illinois Press, 2013). The representations of the new theme as part of longer drafts of the development are found on pp. 34–9 of the sketchbook, and these all show only the lower line (for the cello) when the theme is first stated in E minor. There are, however, clues of a two-part counterpoint elsewhere in these pages, where Beethoven restates the theme in A minor and again in E♭ minor.

15. F. G. Wegeler and F. Ries, *Remembering Beethoven*, trans. F. Noonan (London: André Deutsch), p. 69.

16. Lockwood and Gosman, eds., *Beethoven's 'Eroica' Sketchbook*, vol. 1, pp. 31 and 35.

17. The idea of that the loss of the g^2–$a♭^2$–g^2 figure in the recapitulation is connected to the premature horn entry was proposed by Milton Babbitt around 1970, in a seminar at Princeton University.

18. In an unnumbered music example in his *Beyond Orpheus: Studies in Musical Structure* (Cambridge, MA: MIT Press, 1979), printed at the bottom of pp. 124–5, David Epstein implies that the flute's $a♭^2$ is an extended upper neighbour note; but his written commentary does not underscore the point.

19. D. F. Tovey, 'Some Aspects of Beethoven's Art-Forms,' *Essays and Lectures on Music* (London: Oxford University Press, 1949), p. 275.

20. See, in particular, the transformations of theme in the first movement of Piano Concerto No. 5 ('Emperor'): compare the minor key theme in the strings at bar 41 with the horn version eight bars later, and the full orchestra version at bar 167. What Beethoven achieves here, however, may best be understood as part of a general trend towards thematic interrelatedness in his middle-period instrumental works, a trend that had far-reaching effects in the course of the nineteenth century.

21. E. Cassirer, *Beethoven und die Gestalt: ein Kommentar* (Stuttgart, Berlin and Leipzig: Deutsche Verlags-Anstalt, 1925), the discussion of the first movement of the *Eroica* covers pp. 3–27.

22. C. Dahlhaus, *Ludwig van Beethoven: Approaches to his Music* (Oxford: Clarendon Press, 1991), pp. 202–18.

23. Schenker acknowledged privately that his own pursuit of this figure as a unifying factor in the *Eroica* was initially stimulated by remarks made by his pupil Robert Brünauer in November 1927. For a transcription and translation of the documents that record Brünauer's 'extraordinarily elegant, visionary observation', see I. Bent, 'Heinrich Schenker and Robert Brünauer: Relations with a Musical Industrialist', in *Festschrift Hellmut Federhofer zum 100. Geburtstag*, ed. A. Beer (Tutzing: Hans Schneider), pp. 35–6.

24. See J. Kerman, 'Notes on Beethoven's Codas', in *Beethoven Studies 3*, ed. A. Tyson (Cambridge: Cambridge University Press, 1982), p. 153. For Kerman, the extreme case is found in the finale of the Eighth Symphony, and this is the only work for which he finds the term 'secondary development' appropriate.

25. Kerman, 'Notes on Beethoven's Codas', p. 150.

26. Chief among these are *m. g.* (probably short for *Mittel-Gedanke*, 'intermediate theme', what we would now call 'second subject'), *2da parte*. later in German *2ter Theil* (marking the start of the development), and *da capo* (start of the recapitulation). Beethoven also used the expressions *mit 2 Theilen* and *ohne 2 Theile* in his sketchbooks to indicate a work in, or not in, sonata form. For a fuller explanation, see W. Drabkin, 'Beethoven's Understanding of "Sonata Form": The Evidence of the Sketchbooks', in *Beethoven's Compositional Process*, ed. W. Kinderman (Lincoln, NB: University of Nebraska Press, 1991), pp. 14–19.

6 The Hero Who Practices Resignation: Beethoven's *Eroica* as 'Late' Work

VASILI BYROS

> Will you practice resignation and renunciation? – . . .
> You are a hero – You are what is ten times more,
> A real man!
>
> – Beethoven, *Tagebuch,* copied from Zacharias Werner, *Die Söhne des Thales*
> (*The Sons of the Valley*), 1803–4

Beethoven in the Garden

Early autumn 1802. Beethoven is still at his country summer home in Heiligenstadt just outside Vienna. Having drafted the first sketches for what would become the *Eroica* Symphony, on 6 and 10 October he finalises the aching yet inspiring words of the Heiligenstadt Testament, and in those same weeks commences work on the oratorio *Christus am Ölberge* (*Christ on the Mount of Olives*). He does so by fixing on a specific passage, taken out of context, on page 90 of the same sketchbook that contains the earliest *Eroica* drafts, now known as Wielhorsky.[1] In it we find Christ in the Garden of Gesthemane resisting his fate with pleading words to God: 'Take the cup of sorrow from me!' This plaintive line is one half of a powerful theme in the oratorio that is dramatically shared by the Heiligenstadt Testament and also several of Beethoven's letters from 1801, when persistent and increasing deafness and tinnitus indicated *'a lasting malady'*.[2] The plea to remove the 'cup of sorrow' represents the human instinct to question, battle or resist one's fate and suffering. In this trope, it is but a first step on a path towards spiritual growth and transcendence. The afflicted later awakens to a spiritual will to rise above the battle, through acceptance, submission and resignation. *Christus am Ölberge* is something of a character study, one that dwells on the human side of Christ's suffering as the context for this spiritual transformation: the climax in the drama's narrative arc is Christ's submission to God's will, which occurs in two stages. When the hour for Christ's arrest and persecution has drawn near, we hear one final plea to remove the cup:

O Father, do let the heavy hours of pain pass O'er me soon; let them fly like the swift winds as it pushes a storm quickly across the sky

But then, immediately, submission:

But not my will, no, Thine only be accomplished.

The same arc is present in Beethoven's epistolary life of 1801–2. In two letters of 1801 to his childhood friend from Bonn, Franz G. Wegeler, we read, on the one hand, Beethoven's wish to have his own 'cup of sorrow' removed: 'Oh, if I were rid of this affliction I would embrace the world'.[3] On the other hand, Beethoven reveals that 'Resignation ... [is] the only [refuge] remaining open to me'.[4] The same pattern is seen in another letter from July of the same year to Karl Friedrich Amenda, Beethoven's closest friend in Vienna: 'Oh, how happy should I be now if I had perfect hearing.' But 'resignation must be my refuge ... I am resolved to rise above every obstacle'.[5] Despair having brought him to thoughts of suicide, at some point during the years 1801–2, he began to accept his suffering, and the Heiligenstadt Testament is in part a documentation of this conversion. In Heiligenstadt, Beethoven is now prepared to drink from the cup given him: 'Perhaps I shall get better, perhaps not, I am ready. – Forced to become a philosopher already in my 28th year.'[6] Nowhere is the theme of resignation so palpable as when Beethoven echoes Christ's words, 'Welcome, death' (which he sets in an embracing *amoroso* style in the oratorio), with perhaps the most passionate lines in the Testament: 'With joy I hasten to meet death ... Come *when* thou wilt, I shall meet thee bravely.'[7]

In the oratorio, Beethoven gives the conversion a specifically musical representation. The text setting for 'But not my will, no, Thine only be accomplished' represents only Christ's external declaration of submission. The spiritual awakening is not enacted by the protagonist but rather described by the oratorio's narrator: the orchestra, often used in theatrical music to express the psychological state of a character. An orchestral interlude sounds between Christ's two phrases: here Beethoven sets an axial chromatic progression in the bass, C–B–A♯–B, with syncopated and shimmering tremolandi strings above it (Example 6.1, bars 20–24). The majority of the *Eroica* symphony was composed the following year, in its now eponymous house at '*Oberdöbling* No. 4, on the *left hand side* of the street going down the hill towards Heiligenstadt'.[8] When Beethoven set quill to manuscript for the symphony's opening theme, his hand followed the same outlines it did a year earlier in expressing Christ's transformation, to draw that very same chromatic progression in the bass, now as E♭–D–C♯–D, and again beneath shimmering and syncopated strings (Example 6.2).

Example 6.1 Beethoven, *Christus am Ölberge*, Op. 85, No. 5, recitativo, bars 18–30

Example 6.2 Beethoven, *Eroica* Symphony, Op. 55, Allegro con brio, bars 1–11

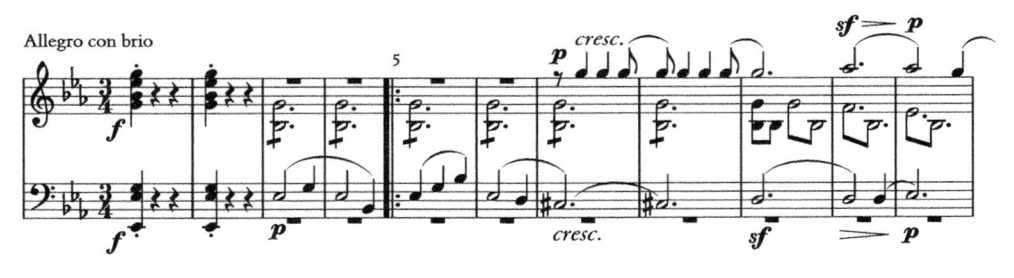

Was this, too, like the Heiligenstadt Testament and *Christus* before it, an act of submission or resignation? Did Beethoven choose, for the Eroica and, by extension, for himself, Christ as a model of the heroic? Is the opening of the Eroica a musico-dramatic expression of Beethoven's own spiritual awakening, as documented in the Heiligenstadt Testament?

Of Heroes, the Heroic and Music Analysis

For many critics, these questions would be decidedly unfamiliar. But they would have found a home in a relatively little-known biography of

Beethoven from 1927, by John William Navin Sullivan – a philosophical meditation on Beethoven's life and works with a pregnant subtitle: *His Spiritual Development*. The Eroica plays an absolutely pivotal role in this story. Sullivan heard the symphony as the 'first piece of music [Beethoven] composed that has a really profound and spiritual content'. He continues, emphatically:

> Indeed, the difference from the earlier music is so startling that it points to an almost catastrophic change, or extremely rapid acceleration, in his spiritual development. We have found that such a change is witnessed to by the Heiligenstadt Testament, and we shall see that the Eroica symphony is an amazingly realized and co-ordinated expression of the spiritual experience that underlay that document ... This is obviously a transcription of personal experience ... Heroism, for him, was not merely a name descriptive of a quality of certain acts, but a sort of principle manifesting itself in life.[9]

What Sullivan means by a 'catastrophic change' is nothing else than 'submission':

> A rigid, strained defiance was no longer necessary. What he came to see as his most urgent task, for his future spiritual development, was submission. He had to learn to accept his suffering as in some mysterious way necessary.[10]

How different this interpretation is from the everyday meanings the *Eroica* carries in the public imagination. A great deal of ink has been spilt on the symphony's alleged programme: a 'Napoleonic *Heldenleben*'.[11] No doubt this is owed in part to an all-too-casual acceptance of the original 'Bonaparte' dedication and later inscription Beethoven had given the *Eroica*. The famous incident of Beethoven dramatically scratching off the inscription, as reported by his friend and pupil Ferdinand Ries, came on the heels of Napoleon's Imperium, when he proclaimed himself Emperor of France in May 1804; but several details in Beethoven's biography from 1796 to 1804 display a relationship with Napoleon that was conflicted at best, negative at worst, and indicate that the Bonaparte dedication was an entrepreneurial move.[12] Beethoven had made definitive plans to move to Paris during this time, when he also dedicated the Violin Sonata in A minor, Op. 47, to Louis Adams and Rodolphe Kreutzer, 'the first pianist and violinist in Paris'. Ries mentions both dedications in the same letter where he announces to the publisher Simrock Beethoven's plans to leave Vienna for Paris.[13] The Bonaparte dedication was, as Maynard Solomon described it, Beethoven's 'musical passport to France'.[14] To be sure, these external circumstances inform our understanding of the symphony in some measure. But a musical work has both an internal and an external life, and when we talk about the 'meaning' of compositions such as the *Eroica*, the question ultimately falls on what the music has to say. The

image of Beethoven violently scratching off the 'Bonaparte' title is a story
involving the work's external life – its cover, packaging and marketing. The
later title *Sinfonia eroica* was given to the Third Symphony only for the first
edition of the orchestral parts published in 1806. And Beethoven never
supplied a programme even when the occasion called for it. He closely
monitored the reception of the symphony, which was met with conflicting
responses.[15] For a performance in Leipzig, reviewed in the *Allgemeine
musikalische Zeitung* on 29 April 1807, 'several precautions' were taken:
'The audience had been made attentive and, as far as possible, prepared to
expect exactly what it was offered, not only by means of a special
announcement on the customary concert program, but also by a short
characterisation of each movement, particularly in regard to the composer's intended effect upon the feelings.'[16] The reviewer's language here
resonates strongly with Beethoven's own words in the sketches on the
Pastoral Symphony:

> The hearers should be allowed to discover the situations . . . [and] the intentions
> of the composer without many titles –
>   Also without titles the whole will be recognized as a matter more of feeling
> than of painting in sounds.[17]

And yet, any survey of published interpretations of the *Eroica* will
quickly reveal something of a detective story component to its reception, filled with programmatic 'paintings'. Critics have judged the book
by its cover, one with a conflicted history and which Beethoven
ultimately destroyed. Whether Napoleon himself, some other contemporary of Beethoven, such as Abercromby or Nelson, or a mythological
character, be it Achilles, Hector or Prometheus, commentators have
sought in vain to identify the alleged protagonist of the *Eroica* – its
hero. This terrain is well trodden in Thomas Sipe's monograph, published as an earlier *Cambridge Handbook* dedicated to the *Eroica* from
1998, and is embodied by the title of Rita Steblin's article from 2006:
'Who Died?: The Funeral March in Beethoven's *Eroica* Symphony'.[18]
Because they begin from the book's cover, interpretive readings commonly encounter dissonances between the alleged programme and
what lies between its covers. Sipe maintains, for his part, that
'Bonaparte was profoundly formative for both the concept and the
structure of the symphony', but admits to 'offer little by way of specific
analytic remarks', and later asks: 'Why does Beethoven bury his hero
long before the end of the symphony?'[19] Steblin offers an answer,
suggesting Beethoven was mourning the death of his patron, the
elector Max Franz, in the Funeral March. But in the end, this too is
only a 'speculative theory'.[20]

A curious element to this detective story is that programmatic interpretations are not grounded in music analysis, even when the project is explicitly music-analytic. No scholar has been more perceptive on this point than Scott Burnham, who illustrated the judging of the book not only by its cover, but also by others' previous reactions to the same cover. In the end, whatever differences a particular interpretation may bring in its details inevitably fall away, and we get repeated 'translations of the same story': the 'triumphant' overcoming of 'a crisis' and 'adversity' (see also Chapter 2).[21] Burnham, too, offers not analysis but a 'composite narrative' of the *Eroica*'s reception, which 'conflate[s] many different versions' into this 'master trope'.[22] The persistent cross-talk in the *Eroica*'s reception combined with the dearth of music analysis raises some serious questions as to the work's meaning:

> Yet the question arises whether the music actually projects such a trajectory for these critics or if the extramusical associations brought on by the designation 'Eroica' may not in fact form the basis for an intertextual tradition of *Eroica* interpretation. In other words, are the programmatic readings largely reacting to one another? ... [T]hey all assume the underlying heroic trajectory and stake their claim to individuality in the designation of specific protagonists ... But is such unquestioned acceptance of the underlying paradigm a function of the power and direction of the music, or of the power and direction of the designation 'Eroica' and its famous associations with the real-life hero Napoleon?[23]

Burnham finds the question 'impossible to answer' and 'ultimately misleading. For it is precisely the conjunction of just this music with just these extramusical implications that has become so firmly planted in our collective musical consciousness.'[24] But these extramusical implications became part of the work's reception only when the former dedication to Napoleon became public knowledge.[25] Burnham himself highlights just how problematic the relationship between music (analysis) and (this alleged) programme is, by, for one thing, 'purposefully limiting the discussion to the first movement', when, as is well known, Beethoven's conception began from the finale and its connection to the Prometheus music of the ballet and later *Eroica* Piano Variations, Op. 35.[26] However, even within the first movement Burnham describes the relationship between music and programme in one crucial instance as 'comic[ally]' dissonant:

> No one denies the overtly heroic effect of the two opening blasts, and it is almost comic to see how programmatic interpreters inevitably rush off with the impetus of these two chords only to stumble a few bars later when they realize that something distressingly less than expeditious heroism is implied by the much-discussed C♯ in bar 7 ... What kind of hero would pause so portentously at the very outset of his heroic exploits?[27]

The answer to this last question may be found in Beethoven's *Tagebuch*, or diary, kept from 1812 to 1818. It contains a lengthy quotation from a dramatic work that is contemporary with the *Eroica*: part one of Zacharias Werner's *Die Söhne des Thales* (*The Sons of the Valley*), titled 'Die Templer auf Cypern' ('The Templars in Cyprus'), a Masonic drama on the fate of the Crusaders, published in 1803, with part two following a year later. Beethoven's citation brings together the following two lines by means of an ellipsis:

> Will you practice resignation and renunciation? – . . .
> You are a hero – You are what is ten times more,
> *A real man!*[28]

For this hero who 'practice[s] resignation', the C♯ deviation, along with the pattern to which it belongs, is not an impediment to the heroic act, but, on the contrary, is coextensive with it. The symphony between the covers tells the story not of a hero who overcomes, but one who transcends: in Beethoven's words, who 'rises above' through 'resignation'. Much of Beethoven's so-called 'heroic period' has been characterized by what Robert Hatten called the 'tragic-to-triumphant schema' of expression exemplified in the Fifth Symphony.[29] Here Beethoven externalised and defeated his 'menace': Fate, personified in C minor, and overcome by C major.[30] This is but one type of 'expressive genre' that Beethoven explored during this time.[31] And, 'forced to become a philosopher', he was apparently aware of its limitations as a philosophical model for life and for music. An altogether different expressive genre would preoccupy his later music and life. In summer 1817, again in Heiligenstadt, Beethoven confessed to the poet Christoph Kuffner that the *Eroica* remained his beloved symphony. At the time he had composed eight of the nine. One reason the *Eroica* remained Beethoven's favourite may be its application of an altogether different 'expressive genre': what Hatten calls the 'tragic-to-transcendent' schema, which is akin to religious drama: 'tragedy that is transcended through sacrifice at a spiritual level. The pathos of the tragic may be understood as stemming from a kind of Passion music, depicting a personal, spiritual struggle; and the "triumph" is no longer a publicly heroic "victory" but a transcendence or "acceptance".'[32] *Christus am Ölberge*, Beethoven's first post-Heiligenstadt work – which, one must be reminded, was composed of his own volition, not commissioned – is the first of Beethoven's works to engage the 'tragic-to-transcendent' schema in a large-scale composition. As an expressive genre in music, it had a broader cultural context, what Hatten identified as the 'cultural unit' of 'abnegation', which is related to 'Christian notions of sacrifice and spiritual surrender': the 'willed resignation and spiritual acceptance of a (tragic)

situation that leads to a positive inner state'.[33] It is defined in Friedrich Schiller's essay 'On the Sublime' from 1794 as a 'state of mind, which morality designates as *resignation* to necessary things, and religion styles absolute *submission* to the counsels of Providence'.[34]

The *Eroica* is the first post-Heiligenstadt instrumental composition to practice such resignation. If the circumstances in Heiligenstadt, when we met Beethoven in the (metaphorical) garden, document the biographical origins of the *Eroica*'s story, the opening chromatic progression the symphony shares with the *Christus* oratorio marks its musical beginning. The musical and expressive connection between Christ's transformation and the opening of the symphony would have been meaningful not only to Beethoven, but also to his contemporary audience(s), because the gesture is a musical convention.

Of Stones Unturned: The Le–Sol–Fi–Sol Schema-Topic

A letter to his Leipzig publisher Breitkopf and Härtel, dated 5 July 1806, suggests Beethoven may have played a role in the publication of the *Eroica*'s first technical analysis. He references both a negative critique of the *Eroica* published in an issue of the Leipzig *Allgemeine Musikalische Zeitung* and an unspecified past disagreement with the editor of the journal, Friedrich Rochlitz, while nonetheless passing on his greetings and earnest praise for Rochlitz's '*very fine articles*'.[35] A few months later, in February 1807, another such fine article was published in the pages of the same journal, the first technical review of the *Eroica*, whose anonymous author has since been identified as Rochlitz.[36] In addition to technical matters, Rochlitz broaches important aesthetic issues, including how an informed technical understanding will impact the work's reception, and cautions would-be casual listeners: 'the entire work, certainly presupposes an audience that . . . at least pays serious attention and can maintain its serious attentiveness'.[37] The first detail demanding such attention is the arresting C♯ moment. Rochlitz begins precisely where later commentators stumble:

> Already in bar 7, where the diminished seventh appears over C♯ in the bass, and in bar 9, where the 6/4 chord appears over D, the composer prepares the listener to be often agreeably deceived in the succession of harmonies. And even this preludising deviation, where one expects to be led formally to G minor but, in place of the resolution of the 6/4, finds the fourth led upward to a fifth, and so, by means of the 6/5 chord, finds oneself unexpectedly back at home in E♭ major – even this is interesting and pleasing.[38]

During the years 2007 to 2009, I conducted a corpus analysis of some 3,000 compositions from 1720 to 1840, from all over Europe, in search of the convention responsible for Rochlitz, myself and others hearing a G minor modulation in bars 6–9: the *Eroica* was the centrepiece of my dissertation on eighteenth-century tonality and historical modes of listening. It illustrated that listening habits are correlated with changes in style and powerfully affected by listeners' varying degrees of familiarity with those styles. In Beethoven's day, the harmonic progression through bar 9 had only one possible tonal meaning: the figured-bass progression $\frac{5}{3}-\frac{6}{4}-\flat\frac{7}{5}-\frac{6}{4}$, over this chromatic turn of phrase in the bass (two descending followed by one ascending semitone), is invariably located on scale degrees $\flat 6$–5–$\sharp 4$–5, with reiterations of scale degrees 1 and 3 in the upper voices (Examples 6.3a–b, f). In the *Eroica*, the larger pattern to which the progression belongs is cut short at its end: the $\frac{6}{4}$ in bar 9 (which displaces and already represents the dominant) would resolve, normatively, to a dominant triad or seventh chord, as part of an authentic or half cadence (compare Examples 6.3g and 6.3a–f). Both the convention and deviation from it are suggested by Rochlitz's language: he uses the adverb *förmlich* ('formally', or 'predictably') to describe the move to G minor, and *unvermuthet* ('unexpectedly') to describe the return to E♭ major. The cause for both the G minor modulation and the experience of a deviation at bar 10 is what I have styled the *le–sol–fi–sol* schema.[39]

Example 6.3 *le–sol–fi–sol* schema-topic:

a) Wolfgang Amadeus Mozart, Requiem in D minor, K. 626, 'Introit: Et lux perpetua', bars 43–6
b) Joseph Haydn, String Quartet in D major, Op. 50, No. 6, 'The Frog', movement 1, bars 138–49
c) Haydn, Symphony No. 101 in D major, 'Clock', movement 1, bars 240–6
d) Mozart, *Grabmusik*, K. 42, aria: 'Felsen, spaltet euren Rachen', bars 142–51
e) Mozart, Mass in C minor, K. 139, 'Credo', bars 126–7
f) Johann Sebastian Bach, *Jesus nahm zu sich die Zwölfe*, BWV 22, aria: 'Mein Jesu, ziehe mich nach dir', bars 29–33
g) Beethoven, *Eroica* Symphony, Op. 55, Allegro con brio, bars 1–11

Example 6.3 (cont.)

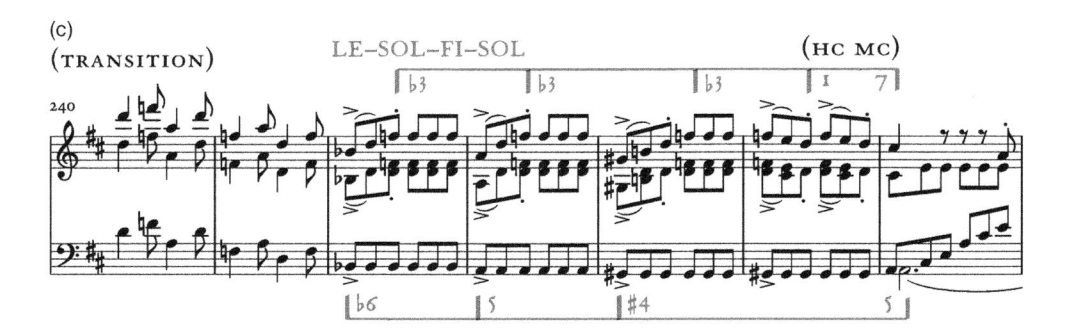

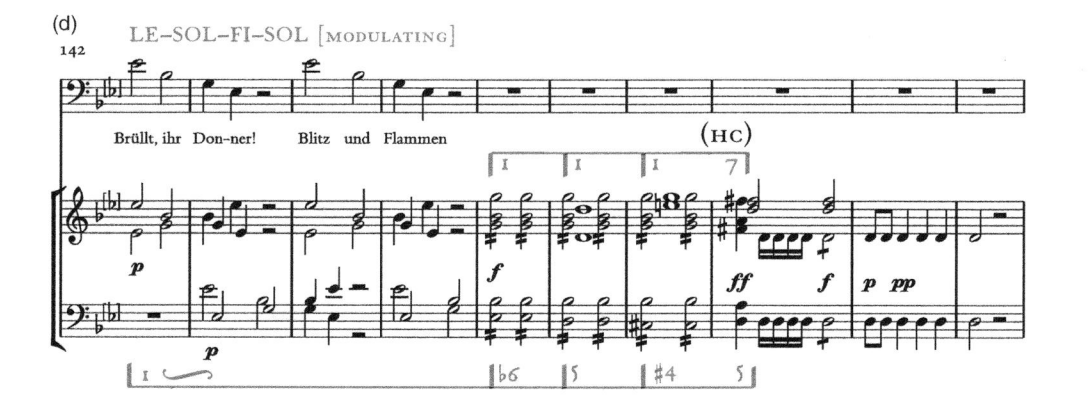

Example 6.3 (cont.)

(e)

(f)

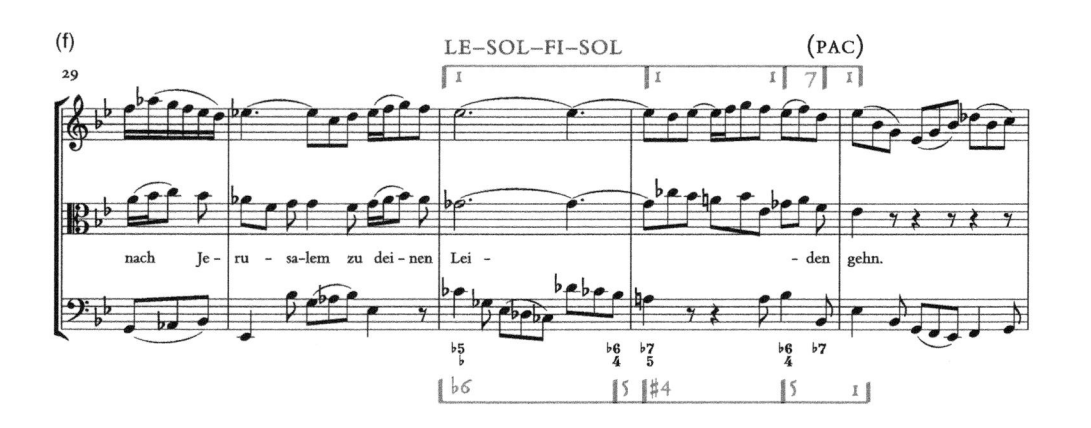

(g)

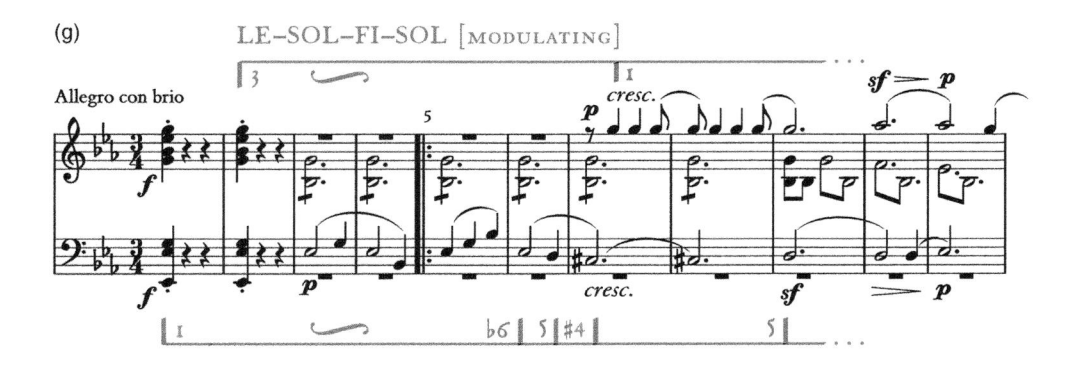

Example 6.4 *le–sol–fi–sol*: abstract representation

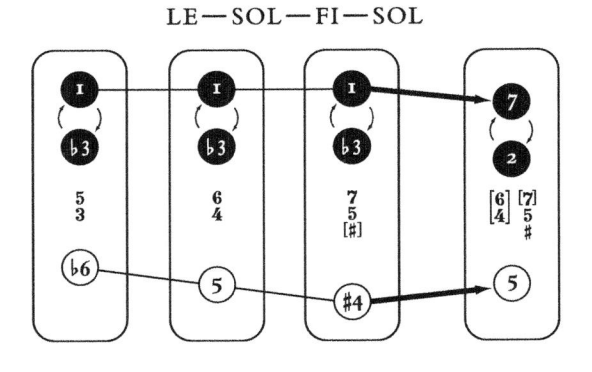

Recurring phrase idioms, with fixed harmony and bass scale degrees, and often paired with a consistent top voice, known as 'schemata' in North America and *Satzmodelle* (compositional models) in Germany, are of great import not only for understanding compositional craft but also for gauging the communicative channel – how composers communicated with their various listeners.[40] In its most common form, shown in the abstract representation of Example 6.4, the *le–sol–fi–sol* is an idiom that appeared 550 times in my *Eroica* corpus. The height of its popularity in this common form is the 1790s, the decade immediately preceding Beethoven's composition of the *Eroica*.[41] By 1803, listeners had been accustomed to hearing this phrase idiom as a common way of effecting a modulation up a third (Examples 6.3b, d), precisely the modulation in question, and, in modulating or non-modulating situations, of making a formal cadence – a half cadence or perfect authentic cadence (Examples 6.3a–f), and typically at the architectural seams of sonata form, what James Hepokoski and Warren Darcy call the cadences of 'essential expositional' and 'structural closure' (Examples 6.3b) and the 'medial caesura' (Example 6.3c).[42] As a closing device, the *le–sol–fi–sol* figures among the 'punctuation formulas' Heinrich Christoph Koch described for realising one of these 'principal resting points of the mind'. Rochlitz's adverb *förmlich* has a likely additional meaning in this connection, as an implicit or explicit reference to Koch's *förmliche Ausweichung*, or 'formal modulation', which specifies a modulation by way of a cadence and formal phrase ending.[43]

Stephen Rumph is among the few modern scholars in Rochlitz's company. In *Beethoven After Napoleon* he describes the modulation to G minor with equally strong language: 'the chromatic opening … settle[s] in G minor'.[44] Independently of this passing reference to the opening theme, Rumph wonders if 'any unturned stone, any unbeaten path', may remain in the 'long parade' of the *Eroica*'s reception, and offers

a perspective that 'flies in the face of a long tradition, newly revived by Burnham and Sipe, of describing the symphony as a heroic military epic'. For Rumph, that unturned stone is the Pastoral Symphony, which 'preserves the legacy of the *Eroica*'.[45] The dominant musical discourse of the *Eroica* Symphony is not military music but pastoral dances. Rumph goes on to highlight the powerful Arcadian imagery of the Heiligenstadt Testament, where Beethoven 'describes his ailment in pastoral terms' and 'chronicle[s] a literal (and literary) flight into the world of nature':[46]

> Thus it has been during the last six months which I have spent in the country . . .
> [W]hat a humiliation for me when someone standing next to me heard a flute in
> the distance and *I heard nothing,* or someone heard a *shepherd singing* and again
> I heard nothing . . . Oh when, Oh Divine One – shall I feel it [real joy] again in the
> temple of nature and of mankind.[47]

By shifting our ears to the pastoral, Rumph also inevitably draws our gaze to the larger garden where that unturned stone lies: it situates the *Eroica* in a larger discourse of meaning-making in eighteenth-century music, now known as topic theory. And if the pastoral remained an 'unturned stone' in that garden, the *le–sol–fi–sol* is a boulder cut from the hill of Golgotha.

The *le–sol–fi–sol* is not only a harmonic-contrapuntal pattern but also a musical topic with specific expressive and extramusical associations.[48] It belongs to the *ombra* style, first discussed by Hermann Abert, later Leonard Ratner, and given book-length treatment by Clive McClelland.[49] *Ombra* music was used both in theatrical- and sacred-style genres to depict mortal and funereal scenes, and generally involved themes of death, burial, the afterlife, the supernatural, ghosts, spirits, furies and so forth. Styles and genres such as the pastoral and *ombra* were a composer's expressive palette and a listener's go-to means for understanding a work's content. Leonard Ratner first defined such musical topics as 'subjects for musical discourse'.[50] In the introduction to *The Oxford Handbook of Topic Theory,* which builds on Ratner's initial formulation, Danuta Mirka writes: 'topics constituted a source of meaning and means of communication in eighteenth-century music. Today they allow one to gain access to its meaning and expression in a way that can be intersubjectively verified.'[51] Avant la lettre, the nineteenth-century music critic and teacher W. S. B. Matthews gave perhaps the clearest exposition of the communicative significance of musical topics in layman's terms:

> [S]ince the substance of music consists only of chords, melodic phrases, rhythms
> and tone-color, in none of which can we find exact equivalents for verbal
> symbols, it is evident that *all story telling by means of music is largely a question of
> convention, imagination and the association of ideas.* What we call 'pastoral'
> movements, 'battles', and the like, arise only when certain tone-successions and

rhythms have been so often used for a single purpose as to have acquired an association of ideas. They then begin to have the force of conventions, or conventional equivalents of a situation or condition. Opera is the great source of this part of musical education.[52]

From everyday musical life, not only opera, but sacred music, *Lieder*, wherever music is paired with text, listeners would learn these conventions. The broader life of the *le–sol–fi–sol* schema-topic, as displayed in the *Eroica* corpus, comprises many variants, nearly 1,500 in total, including the version in the *Christus* oratorio, which modulates by fifth (Example 6.1).[53] In music with a text, in both theatrical and sacred music environments, the *le–sol–fi–sol* is used to set deathly and supernatural scenes, with characteristically *ombra* textures. These include 'diminished seventh' harmony and 'chromatic stepwise movement' (already contained in the harmony and syntax of the pattern), 'minor keys', 'tremolo effects', 'repeated notes' and 'syncopation', among other features.[54] Its extramusical associations were well known already to young Mozart, who aged 11 used the *le–sol–fi–sol* in his 'Gravemusic', K. 42 (1767) to depict 'roaring thunder, lightning, and flames' (Example 6.3d). He would later use it in the Requiem K. 626 (1791) to represent eternal life (Example 6.3a), and treat it thematically in *Don Giovanni*: the *le–sol–fi–sol* stages the very moment that the Commendatore is fatally wounded by Don Giovanni, and several variants of the schema are used in the 'O statua gentilissima' duet of Act 2, where the Commendatore returns to life in ghost form.[55]

Graves, death, spirits, eternal life: these are the subjects of *ombra* music in the theatre and in church. They were ever-present in Beethoven's musical life from an early age. In Vienna he certainly studied a good deal of sacred music with Albrechtsberger. But already in Bonn, Beethoven was appointed deputy organist by the elector Maximilian Franz in 1784, filling in for his teacher and court organist Christian Gottlob Neefe, and, as a violist in Bonn's court orchestra, played numerous operas, including Mozart's *The Abduction from the Seraglio*, *The Marriage of Figaro* and *Don Giovanni* in 1789–90.[56] Both at the opening of the *Eroica* and in the *Christus* transformation, the *le–sol–fi–sol* appears in the same topical dress in which Beethoven encountered the pattern while playing the viola: tremolandi strings, tempestuous syncopations in the first violins, along with the angular chromaticism and diminished seventh harmony of the *le–sol–fi–sol*'s grammar.

The G minor *ombra* music of the *le–sol–fi–sol* communicates a death already in the *Eroica*'s opening bars, owing simply to the

convention's general association of ideas. But as story-telling devices in instrumental music, musical topics depend on the contexts in which they are used: on their interaction with other topics, harmony, tonality and form.

To Die Three Deaths, Only to Live Again

The First Death: The Plea for Life

The 'literary' element that Rumph identifies in the Heiligenstadt Testament is not confined to pastoral imagery. Nor was he the first to read the document in literary terms[57] or to hear the pastoral tone of the *Eroica*. Maynard Solomon deemed the Heiligenstadt Testament the *Eroica*'s 'literary prototype', one oriented to the theme of death: a 'funeral work' in which Beethoven 'metaphorically enacted his own death in order that he might live again', in a profound statement of 'heroism, death, and rebirth'.[58] In his *Late Beethoven* of 2003, Solomon also identifies a pastoral sentiment, but one whose immediate disruption by the chromatic descent in bars 6–7 causes an affective dissonance in the symphony's opening theme that resonates well into the finale:

> On one conspicuous occasion [Beethoven] unveiled a pastoral moment at the very instant of its fracture by disruptive forces. The two crashing chords that open the Eroica Symphony introduce a flowing pastoral negotiation of the common chord [the tonic triad], a shepherd's yodel or an alphorn call that lasts less than two bars . . . until it is tipped into disequilibrium by a decisive descent through D to C♯ at bars 6–7. In a half step, Arcadia has been lost, thus launching a prolonged heroic narrative that will revert to the pastoral mode only in its contredanse finale.[59]

Arcadia here is represented by the *Ländler* style, a rural dance widespread in Austria and Germany in the later eighteenth and nineteenth century.[60] The oom-pah | oom-pah | oom-pah-pah | pah rhythmic pattern in bars 3–6 and 10–15 is a common feature of the *Ländler* as well as of its close relative, the 'German dance' (*deutsche Tanz* or *Deutscher*), often used in combination with tonic pedals and arpeggiation, as in the *Intrada* to Mozart's early pastoral *Singspiel*, *Bastien und Bastienne* (1768), whose main theme is commonly identified as an anticipation of Beethoven's opening in the *Eroica*. The connection is not an intertextual one, but results from the common use of a convention.[61] If 11-year-old Mozart knew to use the *le-sol-fi-sol* for capturing the affect of 'grave music', 12-year-old Mozart knew to use the *Ländler* to communicate pastoral simplicity. By 1803, listeners would have heard passages like bars 3–6 of the *Eroica* in the German

dances of Mozart, Beethoven and their contemporaries, and various instrumental works that call on the style. The Trio of Beethoven's 'German Dance', WoO 8 No. 3, features a *Ländler* with a literal horn call. In the *Eroica* the horn call is initially scored only for strings (bars 3–6), and later becomes literal in subsequent restatements and reworkings of the theme. What all this music shares, as Ratner described the *Ländler*, is a 'rustic and buoyant' character, which defines much of the *Eroica*'s overall stylistic register.[62]

The deathly connotation of the *Eroica*'s opening modulation to G minor depends greatly on its interruption of E♭ major rustic music. The *le–sol–fi–sol* is the 'disruptive force' that induces a change of key, style and semantics in one fell swoop. In turn, the opening E♭ *Ländler* becomes a metaphor for life – a representation of the 'real joy' that Beethoven longed to 'feel again in the temple of nature'. Pastoral music in E♭ and *ombra* music in G minor are mutually 'disruptive forces'. Despite the prevalence of pastoral music in the *Eroica*, Rumph concedes, 'Any serious interpretation must come to terms with the funeral march whose shadow lowers over the entire symphony.'[63] This macrolevel semantic dissonance occurring between movements obtains at the microlevel in the symphony's opening bars. The opening conflict between dance (life) and funeral (death) reverberates across the *Eroica*. Within the first movement, after the *le–sol–fi–sol* is itself disrupted at bar 10, there is an escape from G minor, from death: *Ländler* is combined with battle music, suggesting a metaphorical battle for life, the plea to remove the cup. But as in *Christus* and in the Heiligenstadt Testament, there is no overcoming. Any serious interpretation, furthermore, must come to terms with the Funeral March as a continuation of the symphony's first 'death' contained in its opening gesture, and its assimilation in the third death of the finale.

The Second Death: Resignation and Submission

In the midpoint of the Funeral March, the entire symphony is left suspended on a single note, A♭, in the first violins (Example 6.5, bar 157). The first time we encounter this A♭ is in bar 10 of the first movement, in the self-same instrument and register, precisely where the music breaks the *le–sol–fi–sol* pattern, to return, as Rochlitz described it, 'unexpectedly' back at home in E♭ via the $^6_5$ chord on D (Example 6.3g). Now, at this critical moment in the Funeral March, it comes at the end of what Rumph identified as the first of 'three interruptions' to the genre's ABA form ('two *minore* marches enclosing a *maggiore* trio').[64] That first disruption is a double fugue that closes with an arresting perfect authentic cadence in G minor at bar 154, which is produced by the very same pattern that first introduced G minor at the beginning of the symphony: an augmented sixth

Example 6.5 Beethoven, *Eroica* Symphony, Op.55, Marcia funebre, bars 145–72

chord variant of the *le–sol–fi–sol* returns in bars 149–54 (Example 6.5) to fully realise the symphony's opening G minor implications with a formal close in G minor, as the goal of the Funeral March's fugal episode (bars 114–54). G minor is once again cast in the *ombra* style. The tremolandi, triplet rhythms and Neapolitan harmony just prior to the *le–sol–fi–sol* cadence are reminiscent of Alceste's arrival in the Underworld, which was staged in Bonn, along with *Orpheus*, in 1783–5. But now G minor's connection with death has taken on an overtly spiritual or sacred component that was only latent in the symphony's opening bars and the *le–sol–fi–sol*'s extramusical associations.

Topics are often combined in such a way that a dominant style is inflected by another, through a process that Hatten calls troping.[65] It concerns not the juxtaposition but the fusing of styles, through the importation of a foreign element. In the first movement, battle music is troped with *Ländler* to communicate a fight for life. In the Funeral March, fugue

Example 6.5 (cont.)

itself is the importation. It conventionally points to the church, which points to divinity. Not only is the double fugue based on a learned-style *alla breve* subject, but just prior to the *le-sol-fi-sol* cadence which concludes

the fugal episode there appears a lengthy dominant expansion with its own strong connections to high church music, what Robert Gjerdingen calls a 'Stabat Mater Prinner', due to its prevalent use in Pergolesi's *Stabat Mater*, the most frequently printed work in the eighteenth century.[66] This dominant pedal with braided 2–3 suspensions is a token of a more general church style-type, discussed in eighteenth-century treatises under the category of the *Orgelpunkt* (organ point). Johann Georg Sulzer's entry in the *Allgemeine Theorie der schönen Künste* describes it 'as a delaying of the conclusion' of 'polyphonic church music', which in general involves the 'final cadence' of fugues, 'but it can be used for other church matters'.[67]

The second death communicated by G minor *ombra* music is both more conclusive and more overtly spiritual. It also brings a clarity to the meaning of the original G minor 'death' communicated by the *le–sol–fi–sol* at the symphony's opening. The idiom had a more specific use in church music. The *le–sol–fi–sol* is regularly encountered in the Credo of a Mass, notably in the 'Et incarnatus est'. It is frequently set to the textual clauses 'et homo factus est', 'Crucifixus etiam pro nobis' and 'passus et sepultus est'.[68] The *le–sol–fi–sol* became something of a trope expressing the theme of sacrificial death, and embodies the idea of spiritual submission. As early as 1723, J. S. Bach used the pattern in the alto aria of the cantata *Jesus nahm zu sich die Zwölfe*, BWV 22, to represent the contemporary Christian's taking up their own cross with Christ: 'I am ready . . . to go to Jerusalem to Your suffering' (Example 6.3f). Via the *le–sol–fi–sol* and the cadence it produces, the *Eroica*'s Funeral March now completes the act of resignation. There is no immediate escape, or plea for life, as in the opening. After the fugue's G minor cadence, the suspended A♭ in the violins is immediately taken up by the basses and assimilated to yet another *le–sol–fi–sol* variant, where ♯4 falls to 4, extending the line to a chromatic tetrachord: the *le–sol–fi–fa–sol*. The tides have turned and A♭ is now powerfully reinterpreted as ♭6 in C minor. Peter Schleuning identified the music that follows (bars 159–68) as a sounding of the 'Last Trumpet'.[69] It is among the most powerful in all of Beethoven's output, and its force was felt during its time: for Rochlitz, it was the 'solemn', 'deeply gripping' second movement that showed 'true *genius*'. The grip of the Last Trumpet passage leads to a recasting of the main theme as a dirge with a long pedal on G, now as dominant of C minor (bar 168ff.). Another pedal follows at bar 186ff., along with brief stints in E♭ and D♭ major (bars 179–82, 213–17), which act as memories of the fallen one's life, before the movement, as Rochlitz describes it, 'dies away like a hero'.[70] That the death is a metaphorical one is made immediately apparent by the Scherzo that follows: back to the country with the most pronounced pastoral music of the entire symphony, filled with feelings of running in the hills. The transition between Funeral March and pastoral

Scherzo reflects the same wavering between groping for joy and submission/death in the Heiligenstadt Testament. Within the movement, E♭ major and G minor are again placed in immediate juxtaposition (e.g., bars 54–93, 312–51). It is here, in the symphony's generic dance movement, that the character of G minor entered the picture in the earliest Wielhorsky drafts, as a G minor Trio within a Menuetto Serioso.[71]

But it is the sounding of the 'Last Trumpet' in the Funeral March, in light of the earlier sacred-music allusions, that is most crucial to the continuation of the *Eroica*'s 'narrative'. In Rumph's words: 'the trumpet call exalts the fallen hero to the highest plane'.[72] It marks the Funeral March's death not as an end, but a passing:

> We shall not all sleep, but we shall all be changed, in a moment, in the twinkling of an eye, at the last trumpet. For the trumpet will sound, and the dead will be raised imperishable, and we shall be changed. (Corinthians 15:52)

The fallen hero on the highest plane, who 'dies away', the hero who practices resignation, finds 'change' or 'resurrection' in the *Eroica*'s finale, in the symphony's alpha and omega. The symphony's conception began here in the creative process and ends here in its psychological drama.

The Third Death: Resurrection/Rebirth; Joy Through Suffering

The finale does not begin. It bursts out, from death – from G minor, with a *fortissimo*, *tempesta*-style *unisono* on the dominant, D, which plummets through cascading scales in the same key, before E♭ major is recovered through its own dominant, and, once again through its seventh, A♭, in bar 4 (Example 6.6). A reviewer writing for the Leipzig *Allgemeine musikalische Zeitung* in January 1807, after a performance in Mannheim, described the opening as one instance of the finale's 'great bizarrerie':

Example 6.6 Beethoven, *Eroica* Symphony, Op. 55, finale, bars 1–6

no composer before Beethoven has dared to begin a piece in E♭ major in such a way that the instruments begin *al unisono* on the leading tone, and then continue with progressions that belong to the scale of G minor, until finally the fourth and following bars are merciful enough to extricate our ear from this predicament and remove us to the actual key![73]

For Rochlitz, an equivalent *unisono* outburst towards the end of the movement 'admittedly sounds rather strange'.[74] This outburst, too, begins 'in G minor', now *on* the tonic G, but explodes into E♭ major. What Beethoven intended by such 'bizarrerie' as these G minor-to-E♭ outbursts in the finale, which Rochlitz generally described as 'very contrived' and 'shrill and strange', is again suggested by the hero conception Beethoven was drawn to in Werner's drama. Several other lines that Beethoven copied into his *Tagebuch* read:

> The hero bravely presents to Fate the harp
> Which the Creator placed in his bosom. [. . .]
> be more than your fate, [. . .] seek
> The great good of self completion in creating!
> You are the mirror image of the Eternal[75]

If the Funeral March is the musical equivalent of Beethoven metaphorically enacting his own death in the Heiligenstadt Testament as the symphony's 'literary prototype', the finale is the 'rebirth' that ensues from that resignation – so that he may live again. If the first movement is the battle *for* life, a plea to remove the cup, and the second movement the inevitable submission or resignation *from* life, to God's will, what Beethoven himself called 'death in life', the finale is a unique and complex representation of (spiritual) rebirth.[76]

Living again is, on the one hand, communicated self-referentially, through a discourse on the creative act itself. The Mannheim reviewer found the presentation of the bass theme following the opening G minor outburst 'a little *too* empty. Are all these peculiarities necessary: per festeggiar il Sovvenire d'un grand Uomo . . . ?'[77] The bare presentation of the theme results from what Rumph described as Beethoven's 'blur[ring] the boundaries between theme and variation, showing the theme as a work in progress rather than an a priori object. He takes us inside Prometheus's workshop to view the creative process itself.'[78] This creative process bursts out from 'death', from G minor, staging it as the (creative) rebirth that results from necessary suffering. The hero who 'practice[d] resignation' in the Funeral March now 'presents to fate the Harp which the Creator placed in his bosom'. The main idiom used for the theme is what Leonard Meyer called the changing-note schema, which has several different top voice and bass

pairings.[79] At the outset of the creative act, at its rather '*too* empty' presentation, Beethoven reduces the pattern to its harmonic essence in the bass, tonic–dominant, dominant–tonic. Out of this, a world is created: building up to the theme's first *tutti* (bars 76–107) is coextensive with composing-out the individual parameters of the changing-note schema which underlies it. As a myth that explains the creation of the world, again through the theme of self-sacrifice, the story of Prometheus becomes a metaphor for the act of creation. But all this creative energy and renewed strength should not be mistaken for some triumphant overcoming. The creative power is directed back whence it came: G minor and death. The Funeral March not only still lowers over the entire symphony. Eventually Funeral March and finale become one and the same.

The most powerful G minor episode, the third and final death communicated by G minor *ombra* music, appears at the affective zenith of the entire symphony: the finale's climactic conclusion, where the symphony turns in on itself and the finale metamorphoses into the Funeral March. Following the first *tutti* statement of the *Thema*, a brief transition (in sonata-form fashion) prepares the second variation: a fugato that begins in C minor (bars 107–16). After a Hungarian dance in G minor (bars 210–56), a second fugato (bars 266–348) prepares the final variation, the Poco Andante (bars 349–96), which several commentators have described as 'recollecting' the Funeral March, whose allusions include the sextuplet *ombra* music of the Stabat Mater Prinner. The finale is as much fugue as it is theme and variations, and its fugatti serve two purposes. Fugue not only inflects the movement with a spiritual element, as it does the Funeral March, but it also provides a goal-orientation that is unachievable by theme and variations alone. The Poco Andante variation is the fugal element's large-scale goal. A variation of the Funeral March itself unites the Promethean creative act with its origins: 'death', submission, resignation. It might have served as the symphony's conclusion, one capped by a coda, perhaps the very coda that Beethoven later writes with the Presto at bar 431. Indeed Rumph describes the Poco Andante's Funeral March allusions and reworkings as 'the catharsis of the entire symphony'.[80] And the audience at the first performance may have been expecting a grand cadence in E♭ major at precisely this moment. But the Poco Andante's reworkings of the second movement mark not the end of the Funeral March's transformation into an E♭ major *contredanse*, but rather the inverse: the finale's transformation into the Funeral March. The Poco Andante never receives a conclusive formal cadence, on account of the *Thema* horn melody being doubled

Example 6.7 Beethoven, *Eroica* Symphony, Op. 55, finale, bars 408–40

in the bass at bars 380–96, which produces a 'tenor cadence' (*clausula tenorizans*).[81] The inconclusive cadence leads to a codetta, but one in A♭ major.

This A♭ codetta morphs into the Funeral March proper. The finale not only imports but also gradually becomes the Funeral March, ultimately leading to the *denouement* of the entire symphony. The transformation into the Funeral March involves what Rochlitz describes as a 'powerful modulation' from A♭ major to G minor (Example 6.7, bars 408–20). It occurs over an ascending chromatic line in the bass. Overall, the path outlines the opening *unisono* progression of the finale in reverse and magnified form: D to A♭ now moves from A♭ (as tonic) to D (as dominant). The goal is a devastating perfect authentic cadence in G minor at bar 420 that presents some of the most awe-filled and grave *ombra* music of the

Example 6.7 (cont.)

entire symphony. The *le–sol–fi–sol* returns here yet again. The ascending chromatic line in the bass results from sequential repetitions of a *le–sol–fi–sol* variant: its inverse, *fi–sol–le* (♯4–5–♭6). In the 'Crucifixus' of a Mass, ascending chromatic bass lines are typically used to represent Christ's *via dolorosa*, as in the 'Crucifixus' of Mozart's 'Coronation' Mass and Haydn's 'Harmony' Mass in B♭ major. These ascending chromatic basses often include inverted *le–sol–fi* progressions, as seen in Haydn's 'Theresa' Mass from 1799 (Example 6.8). The whole of the finale and thus the drama of the entire symphony is oriented to these arresting bars, which adopts music conventionally used to represent Christ bearing his cross up the hill of Golgotha. The imposing G minor cadence itself is a learned-style *cadenza doppia*, one of the hallmarks of closure in church music.[82] Following the sublime and terrifying cadence, the dirge from the Funeral March returns: the pedal point G is now a tonic as opposed to a dominant, and again cast with a characteristic *ombra* instrumentation – flutes, bassoons, and strings (bars 420–30).[83] The entire symphony closes in (dies with) G minor. The E♭ major *fanfare* that follows (bar 435) is no resolution: it explodes from the G minor dirge, unexpectedly as yet another 'disruptive force', in the same way that G minor erupted from the Scherzo. All of the finale's creative energies, which burst out from death (D-as-dominant *unisono*), are oriented back to death, to G minor, only to burst out, yet again, in a circular manner, back to E♭ major, through another *tempesta*-style outburst: G-as-tonic *unisono*. Within itself, too, this E♭ *fanfare* is no

Example 6.8 Haydn, 'Theresa' Mass in B♭ major, 'Crucifixus', bars 79–82

overcoming. It remains unresolved: a perfect authentic cadence or formal cadence in E♭ major, by either historical or modern standards, is scrupulously avoided. *Unisono* textures override the attempts at a formal cadence at bars 447–53, and the remaining 21 bars consist of nothing but an E♭ major triad. To hear its absent dominant and formal cadence, one need only compare the finale's *fanfare* to the closing coda music of the first movement, which features lengthy dominant pedals and two grand *cadenze lunge* ('long cadences') (bars 603–73).[84] The last formal cadence of the entire symphony remains in G minor. The E♭ major *fanfare* is thus not an ending but another re-beginning – a 'rebirth'. The key relationship, down a third to a major key, is among the three most common tonal transitions used to express the resurrection, between the 'Et incarnatus est' and the 'Et resurrexit' in the Viennese Mass.[85]

In its conclusion, the finale implodes, while the symphony writ large also collapses in on itself, not only by becoming the Funeral March, but also by returning to its beginning in a circular manner, to present the same tonal conflict set out in the symphony's opening gesture. The finale becomes the Funeral March while also projecting the symphony's very opening conflict between E♭ major and G minor in magnified form. The opening 'fracture' of E♭ *Ländler* music by G minor *ombra* now becomes a large-scale dissolution of another pastoral dance in E♭ major, the *contredanse* of the theme, which succumbs to G minor Funeral March. And, once again G minor death music is interrupted by E♭, now through a *fanfare*, as E♭ major interrupted the *le–sol–fi–sol* in bar 10 of the opening theme. The symphony presents no triumphant overcoming, but a paradox. The two keys are held in tension throughout the *Eroica*. Neither ever wins out. E♭ major yields to and becomes G minor, G minor succumbs to and becomes E♭. As is characteristic of 'religious drama' in general, there is no musical resolution: 'the serene transcendence of a spiritual victory, won not only through heroic striving . . . but through profound abnegation in the face of a tragic reality that cannot be

cancelled'.[86] Nor is G minor cancelled or overcome: 'transcendence or acceptance goes beyond the conflicts of the work (after having fully faced them)'.[87] The end is the beginning is the end. What this paradox means to the hero who practices resignation is best explained by Beethoven's own words, in a rephrasing of a Christian-philosophical tenet, written to the Countess Anna Marie Erdödy in a letter from Vienna, dated 19 October 1815: 'We finite beings, who are the embodiment of an infinite spirit, are born to suffer both pain and joy; and one might almost say that the best of us obtain *joy* [E♭ major] *through suffering* [G minor].'[88]

The Eroica as a 'Late' Work: The Tragic-to-Transcendent Expressive Genre

An early review published in *Freymüthige*, 17 April 1805, relates how the *Eroica* 'divided ... musical connoisseurs and amateurs ... into several parties':

> One group, Beethoven's very special friends, maintains that precisely this symphony is a masterpiece, that it is in exactly the true style for more elevated music, and that if it does not please at present, it is because the public is not sufficiently educated in art to be able to grasp all of these elevated beauties ... The other group utterly denies this work any artistic value and feels that it manifests a completely unbounded striving for distinction and oddity, which, however, has produced neither beauty nor true sublimity and power ... The third, very small group stands in the middle.[89]

That Beethoven's music was misunderstood or difficult to understand, its 'strange modulations and violent transitions' found by some contemporaries to be 'bizarre', is understandable and to be expected. A *BBC* television film that dramatises the first performance of the *Eroica* in the Lobkowitz Palace carries the subtitle 'The day that music changed forever' (see also Chapters 11 and 12).[90] What changes with the *Eroica*, truly, is that Beethoven began to ask of music things that had previously not been required of it. Himself 'forced to become a philosopher', Beethoven began to engage music as a kind of philosophy, or to write philosophy in music – a kind of music that pits a rustic major mode against a deathly minor in a paradoxical relationship, leaving it to the listener to reconcile the conflict. Such are the musical consequences of the 'catastrophic change in [Beethoven's] spiritual development' of which Sullivan wrote, and they placed unprecedented meaning-making demands on listeners. Mark Evan Bonds, looking at the 'Serioso' Quartet in particular, and the late music in general, writes:

Opus 95 also reflects . . . a broader shift from an aesthetics based on the principles
of rhetoric, in which the artist bears the burden of intelligibility, to an aesthetics
based on the principles of hermeneutics, in which the audience assumes
responsibility for comprehending a given text. Beethoven's 'late' works, often
regarded as products of self-critique or turning inward, can thus be heard as part
of a wider effort to engage audiences as active participants in a community
dedicated to a dialectic of critique.[91]

These greater demands were already present in the *Eroica* Symphony,
and they were felt, resisted and questioned even by devotees of Beethoven's
music. Despite expressing admiration for the *Eroica* and Beethoven's
music in general, while reflecting on the finale in the closing paragraphs
of his review, Rochlitz voices important concerns regarding the boundaries
the *Eroica* pushes, in regard to the 'technical and mechanical' as well as the
'artistic and aesthetic' side. There exists a '*Nimium*', an excess, and
'Beethoven's genius . . . show[s] its particularity by touching on it so will-
ingly'. In pushing aesthetic demands, the genius is:

> limited only (and may it happen here!) by the unalterable laws of mankind's
> aesthetic capability. And if he, the genius, is distinguished precisely by the
> willingness to expect more of this capability than is compatible with those laws,
> then he must bear that distinction in mind, so that he may be allowed to become
> a law unto himself and not simply scatter his creations out into the unknown.

The context of these 'laws' to which Rochlitz refers is important. He
begins his critique of the finale by stating that the 'merits' of a work
should be 'discovered and enjoyed, as they must be, in the very
moment of their appearance, and not for the first time on paper
afterwards'. The *Eroica*'s 'merits', meanwhile, 'lie somewhat hidden'.
To understand a music that is a kind of philosophy, one cannot
begin from the premise of a consumptive mode of engagement. And,
his reservations notwithstanding, Rochlitz himself opens the door to
analytic, contemplative listening – by publishing an apologetic technical review, in which he not only calls listeners to be 'serious[ly]
attentive', but also compares music's 'working-out of elevated,
abstract subject matter' to 'any extremely rich painterly or poetic
composition', which demands contemplation, and then locates the
antecedents of this quality of Beethoven's music 'in the greater works
of the unceasingly (and, needless to say, most rightly) praised *Bachs*'.[92]
Perhaps it was not coincidental that Rochlitz's next paragraph discusses edition(s) for keyboard, precisely where listeners could
explore further, 'on paper', and 'discover' the work's 'hidden merits'
in contemplation. Such a contemplative meditation on the *Eroica*'s
hidden merits was published in a 'Miscellaneous' entry for the
Leipzig *Allgemeine musikalische Zeitung* on 30 November 1814, by

one K. B., who grasped its essential meaning of transcendence, of life through resignation:

> [T]he departed one now walks in the kingdom of clarity and light – refreshingly soothing melodies tell us this in the language of heaven perceptibly enough . . . only through resignation can we at last tear ourselves from this place in order to plunge into life's rushing stream and at least to drink forgetfulness from this Lethe![93]

This idea of transcendence through resignation preoccupied Beethoven's late music and life, but it originates, musically, in the *Christus* oratorio. It is the first creative manifestation of a man struggling to find purpose in his suffering, by looking to others as models. Beethoven himself was explicit about Christ as an exemplar in a conversation book entry from 1820: '*Socrates* and *Jesus* were models for me.'[94] *Christus* was one of several philosophical-spiritual exercises to musically realise this model, which Beethoven revisited persistently throughout his compositional output. The *Eroica* is yet another early and untexted chapter in what became a life-long narrative, 'a long and hard journey, a *via dolorosa*'.[95] Historical and individual styles do not map conveniently onto divisions of time. The *Eroica*, accordingly, is among Beethoven's first late works, if 'lateness' is defined not temporally, but conceptually – in terms of what Carl Jung called second-half-of-life thinking.[96] As a philosophical testament, or treatise, it is similar in ethos to the kinds of literary and philosophical essays in whose pages Beethoven himself found solace. In one of the 1801 letters to Wegeler, we learn that '*Plutarch* has taught me *resignation.*'[97] Plutarch's works, both the *Lives* and the *Moralia*, are philosophical treatises that take biographies of great men as models for the moral education of his readers: they offer ways of life. That Christ offered a way of life for Beethoven is by no means limited to the *Christus* oratorio.[98] The C major Mass, whose Kyrie Beethoven described as 'heartfelt resignation',[99] and the *Missa Solemnis*, of course, powerfully continue that story, which is also traced in volumes from Beethoven's library. We know from his *Nachlassverzeichniss* that he owned the fifteenth-century monastic treatise *The Imitation of Christ* (*c*.1427) by Thomas à Kempis, who advises his readers to 'Learn to die to the world now, that then you may begin to live with Christ.'[100] The same theme, along with those of sacrifice, suffering and rebirth, is reinforced by Beethoven's own markings in his copy of Christoph Christian Sturm's *Reflections on the Works of God in the Realm of Nature* from 1772, in which, again, we can see a man struggling to find meaning and purpose in his affliction, not in overcoming it. The title of the following passage was 'marked with three emphatic consecutive lines

in [the] margin', and may well be the most illustrative example of Beethoven's attempts to reconcile himself and submit to his affliction and fate, by understanding his suffering as part of a larger, necessary plan overseen by Divine Providence: 'What God has chosen for me, That shall and must take place; . . . I have surrendered myself unto him. To die and to live.'[101]

If there is a composite narrative to the *Eroica*, it is one Beethoven wrote himself. The hero philosophy that begins to take hold in the years 1801–4, which is given dramatic expression in the Heiligenstadt Testament, and that persisted throughout his life is not about overcoming suffering, but its acceptance and endurance in order to attain a higher self. This practice of resignation runs through the *Tagebuch* entries, as a documentation of Beethoven's spiritual study:

> Submission, deepest submission to your fate, only this can give you the sacrifices . . . You must not be a *human being, not for yourself, but only for others*: for you there is no longer any happiness except within yourself, in your art. O God! give me strength to conquer myself, nothing at all must fetter me to life.
>
> Show your power Fate! We are not masters of ourselves; what has been decided must be, and so be it!
>
> Resignation. Resignation. Thus we profit even by the deepest misery and make ourselves worthy, so that God our mistakes – [102]

In another letter to the Countess Erdödy, dated 13 May 1816, we find the same article of faith: 'Man cannot avoid suffering; and *in this respect his strength must stand the test*, that is to say, he must *endure without complaining and feel his worthlessness* and *then again* achieve *his perfection*, that perfection which the Almighty will then bestow upon him.'[103] These are only a few of countless instances from Beethoven's musical and literary life that reflect a paradoxical Christian theme: 'He who loses his life for my [God's] sake will gain it' (Matthew 10:39).[104]

Beethoven's most trusted biographer, Alexander Thayer, defined the years 1798–1808 as heroic on the same terms, highlighting the same arc of despair, submission, and transcendence:

> [First] the anxiety caused by earliest symptoms; then the profound grief bordering upon despair when the final result had become certain; and at last his submission to and acceptance of his fate. There is in truth something nobly heroic in the manner in which Beethoven at length rose superior to his great affliction. The magnificent series of works produced in the ten years from 1798 to 1808 are no greater monuments to his genius than to the godlike resolution with which he wrought out the inspirations of that genius under circumstances most fitted to weaken its efforts and restrain its energies.[105]

The same heroism carried Beethoven through the difficulties of his last years. In a letter to Moscheles from the final year of his life:

> Truly, a hard lot has befallen me! But I yield to the will of fate and only pray that God in His divine will so order it that as long as I have *to endure this death in life* I may be protected against want. This will give me strength to endure my lot, hard and terrible though it may be, with submission to the will of the Most High.[106]

The *Eroica* symphony, beside the *Christus* oratorio, is among Beethoven's first attempts to work out this philosophical position in musical terms: a lesson, conceived in music, in learning to die now, to 'endure this death [G minor] in life [E♭ major]', in order to live again. With the *Eroica*, Beethoven himself becomes an exemplar for a way of life. As Sullivan put it, it is 'a transcription of personal experience', 'heroism as a principle manifesting itself in life', in which one 'accept[s] … suffering as in some mysterious way necessary'. If the *Eroica* has a message, it is Beethoven's own words from the Heiligenstadt Testament: 'May the poor unfortunate take comfort in finding one of his own kind.'[107]

Notes

1. See T. Albrecht, 'The Fortnight Fallacy: A Revised Chronology for Beethoven's *Christ on the Mount of Olives*, op. 85, and Wielhorsky Sketchbook', *Journal of Musicological Research*, 11 (1991), pp. 263–84; L. Lockwood, 'Beethoven's Earliest Sketches for the *Eroica* Symphony', *The Musical Quarterly*, 67 (1981), 457–78; and *Kniga eskizov Beethovena za 1802–1803 gody* (The 'Wielhorsky' Sketchbook), facs., transcription, and commentary by N. L. Fischman (Moscow: Muzgiz, 1962).

2. A. W. Thayer, *Thayer's Life of Beethoven*, ed. E. Forbes (Princeton, NJ: Princeton University Press, 1980), pp. 280–7 and 304–6 (hereafter *Thayer-Forbes*); Barry Cooper, 'Beethoven's Oratorio and the Heiligenstadt Testament', *The Beethoven Journal*, 10 (1995), pp. 19–24; O. Jander, 'The Rhetorical Structure of Beethoven's Heiligenstadt Testament', *The Beethoven Journal*, 22 (2007), pp. 17–24.

3. 16 November 1801, *Thayer-Forbes*, p. 286.

4. 29 June 1801, ibid., p. 284.

5. 1 July 1801, ibid., p. 282.

6. Ibid., p. 305.

7. Ibid.

8. *The Letters of Beethoven*, 3 vols., ed. E. Anderson (London: Macmillan, 1961), vol. 1, no. 80, p. 95 (emphasis original). The date of 1803 for this letter is inconclusive; it may be from 1804. But Beethoven apparently spent parts of both summers in Döbling. See *Thayer-Forbes*, pp. 335 and 353–5; and *Briefwechsel Gesamtausgabe*, ed. S. Brandenburg (Munich: Henle, 1996), nos. 148 and 185, vol. 1, pp. 172–3 and 215–16.

9. J. W. N. Sullivan, *Beethoven: His Spiritual Development* (New York, NY: Vintage Books, 1960), pp. 90 and 95.

10. Ibid., p. 78.

11. N. Mathew, *Political Beethoven* (Cambridge: Cambridge University Press, 2013), p. 44.

12. See M. Solomon, *Beethoven*, 2nd rev. edn (New York, NY: Schirmer Books), pp. 173–85.

13. *Letters to Beethoven & Other Correspondence, Volume 1: 1772–1812*, ed. and trans. T. Albrecht (Lincoln, NB: University of Nebraska Press, 1996), pp. 119–22.

14. M. Solomon, *Beethoven Essays* (Boston, MA: Harvard University Press, 1988), p. 112.

15. See *The Critical Reception of Beethoven's Compositions by His German Contemporaries*, ed. W. M. Senner, R. Wallace and W. Meredith, 2 vols. (Lincoln, NE: University of Nebraska Press, 2001), vol. 2, pp. 15–42.

16. *Allgemeine musikalische Zeitung*, 9 (1807), cols. 497–8; trans. in *The Critical Reception of Beethoven's Compositions*, ed. Senner et al., vol. 2, p. 33.

17. *Thayer-Forbes*, p. 436.

18. T. Sipe, *Beethoven: Eroica Symphony* (Cambridge: Cambridge University Press, 1998); R. Steblin, 'Who Died?: The Funeral March in Beethoven's *Eroica* Symphony', *The Musical Quarterly*, 89 (2006), pp. 62–79.

19. Sipe, *Beethoven: Eroica Symphony*, pp. ix and 96.

20. Steblin, 'Who Died?', p. 62.

21. S. Burnham, *Beethoven Hero* (Princeton, NJ: Princeton University Press, 1995), pp. 27 and 3.

22. Ibid., pp. 3 and 24.

23. Ibid., pp. 26–7.

24. Ibid., p. 27.

25. This can be seen, for example, in the marked differences between A. B. Marx's first (1824) and second (1859) essays on the *Eroica*. The first is translated in *The Critical Reception of Beethoven's Compositions*, ed. Senner et al., vol. 1, pp. 59–77, the second in *Musical Form in the Age of Beethoven: Selected Writings on Theory and Method*, ed. and trans. S. Burnham (Cambridge: Cambridge University Press, 1997), pp. 158–88.

26. See Lockwood, 'Beethoven's Earliest Sketches' and C. Floros, *Beethovens Eroica und Prometheus-Musik* (Wilhelmshaven: Heinrichshofen, 1978).

27. Burnham, *Beethoven Hero*, pp. 4–5.

28. Solomon, *Beethoven Essays*, p. 263; for the English and German, see M. Solomon, 'Beethoven's Tagebuch of 1812–1818', in *Beethoven Studies 3*, ed. A. Tyson (Cambridge: Cambridge University Press, 1982), pp. 236–41.

29. R. Hatten, *Musical Meaning in Beethoven: Markedness, Correlation, and Interpretation* (Bloomington, IN: Indiana University Press, 1994), p. 79.

30. Sullivan, *Beethoven*, p. 95.

31. Hatten, *Musical Meaning in Beethoven*, pp. 67–90.

32. Ibid., p. 79.

33. Ibid., pp. 281 and 298.

34. F. Schiller, *Aesthetical and Philosophical Essays* (Boston, MA: Cassino, [1772–95] 1884), p. 137. Emphasis added.

35. Anderson (ed.), *Letters*, vol. 1, no. 132, pp. 150–1 (emphasis original).

36. M. Geck and P. Schleuning, '*Geschrieben auf Bonaparte*'. *Beethovens 'Eroica': Revolution, Reaktion, Rezeption* (Reinbeck bei Hamburg: Rowohlt, 1989).

37. *Allgemeine musikalische Zeitung*, 9 (1807), cols. 321–33; trans in *The Critical Reception of Beethoven's Compositions*, ed. Senner et al., vol. 2, p. 24.

38. Ibid., p. 21. Translation adapted.

39. See V. Byros, 'Foundations of Tonality as Situated Cognition, 1730–1830: An Enquiry into the Culture and Cognition of Eighteenth-Century Tonality, with Beethoven's *Eroica* Symphony as a Case Study' (PhD diss., Yale University, 2009); V. Byros, 'Meyer's Anvil: Revisiting the Schema Concept', *Music Analysis*, 31 (2012), pp. 273–346; and 'Towards an "Archaeology" of Hearing: Schemata and Eighteenth-Century Consciousness', *Musica Humana*, 1 (2009), pp. 235–306.

40. In addition to the sources in n. 39, see for example R. Gjerdingen, *Music in the Galant Style* (Oxford: Oxford University Press, 2007); L. Meyer, *Style and Music: Theory, History, and Ideology* (Ann Arbour, MI: University of Pennsylvania Press, 1989); G. Sanguinetti, *The Art of Partimento: History, Theory, and Practice* (Oxford: Oxford University Press, 2012); G. Sanguinetti, 'Editorial', *Eighteenth-Century Music*, 11 (2014), pp. 3–9; V. Byros, 'Mozart's Vintage Corelli: The Microstory of a Fonte-Romanesca', *Intégral*, 31 (2017), pp. 63–89; V. Byros, 'Trazom's Wit: Communicative Strategies in a "Popular" Yet "Difficult" Sonata', *Eighteenth-Century Music*, 10 (2013), pp. 213–52; D. Mirka and K. Agawu (eds.), *Communication in Eighteenth-Century Music* (Cambridge: Cambridge University Press, 2007); H.-U. Fuß and O. Schwab-Felisch (eds.), *Zeitschrift der Gesellschaft für Musiktheorie:*

Satzmodelle, 4 (2007); O. Schwab-Felisch, 'Satzmodell', in *Lexikon der Systematischen Musikwissenschaft: Handbuch der Systematischen Musikwissenschaft*, 6 (Laaber: Laaber-Verlag 2010), pp. 415–19.

41. Byros, 'Meyer's Anvil', pp. 290–314; Byros, 'Foundations of Tonality' (Appendix B), pp. 137–77, Appendix B.

42. James Hepokoski and Warren Darcy, *Elements of Sonata Theory: Norms, Types, and Deformations in the Late-Eighteenth-Century Sonata* (Oxford: Oxford University Press, 2007).

43. On these general aspects of Koch's theory and the specific cadential, form-functional, and modulatory aspects of the *le–sol–fi–sol*, see V. Byros, '"*Hauptruhepuncte des Geistes*": Punctuation Schemas and the Late-Eighteenth-Century Sonata', in M. Neuwirth and P. Bergé (eds.), *What Is a Cadence? Theoretical and Analytical Perspectives on Cadences in the Classical Repertoire* (Leuven: Leuven University Press, 2015), pp. 215–51; V. Byros, 'Topics and Harmonic Schemata: A Case from Beethoven', in Danuta Mirka (ed.), *The Oxford Handbook of Topic Theory* (Oxford: Oxford University Press, 2014), pp. 383–6; and Byros, 'Meyer's Anvil', pp. 290–305.

44. S. Rumph, *Beethoven After Napoleon: Political Romanticism in the Late Works* (Berkeley, CA: University of California Press, 2004), p. 90. On the reception history and tonal hearings of the *Eroica*'s opening, see Byros, 'Foundations of Tonality' (Chapter 1), pp. 1–72; and 'Meyer's Anvil', pp. 283–90, 310–13.

45. Rumph, *Beethoven After Napoleon*, pp. 58 and 73.

46. Ibid., p. 75.

47. *Thayer-Forbes*, pp. 304–6.

48. Byros, 'Topics and Harmonic Schemata'.

49. Hermann Abert, *Niccolò Jommelli als Opernkomponist* (Halle: M. Niemeyer 1908); Leonard Ratner, *Classic Music: Expression, Form, and Style* (New York, NY: Schirmer, 1980); Clive McClelland, Ombra: Supernatural Music in the Eighteenth Century (Lanham, MD: Lexington, 2012); and Clive McClelland, 'Ombra and Tempesta', in Mirka (ed.), *The Oxford Handbook of Topic Theory*, pp. 279–300.

50. Ratner, *Classic Music*, p. 9.

51. Danuta Mirka, 'Introduction', in Mirka (ed.), *The Oxford Handbook of Topic Theory*, p. 1.

52. W. S. B. Matthews, *Music, Its Ideals and Methods* (Philadelphia, PA: Presser, 1897), p. 33 (emphasis added).

53. See Byros, 'Foundations of Tonality' (Appendix B: Topics and Harmonic Schemata), pp. 401–2.

54. McClelland, 'Ombra and Tempesta', p. 282.

55. On these and other *ombra* uses of the *le–sol–fi–sol* in music with text, see Byros, 'Topics and Harmonic Schemata', pp. 393–7.

56. *Thayer-Forbes*, pp. 95–9.

57. See also Jander, 'The Rhetorical Structure of Beethoven's Heiligenstadt Testament'.

58. Solomon, *Beethoven*, pp. 157–8.

59. M. Solomon, *Late Beethoven: Music, Thought, Imagination* (Berkeley, CA: University of California Press, 2003), p. 75.

60. E. McKee, 'Ballroom Dances of the Late Eighteenth Century', in Mirka (ed.), *The Oxford Handbook of Topic Theory*, pp. 174–6; and E. McKee, *Decorum of the Minuet, Delirium of the Waltz: A Study of Dance-Music Relations in 3/4 Time* (Bloomington, IN: Indiana University Press, 2012); Byros, 'Topics and Harmonic Schemata', pp. 398–9; and D. Heartz, *Mozart, Haydn, and Early Beethoven: 1781–1802* (New York, NY: Norton, 2009), pp. 517 and 643.

61. Beethoven most likely did not know of the work. See Sipe, *Beethoven: Eroica*, p. 98.

62. Ratner, *Classic Music*, p. 9.

63. Rumph, *Beethoven After Napoleon*, p. 78.

64. Ibid., p. 80.

65. Hatten, *Musical Meaning in Beethoven*, pp. 170–71; R. Hatten, *Interpreting Musical Gestures, Topics, and Tropes: Mozart, Beethoven, Schubert* (Bloomington, IN: Indiana University Press, 2004), pp. 68–71; and R. Hatten, 'Troping of Topics in Mozart's Instrumental Works', in Mirka (ed.), *The Oxford Handbook of Topic Theory*, pp. 514–36.

66. Gjerdingen, *Music in the Galant Style*, pp. 442–8; See also R. Ivanovitch, 'Mozart's Art of Retransition', *Music Analysis*, 30 (2011), pp. 1–36.

67. Cited and translated in Byros, 'Topics and Harmonic Schemata', pp. 398 and 410.

68. Ibid., pp. 395–7.
69. Geck and Schleuning, '*Geschrieben auf Bonaparte*', pp. 128. See also Rumph, *Beethoven After Napoleon*, p. 81.
70. *Allgemeine musikalische Zeitung*, 9 (1807), cols. 321–33; trans in *The Critical Reception of Beethoven's Compositions*, ed. Senner et al., vol. 2, p. 24.
71. *Kniga eskizov Beethovena*, ff. 44–5; See also Byros, 'Foundations of Tonality', pp. 18–22; and Lockwood, 'Beethoven's Earliest Sketches', pp. 460 and 471–2.
72. Rumph, *Beethoven After Napoleon*, p. 81.
73. *Allgemeine musikalische Zeitung*, 9 (1807), cols. 285–86; trans in *The Critical Reception of Beethoven's Compositions*, ed. Senner et al., vol. 2, p. 19.
74. *Allgemeine musikalische Zeitung*, 9 (1807), cols. 321–33; trans in *The Critical Reception of Beethoven's Compositions*, ed. Senner et al., vol. 2, pp. 29–30.
75. Solomon, *Essays*, p. 263.
76. *Thayer-Forbes*, p. 1036.
77. *Allgemeine musikalische Zeitung*, 9 (1807), cols. 285–86; trans in *The Critical Reception of Beethoven's Compositions*, ed. Senner et al., vol. 2, p. 19.
78. Rumph, *Beethoven After Napoleon*, p. 84.
79. Meyer, *Style and Music*, 226–30; Gjerdingen, *Music in the Galant Style*, pp. 111–38.
80. Rumph, *Beethoven After Napoleon*, p. 85.
81. Gjerdingen, *Music in the Galant Style*, pp. 140–1 and 164–66; and V. Byros, 'Prelude on a Partimento: Invention in the Compositional Pedagogy of the German States in the Time of J. S. Bach', *Music Theory Online*, 21 (2015), [2.4]–[2.5].
82. Gjerdingen, *Music in the Galant Style*, p. 169; and Sanguinetti, *The Art of Partimento*, pp. 107–11.
83. McClelland, *Ombra*, pp. 134–6.
84. Gjerdingen, *Music in the Galant Style*, pp. 169–70; and Sanguinetti, *The Art of Partimento*, pp. 106–8.
85. B. C. MacIntyre, *The Viennese Concerted Mass of the Early Classic Period* (Ann Arbor, MI: UMI Research Press, 1986), p. 325; Byros, 'Topics and Harmonic Schemata', pp. 404–5.
86. Hatten, *Musical Meaning in Beethoven*, p. 286.
87. Ibid., p. 79.
88. Anderson (ed.), *Letters*, vol. 2, no. 563, p. 527 (emphasis original).
89. *Der Freymüthige*, 3 (1805), col. 332; trans in *The Critical Reception of Beethoven's Compositions*, ed. Senner et al., vol. 2, p. 15.
90. *Eroica* [BBC Film], directed by Simon Cellan Jones (London: Opus Arte, 2005).
91. M. E. Bonds, 'Irony and Incomprehensibility: Beethoven's "Serioso" String Quartet in F Minor, Op. 95, and the Path to the Late Style', *Journal of the American Musicological Society*, 70 (2017), p.356.
92. *Allgemeine musikalische Zeitung*, 9 (18 February 1807), cols. 321–33; trans in *The Critical Reception of Beethoven's Compositions*, ed. Senner et al., vol. 2, p. 30.
93. *Allgemeine musikalische Zeitung*, 16 (1814), col. 811; trans. in *The Critical Reception of Beethoven's Compositions*, ed. Senner et al., vol. 2, pp. 38–9.
94. Solomon, *Late Beethoven*, p. 170.
95. Ibid., p. 164.
96. C. G. Jung, *The Collected Works of C. G. Jung, Vol. 8, The Structure and Dynamics of the Psyche* (London: Routledge and Kagan Paul, 1969). For a recent broad assessment of the problem of lateness in the arts, see *Late Style and its Discontents: Essays in Art, Literature, and Music*, ed. G. McMullan and S. Smiles (Oxford: Oxford University Press, 2016).
97. 29 June, *Thayer-Forbes*, p. 284.
98. See also Cooper, 'Beethoven's Oratorio and the Heiligenstadt Testament', p. 22
99. Anderson (ed.), *Letters*, vol. 1, no. 295, p. 309.
100. Thomas à Kempis, *The Imitation of Christ*, trans. A. Croft and H. Bolton (Peabody, MA: Hendrickson, 2004), p. 27.
101. C. Witcombe, R. Portillo, H. Melas, H. Liebmann and W. Meredith, 'An English Translation of the Passages Beethoven Marked in His 1811 Edition of Sturm's Betrachtungen über die Werke Gottes im Reiche der Natur und Vorsehung auf alle Tage des Jahres (Revised and Complete in One Part)', *The Beethoven Journal*, 18 (2003), p. 94. See also Byros, 'Topics and Harmonic Schemata', p. 401.

102. Solomon, *Beethoven Essays*, pp. 246, 271 and 272.

103. Anderson (ed.), *Letters*, vol. 2, no. 633, p. 578 (emphasis original).

104. For a powerful reappraisal of Beethoven's Catholicism in light of contemporary Christian-intellectual currents, see N. J. Chong, 'Beethoven's Catholicism: a Reconsideration' (PhD diss., Columbia University, 2016); N. J. Chong, "Aufklärung, Katholizismus und die religiöse Anschauung Beethovens," trans. and ed. S. Rampe, in *Das Beethoven-Handbuch 5: Beethovens Welt* (Laaber: Laaber-Verlag, 2019).

105. *Thayer-Forbes*, p. 248.

106. *Thayer-Forbes*, p. 1036; added emphasis.

107. L. van Beethoven, *Heiligenstädter Testament: Faksimile der Handschrift mit Übertragung und Kommentar*, ed. S. Brandenburg, new issue (Bonn: Beethoven-Haus, 2017), p. 12.

7 Registering the *Eroica*

NICHOLAS MARSTON

Ever tried. Ever failed. No matter. Try again. Fail again. Fail better.
— SAMUEL BECKETT, *WORSTWARD HO* (1983)

Registering the Opening

A 'brute force to which the symphonic self is exposed from the very beginning':[1] among the many contrasts that the opening of the *Eroica* Symphony presents is that between the vertical – the 'brute force' of the two opening *tutti* chords – and the horizontal – the entry of the famous cello theme, now *piano*, accompanied by strings alone for the next ten bars. But for all the contrasts, there are continuities also to be observed: the violin I g^2 within the *tutti* chords is picked up in bar 7 and raised to ab^2 and (fleetingly) bb^2 before resolving an octave lower on eb^1 in bar 15. By that time, the upper woodwind and horns have crept back in, and the violin's concluding eb^1 overlaps with the return of the triadic main theme across two octaves (eb^1–eb^3) in horn I, clarinet and flute. While horn and clarinet present the complete four-bar unit, however, the flute ceases after the second return to the tonic note (bar 17: eb^3); it does not join in the further triadic ascent $\hat{1}$–$\hat{3}$–$\hat{5}$ before the fall back to the concluding $\hat{1}$.

This cessation is the first indication in the symphony of Beethoven's handling of the registral possibilities and limitations of the flute, which provides the highest registral layer of the score. In Colin Lawson's opinion, 'the upper part of the [flute] range became one of the most controversial aspects of all Beethoven's wind writing'. As Lawson notes, the range of the flute part in the *Eroica* 'is essentially g^1 to g^3, with occasional ab^3 and $a\natural^3$ in the first movement'.[2] As we shall see, neither of these upper notes is confined to the first movement alone, and ab^3 will turn out to be more significant than the description 'occasional' implies. But the larger issue here is Beethoven's consistent avoidance of bb^3, which was not impossible to produce on the flute of his time, but a 'difficult' pitch that he evidently preferred to avoid.

This avoidance is palpable again at the *fortissimo* reassertion of the theme at the textural extremes, along with inner doubling, at bar 37, the first bar of the eight-bar unit that leads to the establishment of V/V at bar

45. But while cellos and basses rise up $\hat{1}$–$\hat{3}$–$\hat{5}$ in bar 39, flute I does not join them, venturing no further than the triadic third, g^3, although that registral extreme will shortly be trumped by the first sounding of ab^3 (bar 43). Subsequent instances make the point. The corresponding phrase to bars 37–44 is bars 440–7; but rather than doubling the theme in the bass, the flutes in this latter phrase insist on the third g^3/eb^3. (This phrase is one of several such climactic moments when the violins join the flutes in unison in the highest octave rather than doubling them at the octave below, as tends to be the norm in this score.) At bar 430 the high-register statement of the theme from bar 37 is reprised, although in the third bar flute I now avoids even g^3 on the second beat, clinging rather to eb^3 (compare bars 39 and 432). It is from this eb^3 that a chromatic ascent to ab^3 will ensue over the next eight bars before that pitch is forced back down to the g^3 of bar 440.

One could also cite bars 482–6, where the three-line octave (i.e., c^3–b^3) is introduced only from g^3 (the same is true, in the differing tonal context of the exposition, of the corresponding passage, bars 79–83); or bars 516–17, which answer the $\hat{5}$–$\hat{3}$–$\hat{1}$ descent in violin I at 512–13; or again, bars 655–62 (compare flute and oboe). Beethoven evidently considered bb^3 an 'unavailable' pitch for the instrument (though he avoids it in the violin also).

It is worth labouring the point about this unavailability of an extreme-register scale degree $\hat{5}$ not merely because triadic themes are so prominent in the *Eroica* but also because the off-limits bb^3 suggests that we might wish to pay careful attention to Beethoven's manipulation of the high-register triadic space remaining to the flute in his scoring practice, specifically $\hat{1}$–$\hat{3}$, or eb^3–g^3. This, and indeed the entire question of register, was not lost on Heinrich Schenker; the theoretical concept of an 'obligatory register', for example, in which the *Urlinie* ('fundamental line') makes its stepwise structural descent from the triadic third or fifth down to the tonic in the course of a composition, had gradually coalesced in his thinking since his 1912 book on Beethoven's Ninth Symphony.[3] In his monumental analysis of the *Eroica*, published in 1930, Schenker regarded the two-line octave as the obligatory register in which the *Urlinie* of all four movements unfolded, and remarked more generally:

> By its very nature, everything that is truly singable is reserved for the middle
> registers; ... The higher registers, on the other hand, serve to promote
> a spatial expansion which not only encourages the generation of new, far-
> reaching diminutions, but also enables the composer to make full use of the
> sonority of an instrument (this is particularly true where the orchestra is
> concerned).[4]

Thus when writing of the flute I entry in bars 13–17, Schenker described it as 'being added for the sake of greater sonority'. More importantly, it was not to be understood as 'an anticipation of the three-line octave and in particular does not anticipate the $e\flat^3$ in bar 37. An obligatory register . . . capable of participating in the change of register . . . would have to be thoroughly elaborated in terms of the voice-leading'.[5] In other words, the two-line octave retains priority as the obligatory register, while the three-line octave is regarded as essentially decorative, or subsidiary.

Building on these observations, Schenker went on to propose:

> Identifying the octave registers in which the voice-leading takes place is a task of the greatest importance for the composer, and especially for the interpreter [*Nachschaffender*] . . . Moreover, the manner in which a change of register occurs reveals the true character of the instrument: every instrument calls for a special kind of registral change.[6]

Yet for all this attention to register, both theoretically and in specific instances, he has nothing to say concerning Beethoven's avoidance of $b\flat^3$ in the flute part throughout the *Eroica*.

Commenting on the very end of the movement, Schenker noted the progression g^3–f^3–$e\flat^3$ in violin I at bars 669, 670 and 673, the initial g^3 having been reached 'by way of the neighbour note $a\flat^3$ in bar 668'. At the same time, 'in bars 671–2 flute I is kept above violin I', that is, the violin $e\flat^3$–d^3 is covered by g^3 in the flute, rising first to $a\flat^3$ from where it descends to f^3 to close in unison with the violin on $e\flat^3$. In Schenker's interpretation, 'this is done intentionally, in order to be able to give precedence, in bars 681–5, to violin I with $a\flat^3$, regardless of the fact that violin I also, in bar 689, finally reaches the end with g^2.'[7]

The context of these remarks is Schenker's observation that 'in bar 631 the structure once more comes to a close on $e\flat^2$. The task of the last section will then be to draw in the three-line octave again in order to achieve a brilliant conclusion.'[8] 'Once more', because the completion of the *Ursatz* ('fundamental structure', comprising the descending *Urlinie* counterpointed by its I–V–I 'bass arpeggiation') – the essential structural closure of the movement, in Schenker's thinking – is understood to have taken place already in bar 547. Admittedly, both flutes and violin I are in unison here as they cadence on $e\flat^2$, approached from the fifth above. But that fifth, $b\flat^2$, in flute I is again a substitute for the unavailable $b\flat^3$, towards which the arpeggiation begun in bar 545 is unmistakably striving. Moreover, while the cadence at bars 546–7 reinforces Schenker's sense of the two-line octave as the obligatory register, he has previously been forced to admit that the $\hat{2}$ of the *Urlinie* 'presents itself as f^3', rather than as f^2.[9] This circumstance comes about because of the register transfer g^2–g^3 across

bars 430–40. But the transfer is effected only in violin I, while the three-line octave is already active. As noted above, the high-register statement of the theme from bar 37 is reprised here in flute I, but now in the context of a chromatic ascent to ab^3 at bar 437, which note is reached by violin I only two bars later and then harmonically mandated to resolve downward to g^3.

This chromatic ascent is one of the many thrilling moments in the *Eroica*, and it is registrally significant also. The violin I ab^3 of bar 439 marks a new highpoint for this instrument, whose previous registral limit had been g^3. And it joins flute I at its own registral limit (apart from a fleeting $a\natural^3$ in bars 245–6). The ab^3–g^3 resolution can be heard to mimic and magnify the parallel two-line octave one of bars 397–8, which launches the recapitulation (flute I again reasserts the three-line octave at that point, with f^3–eb^3). The next occasion on which the two instruments will converge on this extreme pitch will be at bar 668, the neighbour note to g^3, which is reached by a comparable chromatic ascent from eb^3 (bar 655) to that commenced at bar 430. And the final assertion of ab^3 in violin I comes at bars 684–5, which brings us back to Schenker's remarks about the roles of flute I and violin I at this point in the movement.

Schenker's notion that Beethoven's scoring in the last twenty or so bars, and particularly the covering of violin I by flute I at bars 671–2, is contrived so as to give 'precedence' to violin I with ab^3 at bars 684–5 suggests (uncontroversially) that he sees that instrument as the main bearer of the obligatory registral space of the movement: it is as though the stringed instrument must outstrip the woodwind here. Sure enough, this is the only instance of an ab^3 that is not simultaneously present in flute I, whose last articulation of that pitch was at bar 672: its ascending arpeggiation from ab^2 (bar 681) in harness with violin I peaks at f^3 (bar 683). Yet violin I reaches ab^3 only to abandon it, plunging down two and a half octaves to d^1, from where it will ascend to its concluding g^2, in accordance with Schenker's registral scheme. The necessary downward semitonal resolution required of ab^3 is provided by flute I, which moves $\hat{2}$–$\hat{3}$ at bars 688–9 rather than $\hat{2}$–$\hat{1}$, so as to introduce g^3. The comparison with bars 439ff. is instructive: the perfect accord there of violin I and flute I in accomplishing the $\hat{4}$–$\hat{3}$ (ab^3–g^3) resolution is in striking contrast to the more fragmented situation at the conclusion of the movement. Bars 439ff. also bear comparison with their exposition parallel, bars 37ff. Notable there is the fact that violin I reaches only to eb^3: it is the flutes that establish g^3/ eb^3, with flute I proceeding at bar 43 to its first ab^3, which of course cannot be registrally exceeded, and is at that point quitted by leap, to eb^3.

The arrival at eb^3 in bar 37 was important for Schenker as the completion of an ascending register transfer eb^2–eb^3 that introduced the three-line octave for the first time (recall his rejection of the significance of flute I's

statement in bars 15–17 in this respect). Nonetheless, he was firm in his view that this higher register was essentially non-structural, and functioned principally to aid 'spatial expansion' and sonority: the return to the three-line octave at the conclusion of the movement was necessary merely to the achievement of a 'brilliant conclusion'.

In contrast to Schenker's essentially 'decorative' or subsidiary sense of the three-line octave in Beethoven's scoring, the analysis developed here proposes that it should be regarded as more 'structural'. And this proposition invites us to pay particular attention to Beethoven's treatment of flute I, from its initial definition of the truncated triadic space $\hat{3}$–$\hat{1}$ (b♭^{3} being unavailable) at bars 15–17 and again at bars 37ff. to bars 430ff., where for the first time violin I accedes to the flute's registral extreme, and the flute I's own a♭^{3}, left isolated in bar 43 (and again at bar 232 in the development), is now incorporated into the climactic $\hat{4}$–$\hat{3}$ resolution. This climax is arguably more 'brilliant' than the conclusion itself, which in bars 684–9 can recuperate the events of that earlier climax in only a fragmented manner. Violin I may achieve 'precedence' over flute I at bars 684–5, but it is unable to meet the voice-leading obligations of its solo a♭^{3}: the resolution to g^3 ultimately belongs to flute I. And just as flute I is essential to the completion of this linear aspect of the music, so too the two tonic chords of bars 689 and 690 answer those of bars 1 and 2.[10] Violin I asserts g^2 in both locations, beginning and end. Flute I, though, exchanges its initial e♭^{3} for g^3 before leaping down to e♭^{2}. If we can read the 'narrative' of flute I in this movement as tracing a path from an initial, *piano* e♭^{3} (bars 15–17) – which may indeed seem merely colouristic or decorative – to an indisputably climactic g^3 (bar 440), the 'framing' chords of bars 1–2 and 689–90 neatly summarise and encapsulate that path. And inasmuch as flute I's overall movement is from $\hat{1}$ to $\hat{3}$ rather than the reverse, that instrument proposes the three-line octave as a still open melodic space, for all the 'brute force' with which the final bars insist upon closure.

Registering the Close

Register as a compositional parameter is foregrounded in a particularly strategic way in the finale of the *Eroica*. Beethoven's reaching back in this movement to his earlier *Fünfzehn Variationen mit einer Fuge*, Op. 35 – the so-called 'Eroica' or 'Prometheus' Variations – is well known. The variation theme itself derives from the even earlier Contredanse WoO 14 No. 7 and the ballet *Die Geschöpfe des Prometheus*, Op. 43. In Op. 35, Beethoven writes an *Introduzione col basso del tema*, presenting the bass line of the eventual theme systematically over four ascending octaves, the last of

which (the two-line octave) is retained for the initial statement of the *tema* itself. The symphony's finale reworks this principle, though with only three iterations of the *basso*: the second and third iterations present the *basso* clearly in the one- and two-line octaves respectively, with surrounding counterpoints. But the first statement, complete with written-out repeats and much octave doubling, already encapsulates the complete registral terrain of the piano work, with individual parts presenting, in Schenker's words, the 'great, small, one- and two-line octaves'.[11]

We hardly need Schenker to tell us that, of course. But the further invocation of his *Eroica* study is pertinent here. If register is 'composed into' the finale in the manner described, it is, even more than in the first movement, a distinctive structural parameter in Schenker's analysis. Schenker reads a $\hat{3}-\hat{2}-\hat{1}$ *Urlinie* that divides unconventionally, at the 'second middleground layer', into two such progressions, each preceded by an upper neighbour note A♭.[12] What distinguishes the two progressions is register: the first (bars 76–277) unfolds in the two-line and the second (bars 315–435) in the three-line octave. Schenker's conception of the *Urlinie* as an always downward movement through triadic space towards the tonic pitch inevitably entails the structural priority of descending over ascending motion; there will be occasion to revisit this issue below.

There arises from this the question of the relative status of the two progressions. In his Figures 44 and 45 Schenker beams them identically, save that only the concluding e♭²/ e♭³ of the second progression is distinguished by the use of a stemmed white note.[13] Both are accorded careted, unbracketed scale degree numerals. The notation of the foreground graph – Schenker's 'Bild 4' – is interestingly different.[14] Here, g² and f² of the first progression are shown as beamed stemmed white notes, while the concluding e♭² (supported by a $\frac{6}{3}$ rather than $\frac{5}{3}$ tonic: 'something', writes Schenker, 'that would stabilize the connection between the two sections to an excessive degree') is a black note.[15] The second beamed descent accords white-note status only to the initial g³; f³ and e♭³ are stemmed black notes. And Schenker writes of the second progression that it is 'basically a repetition, or, to be more precise, a coupling of the two-line and three-line octaves *which contributes nothing new to our under-standing of the Ursatz*'.[16] This appears to imply that the first, two-line-octave progression carries more structural weight; and after all, Schenker's 'first middleground layer' shows a single, undivided $\hat{3}-\hat{2}-\hat{1}$ progression in the (obligatory) two-line octave.

Not all commentators agree on this interpretation; and while Derrick Puffett inclines towards it, he freely admits of Schenker's italicised claim above that 'whether one goes along with such an explanation, which implies that the movement is more or less over by bar 277, is of course

another matter'.[17] But Schenker himself shores up precisely this reading: while he provides a detailed prose commentary supporting the graphic analysis up to bar 348, where the second neighbour note to the forthcoming second $\hat{3}$ is achieved in the three-line octave, he dispenses with bars 348–473 (and the unique square brackets around these bar numbers tell their own story) in fewer than three lines:

> [**Bars 348–473**] In view of what has been said above concerning Figs. 44 and 45, and the precise indications in the Foreground Graph, an even more detailed explanation of this last section seems superfluous.[18]

Moreover, the 'precise indications' are considerably more sparse here than in the preceding section of Schenker's graph.

Precisely this sparseness in the graph throws into relief two asterisks placed above $b\flat^2$ in bars 377 (oboe I) and 381 (flute I).[19] These are the counterparts to a third such 'indication', above $b\flat^2$ in bar 96;[20] all three also appear in Schenker's Fig. 45, a deep-level graph that clarifies 'changes of registers' among other things.[21] In his commentary Schenker refers to the asterisked $b\flat^2$ in bar 96; but he is curiously silent about the later pair. The issue has to do with his analysis of the *tema*, which he reads as a stepwise ascent from g^2 (bar 76) to $b\flat^2$ (bar 96, repeated at 104) via the passing note $a\natural^2$, followed by a fifth-progression down to $\hat{1}$. The $a\natural^2$ is vital to 'the meaning of the theme':

> That the treble is intended to describe a fifth $[\hat{5}-\hat{1}]$ is proven beyond all doubt by the chromatic passing note a^2 in bar 95: in a manner of speaking, this note embodies the urge of a^2 to reach $b\flat^2$.[22]

Indeed, the $a\natural^2$ is crucial in overcoming the urge of $a\flat^2$ (bars 95 and 104), as a dominant seventh, to fall back to g^2. But there is a potential problem here, and Schenker is alert to it. The *tema*, together with its supporting *basso*, 'comes close to expressing the Urlinie-progression $\hat{5}-\hat{1}$ ... and is thus in conflict with the adumbration of g^2 in bar 76 by the neighbour note $a\flat$ at the beginning of the finale'.[23] Hence the asterisked $b\flat^2$ in bar 96. But he subsequently dismisses the matter out of hand:

> The question of whether the fifth of the theme in the treble has finally overcome the third in bar 76, a note to which the previous descending lines ... have alluded – to say nothing of the neighbour note in bars 7–11 – has already been settled in favour of g^2 as $\hat{3}$.[24]

Whatever the competing claims of scale degrees $\hat{3}$ and $\hat{5}$ for *Kopfton* ('head note', the initial, highest *Urlinie* note) status in the movement as a whole, it is also the case that the *Urlinie*-like $\hat{5}-\hat{1}$ descent that Schenker reads in the *tema* is somewhat manufactured; in particular, the melodic line presents no explicit scale degree $\hat{4}$, and scale degree $\hat{3}$ is, properly speaking, an

appoggiatura to $\hat{2}$ rather than a harmonically supported pitch. The situation is far from uncommon in a Schenkerian context, and would hardly raise eyebrows. But since this present analysis is concerned with 'registering', closely, the foreground experience of this music, such differences matter. More than this: the fact that the *tema*, having reached bb², then ascends a further tone to c³ leaves bb² implicitly active while the melodic line plunges down to its close. That is, c³ implicitly returns to bb² over the harmony of bar 98 (Example 7.1); though to make this point admittedly requires one to invoke precisely the same kind of abstract voice-leading model that allows Schenker to 'provide' scale degree $\hat{4}$ in bar 97.

To read the *tema* in this way is to hear a strong ascent from $\hat{3}$ to a climactic arrival at $\hat{5}$ followed by a broken descent to $\hat{1}$ that does not adequately expunge $\hat{5}$ from the ear. In this respect the *tema* closely mimics its supporting *basso*. Schenker observes that the *basso del tema* can be understood not just as 'the bass of an outer-voice structure' but also 'as the treble of a two-voice structure', functioning above what he calls a 'hidden bass'.[25] In either case, he understands the *basso* as a stepwise ascent through the fifth Eb–Bb followed by a leap back to the starting note. As in the *tema*, then, strongly directed stepwise motion up to $\hat{5}$ is not matched by similar stepwise motion back to $\hat{1}$; in the case of the *basso* the $\hat{5}$–$\hat{1}$ space is left entirely void.

Schenker may have lost no sleep in deciding 'whether the fifth of the theme in the treble has finally overcome the third'; but the foregoing remarks highlighting the significant positioning of $\hat{5}$ within the *tema* and its *basso* – the raw matter of the *Eroica* finale, after all – may keep us awake a little longer. And just as the prominence of register in Schenker's analysis means that a study such as this one can hardly avoid engaging with it, even if by disagreeing with it, our concern must be not just with scale degree $\hat{5}$ in general but with its specific registral instances.

We may begin by worrying anew at the pitch bb², in light of the distinction that Schenker seeks to sustain between it and g² in relation to the larger structure of the movement. Writing of the initial statement of the *basso del thema* (bars 12–43), he asserts that 'neither the higher octave

Example 7.1 Beethoven, *Eroica* Symphony, Op. 55, fourth movement, cf. bars 94–9

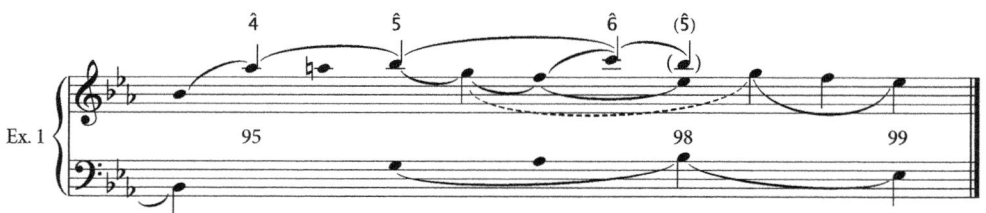

registers of the unison strings nor those in the wind rob the double bass part ... of the primary significance of the great octave'.[26] Here he presumably wants to reinforce the connection between the symphony finale and the *Fünfzehn Variationen*, Op. 35. But there is no getting away from the fact that flutes I and II in unison introduce the two-line octave in bars 20–7, the written-out repeat of the first eight-bar half of the *basso*. Then B♭ is hammered out, *fortissimo*, across four octaves in bars 29 and 31; the fact that these are hypermetric 'offbeats' within the eight-bar phrase (bars 28–35) only adds to the effect, and brings the highest register, bb^2 in the upper woodwinds, into greater prominence. The written-out repeat, bars 36–43, while it fills in the previously silent bars, undoing the previous syncopation, simultaneously redoubles the presence of the repeated B♭ in woodwinds, brass and timpani; meanwhile, the thinning of the texture (the oboes withdraw) in the final four-bar phrase leaves the two-line octave – and bb^2 – to flutes I and II.

The settings *a tre* and *a quattro* of the *basso* (bars 44–59 and 60–75) are for strings alone, so that it is only with the appearance of the *tema* itself that woodwind and brass re-enter. The melody is carried in oboe I, beginning on g^2. But above this, at the top of the texture, flute I introduces a pedal on bb^2, a pitch that by now is become almost emblematic. In the written-out repeat the pedal will be carried by flute II, while flute I operates around eb^3 above. The flutes fall silent for the first statement of the second half of the *tema* (bars 92–9), while in the second (bars 100–7) they reiterate the threefold bb^2 of bars 29 and 37 (the quaver rest now at the beginning rather than the end of the bar), in bar 101 juxtaposing with the violins' ab^2 precisely the climactic pitch one tone higher to which violin I will accede in bar 104. By this time flute I has again moved into the three-line octave where it executes a complete $\hat{1}$–$\hat{2}$–$\hat{3}$–$\hat{2}$–$\hat{1}$ motion (bars 104–7), introducing thereby a new registral highpoint, g^3, in the movement. That highpoint will be reinforced a few bars later, with the arrival on V/c in bars 115–16, prior to the commencement of the fugato; but before reaching up to g^3 again, flute I introduces $b\natural^2$, which breaks the hold, as it were, of bb^2 and opens up the possibility of a further linear ascent, to c^3 and beyond.

Sure enough, the next appearance of the flutes, with a false entry of the fugato subject, establishes c^3 as an upper pedal in bars 145–53. Violin I enters the three-line octave from bar 156, with flute I joining it at bar 159. Together they touch on db^3 and d^3, but the overall direction of motion here is a return to $b\natural^2$, in the context of dominant ($^4_2$) harmony in C minor (compare bar 116), at bar 163. That same harmony, now in root position, returns at bars 173–4, by which time the flutes have established the pair d^3/f^3; the higher of these two will edge upward to $f\sharp^3$ at bar 175, when V^7/c resolves deceptively as an augmented sixth (E♯ masquerades as F♮),

launching what, despite its B minor opening, will be a complete reprise (or variation) of the *tema* in D major (bars 175–206).

We shall return to the D major reprise below. For the present, it suffices to say that taken as a whole it firmly establishes d^3 as a stable new registral 'marker' in the upper voice, particularly as represented by flute I. And that marker is carried forward through the martial section in G minor that follows, even though flute I reaches up beyond d^3 to cadence on g^3 (bar 254: compare bars 115–16). The ensuing partial statement in flute I of the *tema* in C major allows d^3 to move upward to $e\natural^3$, and thence locally through f^3 to g^3 (bars 258–62); but the half-cadence in the eighth bar (265) returns the larger line to d^3.

The passage subsequent to this C major statement corresponds to that in which, in Schenker's interpretation, the first, two-line-octave iteration of the $\hat{3}$–$\hat{2}$–$\hat{1}$ *Urlinie* progression completes. As he puts it, 'the flute [I] finally makes a point of playing f^2 in bar 274, and the Urlinie descends to eb^2 in bar 277'.[27] But this conveniently ignores the bb^2 which follows f^2, underscored by Beethoven's open *crescendo* marking (note the placement, here and in the clarinet part, of the succeeding *diminuendo* underneath the doubling second part, rather than above the stave: it is as though the *crescendo* continues in the upper octave, even though both these wind parts now disappear). To the extent that we may, in accordance with Schenker's reading, understand a new beginning at this point in the movement, flute I's reassertion of bb^2, the starting point of the registral activity we have been tracing largely through that particular instrumental voice, is pertinent (compare flute I, bar 76ff.).

The next entry reinforces the sense that bb^2, on the lips of a flautist, is not just another pitch in this unfolding movement; rather than joining in the strings' counter-exposition of the inverted fugato subject, both flutes, on their re-entry, present a rhythmically displaced statement of the *tema* opening in the prevailing two-line octave that reaches its climactic bb^2 one crotchet early. And that same pitch is grasped again, after another 19-bar silence, as the flutes confirm the establishment of the three-line register just accessed in the ascent by violin I to a fleeting g^3 at bar 315. The eb^3 that follows at bar 318 can in a broader sense be understood to connect back to d^3 at bar 265; and that pitch will be reasserted in bar 328, where there commences the dominant pedal that will extend over the next 21 bars – but not before flute I has exceeded both eb^3 and g^3 to touch, for the first time in this finale, ab^3 in the previous bar (327). (That d^3 in bar 328 is a substitute for the flute's bb^3 is made clear by oboe I, to which flute I has been locked in octave doubling since the end of bar 321.) And ab^3, reached from d^3 in flute I (bars 338–9 and 346–7), soon reappears to crown the massive dominant seventh to which this section of the movement gravitates. In terms of

sonority and scoring it is a moment that vividly recalls the corresponding penultimate harmony of the first movement (bars 681–5), within which violin I uniquely displaced flute I in its 'possession' of ab^3. But whereas in that earlier movement the obligations of V^7 were immediately realised, here in the finale matters are left poised on the brink.

Example 7.2 seeks to summarise the rather dense foregoing discussion of the surface melodic activity of the finale up to bar 348. Above all, it proposes a single, unified *ascending* trajectory, carried largely by flute I, that connects bb^2 (bar 29) to ab^3 (bar 348). This is in distinct contrast to Schenker's reading, the downward orientation of which follows ineluctably from his concept of *Urlinie* as an always *descending* motion towards the tonic pitch, already reached from g^2 in the two-line octave at b. 277, after which there follows a mere 'repetition' of the same events an octave higher.

The return at bar 349 to the complete *tema*, now Poco Andante, immediately brings matters back down to the two-line octave. But the seeming thematic recuperation here exhibits some subtle features needing careful observation: this is not simply a return to the *status quo ante* of bars 76–107. The principal difference concerns the final four bars (369–72, repeated 377–80), where the $\hat{5}$–$\hat{6}$–$\hat{5}$ motion around bb^2 that is implicit in the initial statement is now made explicit: the upward motion through $a\natural^2$ to bb^2 (bar 369: note that $a\natural^2$ now displaces bb^2 from the downbeat) continues with $b\natural^2$–c^3, whereupon flute I reiterates $a\natural^2$–bb^2 (bar 371) while the thematic line, rather than plunging down to eb^2, goes no further than g^2, bringing bb^2 back down to this pitch through ab^2 (Example 7.3). The stepwise ascent to c^3 is already adumbrated in oboe I in bar 367, such that the flute I entry on d^3–eb^3 (bars 369–70) acts effectively as a continuation; the thematic line, from the initial g^2 of bar 349, traces an ascent of a sixth (made even clearer in the repeat at bar 378, when $b\natural^2$–c^3–d^3–eb^3 appears conjunctly, and flute I maintains eb^3 at the cadence in bar 380). This ascent, though, is subsidiary to the more underlying reshaping of the *tema* within the arch-like space $\hat{3}$–$\hat{4}$–$\hat{5}$($-\hat{4}$–$\hat{3}$) rather than $\hat{5}$–$\hat{1}$.

The peak of that arch, bb^2, now emerges again as an upper pedal, in flute I reinforced by oboe I and subsequently violin I, while the *tema*, now in its original melodic form, passes to the lowest voice: *basso* becomes *tema*. The extreme registral separation between upper-voice pedal and *tema* here might be heard in terms of a radical rewriting of the pedal-*tema* combination of the initial statement at bar 76, so as to set the two elements graphically and sonically apart.

The new emphasis accorded to bb^2 through the subtle melodic changes wrought by the Poco Andante brings us to that point in the movement where, in Schenker's Fig. 45 and his foreground graph, unexplained asterisks highlight bb^2 in bars 377 and 381 respectively.[28]

Example 7.2 Beethoven, *Eroica* Symphony, Op. 55, fourth movement, cf. bars 29–348

Example 7.3 Beethoven, *Eroica* Symphony, Op. 55, fourth movement, cf. bars 369–72

He had been originally concerned to argue for the primacy of g^2, as $\hat{3}$, over bb^2 as a potential *Urlinie Kopfton* $\hat{5}$. From the perspective of the present analysis, however, bb^2 seems more and more a melodically prominent pitch – above all, one from which significant *ascending* rather than *descending* events follow. It was noted that flute I established eb^3 above the bb^2 pedal at the cadence in bars 379–80. Now in this *basso* iteration of the *tema* it reaches higher again, over-stepping eb^3 and f^3 through $f\sharp^3$ to touch on g^3 at bar 393 before cadencing back on eb^3 in bar 396.

$F\sharp^3$ will again be the gateway to the next appearance of g^3 in flute I, at bars 416–20: these pitches also mark a new registral highpoint for violin I, which then drops in register while flute I continues to operate in the three-line octave, ready for the Presto stepwise descent to eb^3 at bars 431–5 which, as the second (and secondary) *Urlinie-Zug*, represents the end of structural business as far as Schenker is concerned. While there is no denying the closural force of the moment, simply to dismiss the remaining 38 bars of the symphony with '*u.s.w.*' ('etc') is insufficient.[29] Until bar 447 all registers repeatedly articulate the $\hat{3}$–$\hat{4}$ (G–Ab) upward movement built into the initial bars of the *tema*: the point is hammered home most insistently in flute I in bars 443–7. The last appearance of ab^3 comes in bar 446, after which g^3 marks the upper boundary of flute I, where it is joined by violin I in bars 458–61, which in scoring and dynamic are akin to bars 440–3 of the first movement. But whereas the close of the first movement left the three-line octave open, thanks to the plunge g^3–eb^2 in flute I, here that instrument closes in register, g^3–eb^3; indeed, the general tessitura of the final tonic chord is higher (or more top-heavy) than its first-movement equivalent. Even so, it is notable that after the stepwise descent g^3–f^3–eb^3 of bars 431–5, both flutes work to keep the $\hat{3}$–$\hat{1}$ space open for the remainder of the movement (only at the end of the Scherzo does flute I offer a complete, stepwise closure of this space).

Registering the Impossible

The attempt, in the preceding analysis, to suggest that bb^2 plays a significant melodic role in the *Eroica* finale is based primarily on close observation of Beethoven's scoring (and its aural consequences) rather than being driven by any specific theoretical aim: it is not my purpose, for example, to suggest that Schenker's $\hat{3}$-line *Urlinie* ought to yield to a $\hat{5}$-line alternative. Nonetheless, we have also observed that the *basso del tema* and the *tema* itself are each characterised by strongly directed motion towards scale degree $\hat{5}$, while the melodic gap between that and the closing scale degree $\hat{1}$ is left void (in the case of the *basso*) or only partially filled (in the case of the *tema*). The achievement of the climactic $\hat{5}$ is all the more dramatic in the *tema* in that the ab^2 that is the goal of the scalic ascents of bars 92–5 and their repetition in bars 100–3 is so powerfully set up, as a dominant seventh, to fall by step to g^2 rather than to rise (the fermata of course makes the expectation of 'normal' dissonance treatment all the more potent). The extended, emphatic V^7/I is something of an iconic harmony – an iconic *sound* – in the *Eroica*. We have already tracked its instances in the first movement (bars 396–7, before the recapitulation; bars 438–9, over a tonic pedal; and bars 681–8, leading to the concluding tonic cadence), and bars 6–11 and the massive build-up across bars 328–48 of the finale. Thus there is something almost transgressive about the $a\natural^2$ that defies the downward pull of harmonic gravity here in the *tema* and enables the melodic line to reach its triumphant goal. The *piano/forte* contrast between the initial upward push (bars 95–6) and its repetition (bars 103–4) only adds to the effect: the first 'testing' of the rules is tentative, but having got away with it once imparts a certain bravado to the repetition.

But what is achieved so satisfyingly – so heroically – here will prove hard to repeat. Following the *basso*-based fugato commencing at bar 117, the *tema* re-emerges at bar 175. This D major reprise follows the 32-bar (8+8+8+8) phrase structure of bars 76–107 exactly, but is otherwise significant on several counts. It foregrounds flute I in a genuinely soloistic role; and given the emphatic tonic–dominant basis of so much of the harmony of this movement (a characteristic obviously conditioned by the structure of the *basso del tema* itself), the oblique harmonic approach to it is anomalous, and sounds so: there is no other moment in the finale, or perhaps the symphony, quite like it. In fact, the approach is doubly oblique, in that the bass A♭ of the diminished seventh harmony of bar 171, following upon the D minor harmony of the previous two bars, is perceived as G♯, which would be expected to rise to A as V/d; that it falls to G (bar 173) to create V^7/c is the first surprise, the second being that this harmony is then quitted as an augmented sixth (F♮ = E♯), to produce the $^6_4$ B minor

harmony that supports the first four bars (175–8) of the *tema* reprise. Finally, the upward semitonal slide from $f^{2/3}$ ($e\sharp^{2/3}$) in violin I and flute I, precisely evokes the $\sharp\hat{4}$–$\hat{5}$ ($a\flat^2$–$b\flat^2$) motion that brings the *tema* itself to its climactic $\hat{5}$ at the beginning of its last quarter.

This D major reprise, then, is clearly marked; placed 'in quotes', as it were. And its unique timbral quality is enhanced by its uniquely high register, which takes flute I up to a repeated $a\natural^3$, previously heard only in the slow movement (see bars 84–95), and fully a tone above the instrument's previous registral peak of g^3 (bars 115–16). The beginning of the second half of the statement (bar 191ff.), where flute I abandons the *tema* for virtuosic figuration in semiquavers, properly prepares g^3 (bars 191 and 193) as V^7; but rather than carrying this up to a^3 via $g\sharp^3$ at bar 195, consistent with the *tema*, g^3 is left isolated until it resolves downward to $f\sharp^3$ at bar 203, the bar corresponding to bar 195 in this repeat of the second half of the *tema* structure. As if to compensate, the four-bar codetta to this 32-bar section does indeed present a direct statement of the complete chromatic ascent $\hat{3}$–$\hat{4}$–$\sharp\hat{4}$–$\hat{5}$ that shapes the upper voice of the *tema*, so that $a\flat^3$ is again reintroduced via $g\sharp^3$ before the cadence on d^3 (bars 207–10).

A second attempt to recuperate the *tema* comes at bar 257: as at bar 175, flute I and violin I have the melody in octaves. But whereas the D major reprise presented the entire 32-bar structure, now only the first eight-bar phrase can be contemplated before the *basso* again predominates (bar 266ff.), despite the efforts of flute I and horns (bars 292, 303) to reassert the opening of the *tema* in the tonic key against the prevailing fugato counterpoint (the metrical displacement of the *tema* perhaps symptomatic of the unevenness of the contest). While the second half of the D major reprise shied away from the chance to carry g^3 back up to $a\flat^3$ via $g\sharp^3$, this second attempt at bar 257 simply never gets that far to start with. Moreover, it is cast not in D but in C major, so that its registral peak reverts from $a\natural^3$ to g^3.

All this may help to recontextualise the arrival in flute I at $a\flat^3$, first in bar 327 and then bar 338, whereupon it persists for almost the next ten bars: following the downturn after bar 210, $a\flat^3$ marks a new attempt to reach up above g^3. Meanwhile, Example 7.2 suggested that this $a\flat^3$ marks the goal of an extended ascent from $b\flat^2$ that is played out through the movement almost from the beginning up to bar 348. This ascent can be understood as a massive expansion of the very opening, with its gradual accumulation of the elements of a powerful V^7/E$\flat$ across bars 1–11. As is widely noted, the movement begins off-tonic on a seeming dominant of G minor, a key that will be realised as a tonic in the martial section beginning at bar 211. The crucial shift from a G minor towards an E$\flat$ major context is effected by the cancellation of A$\natural$ by A$\flat$ in bars 3–4; in

other words, the reverse of the semitonal succession that is so important to the climax of the *tema*. And it is the lead-up to that climax that offers another context for the expanded ascent bb^2– ab^3 of Example 7.2: on this reading, V^7 at bar 348 corresponds to the equivalent harmony in the twentieth bar of the *tema* and its repeat; and by this point in the movement we know what should happen next.

It does not happen, of course; Beethoven could not, or would not, allow it to happen. Given the accumulated 'brute force' of bars 328–48, the succeeding Poco Andante risks seeming a damp squib (compare the first emergence of the *Freude* theme in the Ninth Symphony, after its grandiose announcement): all that, for *this*? We have noted, too (Example 7.3), the changed ending of this iteration, which substitutes melodic closure on $\hat{3}$ for that on $\hat{1}$, and also promotes the sense of $\hat{5}$ (bb^2) as lingering over that closure. Nonetheless, the Poco Andante at last succeeds in recuperating, in the tonic key, the *tema* in its complete, 32-bar form, something that the two previous such attempts had failed to do (the last, beginning in bar 404 in A♭ major, will falter earlier still, just six bars in). Rather than representing some kind of *telos*, might the Poco Andante be better understood as marking a new beginning (as, indeed, is the import of Schenker's analysis)?

The shift in the last several paragraphs to a more avowedly hermeneutic mode is not accidental. I have endeavoured to sketch an emerging narrative of failure, one centrally bound up with extreme high register and what has hitherto been deemed an 'unavailable' pitch, namely bb^3 in flute I. This renders always impossible the completion in the three-line octave of the upward-striving $\hat{3}$–$\hat{4}$–$\sharp\hat{4}$–$\hat{5}$ progression of the *tema*. The appearance of $a\natural^3$ in the D major *tema* reprise in principle holds out some promise of completion, in that that pitch ($\sharp\hat{4}$) is the crucial vehicle for the ascent to $\hat{5}$: recall Schenker's sense of 'the urge of a^2 to reach bb^2' in the *tema*;[30] but it will not reappear to lift ab^3 after bar 348.

Are we too comfortable with the Beethovenian narrative of striving *per ardua ad astra*? Certainly, to suggest that in the *Eroica*, of all pieces, striving *fails* is likely to invite accusations of perversity. Adorno, too, attached a sense of failure to the *Eroica* finale, in that Beethoven 'over-reached himself' in relation to the attempt to synthesise 'closed' and 'open' forms, namely variations and counterpoint. Adorno found the proportions of the movement skewed also: 'the *andante* section seems to me relatively too long, whereas the *presto*, in particular, is much too short'.[31] The mere five-bar Presto denouement of Schenker's second $\hat{3}$–$\hat{2}$–$\hat{1}$ *Urlinie* descent may indeed strike even his sympathisers as implausible in relation to the 430 bars of music that precede it. And whereas for Schenker the melodic closure on $\hat{1}$ at bar 435 was the entirely positive outcome of the movement's overall linear, *Urlinie*-shaped

'mission', from the perspective developed here it stands as the sign of the impossibility of triadic movement upward from g^3. The insistent hammering away at $g^3 - ab^3$ in flute I from bar 439 onward tells its own tale: insistent, but impotent.

We could go further. Brian Hyer, in an extended review of Scott Burnham's *Beethoven Hero*, reminds us of the association of musical cadence with death: 'the long-range motion to the tonic, that is – the harmonic, melodic, and metrical convergence of the music on its moment of closure – embodies a musical death-drive, a merger of *telos* with *thanatos*'. For Hyer, 'the furious insistence on the tonic in [Beethoven's] heroic codas . . . the complete saturation of the music with the tonic betrays a certain defensiveness, a terrified attempt to cover over and disavow a musical absence'. He cites in particular the coda to the *Egmont* Overture, in which 'the monumental arrival on the tonic in the coda is doubly ironic, since it enacts the death of Egmont, but also enunciates his heroic transcendence . . . one more reason to distrust the heroism of this music'.[32] In the reading of the finale offered here, failure is in a sense self-ordained, given the conflict between Beethoven's melodic materials and his scoring practice: *per ardua* . . . but the furthest, highest 'star' will always be out of reach. One might yet discern heroism in the very attempt itself. And one might endeavour, too, to register in the final forty or so bars of the *Eroica* how music so routinely taken as quintessentially 'utopian' and representative of 'bliss'[33] can teach us not just how to fail, but how to 'fail again. Fail better'.

Notes

1. M. Geck, *Beethoven's Symphonies: Nine Approaches to Art and Ideas*, trans. S. Spencer (Chicago: University of Chicago Press, 2017), p. 84.
2. C. Lawson, 'Beethoven and the Development of Wind Instruments', in *Performing Beethoven*, ed. R. Stowell (Cambridge: Cambridge University Press, 1994), p. 84.
3. Schenker's concept indeed often appears only *theoretically* 'obligatory' in that registral manipulation of structural pitches at the musical surface is frequently encountered. For a study that invokes register strongly in a Schenkerian context, see N. Marston, 'Analysing Variations: The Finale of Beethoven's String Quartet Op. 74', *Music Analysis*, 8 (1989), pp. 303–24.
4. H. Schenker, 'Beethoven's Third Symphony: Its True Content Described for the First Time', trans. D. Puffett and A. Clayton, in *The Masterwork in Music: A Yearbook, Volume III (1930)*, ed. W. Drabkin (Cambridge: Cambridge University Press, 1997), p. 23.
5. Schenker, 'Beethoven's Third Symphony', p. 12.
6. Ibid., p. 13.
7. Ibid., p. 34.
8. Ibid.
9. Ibid., p. 33; compare n. 3 above.
10. A similar observation is found in D. Epstein, *Beyond Orpheus: Studies in Musical Structure* (Cambridge, MA: Massachusetts Institute of Technology, 1979), p. 133.
11. Schenker, 'Beethoven's Third Symphony', p. 51.

12. The unconventionality of Schenker's reading resides in the fact that division, or 'interruption', of the *Urlinie* properly takes the form $\hat{3}-\hat{2}//\hat{3}-\hat{2}-\hat{1}$ (or $\hat{5}-\hat{2}//\hat{5}-\hat{1}$). See my 'The Development of Schenker's Concept of Interruption', *Music Analysis*, 32 (2013), pp. 332–62.

13. Schenker, 'Beethoven's Third Symphony', p. 52.

14. Ibid., pp. 103–15.

15. Ibid., p. 51.

16. Ibid. (Emphasis added.)

17. Derrick Puffett, 'Schenker's "Eroica"', *The Musical Times*, 137 (1996), p. 19, n. 29.

18. Schenker, 'Beethoven's Third Symphony', p. 59.

19. Ibid., p. 113.

20. Ibid., p. 105.

21. Ibid., pp. 51–2.

22. Ibid., p. 54.

23. Ibid, p. 53; the analysis of the *tema* is p. 54, Fig. 47.

24. Ibid., p. 54.

25. Ibid., pp. 53, 54; and Fig. 46.

26. Ibid., p. 54.

27. Ibid., p. 58.

28. Ibid., pp. 52, 113.

29. Ibid., p. 115.

30. Ibid., p. 54.

31. T. W. Adorno, *Beethoven: The Philosophy of Music*, ed. R. Tiedemann, trans. E. Jephcott (Cambridge: Polity Press, 1998), p.106.

32. B. Hyer, 'Review of S. Burnham, *Beethoven Hero* (Princeton, NJ: Princeton University Press, 1995)', *Music Theory Spectrum*, 20 (1998), p. 130. See also p. 124 for Hyer's discussion of Burnham's own assessment of the *Egmont* Overture coda as 'enforced bluster'.

33. S. Rumph, *Beethoven After Napoleon: Political Romanticism in the Late Works* (Berkeley, CA: University of California Press, 2004), p. 52; T. Sipe, *Beethoven: Eroica Symphony* (Cambridge: Cambridge University Press, 1998), p. 116.

8 After Invention: Traces and Materials in the *Eroica* Finale

ELAINE SISMAN

The *Eroica* finale is its most contested movement. It is at once Beethoven's earliest unique structure, departing from any known formal precedent, and the only piece he based on his own earlier compositions. The theme comes from his 'heroic-allegorical' or 'allegorical-historical' ballet, *The Creatures of Prometheus*, Op. 43, first performed in March 1801. The following year he wrote the Variations for piano in E♭ major, Op. 35, on that theme, and sought to have the title page identify the theme's source as his 'allegorical ballet Prometheus'.[1] And, as Lewis Lockwood has shown, immediately upon completion of the variations Beethoven sketched out a movement-plan for a symphony in E♭ major, the projected finale of which is inferably to be based on Op. 35.[2] It seems to have been the theme and its variations, then, that formed part of the 'invariant concept' of the symphony, in Lockwood's words.[3] What was it about this theme that drew Beethoven to compose with it *after* its invention was complete, to start to elaborate it anew, and in such different genres?[4] This chapter seeks to explore the traces of these earlier works in the *Eroica* and to consider which of them Beethoven found essential to his symphonic conception. In particular, it will bring together his letters concerned with the counting of variations in Op. 35 and a sketch page suggesting that the theme of the *Eroica* finale will be 'varied and deduced', which have not yet made an impression on analytical understandings of the movement. Ultimately, these material traces will be used to illuminate the intersection between variation form and symphonic discourse.

A Contredanse in a 'Heroic-Allegorical' Ballet

The theme of the *Eroica* finale started life as the finale of Beethoven's first work for the theatre in Vienna: his music to Salvatore Viganò's ballet *Die Geschöpfe des Prometheus* premiered on 28 March 1801. The scenario concerned a Titan who, fleeing the wrath of Zeus, created two creatures from clay and enabled them to achieve humanity by means of an education in the arts from the muses and gods of Parnassus. The impetus for

the work came from the music-loving Empress Marie Thérèse, the second wife of Emperor Francis; Viganò's first biographer even claimed that her love and patronage of the arts made her the allegorical subject of the ballet.[5] Perhaps concluding with a contredanse reflects her preference, and John A. Rice suggests that Beethoven and Viganò included a contredanse especially for the empress because her own Parnassian ballet scenario expressly called for one in the same position.[6] Beethoven's Eb major theme, a felicitous invention, launches a rondo with three refrains, its melody given chiefly to the violins (Example 8.1). Winds and horns play the dance-like accompaniment in the first and last phrases, lending an air of the oom-pah dance band. When the melody slows to a single Bb per beat in bars 5–6 but the harmonic rhythm doubles, the second violins speed up to semiquaver-note elaborations of the opening melody. In the penultimate bar of the first reprise (bar 7), violins and bass line keep pace as the harmonic rhythm doubles again to a chord change on every quaver note. Perhaps as compensation, the contrasting phrase in the second reprise (bars 9–12) is all on the dominant. In the three repeated dominant seventh chords in bar 10, the entire orchestra plays, *fortissimo*; the echo of that chord, in bar 12, is *piano*, with only clarinets and horns joining the strings, and is marked by a fermata. This series of hammer-blows and the fermata were almost certainly related to choreographic gestures. One wonders if a fermata signalled an improvisatory opportunity to a dancer, as it would to a musician. Certainly the fermata is present the first time Beethoven sketches out the second reprise of the contredanse on p. 129, staff 5, of the sketchbook that contains all the materials for Prometheus, Landsberg 7.[7]

The finale was one of the most popular numbers in the ballet, which was performed twenty-eight times in 1801 and 1802. It had an exciting conclusion, because the rondo gave way to a fast fugato (based on the theme of the overture) comparable in some ways to the fugal writing in the overture to *The Magic Flute*, and a final stretto with prolonged and noisy cadencing. Critical reaction was muted. The two published reviews found Beethoven's music either too 'learned' or too 'contrived' (*künstlich*) for what was supposed to be a divertissement, not an opera.[8] The choreography did not entirely please either, and opinions of the music may have suffered as a result. Both the finale's theme and one of its episodes were arranged as separate contredanses for the public balls of the following winter season in Vienna (WoO 14 nos. 7 and 11, 1801), suggesting that the theme might have become, briefly, as well known as Mozart's 'Non più andrai' from *The Marriage of Figaro*, which he arranged as a contredanse in 1791 (K. 609, no. 1).[9] Thus a contredanse 'topic' in a ballet or opera could turn into an actual contredanse for social

Example 8.1 Beethoven, *Die Geschöpfe des Prometheus*, Op. 43, No. 16, finale. Allegretto, theme

dancing rather than a stylised representation of one. The line separating kinds of dance practices, and the musical topics and styles related to them, was thin.[10] Also performed in concerts at the Augarten, as noted by Beethoven's brother, were the Overture, the exciting timpani-fuelled dance of Bacchus (no. 8), much of it a march, and Pan's fluting Pastorale (no. 10).[11] A piano arrangement of the complete work

Example 8.1 (cont.)

published by Artaria in 1801 and selections by Hoffmeister in 1803 attested to continuing interest.

When the prestigious Leipzig journal *Allgemeine musikalische Zeitung* (*AmZ*) reviewed Beethoven's Variations and Fugue in E♭, Op. 35, in 1804,

the theme's source in the Prometheus ballet was identified.[12] But when the *AmZ* reviewed the *Eroica* Symphony in 1807 upon publication of the score, the theme was identified only as one that he had already worked on (*bearbeitet*) for piano.[13] Whatever memories of the ballet survived into the time of the *Eroica's* public premiere in 1805, by 1807 it was the piano work that was the better known, at least to readers of the *AmZ*. Why did Beethoven return to the theme for the symphony, and in particular, why did completing Op. 35 seem to put thoughts of a symphony in Eb in his head? Perhaps the contredanse's position as the culmination of the ballet's allegorical programme suggested that it could be a meaningful symbol in other instrumental works. Perhaps it was 'rich in solid musical facts', as Tovey said of the maligned theme of the Diabelli variations.[14] Perhaps Beethoven's brilliant stroke in separating the bass from the melody in Op. 35 suggested to him a new universe of thematic generation in the symphony.

Making Variations Count

If the *Prometheus* ballet was Beethoven's first work for the theatre in Vienna, his Variations in Eb, Op. 35, paired with the Variations in F, Op. 34, were his first variations to be assigned opus numbers, at his insistence. In a letter to Breitkopf of 18 October 1802, his brother and business representative, Kaspar Karl, referred to each set as having the 'worth of a Work' because 'it is a completely new invention to make variations in this way' ('weil es eine ganz neue Erfindung ist, Variationen auf dieser Art zu machen').[15] He added that 'one piece can be counted as 8, the other as 30 variations' ('Eine Partie kann man zu 8, die andere zu 30 Variationen rechnen').[16] Beethoven added his own letter the same day, expanding on these details with an evident interest in numbers and counting that go beyond possible remunera-tion. His language also exceeds that of his brother in marking the works as something special:

> I have composed two sets of variations, one of which can be counted [reckoned] as 8 variations [*wovon man das eine auf 8 Variationen berechnen*] and the other as thirty. Both sets are worked out in quite a *new manner* [*eine wircklich ganz neue Manier bearbeitet*], and each in a *separate and different way* [*auf eine andre verschiedene Art*] . . . –Each *theme is treated in its own way and in a different way from the other one.* Usually I have to wait for other people to tell me when I have new ideas, for I never know this myself. But this time – I myself can assure you that in both these works the *method* [*Manier*] is completely *new for me.*[17]

The language reminds us of Haydn's calling attention to the 'new and special way' ('neu, gantz besonderer Art') of his quartets of 1781, Op. 33, in letters to prospective subscribers.[18] But it must be read in conjunction with other letters from Beethoven, both concerned with newness and numbers. The first, of 18 December 1802, informs Breitkopf that his variations must carry a kind of certificate of authenticity, lest the idea of a brand-new kind of variation cause confusion among the 'Nichtkenner', who might mistakenly associate his new approach with Anton Reicha's 'new method' for writing fugues, 'which means only that the fugue is no longer a fugue'.[19] In Reicha's *Trente-six fugues d'après une nouvelle système*, Op. 36, published in 1803 and dedicated to Haydn, the fugal answers do not need to maintain an adherence to the dominant and may begin anywhere. That work may also have enraged Beethoven with the stagey agreement of number of fugues with opus number, and with the closeness of Op. 36 to Beethoven's own Op. 34 and 35. In any case, Beethoven asked that a notice be printed on the edition to point out that 'as these variations are distinctly different from my earlier ones, instead of indicating them like my *previous ones* by means of a number (such as, for instance, Nos. 1, 2, 3 and so on), I have included them in the actual numeration [*Wirkliche Zahl*] *of my greater musical works*, the more so as their themes were composed by me'. The importance of numbering thus extends to the opus concept, which Beethoven was the first to require his publishers to follow and to coordinate, assigning works he deemed significant enough to a 'greater' series.[20] His so-called lesser works, like the many sets of variations on themes by other composers, he also assigned to a series, though without the opus designation.[21]

Numbering posed a problem within variation sets. Kaspar Karl van Beethoven wrote again to Breitkopf on 12 February 1803, with the desired dedicatees of each set, changing the original eight and thirty to seven and twenty-four. Breitkopf pushed back on 3 March, saying they saw only six and fifteen variations, for Op. 34 and Op. 35, respectively.[22] Beethoven finally responded on 8 April with this resonant justification, offering to point out to them what he means on the proof copy:

> As to the variations, about which you think there are not as many as I stated, you are certainly mistaken; my difficulty was that they could not be indicated in the same way; for instance, in the grand ones where the variations are merged together [*verschmolzen*] in the Adagio, and the Fugue admittedly cannot be called a variation; and similarly the introduction to these grand variations which, as you yourself have already seen, begins with the bass of the theme and then becomes two, three, and finally four voices; and [only] then the theme appears, which again cannot be called a variation, and so forth.[23]

Example 8.2 Beethoven, Variations in E♭ major, Op. 35, finale. Alla Fuga: a) bars 1–9; b) bars 51–7; c) bars 89–94

There is in fact no Adagio: for the variations 'merged together in the Adagio', Beethoven could be referring to the varied repeats in the Largo, Variation 15, but more likely he means the two Andante con moto variations that succeed the fugue in the finale. In effect, Beethoven wanted to be credited with the effort of writing so many varied versions: in the introduction, in the finale, in the fugue. The fugue contains several techniques treated successively: a fugue on the subject derived from the head of the *Basso del Tema* (bars 1–50) (Example 8.2a); a double fugue on the bass and melody of the theme (bars 51–89) (Example 8.2b); and a fugue with the inverted bass subject (bars 90–111) (Example 8.2c), which after the dominant pedal seems to flow into a variation of the second reprise of the bass theme (bars 112–32).

Demanding recognition for a larger number of variations than can properly be assigned a number, while at the same time demanding an opus number for the work, neatly encapsulates two meanings of 'work', the

labour involved and the final result. Indeed, two hundred years after Listenius (1537) first referred to an opus as 'the work that is left behind after the labour of completing it is over', eighteenth-century definitions still laboriously made this point. Johann Heinrich Zedler's massive *Grosses Vollständiges Universal-Lexicon aller Wissenschaften und Künste* (vol. 25, 1740) defined it this way: 'o p u s, a work, is properly that which either has been constructed and finished or else is still to be constructed and yet to be finished; and therefore distinguished from the elsewise familiar word Opera in this manner: that the former indicates precisely the construction to be built or piece to be completed itself, but the latter only the effort or labor to be employed upon it.'[24] Beethoven wanted both labour and result to count. His publisher disagreed.

Counting and numbering were a preoccupation. Op. 34 and Op. 35 join the numbered series of major works by being granted a number. The counting of their variations – the total number of varied segments – expands to include kinds of pieces that are not normally counted. In saying 'the fugue cannot be called a variation', Beethoven did not imply that the fugue is *not* a variation (although it has been interpreted that way). Bach's Goldberg Variations, with its tenth variation labelled fughetta and sixteenth variation labelled Ouverture, with slow introduction and fugue, had just been published in Vienna. Various scholars have tried to re-count the Prometheus variations according to these guidelines to see what Beethoven might have included; as far as I know, only Barry Cooper has made it to thirty, by counting the fugue as four variations.[25] Christopher Reynolds has shown that Beethoven numbered some of the sketches for the Op. 35 variations, most of them unrelated to final placement, and those numbers went up to seventeen.[26] Writing variations on his own well-known theme meant that he could not call the theme Variation 4 when it arrived. As a result of building up to the contredanse with contrapuntal variations on its bass, he had to relegate four full numbers to a single 'Introduction'.

The question of what Beethoven counted as a variation in Op. 35 is relevant to the *Eroica* finale, even though composers had long since stopped labelling variations in orchestral music. Not one of Mozart's piano concerto variation movements numbers its variations, and Haydn's last numbered variations in symphonies were the finale of No. 31, the 'Hornsignal', a concertante work with soloistic variations (1765), and the slow movement of Symphony 75 (1779); in fact, the latter was Haydn's penultimate use of numbered variations in any major genre. At issue is the musical value placed upon variations. If Beethoven considered a fugue to be doing the work of a variation even if it could not be so numbered and called, then the *Eroica* is a self-conceived variation movement, however unusual, expanded, continuous, or ground-breaking. However, if variation form is understood as a 'rigid' succession,

Example 8.3 Beethoven, Variations in E♭ major, Op. 35, Introduzione col Basso del Tema, bars 1–8

then the *Eroica* finale cannot be named a variation form. And yet it includes exactly the kinds of pieces that Beethoven said cannot be named but that he wanted to be credited to his variation account. I will return to this point.

In the Op. 35 variations, which brighten the ballet theme's initial tempo from Allegretto to Allegretto vivace, the Introduzione begins with an assertion of the keyboard's power and sonority in a *fortissimo* tonic chord with G on top – the same voicing as the symphony's opening chords. When the fermata fades, the *Basso del Tema* is sounded in its penumbra, *pianissimo* (Example 8.3). The bass notes of the ballet theme were quavers; here they are minims, looking less like a contredanse than like an antique 'white-note' topic. Quickly dispelled by staccatos in the faster note values of bars 5–8, and utterly forgotten in the empty bar and hammer blows, that style nonetheless resonates with the cantus-firmus presentation of every introductory variation, each labelled not as a variation but with the number of voices. Yet at the same time that the note values and contrapuntal treatment bespeak 'learned style', the gestural potential of the fermata becomes explicit: both the *a due* and the *a tre* variations embellish the moment with a brief cadenza, respectively Poco adagio and Adagio. (In the regular series of variations, only Variation 2 embellishes the fermata, with a lengthy Presto cadenza.) As the *Basso del Tema* rises into the treble *Tema*'s register, it also increases in dynamics, from *pp* to *p* to *f*.

The *Tema* is *piano* and *dolce*, more fully voiced than the piano reduction of the ballet published by Artaria; with two voices in the right hand, it would be somewhat harder to play. After the intensity of the *a quattro* in Op. 35, the *Tema* is a point of recognition and relaxation, a graceful oasis. Was a variation *theme* ever a point of arrival before this? The first variation is the only one in the set to maintain the dance bass. Beethoven's awareness of the origin of the theme in dance is also perhaps shown in the marking *cantabile* for the theme of Op. 34: one work dances, the other sings. Although the parts of Op. 35 most specifically analogous to the *Eroica* finale are the Introduction, the fugue, and the final slower variations, the minor mode variations also have a connection. The two in C minor – no. 6

and the Coda to no. 15, the Largo – reharmonise the theme at the same pitch level. The E♭ minor, no. 14, returns the *Basso del Tema* to the upper voice in a two-part counterpoint with a variation of the melody. Relevant segments for comparison in the symphony are the C minor fugue (bar 117), the variation that begins in B minor (bar 175) by reharmonising the theme at the same pitch level (before turning to D major), and the C major variation that turns to C minor (bar 257), sounding theme and bass in counterpoint just before the inverted fugue begins in the tonic.

The 'Movement Plan' and Its Meanings

To return to the point that some kind of transformation of Op. 35 was always going to become the finale, this means the symphony was directed specifically towards its variation theme as a complex of bass and treble.[27] It is plausible that Beethoven thought to reverse-engineer the first movement to create a sense of teleology on precisely that point. Not only was the theme of the first movement given a thirds and fifths motion and shape similar to the variation theme, but also the bass register as an arena for thematic action appears in both movements by way of Op. 35. Tellingly, the climactic thematic statements of first movement and finale appeared in the bass register, an idea deriving from the Op. 35 finale, where it served as one of Beethoven's uncounted variations. The finale sketches appear on pp. 70–91 of Landsberg 6, with a movement-plan or set of 'concept sketches' on the first four staves of p. 70.[28] Aspects of these staves and their relationship to the rest of the page have not been fully taken into account, and it is to this page that I now turn (see Illustration 8.1).

There are four musical ideas on these four lines, and ten words or word-combinations. They are, in order:

Staff 1: The first four notes of the bass line, written as one quaver per bar with rests, then the words 'Varia[tions] Clarinetto Solo Corno Solo'.

Staff 2: The word 'principio' is written under the staff and might refer to the bass line in staff 1. After it, and possibly unrelated to it, is a first attempt at the initial orchestral unison passage: five bars of semiquavers on the dominant of G minor, in the bass register, turning to the dominant of E♭, and ending with four repeated semiquavers on the dominant of E♭ major, in a higher and then lower octave. (The lower four notes occupy the beginning of the third staff.) After the final notes on the third staff, he continues *etc.* and *dopo*.

Staff 3: [continued]: Marked 'Fuga', the bass line as fugue subject with the first four notes in minims, and a version of the continuation that is hard to decipher. Lockwood points out that the fugue could be read either in C minor if treble clef or E♭ major if bass clef. However, at the end of the staff are the words

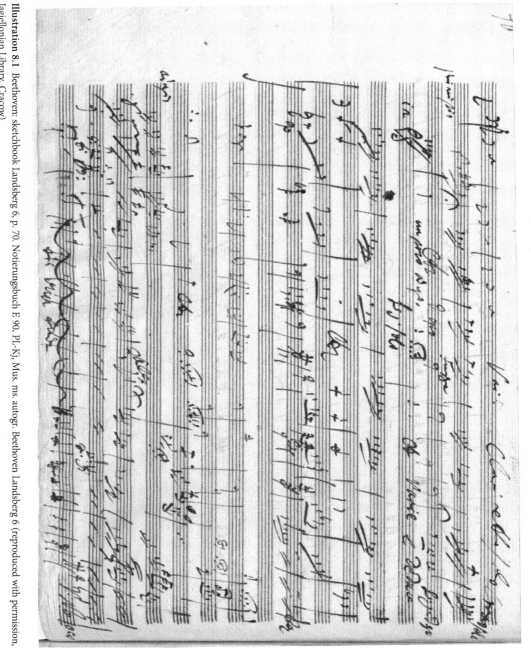

Illustration 8.1 Beethoven: sketchbook Landsberg 6, p. 70 Notierungsbuch E 90, PL-Kj, Mus. ms. autogr. Beethoven Landsberg 6 (reproduced with permission, Jagiellonian Library, Cracow)

'B[las] i[nstrumente] dopo', and on the next staff: 'In Es'. One could interpret this as 'Fugue in C minor – segments with wind instruments – then another fugue in E♭'. That is the final version; perhaps a different original reading was possible.

Staff 4: After the 'In Es', the words 'Un poco adagio' precede the first two bars of the hymn variation's melody, simplified, underneath which are the words 'B[las] i[nstrumente] solo'. After a large 'etc.', at the end of the stave in very clear cursive appear the words 'varie e deduce'.

There is much to interpret here. While Lockwood reads the lines as an 'internal' movement plan against the final version and sees Beethoven changing his mind about specifics, I see more a series of concept sketches, setting out the aspects that Beethoven thinks must be included.[29] If the finale was the 'invariant conception' towards which the entire symphony was heading, then the first four lines of p. 70 show what Lockwood elsewhere calls a 'conceptual image', the features considered essential however they might be fine-tuned:

1. The main theme of the movement is the bass line.

2. There will be variations.

3. Variations will feature one or more *concertante* instruments.

4. The introduction of the piece will be a faster line moving from G minor to V^7. (Again, it is unclear what music the word 'principio' refers to, though from the facsimile it appears closer to the bass theme.)

5. A fugue subject will be derived from the bass theme, as in Op. 35.

6. A slow variation will derive from the Prometheus theme of Op. 35, and will be played by solo wind(s).

7. The placement and emphatic size of the words 'varie e deduce' connect them to working out both the Fuga and the Poco adagio, meaning to both the bass and the treble themes. But the phrase exists in no one language, and is not even a polyglot combination of French, Italian and Latin; Lockwood renders the words as though they were French, with é as the last letter. 'Varie' is closest to having a meaning (varied or various) in all three languages; but as a participle comparable to 'varié' the other word should be *déduit, dedotto,* or *deductus; dēdūce* is imperative. (Perhaps Beethoven is telling himself what to do!) The connotations of both words are suggestive. *Varie* suggests variation, which refers to evolving methods of treating constant and changing elements of a theme, as in the Op. 35 variations. *Deduce,* as derived from *deducere,* leads us to 'deduction', which is less clear in a musical application. It opens a rich semantic field in contemporaneous and historically suggestive thought, and puts a different spin on the term 'concept sketch'. In some branches of fugal theory, the *comes* is deduced from the *dux,* and logical deduction reveals the seriousness of thought that the fugue requires. For the fifth edition of the *Dictionnaire de l'Académie Royale* (Paris, 1798), the meaning of 'déduire' (together with 'deduction', always referenced in terms of the Latin *deducere*)

adds another gradation of meaning to the definition 'to narrate, tell at length and in detail', namely inference: 'Il signifie encore inférer, tirer comme conséquence' (as in, 'Cette consequence est mal déduite'). The final paragraph of Reicha's introductory remarks to the *Trente-six fugues* reviled by Beethoven, begins, 'It is reserved for philosophers and to the geniuses who follow our epoch to draw out [*tirer*] all the consequences of this important system.'

Sulzer's article on 'Erfindung', in the encyclopedic *Allgemeine Theorie der schönen Künste* (consulted by Beethoven in autumn 1802),[30] divided invention into two types: in the first, already knowing the intention or goal of the work, the artist finds the means, the appropriate theme(s) needed to attain it; or in the second type, happening upon the theme, the artist 'discovers that it might be useful for attaining a specific goal, which is to say, that it is suitable for certain intentions'.[31] He concludes, 'The most important inventions probably do not arise through the first deductive manner described above, but rather by the second way: the main subject appears only dimly at first to the artist; he recognizes its importance and takes time to think about its contents so it can be set in its proper light.'[32] The process of drawing out the potentialities both of the theme and of the contexts in which it may be embedded became critical to Beethoven's symphonic thinking, or as Lockwood describes in the case of the *Eroica*, 'his most profound and searching effort to deepen the logic of his musical discourse'.[33] In that sense, Beethoven's sketch could almost be channelling the proemium to Ovid's *Metamorphoses*:

> My mind inclines me to speak about bodies changed into new forms. You, Gods – for you are the ones that alter these, and all other things – inspire my attempt and spin out my song in a continuous thread of words from the very beginning of the world down to my own times.[34]

The metaphor of *deducere carmen*, the poet's weaving of poem or song, is antique, but so strikingly connected to the drawing out of implications that it surfaced in later ages. Physically, one draws down the rudiments of thread (*deducere filum*) from the mass of wool, then spins them into thread (also *deducere*) and finally weaves the threads into a fabric. Extending the metaphor to rhetoric, Gianpiero Rosati notes that 'in rhetorical terms one could say that spinning corresponds to the *inventio* ('invention, devising'), weaving to the *dispositio* ('arrangement') and *elocutio* ('style')'.[35] Spinning an unbroken thread meant that its origins could be recognisable. What we have here in this process of 'deduction' is nothing less than *il filo*, the thread of continuity that Leopold Mozart and his contemporaries found so essential in creating comprehensible music.[36] Metaphors of spinning and weaving, invention and elaboration, turned melody and counterpoint, as warp and weft, into a continuous fabric (*textus*) of recognisable metamorphoses.[37]

Beethoven's theme and its initial treatment had already been invented, and the subjects of variation and fugue had already been worked through as its appropriate treatments for piano in Op. 35. Deducing new possibilities from the new goal – concluding a symphony intended to be heroic in scale – he had now to keep the thread going, weaving in material traces from his earlier works. As I have demonstrated elsewhere, separating his theme into individually profiled bass and melody enabled Beethoven to vary them in turn, using a model of alternating variations with which Haydn had been pre-eminently associated.[38] He varies them according to the questing sensibility of this symphony, which seeks to transform its materials gradually and to create long-term arcs of resolution (or of dissolution, in the case of the Marche funebre). Thus, in the finale Beethoven organises groupings of variations on bass and melody in successive waves that drop down to soft, thin textures and then rise registrally and dynamically to different forms of arrival. This method of structuring, highlighted by orchestral contrast, puts more focus on the bass at the beginning and on the melody at the end. Each wave highlights powers of invention and deduction: the first wave makes the creation of space and time a theme, the second wave keeps rhythmic action at the forefront, the last wave stages a confrontation between melody and bass, creating the climax in the bass register towards which the symphony has been heading and that is needed to bring the symphony to an end. After the climax, however, a kind of orchestral fantasia echoes a passage from the Marche funebre.

What we learn from the finale's concept sketch is that a figured passage moving from G minor to V^7 was going to introduce that element of fantasia already from the outset. Even if the drive to the dominant seventh is accomplished in barely five bars (and emphasised for another six), the rhythmic action involved in beginning before the beginning and concluding after the end forms one of the topics of the first page of finale sketches. Immediately after the words 'varie e deduce', staff 5 is a line of semiquaver triplet figuration. Triplets constitute an important marker of rhythmic identity in this symphony, forming the most intense climaxes in both the Marche funebre and the finale. Beethoven's first two symphonies had used triplets very sparingly: in the Andante of the First, and the first movement of the Second. In each movement of the *Eroica*, by contrast, triplets underlie extended sections as either broken-chord accompaniment (as in the Maggiore of the Marche funebre) or pulsing chords in which all voices may join (as in the second reprise of the D major Variation 5). Both the hair-raising A♭ major interruption in the second movement and the triumphant final bass variation in the finale generate a dynamic climax that dissolves

Example 8.4 Beethoven, Variations in E♭ major, Op. 35, finale. Andante, final variation, bars 164–8

into a passage of nearly identical off-beat semiquaver triplets (bars 160–80 and 408–30, respectively). The latter passage was a principal focus of the finale sketches, beginning already on the first page. With its chromatic rising bass line and treble rising by thirds, this part of the coda returns to a position of precariousness that the triplets help exacerbate. In Op. 35, triplet figuration is found only in Variations 2 and 13, but, forecasting the symphony, it accompanies the final Andante variation with the theme in the bass register (see Example 8.4), as well as the coda.

Making Alternating Variations Count

Bringing the fugue-variation more into the fabric of the series, instead of saving it for the finale, made it count: it gave Beethoven the means to create an immense cycle of alternating variations on the counterpoint-identified bass theme and the dance-identified melody. In what follows, I replace *Basso del Tema* and *T* with the more diagram-friendly A and B. Let us imagine the movement as a set of (numbered) variations using the criteria of counting that Beethoven wanted to apply to Op. 35, while at the same time ordering his doubled theme in the structure of alternating variations in successive waves.[39]

Wave 1: Introduction, A, A1, A2, B: The Creation of Space and Time, Bars 1–116
Introduction: orchestral fantasia, V/G minor to V^7 of E♭

By 'fantasia', I mean a freely constructed passage that may function to create an image (the original meaning of the term), induce mental movement to ready the scene (places, everyone!), stand outside the frame. Surely the movement could not begin flat-footed with the *Basso del Tema* after the exciting race that ended the Scherzo. The passage introduces the string vs. wind sonorities and echo effects that will pervade the finale, so that after the *fortissimo* tutti cadence, the *pizzicato* of the theme and the string textures of the first three variations are thrown into higher relief (see Example 8.5).

1. Theme [= *Basso del Tema*; pizzicato; with reorchestrated reprises] [A]
2. Variation 1 [3 voices, strings only, repeated-note countersubject] [A1]
3. Variation 2 [4 voices, strings only, with solo viola and solo cello in triplets] [A2]

The theme and first two variations set out the parameters of contrapuntal space, a direct descendent of Op. 35, and assign it to the strings. They also establish the temporal unit of the theme, so that later expansions and transitions make more of an effect.

4. Variation 3 [= *Tema*, fully scored] [B]

The effect of the winds playing the familiar melody in Variation 4, with violin figuration and the pizzicato bass supporting the dance accompaniment, turn this theme-variation (if we may call it that) into the goal of the first wave, as if the opening numbers have suddenly turned from black and white to technicolour. The addition of the melody and the orchestra has a prismatic effect, radiating colour everywhere. But what kind of piece instantly leaves its theme once it is reached? Op. 35 did not do that, of course. Now Beethoven threads the needle a different way, using the ascending figure from bar 9 of the theme, allowing a brief transition on a series of accented diminished-seventh chords to end the idyll.

Wave 2: A3, B1, A4, B2: Actions, Bars 117–276

5. Variation 4 [= Fugue in C minor, on the bass theme] [A3]

The second wave has a decidedly rhythmic cast: each one of its variations is strongly rhythmically profiled. The first fugue raises the temperature of the counterpoint present in the first wave: the space has been cleared for action with a stark inevitability. The first statement of the subject begins misleadingly, with the supposed countersubject from Variation 1 in cello, clarinet and bassoon. In fact, this is the end of the wind colour in the fugue's exposition, and that countersubject does not return, although it gives rise to two different versions of the real countersubject.

Example 8.5 Beethoven, *Eroica* Symphony, Op. 55, finale, bars, 1–15

Both have emphatic repeated quavers, which impart a martial air. The second countersubject, beginning in the violins in bar 131, pushes against those quavers with an expressively accented upper neighbour on the weak beat (bars 134, 136). The return of wind scoring in bar 138

offers opportunities for stretto. Dissonant stretto octaves beginning in bar 165 generate a *fortissimo* passage that resolves by augmented sixth to the next variation.

6. Variation 5 [B minor/D major] [B1]

Beginning as a theme reprise, the fifth variation turns into a virtuosic flute variation (Paul Bertagnolli calls it 'military fifing') without any bass register at all. Its final reprise is a tutti triplet climax with reiterated cadence. The action has moved from the individual to the group, each highly differentiated in register and self-assertion.

7. Variation 6 [G minor-C minor] [A4]

This dotted-rhythm march variation returns the *Basso del Tema*, reduced to its first four notes, to the centre of attention, and, even though there are no double bars, it sounds like the first segment since the *Tema* to have literal repeats. (Only the upward string flourishes become more thickly harmonised at each iteration.) As a characteristic piece, meaning a recognisable dance type (march, waltz) or referential style (pastorale, tempest), the Hungarian stylistic referents of its dotted rhythm in conjunction with a snaking melody give it considerable presence: it is often described as being the 'centre' of the movement. Rather it is a crest, notable for its singularities: the only variation entirely in minor, a single set of repetitive rhythms, in a single dynamic (forte), and single-mindedly reiterating the first four notes of the bass theme. As such it is a reminder of the bass's generating power, and the climax of Wave 2. It is the only variation to pause after its final (extended) cadence in G minor, with the horns holding over into the next variation. Its array of topics and styles – contrapuntal (Variation 5), virtuosic (Variation 6) and characteristic (Variation 8) – are matched by its parade of tonalities. As the crest of the second wave, the homophonic G minor march takes contrapuntal necessity away from the bass theme, thus allowing the melody to meet the bass as an equal in the transitional Variation 7 and even to appear as a syncopated countermelody in Variation 8, the inverted fugue.

8. Variation 7 [C major–C minor] [B2]

This shortened, transitional variation is the last one in a key other than the tonic, and forms a link between Wave 2 and Wave 3. In some ways it participates in both: perhaps it is an eddy. Beginning like the theme reprise in D major (Variation 5), Variation 7 turns after only eight bars into a minor-mode clash of the melody and bass as simultaneous counterpoints, exacerbated by the violin and viola sonorities of B and the oboe and horn sonorities of A. There are harmonic reasons to hear this variation

as part of a middle section in foreign tonalities. But as a transition between the climactic march variation and the beginning of the next fugal wave, it is comparable to the C minor coda (so labelled) of Op. 35 that concludes the regular series of variations. The coda also uses only the first reprise of the theme and ends on a half cadence in C minor. Beethoven must have been counting it.

Wave 3: A5, B3, B4: The Melody and Bass Engage Contrapuntally, and the Basso del Tema Bids Adieu, Bars 277–473

9. Variation 8 [Inverted Fugue in E♭] [A5]

The fugue that inverts the bass subject returns to the tonic E♭ major for the first time since the end of the first wave (Variation 4, the first appearance of the *Tema*, B). It is almost entirely for strings, and with the running semiquaver countersubject it connects across the work to variations chiefly for strings with an accelerating rhythm (A1, A2, A3, A5), making the alternations even more vivid. But the winds here are potent: first the flute and then the horns play the melodic theme in the syncopated version Beethoven introduced in the middle section of the fugue of Op. 35 (bar 51) (Example 8.6). In that piece, Beethoven had separated the double fugue from the inverted fugue, but here the scoring enables the B theme to encroach on the A theme's last bit of territory. As the subject reaches its own climactic statement with winds, horn and timpani playing *fortissimo*, a dominant pedal with layered sonorities leads to the next crest.

10. Variation 9 [Andante, hymn-like, winds, E♭ major] [B3]
11. Variation 10 [Andante, theme in bass register, E♭ major] [B4]

Example 8.6 Beethoven, *Eroica* Symphony, Op. 55, finale, bars 292–6

If the sudden stillness and spotlight on the first Andante variation completes the trajectory of the wave that began with Variations 7–8, the second Andante variation completes the trajectory of the entire symphony. But even that very clear teleology is not enough to end the symphony. Shockingly, the *Allgemeine musikalische Zeitung* reviewer of 1807 considered the entire Andante an 'interruption', just as he had taken the *Tema* for a 'countersubject' to the *Basso del Tema*. (Apparently neither Prometheus nor Op. 35 were in his mind.)

Coda: orchestral fantasia, mm. 396–473

Beethoven completes the movement with a passage that spins out of Variation 10, first as a codetta (with the version of triplet figuration noted on the concept sketch on Landsberg 7, p. 70), then with a partial variation in the subdominant (bar 403). The chromatic process that occupied so much of the sketchbook is a continuation of the A♭ variation in bar 409, expanding on the rhythmic motif of the fifth and sixth bar of the *Tema* (crotchet–crotchet–minim). Referring also to the repeated quavers in the *Basso del Tema*, the motif enhances the chromatic crescendo to G minor. Now we are in a better position to understand the offbeat repeated-note pattern that rhymes with the Marche funebre: it is the last thread of the bass and melody working together. The opening fantasia returns, now bypassing the *Basso* and heading straight for the *Tema*, so that the final *gradatio* of the coda, like that of Op. 35, is then able to produce what the *Allgemeine musikalische Zeitung* reviewer called 'a true jubilation of all the instruments'.

Beethoven might not have been happy with a total of only ten variations for the *Eroica* finale. Including the varied reprises (Variations 5, 9 and 10) brings the total to thirteen, and adding the final coda, with its truncated A♭ major variation, makes fourteen. And counting the *gradatio* of repeated iterations of the head of the theme, in increasingly exciting orchestral presentations, brings the total to fifteen. Could the number of official variations in Op. 35 have been a subliminal goal for Beethoven in the *Eroica*? Every variation, no matter how contrapuntally or melodically focused, finds its place in a continuous fabric that draws its threads from the series of ideas Beethoven considered most essential to his 'conceptual image': the *Basso del Tema* as subject; the *Tema* as agent of tempo change and bringer of wind colour; the fugue as variation; and several series of running and pulsating harmonies to draw even more tightly the sense of inevitability at the close of the symphony.

To Beethoven, the labour of writing variations included all manner of varying and deducing, of spinning and weaving the threads of his source material, depending on the genre. He railed against a rigid

conception of what counts as a variation, so there is no reason to adopt it as the model of what the *Eroica* is thought to be departing from. After an invention for dancing in the ballet came the separation of its bass and treble threads in the Variations. With the symphony came an elaborate re-weaving of their gestural possibilities, and new modes of thinking and action in an alternating pattern. Without Beethoven's words we might not have those metaphors, but at least we know what he was counting on.

Notes

1. Letter to Breitkopf & Härtel of late May/early June 1803, *Ludwig van Beethoven. Briefwechsel: Gesamtausgabe*, 7 vols., ed. S. Brandenburg (Munich: Henle, 1996–8) (BGA), 140, vol. 1, pp. 166–7.

2. L. Lockwood, 'Beethoven's Earliest Sketches for the *Eroica* Symphony', *Musical Quarterly*, 67 (1981), pp. 457–78; L. Lockwood, 'The Compositional Genesis of the *Eroica* Finale', in *Beethoven: Studies in the Creative Process* (Cambridge, MA: Harvard University Press, 1992), pp. 151–66. Lockwood introduced the term 'movement-plan' in 'Beethoven's Earliest Sketches', p. 460.

3. Lockwood, 'Earliest Sketches', p. 461. He asserts that the finale, 'in content rather than in form', was the 'springboard' to the symphony.

4. Erica Buurman notes that 'No other theme by Beethoven appeared across such a wide range of musical genres': stage music, social dance music, domestic music and serious concert music. E. Buurman, 'Beethoven's Compositional Approach to Multi-Movement Structures in His Instrumental Works' (PhD diss., University of Manchester, 2013), p. 108.

5. See M. A. Smart, 'Beethoven Dances: Prometheus and His Creatures in Vienna and Milan', in N. Mathew and B. Walton (eds.), *The Invention of Beethoven and Rossini: Historiography, Analysis, Criticism* (Cambridge: Cambridge University Press, 2013), pp. 210–35; P. Bertagnolli, *Prometheus in Music: Representations of the Myth in the Romantic Era* (London: Routledge, 2007), pp. 1–91; J. A. Rice, *Empress Marie Therese and Music at the Viennese Court, 1792–1807* (Cambridge: Cambridge University Press, 2003), pp. 248–52.

6. Rice, *Empress Marie Therese*, 249. There are convincing metric and rhythmic reasons to identify the theme as a contredanse, but Beethoven's separate publication of it as a contredanse is conclusive.

7. The sketchbook is digitized at https://digital.staatsbibliothek-berlin.de/ and transcribed in K. Mikulicz, *Ein Notierungsbuch von Beethoven aus dem Besitz der Preussischen Staatsbibliothek zu Berlin* (Leipzig: Breitkopf & Härtel, 1927). For the inventory, see D. Johnson, A. Tyson, R. Winter (eds.), *The Beethoven Sketchbooks: History, Reconstruction, Inventory* (Berkeley and Los Angeles, CA: University of California Press, 1985), pp. 107–11.

8. The review in *Journal für die elegante Welt*, 1 (April 1801), pp. 485–7 is translated in *The Critical Reception of Beethoven's Compositions by His German Contemporaries*, ed. W. M. Senner, R. Wallace and W. Meredith, 2 vols. (Lincoln, NE: University of Nebraska Press, 2001), vol. 1, pp. 215–16. The review in *Journal des Luxus und der Moden*, 16 (June, 1801), p. 303ff., dated 17 April 1801, is given in E. Voss, 'Schwierigkeiten im Umgang mit dem Ballett "Die Geschöpfe des Prometheus" von Salvator Viganò und Ludwig van Beethoven', *Archiv für Musikwissenschaft*, 53 (1996), pp. 38–40.

9. The most recent research shows that the ballet was written first, though it has often been assumed that Beethoven arranged his contredanse for the ballet. See K. Dorfmüller, N. Gertsch and J. Ronge, eds., *Ludwig van Beethoven: thematisch-bibliographisches Werkverzeichnis* (Munich: Henle, 2014), pp.232–3.

10. On dances as topics, see W. J. Allanbrook, *Rhythmic Gesture in Mozart: Le Nozze di Figaro and Don Giovanni* (Chicago: University of Chicago Press, 1983); E. McKee, 'Ballroom Dances of the Late Eighteenth Century', in *The Oxford Handbook of Topic Theory*, ed. D. Mirka (New York, NY: Oxford University Press, 2014).

11. Letter of Kaspar Karl van Beethoven to Breitkopf, 22 Jan 1803, BGA 125, vol. 1, pp. 149–51.

12. *Allgemeine musikalische Zeitung*, 6 (1804), cols. 338–45; trans. Senner et al., *The Critical Reception of Beethoven's Compositions*, vol. 1, pp. 190–4. Perhaps in mentioning the ballet, the Breitkopf-owned journal was atoning for not having acceded to Beethoven's wish to put 'theme from Prometheus' on the title page, as Beethoven had requested (BGA 140, vol. 1, pp. 166–7).

13. *Allgemeine musikalische Zeitung*, 9 (1807), cols. 319–33; trans. Senner et al., *The Critical Reception of Beethoven's Compositions*, vol. 2, pp. 26–31.

14. D. F. Tovey, *Essays in Musical Analysis: Chamber Music* (London: Oxford University Press, 1944), p. 124.

15. BGA 107, vol. 1, pp. 125–6.

16. Translations are my own unless otherwise noted.

17. BGA 108, vol. 1, pp. 126–7; translation modified from E. Anderson, *The Letters of Beethoven* (New York, NY: Norton, 1985), no. 62 (emphasis original), pp. 76–7.

18. *Joseph Haydn: Gesammelte Briefe und Aufzeichnungen*, ed. D. Bartha (Kassel: Bärenreiter), pp. 106–7.

19. He crossed out Reicha's name and identified him only as 'our neighbor the Gallo-Frank'. BGA 123, vol. 1, pp. 145–6.

20. On the opus concept, see E. Sisman, 'Six of One: The Opus-Concept in the Eighteenth Century', in S. Gallagher and T. F. Kelly (eds.), *The Century of Bach and Mozart* (Cambridge, MA: Harvard University Press, 2008), pp. 79–107.

21. On the smaller numbered list, see R. Nosow, 'Beethoven's Popular Keyboard Publications', *Music & Letters*, 78 (1997), pp. 56–76.

22. BGA 127, vol. 1, pp. 153–4; BGA 128, vol. 1, p. 155.

23. BGA 133, vol. 1, pp. 159–60.

24. Sisman, 'Six of One', 80–2.

25. B. Cooper, *Beethoven*. Master Musicians Series (Oxford: Oxford University Press, 2000), p. 127.

26. C. Reynolds, 'Beethoven's Sketches for the Variations in E♭, Op. 35', in *Beethoven Studies 3*, ed. A. Tyson (New York, NY: Norton, 1983), pp. 47–94, Appendix II.

27. See n. 1 and *Beethoven's Eroica Sketchbook: A Critical Edition*, 2 vols., ed. L. Lockwood and A. Gosman (Urbana, IL: University of Illinois Press, 2013). The following discussion of the sketches is indebted especially to the edition.

28. The term 'concept sketch' was introduced by Alan Tyson in 'The 1803 Version of Beethoven's *Christus am Oelberge*', *Musical Quarterly*, 56 (1970), p. 571.

29. Lockwood, 'Compositional Genesis', pp. 154–6.

30. R. Kramer, 'Beethoven and Carl Heinrich Graun', in *Beethoven Studies*, ed. A. Tyson (New York, NY: Norton, 1973), pp. 18–44.

31. J. G. Sulzer, *Allgemeine Theorie der schönen Künste* (Leipzig, 1771–4), vol. 1, pp. 338–40; trans. Thomas Christensen in *Aesthetics and the Art of Musical Composition in the German Enlightenment: Selected Writings of Johann Georg Sulzer and Heinrich Christoph Koch*, ed. and trans. T. Christensen and N. K. Baker (Cambridge: Cambridge University Press, 1995), p. 55.

32. Ibid., p. 61.

33. L. Lockwood, 'From Conceptual Image to Realization: Some Thoughts on Beethoven's Sketches', in *Genetic Criticism and the Creative Process: Essays from Music, Literature, and Theater*, ed. W. Kinderman and J. E. Jones (Rochester, NY: University of Rochester Press, 2009), 116.

34. Translation adapted from A. S. Kline (2000), www.poetryintranslation.com/PITBR/Latin/Metamorph.php (accessed 15 July, 2019): 'In nova fert animus mutates dicere formas / corpora; di, coeptis (nam vos mutatis et illa) / aspirate meis primaque ab origine mundi / ad mea perpetuum deducite tempora carmen.'

35. G. Rosati, 'Form in Motion: Weaving the Text in the *Metamorphoses*', in *Oxford Readings in Ovid*, ed. P. Knox (Oxford: Oxford University Press, 2006), pp. 334–50.

36. L. Mozart, Letter of 13 August 1778, in *Mozart: Briefe und Aufzeichnungen*, ed. W. Bauer and O. E. Deutsch (Kassel: Bärenreiter, 1962), no. 476, p. 444. Robert Gjerdingen devotes a chapter to this concept in *Music in the Galant Style* (New York, NY: Oxford University Press, 2007), pp. 367–97.

37. Pierpaolo Polzonetti explores some of these Ovidian metaphors for Haydn's musical thinking as well as for the referential awareness of Haydn's age: P. Polzonetti, 'Haydn and the

Metamorphoses of Ovid', in *Engaging Haydn: Culture, Context, and Criticism*, ed. M. Hunter and R. Will (Cambridge: Cambridge University Press, 2012), pp. 211–39.

38. E. Sisman, 'Tradition and Transformation in the Alternating Variations of Haydn and Beethoven', *Acta musicological*, 62 (1990), pp. 152–82; E. Sisman, *Haydn and the Classical Variation* (Cambridge, MA: Harvard University Press, 1993), pp. 255–60; E. Sisman, s.v. 'Variations', in *The New Grove Dictionary of Music and Musicians*, 2nd edn, ed. S. Sadie and J. Tyrrell (New York, NY: Macmillan 2001), vol. 26, pp. 284–326.

39. Haydn never numbered any of the variations in his alternating variation movements.

Reception

9 Who is the Hero? The Early Reception of the *Eroica*

BEATE ANGELIKA KRAUS

Beethoven's Third Symphony, first performed in 1804 at Prince Lobkowitz's city palace in Vienna, differs in many respects from the First and the Second Symphonies. This had consequences for its reception. When the first reviews of the work appeared in 1805, the symphony was not yet published. But it had already been performed together with the Second Symphony in Vienna at one of the concerts given by the wholesaler and banker Joseph von Würth. On this occasion a critic was ambivalent about the work: 'A very new symphony by Beethoven ... written in a very different style. This long, and extremely difficult to perform composition is actually a greatly elaborated, bold, wild Fantasia.'[1] Later, after another performance directed by Beethoven himself, the same critic went so far as to suggest some modifications and even that the work should be shortened:

> To be sure, this new work of B. has great and daring ideas, and, as one can expect from the genius of this composer, great power in the way it is worked out; but the symphony would improve immeasurably (it lasts an entire hour) if B. could bring himself to shorten it, and to bring more light, clarity, and unity into the whole ... Here, for example, in place of the Andante, there is a funeral march in C minor, which is subsequently developed fugally. But every fugal passage delights simply through a sense of order in apparent confusion ... The symphony was also lacking a great deal else that would have enabled it to have pleased overall.[2]

The first commentaries on the *Eroica* Symphony are very similar to those on other works by Beethoven, such as his piano sonatas or string quartets: there is a mixture of admiration and shock, and the critics are often equivocal. Soon after the publication of the symphony, reviews appeared that analyse all the movements of the symphony and even give musical examples to help the reader or the listener to recognise certain themes and passages. The very long review in the *Allgemeine musikalische Zeitung*, published in February 1807, is a good example of this kind of approach. The author defines his aim clearly:

> in this essay the aesthetic aspects will certainly not be completely passed over, but inquiry will be made primarily into the technical and mechanical ones. The fact that the author will in the process deliver a series of individual observations and

analyses that offer little to those who read only for entertainment, and will even seem dry to them, cannot be changed and lies in the nature of the thing. One must not always wish only to be entertained![3]

The critic's position is clear: Beethoven's music demands insight and comprehension, and the public will only appreciate the new work when they make the effort to study and understand it. The writer makes the point that even if listeners find some passages beautiful, and so might think that they do not need further explanation, they should nonetheless try to analyse the reason behind their aesthetic responses, to gain further insight. For example, concerning the Marcia funebre, the author addresses those who criticise extensive explanations: 'Let us just simply inform these people that this passage, the beautiful effect of which they hopefully will not deny, is actually a double fugue in which the countersubject is stated in half notes.'[4]

Very soon, reviewers dared not criticise Beethoven's *Eroica* Symphony. The *Allgemeine musikalische Zeitung* reports in April 1807: 'The most educated friends of art in the city [Leipzig] were assembled in great numbers, a truly solemn attentiveness and deathlike silence reigned . . . Each movement unmistakably had the effect that it should have, and each time at the end of the entire piece loud demonstrations of applause gave vent to well-founded enthusiasm.'[5] There are other reviews in the same style. Words used to describe the symphony include 'colossal', 'grand', 'rich', 'sublime' and 'ingenious'. Here the aesthetic of the sublime, which became important in the eighteenth century and later in the Romantic period, is clearly operating. The *Eroica* Symphony is placed in one of the most highly valued aesthetic categories of the time. The sublime, often associated with grandeur, refers to extraordinary experiences. A cultivated audience (and only such an audience was thought to be able to understand the sublimity of a work) would understand that there was a specific definition of the sublime, as distinct from the beautiful.

At times the praise might be even more extreme, for example, in the *Journal des Luxus und der Moden*:

Beethoven's new grand *Eroica* Symphony, the greatest, most original, most artistic and, at the same time, most interesting of all symphonies. It is a product that will remain an eternal monument to the outstanding genius, the rich imagination, the deep feeling, and the highly developed art of its composer. Indeed, one could offer it as a high ideal of this genre without thereby doing an injustice to the excellent symphonies of *Mozart* and *Haydn*, and without forgetting that this ingenious and grand work of art would itself not exist as it is now if these wonderful earlier symphonies (including Beethoven's earlier ones) had not led the way.[6]

Not Just for Pleasure

In 1809 Carl Maria von Weber began his ultimately incomplete novel *Tonkünstlers Leben (The life of a Composer)*, which occupied him on and off until 1820/1. Among the fragments of this novel is the description of a dream. In this dream, the assembled instruments of an orchestra are getting excited about a symphony by a contemporary composer, and are discussing his music. The composer is not named, but Beethoven is certainly meant. At the end of this scene, the director appears and the instruments have to perform Beethoven's *Eroica* Symphony. This text was first printed in a German journal, *Morgenblatt für gebildete Stände*, on 27 December 1809. An English translation was published in *The Harmonicon* in 1829. The dialogue between the director and the instruments begins as follows:

> At this moment, the Director entered the apartment; all was agitation and alarm, and the different instruments huddled into the corner together; they knew whose powerful hand could call forth and combine their powers.
>
> 'What!' cried he, 'again in open rebellion! Now, mind me – the *Sinfonia Eroica* of Beethoven is about to be performed; and every one of you who can move key or member will be then put in active requisition'.
>
> 'Oh, for heaven's sake, anything but that!' was the general exclamation.
>
> 'Rather', said the Viola, 'let us have an Italian opera; then we may occasionally nod'.
>
> 'Nonsense!' replied the Director, 'you must accomplish the task. Do you imagine that, in these enlightened times, when all rules are set at nought, and all difficulties cleared at a bound, a composer will, out of compliment to you, cramp his divine, gigantic, and high-soaring fancies? Thank heaven, there is no longer any question as to regularity, perspicuity, keeping, and truth of expression; these are left to such old-fashioned masters as Gluck, Handel, and Mozart. No! attend to the materials of the most recent symphony that I have received from Vienna, and which may serve as a recipe for all future ones'.[7]

This text has elements typical of the early criticism of Beethoven's works: the execution is considered very difficult, so the performers have to be skilled (see also Chapter 11). This is certainly not the kind of music one could play just for pleasure and without rehearsal. It is the music of a giant, worth the effort: one should accept the challenge to discover and understand the work. On the other hand, this means that 'true' performers of and listeners to Beethoven's music – a small elite of connoisseurs – can make fun of those who are too lazy or too stupid to understand the *Eroica* Symphony. Thus Beethoven's Third Symphony polarised the public at an early stage. One example of this polarisation, from a time when the public already knew eight of Beethoven's symphonies, can be found in the *Berliner allgemeine musikalische Zeitung* in 1824:

> The royal general music directorship is to be thanked for the great satisfaction given by the magnificent *Eroica* Symphony of Beethoven, performed with the utmost precision at the concert that it organized on 19 January [in Berlin]. The audience, small in number but thoroughly sensitive to art, took up this rare gift with the greatest of thanks, which could be recognized in the loudest possible applause accorded to the creator of these harmonies and to the royal orchestra.[8]

Again, a certain exclusiveness is apparent in this review. The critic underscores this aspect of Beethoven's music, and the high degree of musicianship and sensitivity of the relatively small number of listeners who can appreciate that it is a privilege to attend the performance of such a masterpiece. Beethoven's music becomes a gift, and the public is grateful.

Whenever there was a crowd, rather than a small audience, and the musicians seemed not only challenged but also happy to perform the *Eroica* Symphony, these aspects were typically mentioned specifically by the critic. A review in the *Allgemeine musikalische Zeitung*, published in January 1811, draws attention to just such an exceptional occasion, which took place in Berlin:

> The second half was filled by Beethoven's grand, ingenious work, the *Sinfonia eroica*, to the lively satisfaction of the extremely numerous listeners, who listened with heightened attention until the final chord. It was performed by the orchestra with unmistakable enjoyment and love, with as much precision and fire, and yet also with as much delicacy as it demands if, with its length of fifty minutes, it is to bring about such an effect upon a mixed public.[9]

The *Eroica* as Political Statement

In addition to purely musical understandings of Beethoven's music, there were various other critical approaches, which included viewing the *Eroica* Symphony as a political statement. Apart from the length and new style of the work, other things also aroused the curiosity of the public: the title raised the question of who might be the hero behind the mask of a *Sinfonia eroica*. The second movement, Marcia funebre, in particular, raised the question: what was the loss that occasioned this mourning?

The title of the symphony, published during Beethoven's lifetime, gave rise to various interpretations. The original edition, published in parts in Vienna in October 1806 by Kunst- und Industrie-Comptoir, clearly states the intention of celebrating the memory of a great man: 'Sinfonia Eroica . . . composta per festeggiare il sovvenire di un grand Uomo.' This is also the title on the score published in Bonn and Cologne in 1822 by Simrock. But another score, published in London in March/April 1809 by Cianchettini & Sperati, is titled *Sinfonia Eroica composta per celebrare la morte d'un*

Eroe, the death of a hero. While 'grand homme' (a great man) might refer to greatness of mind, 'la morte d'un Eroe' implies a military hero, killed in battle. As we shall see, certain writers proposed a specific background to this difficult new symphony by trying to identify an actual hero, or an instance of heroism, that Beethoven perhaps had in mind. In this way, Beethoven's Third Symphony became a piece of programme music, although it was to prove almost impossible to find an interpretation that would include all four movements.

In England, a connection between the work and Napoleon seems to have been accepted as a fact, and the Marcia funebre was a focal point. A review published in 1836 in *The Musical World*, for example, underscored the idea that Beethoven's music required an educated public and that listeners might be overwhelmed by its effects; then the critic focuses on the Marcia funebre:

> The Sinfonia Eroica, which, but for his worthless ambition, would have been identified with Napoleon, is as massive in construction, and gorgeous in detail, as any descriptive poem of the same character, that ever was composed. A person of imagination, and unacquainted even with the commonest musical constructions, described the effect of the 'Marcia funebre,' what to his sense of seeing would be a multitudinous procession clad in *dark purple*. Such relative criticism (if criticism it may be called) may be nonsense to the man of musical science; the poet and the painter, however, would at once appreciate the full effect which that noble movement conveyed to the mind of this unlearned listener. The whole of this symphony was played as the best musical audience in the world deserve to have it played to them.[10]

In the same year, 1836, *The Musical World* published an anecdote about Beethoven dedicating his Third Symphony to Napoleon:

> It is not generally known that Beethoven intended to have dedicated his 'Sinfonia Eroica' to Buonaparte, entitling it the 'Sinfonia Napoleon.' When the news, however, arrived, that the *First Consul* was about to assume the title of *Emperor*, the bluff musician exclaimed: 'Oh! he is making an emperor of himself, is he? then he is no better than *the rest of them*: – He shall not have my symphony!' – Shocking old radical! No wonder he died poor.[11]

Beethoven's supposed reaction to Napoleon was disseminated by Franz Gerhard Wegeler and Ferdinand Ries in their *Biographische Notizen über Ludwig van Beethoven*, published in 1838, after which the anecdote was quoted many times and in several languages. Ries, a former student of Beethoven, had lived in London between 1813 and 1824, and he may have already told this story in England. There is also a letter written by Ries in Vienna in October 1803 to the publisher Nikolaus Simrock in Bonn, in which he reports, concerning the Third Symphony: 'He [Beethoven] is very much inclined to dedicate it to Bonaparte; if he does not do so,

because Lobkowitz wants to have it for half a year and to give 400 gulden, then he will entitle it Bonaparte.'[12] This account fits closely with Beethoven's first intentions as reported in *The Musical World*. As we shall see, though, it is unlikely that the scene happened exactly as recounted by Ries:

> In this symphony Beethoven had thought about Bonaparte during the period when he was still First Consul. At that time Beethoven held him in the highest regard and compared him to the greatest Roman consuls. I myself, as well as many of his close friends, had seen this symphony, already copied in full score, lying on his table. At the very top of the title page stood the word 'Buonaparte' and at the very bottom 'Luigi van Beethoven', but not a word more. Whether and with what the intervening space was to be filled I do not know. I was the first to tell him the news that Bonaparte had declared himself emperor, whereupon he flew into a rage and shouted: 'So he too is nothing more than an ordinary man. Now he also will trample all human rights underfoot, and only pander to his own ambition; he will place himself above everyone else and become a tyrant!' Beethoven went to the table, took hold of the title page at the top, ripped it all the way through, and flung it on the floor. The first page was written anew and only then did the symphony receive the title *Sinfonia eroica*.[13]

Anton Schindler also underscored the composer's political ideas and his relationship with Napoleon. Schindler had much influence on Beethoven's reception, since he claimed to have been very close to Beethoven in Vienna; he claimed that many details that subsequently appear in his Beethoven biography were communicated to him by Beethoven himself. In the first edition of his biography of Beethoven, published in 1840, Schindler wrote of Beethoven's politics: 'In his political sentiments Beethoven was a republican; the spirit of independence natural to a genuine artist gave him a decided bias that way.'[14] Schindler goes on to argue that Beethoven believed that Napoleon was the man to republicanise France, and therefore in autumn 1802 he planned to pay homage to Napoleon in a grand instrumental work. Regarding the *Eroica* Symphony, Schindler brings into play the French General Jean-Baptiste Bernadotte, who had been in Vienna: 'The original idea of that Symphony is said to have been suggested by General Bernadotte, who was then French ambassador at Vienna and had a high esteem for our Beethoven.'[15] Then Schindler reports that, having finished his Third Symphony, Beethoven had intended to send a handwritten copy of it to Paris. His version of the story continues:

> A fair copy of the musical work for the first consul of the French republic, the conqueror of Marengo, with the dedication to him, was on the point of being despatched through the French embassy to Paris, when news arrived in Vienna

that Napoleon Bonaparte had caused himself to be proclaimed Emperor of the French. The first thing Beethoven did on receiving this intelligence was to tear off the title-leaf of this Symphony, and to fling the work itself, with a torrent of execrations against the new French Emperor, against the 'new tyrant', upon the floor, from which he would not allow it to be lifted. It was a long time before Beethoven recovered from the shock, and permitted this work to be given to the world with the title of 'Sinfonia Eroica', and underneath it this motto: 'Per festegiare il sovvenire d'un gran uomo'. I shall only add that it was not till the tragic end of the great Emperor at St. Helena, that Beethoven was reconciled with him, and sarcastically remarked, that, seventeen years before, he had composed appropriate music to this catastrophe, in which it was exactly predicted, musically, but unwittingly – alluding to the Dead March in that Symphony.[16]

Schindler's story was reprinted in later editions of his biography, and it was translated into many other languages. For a long time the public did not question its truth, possibly because certain details of this story seem to be close to those that Wegeler and Ries had already published in 1838. In fact Schindler did not have any contact with Beethoven until 1822. So he may have been a witness during Beethoven's last five years, but certainly not in the period of Bernadotte's visit to Vienna and the *Eroica* Symphony.

A crucial detail cannot be confirmed by the the material evidence: Ries's anecdote that Beethoven tore off the entire sheet of the title page of the score is not supported by the title page of the existing copy of the symphony. On this title page, the title originally read 'Sinfonia grande / intitolata Bonaparte / del Sigr / Louis van Beethoven'. Beethoven removed the second line ('intitolata Bonaparte') by heavy erasure, but later he added in pencil the words: 'geschrieben auf Bonaparte' (written on/about Bonaparte).[17] In a letter written in Vienna on 26 August 1804 to the publisher Breitkopf & Härtel in Leipzig, Beethoven wrote: 'die *Simphonie* ist eigentlich betitelt *Ponaparte*' (the true title of the symphony is Ponaparte).[18]

Regarding the reviews connecting Napoleon and the *Eroica* Symphony, one point was never really discussed: there is a distinction to be made between choosing Napoleon as the title or subject of the work (which has to do with the inspiration, content and interpretation of the work) and choosing Napoleon as the intended dedicatee. The two matters became blurred in the reception history. But Beethoven always dedicated his large-scale works to a person who could be useful for his career and/or pay for the dedication. What is clear is that ultimately, in the case of the *Eroica* Symphony, this person was Prince Franz Joseph Maximilian von Lobkowitz.

The French Tradition

The way the public and critics understand a new work of music is always influenced by their own cultural heritage and the context in which the music is performed. In this respect, the French reception of Beethoven's symphonies was different from that in other European cities, and the *Eroica* Symphony is a prime example. In France there was a strong tradition of funeral marches, especially after the French Revolution. They were played in public, and it is clear that the political aim was not only to mourn the death of a person but also to salute the victims of the Revolution and to underline the hope of a glorious future. Pathos combined with a vibrant character, expressed in a relatively fast tempo suggesting a people on the move, typifies this French tradition. Examples are the famous *Marche lugubre* by François-Joseph Gossec (1790) or Luigi Cherubini's *Hymne funèbre sur la mort du General Hoche* (1797).[19] Beethoven knew about this tradition. The third movement of his Sonata Op. 26 in Ab major (1801/2), for instance, is entitled *Marcia funebre sulla morte d'un Eroe*. Later, an arrangement of this movement was played in Paris during the transfer of the mortal remains of Marshal Jean Lannes to the Panthéon. Lannes, a personal friend of Napoleon, had been fatally wounded in the battle of Aspern-Essling near Vienna in 1809.

François-Antoine Habeneck's performances of Beethoven's music in Paris at the *Société des Concerts du Conservatoire* after 1828 were particularly important in early Beethoven reception. This excellent orchestra performed all the symphonies of Beethoven regularly and at a high level, and the *Eroica* Symphony was the first piece played in the opening concert of the series on Sunday 9 March 1828. One can fairly say that this orchestra was founded upon the *Eroica* Symphony. On Saint Cecilia's day in 1826 Habeneck had invited some musicians to come to his home for lunch and to bring their instruments. The music he had prepared for informal rehearsal was Beethoven's Third Symphony, and the musicians were so fascinated that they nearly forgot their meal.[20]

The Marcia funebre was always in the foreground and served as a key for understanding the work. Often the Marcia funebre was performed separately, in concert and on special occasions; this led Hector Berlioz to demand in 1838 that the symphony always be played in its entirety.[21] Other reviewers confirmed that the public admired only this movement. For example, Joseph d'Ortigue wrote in 1844 that the symphony 'seems too long and, except the Marche funèbre, it makes little effect' on the listening public.[22] This third movement was admired as a 'hymn of sorrow and pain ... a funeral song'.[23] And François-Joseph Fétis noted: 'A delightful melancholia reigns in the first motive of the funeral

march.'[24] Thus the question arose of the subject, and the trigger event, behind the work.

Berlioz insisted that the title of the work was 'Symphonie héroïque pour célébrer l'anniversaire de la mort d'un grand homme', and even called it an 'oraison funèbre' (funeral oration). His interpretation reads as follows:

> It is a mistake to truncate the title that the composer provided for the symphony. It reads: *Heroic symphony to celebrate the anniversary of the death of a great man.* As will be seen, the subject here is not battles or triumphal marches, as many people, misled by the mutilation of the title, might expect; but rather deep and serious thoughts, melancholy memories, ceremonies of imposing grandeur and sadness, in short a *funeral oration* for a hero. I know not a single example in music of a style where sorrow has been so unfailingly conveyed in forms of such purity and such nobility of expression.[25]

In the following review from 1837, Berlioz evoked a concrete programme, quoting verses from Virgil's *Aeneid*, and referring to the funeral procession of young Pallas:

> The funeral march is a drama in its own right. One believes one finds there a translation of Virgil's beautiful verses on the funeral procession of the young Pallas: '*The richest spoils, gifts from the Laurentine battle, surround the last bed of the warrior; then follow chariots drenched with Rutulian blood; and the unhappy old man Acoetes, marring his face with his nails, bruising his chest with his fists; behind went the war-horse, Aethon, without his trappings, with hanging mane, follows the corpse of his master, wetting his face with great tear drops.*' The ending in particular is deeply moving. The theme of the march returns, but now in a fragmented form, interspersed with silences, and only accompanied by three *pizzicato* notes in the double basses. When these tatters of the sad melody, left on their own, bare, broken and lifeless, have collapsed one after the other onto the tonic, the wind instruments utter a final cry, the last farewell of the warriors to their companion in arms, and the whole orchestra fades away on a *pianissimo* pause.[26]

Such references to antiquity are common in the French reception of the *Eroica*. In 1835 the *Gazette musicale de Paris* gave the following summary of a concert: 'The *Eroica* symphony . . . reappeared greater and nobler and more admirable of ancient grief than ever.'[27] In French dictionaries, the terms 'héros' and 'héroïque' refer to antique heroes such as Hercules or Alexander the Great, excelling in physical strength and bold military undertakings; so this kind of interpretation is not surprising.[28] We can observe the same construction from commentators in other Romance languages: in Italy in 1884, the critic Ippolito Valetta interpreted the Marcia funebre of the *Eroica* Symphony as the funeral of an ancient Roman hero.[29]

Berlioz, an influential writer as well as composer, was among the few who did not merely concentrate on the interpretation of the funeral march. He analysed all the symphonies of Beethoven in long articles, mostly published in the *Revue et Gazette musicale de Paris*. He began his description of the beginning of the *Eroica* Symphony as follows:

> The first movement is in triple time and in a tempo that is almost that of a waltz. What could be more serious and more dramatic than this *Allegro*? The energetic theme on which it is built is not at first presented in its complete form. Contrary to normal practice, the composer initially provides only a glimpse of his melodic idea, which is only revealed in its full power after a few bars' introduction.[30]

Berlioz's style of writing about the music is meant to arouse interest. He understood that listeners might be surprised by certain aspects of Beethoven's music, and so he explained points where Beethoven did not meet the audience's expectations. In this way, Berlioz was not only one of the most important critics in the early reception of Beethoven but also an influential teacher. An example of his explanatory stance is found in his comments on the meaning of the Scherzo:

> The third movement is entitled *Scherzo*, following normal practice. The Italian word means play, or jest. It is hard to see, at first sight, how this kind of music can find a place in this epic composition. It has to be heard to be understood. The piece does indeed have the rhythm and tempo of a *Scherzo*; these are games, but real funeral games, constantly darkened by thoughts of grief, games of the kind that the warriors of the *Iliad* celebrated around the tombs of their leaders.
>
> Even in his most imaginative orchestral developments Beethoven has been able to preserve his serious and sombre colouring, the deep sadness which of course had to predominate in such a subject.[31]

True to French interpretations of the *Eroica* Symphony, Berlioz invokes ancient culture with his reference to the *Iliad*. Treating the work as comparable to outstanding examples of past cultures gives a sense not only of its greatness but also its authenticity. In his conclusion Berlioz emphasises that Beethoven's Third Symphony, with its poetic form, is in his eyes one of the composer's very greatest works. As it is typical of Berlioz, he reaches for depth of sentiment as a measure of greatness, and his own personal impressions are linked to thoughts of the ancient world when he says: 'Un sentiment de tristesse grave et pour ainsi dire antique me domine toujours pendant l'exécution de cette symphonie' ('Whenever this symphony is performed I am overcome with feelings of deep and as it were ancient sadness').[32] One could conclude that he was trying to establish the canonic status of the work, by appealing to the longevity of the feelings it inspires, even if the work itself was relatively new and not yet really understood by the public.

For a long time, the possible connection between the *Eroica* Symphony and Napoleon Bonaparte was completely ignored in French reception. The first French review of a concert in which the name of Bonaparte was quoted appeared in 1841 in *Le Monde musical*. The author mentions Napoleon's burial in Les Invalides in Paris in December 1840, and suggests what Beethoven's attitude to the occasion might have been:

> No doubt that if the great German composer had lived until this day, in the presence of the enthusiasm with which France had hailed the return of the glorious remains of her emperor, he would have returned his symphony to its first destination. And which music other than this sublime funeral march could have welcomed with more dignity the mortal remains of Napoleon at their entry into the chapel of Les Invalides![33]

The author recalls Ries's anecdote, but does not discuss whether the *Eroica* Symphony had been written for or about Napoleon. Rather, the critic seems to construct a posthumous reconciliation between Beethoven and Napoleon, writing that the *Eroica* Symphony would have been a wonderfully appropriate piece of music, in the tradition of the French *Marche lugubre*, for a ceremony like that of the funeral of a former statesman or emperor.

Napoleon and Other Heroes

In 1841 Richard Wagner published his interpretation of the *Eroica* Symphony in France, as 'Une Soirée Heureuse, Fantaisie sur la musique pittoresque' in the *Revue et Gazette musicale de Paris* (this French text was the first version to be printed).[34] The fact that young Beethoven was once fascinated by the young and victorious Napoleon, and thus inspired to write this work, was a new idea for the French public. Wagner underlined that there was no reason to understand the music as a 'symphonie biographique de Bonaparte' ('biographical symphony of Bonaparte').[35] This work itself was a feat, according to Wagner, and thus Beethoven was himself the hero of this heroic deed.

In Austria, another hero joined the reception story: Louis Ferdinand, Prince of Prussia (1772–1806). In 1843 The *Allgemeine Wiener Musik-Zeitung* published a contribution to the mythology around Beethoven's heroic symphony ('Zur Schicksalsgeschichte der heroischen Symphonie von Beethoven'). The article is about a cavalier who, after having seen that the public did not understand Beethoven's new symphony, had already left Vienna for one of his country houses when Prince Louis Ferdinand announced his visit. In order to surprise the Prince, another performance

of the symphony was organised, and Louis Ferdinand, very moved and fascinated by this new music, asked to listen to the work a second time. After this encore, Louis Ferdinand, even more impressed, asked if, after a break for the musicians, he could hear the symphony again, and thus it was performed for the third time. The article concludes by reporting that the day after this success Beethoven received a gift from the cavalier, but that the Prince would never hear this music again, because a short time later he died a heroic death.[36]

The unnamed cavalier in this article was Prince Franz Joseph Maximilian von Lobkowitz, who was at Raudnitz castle (Roudnice) in Bohemia when Louis Ferdinand of Prussia joined him and attended a performance of the yet unpublished *Eroica* Symphony. Louis Ferdinand, a brilliant pianist and talented composer, had met Beethoven several times since 1796; and he visited Prince Lobkowitz at the end of September 1806 before he re-joined the army. He was killed by a French marshal on 10 October 1806 during a battle near Saalfeld. Even though the *Allgemeine Wiener Musik-Zeitung* writer did not conclude that Prince Louis Ferdinand was the intended dedicatee when the *Eroica* Symphony was published later in the same month, the Prince's name still appears in the lengthy journal article. Later authors, among them Walther Brauneis, believed that the *Eroica* Symphony, while officially dedicated by Beethoven to Prince Lobkowitz, was somehow anonymously dedicated to Prince Louis Ferdinand.[37] Surely Beethoven could not have had in mind Prince Louis Ferdinand's death in 1806 when he composed his Third Symphony, since it had long since been publicly premiered in Vienna.

Apart from published interpretations of the work, other attempts have been made to construct a political context for the *Eroica* Symphony. Otto Jahn, in his handwritten records, refers to Dr Joseph Bertolini (1774–1857), one of Beethoven's doctors in Vienna. Bertolini had been the student and assistant of Beethoven's doctor and friend Johann Baptist Malfatti and so came into contact with Beethoven. According to Jahn's notice from 1852, Bertolini recorded that Beethoven first had the idea of composing the *Eroica* Symphony when he heard about Bonaparte's campaign in Egypt; he also observed that the rumour of Admiral Horatio Nelson's death in the battle of Abukir was the origin of the funeral march.[38] In fact, Nelson (1758–1805) was only wounded on 1 August 1798; it seems very unlikely that this event influenced the composition of a work that Beethoven began to sketch no earlier than 1802/3.

In the notes of Carl Czerny (1791–1857), who knew Beethoven personally, Dr Bertolini is again invoked. Czerny wrote: 'After the indication of his close friend for many years, Dr Bertolini, the first idea for the *Sinfonia*

eroica was given by the death of the English *General Abercrombie*.'[39] Ralph Abercromby had defeated the French in the battle of Alexandria on 21 March 1801, where he was wounded, and died on 28 March 1801. Despite the fact that this was not when Beethoven started composing his Third Symphony, and that Bertolini attended Beethoven only from 1806, there was a second effort to understand the *Eroica* as tribute in honour of Napoleon's English war opponents when he was still first consul. However, it seems that this idea did not really convince the critics and the public, even though the possible connection to Napoleon was often discussed. Czerny wrote that perhaps Beethoven, known for his changeable mood, may have had in mind a connection between the *Eroica* Symphony and Napoleon.[40] Since Abercromby and Nelson are both key figures in British history, one might assume that English authors would be interested in making any possible connection between them and Beethoven's music. Yet British music critics did not make any connections at all between Beethoven's *Eroica* Symphony and British history.

The first half of the nineteenth century produced not only many performances of the *Eroica* Symphony, but also manifold documents of its reception. On the one hand, there were authors specifically interested in music, who studied the score and tried to help others to understand Beethoven's art of composing. On the other hand, there were writers – among them composers such as Weber, Berlioz and Wagner – who gave literary interpretations, and did not write as music experts in the narrow sense. In doing so, they communicated to their readers their own understandings of what constitutes a musical masterpiece, and their own reception of Beethoven's work in particular.

There has always been a strong desire to understand music by relating it to biography – and this tendency increased as the nineteenth century wore on. In the case of the *Eroica* Symphony the result was a focus on the title, and on the unnamed great man or hero (which is perhaps also the case with the Piano Sonata, Op. 26). Today, the public is still interested in such stories, factual or fictional, which reappear in CD booklets, films and concert programmes and in biographical literature. They have made Beethoven's Third Symphony one of the best-known works of classical music. This thirst to link works and biography means that even today the *Marcia funebre* remains a focus of interest, like the finale of Beethoven's Ninth Symphony and the first movement of the *Sonata quasi una fantasia*, Op. 27, No. 2.

The early reception of Beethoven's *Eroica* proves to be a complex phenomenon, in which several strands intertwine: especially influential in this reception history was the emergence of new forms of organisation in musical life, with new orchestral cultures and new audiences interested in

understanding music through listening and reading. The question of performance practice is linked to these changing circumstances. The changing image of Beethoven, and the status of his works, played and play an important role in determining performance practices. It makes quite a difference, especially to the Marcia funebre, if it is played in the manner of French revolutionary music, or in a sad and slow tempo, close to the funeral procession after Siegfried's death in Wagner's *Twilight of the Gods* (*Götterdämmerung*). It makes a difference for the performance practice, and for the listeners, if the symphony is understood as part of a political statement in the time of Napoleonic wars, or if it is associated with the idea of the sublime and of timeless grandeur. As the reception of the *Eroica* Symphony changes, so too does performance practice, and vice versa.

Notes

1. *Allgemeine musikalische Zeitung,* 7 (1805), col. 321. Translations are by the author unless stated.
2. Ibid., cols. 501–2; trans. R. Wallace in W. Senner, R. Wallace and W. Meredith (eds.), *The Critical Reception of Beethoven's Compositions by His German Contemporaries,* vol. 2 (Lincoln and London: University of Nebraska Press, 2001), p. 17.
3. *Allgemeine musikalische Zeitung,* 9 (1807), col. 322; trans. R. Wallace, *Critical Reception,* p. 20.
4. Ibid., col. 325; trans. R. Wallace, *Critical Reception,* p. 25.
5. Ibid., col. 497; trans. R. Wallace, *Critical Reception,* p. 33.
6. *Journal des Luxus und der Moden,* 22 (1807), p. 444; trans. R. Wallace, *Critical Reception,* p. 35–6 (emphasis original).
7. *The Harmonicon,* 7 (1829), pp. 32–3.
8. *Berliner allgemeine musikalische Zeitung,* 1 (1824), p. 41; trans. R. Wallace, *Critical Reception,* p. 40.
9. *Allgemeine musikalische Zeitung,* 13 (1811), col. 66; trans. R. Wallace, *Critical Reception,* p. 38.
10. *The Musical World, A Weekly Record of Musical Science, Literature, and Intelligence,* 1 (1836), p. 173.
11. Ibid., p. 10.
12. *Ludwig van Beethoven. Briefwechsel: Gesamtausgabe,* 7 vols., ed. S. Brandenburg (Munich: Henle, 1996 -8) (BGA), 165, vol. 1, p. 190.
13. F. G. Wegeler and F. Ries, *Biographische Notizen über Ludwig van Beethoven* (Koblenz: K. Bädeker, 1838), p. 78; trans. F. Noonan in *Remembering Beethoven. The Biographical Notes of Franz Wegeler and Ferdinand Ries* (London: Deutsch, 1988), p. 68.
14. A. Schindler, *Biographie von Ludwig van Beethoven* (Münster: Aschendorff, 1840), p. 56; trans. in I. Moscheles, *The Life of Beethoven, Including His Correspondence with His Friends, Numerous Characteristic Traits, and Remarks on His Musical Works,* vol. I (London: Henry Colburn, 1841), p. 89.
15. Ibid., p. 55; trans. Moscheles, *Life of Beethoven,* p. 88.
16. Ibid., pp. 56–7; trans. Moscheles, *Life of Beethoven,* pp. 90–1.
17. See Beethoven's score, copied by Benjamin Gebauer, housed in Vienna, Gesellschaft der Musikfreunde, A 20; Ludwig van Beethoven, *Symphonie Nr. 3 Es-Dur op. 55 "Eroica", Partitur-Manuskript (Beethovens Handexemplar), Vollständige Faksimile-Ausgabe im Originalformat,* vol. 1, ed. O. Biba (Vienna: Gesellschaft der Musikfreunde, 1993).
18. BGA 188, vol. 1, p. 219.
19. See F. Robert, 'Beethoven en France', *Europe,* 48 (1970), p. 119.
20. A. Elwart, *Histoire de la Société des Concerts du Conservatoire Impérial de Musique* (Paris: Librairie Castel, 1864), p. 62.
21. *Revue et Gazette musicale de Paris,* 5 (1838), p. 34.
22. *La France musicale,* 7 (1844), p. 73.

23. *Revue musicale*, 15 (1835), p. 230.

24. Ibid., p. 26.

25. *Gazette musicale de Paris*, 4 (1837), p. 122.

26. Ibid., p. 122.

27. *Revue et Gazette musicale de Paris*, 2 (1835), p. 31.

28. See, for example, A. Furetière, *Dictionnaire Universel, contenant généralement tous les mots françois, tant vieux que modernes, & les Termes de toutes les Sciences et les Arts: Divisé en trois tomes*, 3 vols. (The Hague and Rotterdam: Leers, 1690); *Dictionnaire de l'Académie Française*, Seconde Édition (Paris: Coignard, 1696); *Encyclopédie, ou Dictionnaire Raisonné des Sciences, des Arts et des Métiers, par une Société de Gens de Lettres* (Neufchastel: Faulche, 1765); E. Littré, *Dictionnaire de la langue française, contenant la nomenclature la plus étendue*, 4 vols. (Paris: Hachette, 1863–72).

29. See W. Witzenmann, 'Zur italienischen Beethoven-Rezeption des Ottocento: Eine Zwischenbilanz', in 'Studien zur italienischen Musikgeschichte', *Analecta Musicologica*, 22 (1984), p. 474.

30. *Revue et Gazette musicale de Paris*, 4 (1837), p. 122.

31. Ibid., p. 122.

32. H. Berlioz, *Voyage Musical en Allemagne et en Italie. Études sur Beethoven, Gluck et Weber. Mélanges et Nouvelles* (Paris: Jules Labitte, 1844), vol. 1, pp. 284–5.

33. *Le Monde musical*, 2 (1841), [p. 1].

34. *Revue et Gazette musicale de Paris*, 8 (1841), pp. 463–5 and 487–9.

35. Ibid., p. 489.

36. *Allgemeine Wiener Musik-Zeitung*, 3 (1843), p. 28.

37. W. Brauneis, "' ... composta per festeggiare il sovvenire di un grand Uomo". Beethovens "Eroica" als Hommage des Fürsten Franz Joseph Maximilian von Lobkowitz für Prinz Louis Ferdinand von Preußen', *Studien zur Wiener Geschichte. Jahrbuch des Vereins für Geschichte der Stadt Wien*, 52/53 (1996/97), pp. 53–88.

38. *Beethoven aus der Sicht seiner Zeitgenossen in Tagebüchern, Briefen, Gedichten und Erinnerungen*, ed. K. M. Kopitz and R. Cadenbach (Munich: Henle, 2009), vol. 1, p. 64.

39. Ibid., p. 227.

40. Ibid.

10 The *Eroica* in the Nineteenth and Twentieth Centuries

LEON BOTSTEIN

Finding Meaning in the *Eroica*

The composition and first performances of the *Eroica* Symphony took place between 1802 and 1805, just a few years after the start of a new century, and a decade after the radical phase of the French Revolution. The revolution of 1789, and not the year 1800, came to be regarded by posterity as the true start of modern history and the nineteenth century. The *Eroica* was linked, by chronology, to a new era, and spiritually to the ideals and history of the Revolution and Napoleon. This influenced how the symphony was heard and understood throughout the nineteenth century. The *Eroica*, by bridging art, history and politics, became a musical mirror of the 'long' century whose end was marked by World War I. But it was a magic mirror, reflecting back to its public not merely echoes of the past but also the political and cultural aspirations of successive generations.

Two lines of arguments prevailed. The *Eroica* was viewed, on the one hand, as an inheritance: the utopian expression in music of the philosophical and spiritual conceits of the eighteenth-century Enlightenment and the Revolution. On the other hand, it was admired as a radical, revolutionary departure from tradition that ushered in a break with the past and suggested a pathway into a new modernity and the triumph of Romanticism. By the end of the century, the *Eroica*'s status as a contested and unique representation of the promise of the new century included a recognition that it was also a reminder of the devastating shortcomings of the nineteenth century, measured against the political and social ideals of the eighteenth. What follows is an account of the intense preoccupation with the *Eroica*, from the mid-nineteenth century to the mid-twentieth, among critics, composers, performers and audiences.

Philip H. Goepp (1864–1936) was an American organist, student of John Knowles Paine (who thought Wagner a dangerous influence), and a lawyer. He served as the programme annotator for the Philadelphia Orchestra for two decades (from 1900 to 1921). In his popular guide to the symphonic repertory, *Symphonies and Their Meaning*, first

published in 1897, Goepp tried his best to explain the elusive and contradictory character of the *Eroica*. The symphony had the 'ring of universality' yet was full of the uniquely unexpected, unprecedented sonorities and even the 'hysterical'. The listener needed to be able to 'distinguish profound joy ... from careless irresponsible abandon'. Beethoven, 'a thinking man' according to Goepp, 'dethroned Beauty and set up Feeling'.[1]

But in the *Eroica* Beethoven also demonstrated 'strongest sympathy with the struggles in France for individual freedom and for the principles on which stand the American republic and national life ... Justice, Equality, Democracy, Common Sense, and ... Universal Brotherhood'. That being said, the *Eroica* also managed to reveal Beethoven as not 'o'ercast with intellectual motives' but possessed of a 'balance of depth and of humanity'. Beethoven's 'elemental simplicity and childlike exuberance' were on full display in the *Eroica*.[2]

Goepp's uncertainty and inability to sort out ambiguities and contradictions in the *Eroica*, and his discomfort in reconciling formal qualities and some manner of meaning derived from the compositional genesis of the work, primarily the association with Napoleon and the idea of the hero, were extreme. These struggles may seem comical and naively American, but Goepp's account confirms the conflicts and currents in the nineteenth-century reception of the symphony relating to its ambitions, form and meaning. Was it a work, Goepp explicitly asked, that celebrated the political ideas of America's Declaration of Independence?[3] Or was it a forceful manifesto of Romantic sentiment that elevated emotion over reason, spontaneity over logic, the subjective and individual over the universal, and the naïve over the sublime? Or perhaps it did both?

Anton von Webern and Felix Weingartner, two quite different composer-conductors in German-speaking Europe whose careers overlapped with Goepp, also sought to come to terms with the symphony. Webern, 23 years old, attended a performance in Vienna, conducted by Felix Mottl, on Sunday 6 November 1904, almost exactly 100 years after the *Eroica*'s composition. He wrote in his diary that the performance had brought him closer to the 'divine' genius of Beethoven and that

> I long for an artist in music such as Segantini was in painting. His music would have to be a music that a man writes in solitude, far away from all the turmoil in the world, in contemplation of the glaciers, of eternal ice and snow, of the sombre mountain giants. It would have to be like Segantini's pictures. The onslaught of an alpine storm, the mighty tone of the mountains, the radiance of the summer sun on flower-covered meadows – all these would have to be in the music, born

immediately out of alpine solitude. That man would be the Beethoven of our day. An *Eroica* would inevitably appear again, one that is younger by 100 years.[4]

The painter whom the *Eroica* inspired Webern to compare Beethoven with was Giovanni Segantini, who died unexpectedly in 1899 at the age of 42.[5] Segantini was widely considered one of the greatest painters of his time. Ludwig Hevesi, Vienna's leading art critic, was among the painter's most ardent admirers. For Hevesi, Segantini's unique synthesis of hyper-realism, achieved by the application of small, highly textured geometric brush strokes, with a compositional strategy of visual and pictorial symbolism made him 'a great philosopher with the brush'.[6] The meticulous beauty of Segantini's representations of life and nature high up in the alpine mountains vindicated Nietzsche's privileging of an artist's vantage point in the search for truth.

The rhetoric of Hevesi's critical assessment of Segantini's art and ambition found its way into Webern's diary. For Hevesi, Segantini crystal-lised reality and turned life into an epic. Suffering and death became real without sacrifice of beauty. Hevesi compared Segantini's disaggregated brushwork with the innovative military strategy of Helmuth von Moltke who led Prussia to victory over Austria in 1866 and France in 1871. Segantini approached the canvas piecemeal, working with seemingly dis-connected detailed gestures only to succeed in depicting a coherent argu-ment in the totality of the artwork. The soul of reality beyond the visible was revealed to the viewer through aesthetic representation.[7] Hevesi, writing in 1906, described Segantini's achievement as the 'humanising of nature'. The 'highest loyalty to reality' led Segantini to the 'secret meaning of appearance, the symbolism of the visible, and the soul of the world of people'.[8] Segantini's painterly means and unique perspective revealed a new way of knowing the world.

Hevesi's comparison of a modern painter to a contemporary military hero suggests the prominence of the aesthetic in the *fin-de-siècle* discourse on modernity and politics. For Webern, the astonishing formal aspects of the *Eroica*, its relentless energy and the constantly surprising ingenuity in thematic development demonstrated the composer's ambition to express something about the course of history. This justified the *Eroica*'s stature as a landmark of the power of artists to create meaning and value.

Listening to the *Eroica*, Webern was reminded of Segantini on account of the grandeur of the symphony and its arresting ingenuity in the elabora-tion of motivic elements. Segantini's revelatory symbolism depicting the confrontation of the human and the natural landscape, and his penetrating gaze and original divisionist technique resembled, for Webern, Beethoven's use of musical procedures in the service of ideas. Both artists

revealed an overt and a covert reality simultaneously, and exposed human ideals through their aesthetic. And both worked in solitude: Segantini by choice and as a result of perpetual statelessness, and Beethoven because of deafness.

Webern's awe at how Beethoven 'humanised' nature and articulated man's place in the world in the *Eroica* was, however, compromised by a sense of loss and absence, widely shared by his generation, regarding the moment of history he found himself in. Segantini's paintings suggested what a modern *Eroica* needed to achieve, and perhaps what it might sound like. But the absence of a Beethoven, someone who might be up to the task of writing another *Eroica*, was pronounced. The spirit of the age seemed to work against the possibility.

Hevesi had pitted Segantini's penetrating idiosyncratic pictorial realism against the soulless power of modern technology, exemplified by the capacity of 'Roentgen rays' (X rays) to produce unprecedented images of reality; the facts hidden by mere appearance were astonishing. But this modern means lacked a soul. It could not discover and assert deeper meanings. Segantini, however, could do so as a result of a contemporary aesthetic vision and style. By using small, 'atomic' strokes, the painter revealed majesty and the play of enduring values by highlighting over-looked details, and reconciling the impressive with the ephemeral, all in contemplation of human life and time in nature.[9] Hevesi and Webern both saw in Segantini an artist capable of evoking new meaning. For Webern the apparent contradictions in the *Eroica* that baffled Goepp could be recon-ciled by imagining its equivalent in modern painting.

Segantini defined for the young composer, overwhelmed by the sound of the *Eroica*, the proper aspiration of the composer of the day. The new Beethoven would have to experience isolation, idealised by Webern as being alone in nature. An *Eroica* could not come from within the trans-formed space of modernity – the city – but only from within a refuge from it. Although Webern construed the solitude of the high mountains of Switzerland metaphorically, the allusion to Nietzsche's attachment to Sils Maria was unmistakable. But most important for Webern, in 1906, was the replication through music of Segantini's harnessing of modern composi-tional strategies to create a coherent transformative totality, a modern *Eroica*, a philosophical vision in music.

Twelve years later, in 1918, at the end of the Great War, Felix Weingartner, the world-renowned 55-year-old composer-conductor, wrote a short essay 'Where is the Modern Eroika?'[10] His spelling (an evocation of Greek antiquity) highlighted the point articulated by Webern, the need for a modern work of comparable stature and power. Weingartner understood, as did Webern, that such a work needed to

emulate the *Eroica* in spirit and ambition but not imitate it. The new 'Eroika', like the original, had to be evocative of and true to its own historical moment, and not deny the passage of time by conceding to a nostalgic aesthetic of restoration that was increasingly popular with concert audiences.

The catastrophic events of the Great War drove Weingartner in a political direction far from the concerns that preoccupied Webern. Weingartner acknowledged that during the war there had been no short-age of new patriotic music, some of it superficially reminiscent of the *Eroica* but more akin to *Wellington's Victory*. But the monumentality of patriotic music (one thinks of Max Reger's 1915 *Eine vaterländische Overtüre*, Op. 140, as opposed to his *Requiem*, Op. 144b, from the same year) emulated the *Eroica* only in terms of scale and the presumed subject matter of heroic deeds in war. This revealed, he thought, too narrow an understanding of Beethoven's *Eroica*.[11]

Weingartner knew that throughout the nineteenth century the best-known aspect of the *Eroica* among musicians and the lay public was its link to Napoleon, rooted in the legend of its original dedication and Beethoven's subsequent striking of it to substitute a nameless hero for commemoration. Generations of listeners understood the unprecedented heroic scale of the opening movement, and the funeral march of the second, as evoking an ideal of heroism rooted in war and politics. The apparent contrasts between the opening movements and the last two, however, remained a puzzle.

Since the *Eroica* was first and foremost an epic narration in music of heroism in wartime, for Weingartner the surprise was that four years of war failed to inspire a new *Eroica*. The turmoil, violence and leadership of the Napoleonic era had provided, after all, the context for Beethoven's masterpiece. 'The truly heroic' was apparently a consequence of war, and therefore the *Eroica*'s guiding essence. Despite the 'limitless' sacrifice of millions of promising young people, the innumerable sufferings tolerated in silence, and the 'belief in a better world' (which applied also to the first decade of the nineteenth century), no work of music had yet appeared that met 'the unprecedented events of contemporary life' with comparable 'profundity'. What the shattered world required, in Weingartner's view, was a work that 'releases in liberating sounds the animating movement of our soul', just as Beethoven had done. What made the *Eroica* immortal was the 'overwhelming picture of greatness', inspired by the events of its time, communicated by music.[12]

For Weingartner, the events of modern history were overwhelming. Technology had so transformed the globe, closing the gaps between peo-ples, that it seemed inconceivable that the uniqueness of the historical

moment would not be revealed in a work of music, much in the way Webern understood Segantini's painting to operate. Weingartner was in search of a work that 'would liberate forever the doors' that imprisoned the highest ideals of the day. The question was whether there was an artist capable of creating a work for all times that also remained true to its historical context, one that could pass the test of time and not become just a 'gradually fading image'.[13]

Despite an uncanny resemblance between the modern world and the time of Beethoven's *Eroica*, there was, for Weingartner, one decisive difference. And that was the absence of a hero in contemporary public life remotely comparable to Napoleon. The cause of modernity's failure to produce a new *Eroica* was not, as Webern thought, the lack of an artist of Beethoven's stature. Rather, the cause was a vacuum in political greatness. A hero in politics was needed to inspire the present, precisely on account of the barbarism of the war; it had derailed the historical momentum of the nineteenth century towards progress. Before 1914 'humanity had been on the best path, guided by truthful understanding, on its way to a cosmopolitan world', Weingartner lamented.[14]

No mere war hero could inspire a modern Beethoven to compose a new 'Eroika'. The need was for charismatic political leadership. The *Eroica* revealed that Beethoven, before 1804, understood Napoleon to have been more than a hero in war. Weingartner observed that Napoleon's ideals transcended violence and conquest, although he relied on and was ultimately defeated by war. Those ideals included the unification of Europe, the liberation of all people, and a belief in equality, liberty and the elimination of conflict between nations and races. There was no modern 'Eroika' because there was no 'true' hero like Napoleon who could 'ignite' the Beethoven of the day to write a new 'Eroika'. Beethoven's achievement was a work that 'understood the language of the destiny and direction of the spirit of the world' and 'faithfully translated' history and politics into music. But heroic deeds in the public realm, not only on the battlefield, remained the necessary pre-conditions for the appearance of great modern art.[15]

Contemplating the Hero: Berlioz and Wagner

Weingartner's certainty about a causal link between political deeds and ideals and the art of music was a symptom of the extent to which, for the nineteenth century, such a link had been defined by Beethoven's *Eroica*. The symphony stood apart on account of its synthesis of aesthetic and formal originality in music and its suggestion of a philosophical and

historical argument expressible in language. That argument possessed an unambiguous, authentic, but ill-defined biographical origin. No account of the *Eroica*, especially in the many concert guides for the lay public, omitted this issue. In his entry on Beethoven in Gustav Schillings's 1835 *Encyclopädie der gesammten musikalischen Wissenschaften*, Adolf Bernhard Marx pointed to the significance of the 'images of the heroic' and the 'sequence of ideas' in shaping the symphony's musical fabric.[16]

Berlioz opened his 1862 account of the symphony with an admonition not to 'tamper' with the description of the work in the first published edition as 'heroic' and as the 'celebration' of the 'memory of a great man'. Berlioz omits any reference to Napoleon or historical specifics. He underscores the absence of particularised imagery and a specific story line. The well-known anecdote about Beethoven striking out Napoleon's name, which Berlioz calls the 'mutilation' of the title, is termed a 'deception', since the symphony lacks an explicit programme or narration. However, for Berlioz it possesses an aesthetic consistency, a prevailing style adequate to the hero's funeral and remembrance. A coherent style and not a story explains the uniqueness of the work and its ability to elevate 'grief' through 'such pure form and such nobleness of expression'.[17]

The *Eroica*, Berlioz concludes, 'possesses such strength of thought and execution, that its style is so emotional and consistently elevated besides its form being so poetical'. For Berlioz, the symphony came to occupy a purgatory between explicitly programmatic instrumental music and symphonic music uncompromised by defining words or descriptive images. It was 'entitled to a rank as equal to the highest conceptions of its composer', despite competition from Beethoven's subsequent six symphonies. Berlioz viewed the 'poetic' aspect of the *Eroica* as evocative of classical antiquity: Virgil in the *Aeneid* (for the funeral march) and Homer in the *Iliad* (for the link between mourning and celebration in the Scherzo).[18]

The most influential voice in the nineteenth century on the character and meaning of the *Eroica* was Wagner. A decade before Berlioz, in his 1852 programme note on the *Eroica*, Wagner pioneered the idea that the entire work possessed a dramatic poetic programme of articulated generic ideals. Wagner detached its presumed poetic content from any connection to the specific history of the French Revolution and the Napoleonic era. Wagner stripped the symphony of its own history and context and elevated its poetic meaning into the realm of metaphysical idealism.[19] In 1870, in the midst of playing the work with Cosima, Wagner stood up and exclaimed, 'The only mortal who can be compared to Shakespeare!'[20] The *Eroica* fuelled Wagner's ambition to transform the genre of opera in

a direction consistent with Beethoven's use of symphonic form as a vehicle for a drama of ideas, whose greatest exponent was for him Shakespeare.

Wagner sought to characterise the *Eroica* in a way more fitting to the mid-century. He had begun to align himself with the political nationalism flourishing in Germany; he developed his image of Beethoven to fit his ambitions and prejudices regarding the intersection between music and poetry; and he took into account the anti-Enlightenment currents in German idealism and Romantic literature and sought to separate the *Eroica* from the political and epistemological ideologies with which Beethoven had aligned himself.

In the mid-1850s, Wagner's inconsistent and self-serving bias against the French had not yet fully blossomed (it had done so by 1870, when he published his seminal essay *Beethoven*). But his affinity with a new aggressive German cultural and political chauvinism had. Wagner shared a suspicion within German intellectual circles of a renewal in France of a mythic obsession with Napoleon (as expressed in Stendhal's *Le Rouge et le Noir* from 1830, and amply demonstrated by Napoleon's re-burial in 1840 in Paris). The link between the posthumous glorification of Napoleon's ambitions, talent and courage and the French appreciation of the *Eroica* rested on the idea that the symphony was a tribute to Napoleon's originality and greatness.[21]

By focusing on the *Eroica*'s place in the evolution of music, poetry and ideas in history, a reinvention that secured Beethoven's identity as German, Wagner sought to undermine this interpretation. Since there was reason to suspect that Beethoven, his rage at Napoleon's naming himself Emperor notwithstanding, harboured some fascination with and admiration for Bonaparte throughout his life, the erasure of a specific history for the *Eroica* was essential. Wagner recognised that the enthusiasm for the music of Beethoven in France at mid-century demanded that the significance of Beethoven's original dedication and the underlying beliefs that led the composer to the idea of the symphony in the first place, be diminished in the eyes of the German public.

Wagner's reframing of the *Eroica* was not only politically well timed but also justified by the fact that the dedication was changed to 'an heroic symphony . . . composed to celebrate the memory of a great man'. The challenge remained how to unify the work's varied musical materials and reconcile, ideologically, the sharp contrasts between the movements as a single poetic drama. Wagner's solution was brilliant. Each of the movements represented parts of a dramatic representation of life. Action was followed by tragedy, serenity and love (in Goepp's simplification of Wagner's argument).[22] Wagner's idea of the hero in the symphony was thereby detached from any narrow association with Napoleon. It referred rather to an idealised vision of human experience.

The word 'hero' in the *Eroica*, Wagner argued, referred to 'the whole, the full-fledged man in whom are present all the purely human feelings – of love, of grief, of force – in their highest fill and strength'. Wagner concluded:

> the artistic space in this work is filled with all the varied intercrossing feelings of a strong, a consummate Individuality, to which nothing human is strange, but which includes within itself all truly Human, and utters it in a fashion that – after frankly manifesting every noble passion – it reaches a final rounding of its nature, wherein the most feeling softness is wedded with the most energetic force. The heroic tendency of this artwork is the progress toward that rounding off.[23]

This decontextualising of the political origins and implications of the symphony came shortly after Wagner's flight from Dresden and his brief career in 1848 and 1849 as a revolutionary dedicated to the older liberal traditions of the universal extension of political rights. This decontexualisation had its impact on subsequent generations. However, Wagner's reading of the *Eroica*, and his recasting of Beethoven in general, inspired opposition and scepticism, as would his own music. Wagner notwithstanding, the idea of the hero as a figure in the public realm, associating the heroic with political power and military prowess as exemplified by Bonaparte, remained associated with the *Eroica*, as Weingartner's conviction that for another 'Eroika' to be written, great leadership capable of world historical actions had to precede the work of art. This reflected a widespread presumption that art, in history, remained consistently contingent on politics.

Weingartner's call for a new hero was a familiar refrain between 1918 and 1920, as testified to by the hero-seeking circle around Stefan George and Max Weber's classic critique of the heroic political saviour in his 1919 Munich lectures, *Wissenschaft als Beruf* and *Politik als Beruf*. The outcome was ultimately tragic. Hitler fulfilled the wish for charismatic leadership. But Beethoven's own inclination to hero worship in politics, which began with Joseph II, remained tied to the ideal of the enlightened despot. Beethoven's fascination with Napoleon was hardly exceptional for the nineteenth century, as Tolstoy's *War and Peace* suggests.

The desire for a strong authoritative ruler defined the second half of the century in German history. It was expressed primarily through the cult of Bismarck. It later persisted and fuelled distrust of the Weimar Republic. In 1802 and 1803 Bonaparte may have represented for Beethoven universal ideals of freedom, brotherhood and the rights of citizens. But the striking of his name from the title page of the *Eroica* inspired Arnold Schoenberg to explain in 1944 that when he undertook to write his *Ode to Napoleon*, the *Eroica* reminded him that it was his 'moral duty' as an artist 'to take a stand against tyranny'. Politics, once again, preceded art.[24]

What fuelled nineteenth-century criticism of Wagner's reading of the *Eroica* was the historical record that Beethoven admired Bonaparte on account of shared 'Enlightenment' political sympathies. Beethoven's out-look, typical of the quite liberal Bonn of his youth, was rooted in a faith in the power of reason, and grounded in an awe of nature. These inheritances from the late eighteenth century were never understood in the nineteenth century to be fundamentally inconsistent with a politics dominated by a single individual, and therefore with the ideal of the great man. It was not autocracy or even despotism that defined the debate in the nineteenth century over the meaning of the origins of the *Eroica*. Rather it was Beethoven's allegiance to universality and reason as criteria of ethical and political principles and epistemological judgement. It was the asser-tion of the universal character of freedom that Wagner sought to deflect and minimise.

Reclaiming the Idealism of the *Eroica*

The opponents of Wagner, such as Carl Reinecke and Max Bruch, saw Beethoven as the prophet of universal virtues, including tolerance and equality, not a nascent radical post-1848 German nationalist whose ideas anticipated a racialist ideology and the substitution of national myth for history. This divide helped deepen a nineteenth-century perception among anti-Wagnerians of a close affinity between Beethoven, Goethe and Kant. The *Eroica* Symphony was understood as a radical departure from the Classical models of Haydn and Mozart, and a harbinger of musical Romanticism (alongside the C minor Fifth Symphony and the Ninth, whose choral movement with its reprise of earlier movements set it apart from the *Eroica*). But this break with past musical models actually under-scored Beethoven's commitment to contemporary sentiments regarding the political freedom of the individual. The *Eroica*'s ideological prestige derived from its being perceived as the purely instrumental evocation of the sentiments expressed explicitly in the last movement of the Ninth. The *Eroica* became the Beethoven symphony most closely associated with the Ninth.

Among sceptics of Wagner's nationalist politics, the implied meaning of the *Eroica* was an argument on behalf of liberty, the idea of natural rights, individuality and therefore a 'cosmopolitan' world, the proper fulfilment of a universal historical destiny. The *Eroica* was not, in this view, an ahistorical evocation of generic human experience. Nor did it prefigure the heroic in the sense evoked by the myths to which Wagner was attached, which idealised his aggressive German chauvinism.

Nowhere is the character of the late nineteenth-century anti-Wagnerian reading of the *Eroica* more evident than in the writings of Paul Bekker, a highly influential critic and partisan of early twentieth-century modernism, particularly Mahler and Schreker. Bekker's *Beethoven* first appeared in 1911. He argued that the *Eroica* was emblematic of an underlying unity within musical expression, which flourished throughout the nineteenth century. This unity, derived from Beethoven, persisted beneath the divisive distinctions between programme music and 'absolute music' that had emerged in the 1860s.[25]

Beethoven, and particularly the *Eroica*, represented the common ground between the opposing camps of the 'New German' school dominated by Liszt and Wagner, and the group around Brahms. The work was exemplary, for Bekker, owing to its classic–romantic synthesis, and the link it created between sound and ideas. However true the *Eroica* was to apparently purely musical values – thematic development, harmonic logic and the use of time in formal structures – it nonetheless shaped the way music could express thought in instrumental music. Beethoven's *Eroica* elevated music as a complex but persuasive system of human communication that articulated ideas – not pictures, events or personalities – with musical means, even without an explicit intention to do so.

The *Eroica* for Bekker marked a radical departure in the use of sonority. The use of solo instruments (such as the horn), and the extremes of dynamic range and contrasts, including the amassing of sound, are audible in all four movements. This sustained novel use of the orchestra lent the work a perceived unity that permitted it to develop a complex argument. Yet the *Eroica*, according to Bekker, still had one foot in Classicism, as evidenced by the absence of the nascent organic form exhibited by the Ninth.[26]

Bekker's most celebrated insight into the *Eroica* was his assertion that precisely because the symphony's structure was not organic but sequential, the source for the motivating ideas behind the work, and therefore the key to its overall argument, lay not in the first or second movements, but in the last. Until Bekker, the nineteenth-century consensus held that the leading idea of the work, the 'heroic', was established in the first movement. The exposition of the hero in the initial movement was a prelude to the hero's subsequent funeral and commemoration. Indeed, the tune of the funeral march had been set to words for Simon Bolivar's funeral in 1830.[27]

Bekker, intrigued by Beethoven's use of material from the 1801 ballet *The Creatures of Prometheus* in the last movement, argued that idea of Prometheus represented the culmination of Beethoven's design and argument. The evocation of Prometheus reconciled the political origins and ideology of the first two movements with the *Eroica*'s larger purpose as an

affirmative celebration of the human potential to command nature and make history. The originality of the music and the form in the *Eroica* for Bekker constituted 'a hymn of praise of a free humanity of action'.[28]

In Bekker's reading, the gift of fire and therefore foresight was the legacy of Prometheus. The symphony opens with the articulation in the first movement of human freedom as individual heroism. With the death of the hero, and the overcoming of grief (the third movement), the Kantian universalisation of practical reason constituted the culmination of freedom as freedom for all. Thus Beethoven shifted the weight in the architecture of the *Eroica* to the figure of Prometheus in the finale. Individual 'great men' – Bonaparte and General Ralph Abercromby (who was killed in the Battle of Alexandria in 1801 and whom Bekker adduced as a possible inspiration for the second movement) – were ultimately transitional factors in history and in the symphony's structure.[29]

Bekker found that, by placing the emphasis in the finale on the mythic figure of Prometheus after traversing the preceding movements, Beethoven could persuasively render his ultimate philosophical objective: the affirmation of the universalising of Prometheus's gift to humankind. The music argued a transition from the individual to the collective. The purely formal procedures of musical art in the last movement – the variation form – represented a closing reconciliation of individual and collective freedom. As to the nature of individual heroes, Bekker observed that 'to their personalities, in the narrow sense of the term, Beethoven remained indifferent'. For Beethoven, Bekker concluded, 'only what was typical, eternal in its appearance: the power of the will, majesty in death, creative power did he fashion together; and he created from this his poem on all that can be great and heroic, and all that human existence can make of itself'.[30]

By reversing the priority of the four movements of the symphony, Bekker integrated the Wagnerian view of Beethoven as musical dramatist and forerunner of the music drama. Following an emphasis on musical form associated with the anti-Wagnerian, Bekker held up the *Eroica* as a masterful breakthrough in musical expression, incomparably reconciling classicism with a typically Romantic freedom of musical expression. He thereby modified the Wagnerian idea of meaning in music by viewing the *Eroica* as a generalised philosophical assertion of human potential in a condition of freedom. This fitted Webern's association of the work with Segantini's capacity to unlock, by aesthetic means, underlying universal truths by penetrating the details and structures in nature.

Bekker's removal of the symphony's meaning from the age of Napoleon was less radical than Webern's, since the ideas Bekker found expressed by the *Eroica* remained true to their historical origins in 1789. The analogy

Webern drew between Beethoven and Segantini focused on what would be required of a modern equivalent to the *Eroica*. This question assumed the distancing of the symphony from its context of origin, a strategy implicit in the assessments of Wagner and Berlioz.

Weingartner was sceptical of both Bekker's analysis and Wagner's highly romantic approach. He remained wedded to the idea that the key to the meaning of the *Eroica* lay in the first two movements. He rejected the composer's metronome markings for the first two movements, added by Beethoven in 1817. They ran contrary to what he believed to be the ideational content of the work. The sixty per dotted minim for the first movement invited, he thought, a trivialisation of the movement and the grandeur of the heroic. Likewise, the eighty to the crotchet indication for the second movement was 'alarmingly quick' and 'could not possibly be the right one', for it violated the funereal idea.[31] Erwin Stein reported on two performances he heard in 1930, one by Toscanini and one by Webern. Toscanini, Stein reported, adhered to an 'old style' that relied on tempo modifications to underscore 'pathos and expression'. By pursuing flexibility in the pacing of the work, Toscanini followed the path of emancipating the *Eroica* from its narrow historical context implied by Wagner and Berlioz but returned the priority of the heroic as definitive of the first movement and the symphony.

Webern's performance seemed to Stein 'more directly impressive'. Webern held to a swift tempo in the first movement without sacrificing expressive contrasts. The 'vehemence' and 'lyrical elements' occurred naturally without losing their unique character. The second movement was 'more flowing' and 'less pathetic' in character. But most remarkable was the last movement. It was 'wonderful', particularly the variations. The impetus with which the symphony closed was 'telling'. Webern sought to highlight the inner structural coherence of the four-movement work, and, as Bekker, underscored the defining presence of the last movement.[32] As Donald Francis Tovey observed in 1935, the finale 'is in a form which was unique when it appeared, and has remained unique ever since'.[33]

The *Eroica* and the Logic of History

The status accorded the *Eroica* during the second half of the nineteenth century by Wagnerians and their detractors derived in both instances from the undeniable suggestion from the composer himself that there was some sort of argument rooted in politics and history that hovered over a work. Unlike the 'Pastoral' Symphony, the *Eroica* has neither a preface nor explicit allusions to nature and visual scenes in the countryside illustrated by tone painting. But unlike the Fifth or the Seventh, the *Eroica* does not

allow one to dismiss assertions of allusions (to 'fate' and the 'apotheosis of the dance' in those cases respectively) as illegitimate. Yet the *Eroica*, despite the resemblances to the Ninth, lacked an explicit setting of text.

The nineteenth-century reception of the *Eroica* reveals that Wagner and his acolytes understood themselves as participants in the march of historical progress and actors in the dawn of a new age. On the other hand, Brahms and his followers remained sceptical of the inevitability of progress in history. The *fin-de-siècle* modernists in the early twentieth century, including Mahler and Schoenberg, absorbed the Wagnerian conceit of progress. But as Webern's 1906 musings and Hevesi's advocacy of contemporary art suggest, the belief in the inevitability of a progressive logic in history had a sharp edge of criticism. The growing dominance of industry, the mechanisation of daily life, the destruction of the natural landscape and the ravages of capitalism were dangers to spiritual and aesthetic progress. By the end of the century, the human soul seemed at risk, as was the purity of nature. But the imperative to create a new art to fit a new age remained.

Running parallel to the Wagnerian enthusiasm for a new art adequate to contemporary life was a pessimistic vision of cultural decline. Progress in material terms, including advances in technology (of which Brahms, ironically, was particularly fond), was accompanied by a sense of foreboding linked to political nationalism, and to a perceived threat to aesthetic and cultural standards posed by democracy and mass culture. Among the consequences of the French Revolution was the destruction not only of the aristocracy of birth and political privileges, but also of an aristocracy of learning and aesthetic patronage and discernment. Nostalgia for pre-modern eras flourished, including the Medieval (visible in the Gothic Revival in architecture) and the Renaissance (the cult of Raphael, Leonardo and Michelangelo). The late nineteenth century witnessed a reassertion of artisan crafts as a counterweight to industrial manufacture (the Arts and Crafts Movement) and a call to rediscover Classicism, particularly Mozart.

Bekker's Beethoven represented a non-Wagnerian liberal defence of the idea of progress. Beethoven pointed to a future marked by the universal encouragement of individuality, an ethics of equality and freedom on behalf of human potential and justice. Weingartner, once an adherent of this view, became more doubtful. In 1912, in a collection of essays that included a plea for a return to Mozart, he confessed that he thought Beethoven marked the high point of music history. The book opened with an affectionate reminiscence of Weingartner's 1898 encounter with an elderly surviving contemporary of Beethoven's. 'Beethoven was everything', she said, and modern music left her cold.[34]

Cultural criticism that excoriated the nineteenth century and raised the alarm at a descent into mediocrity gained in prominence after 1860.

Matthew Arnold published *Culture and Anarchy* in 1869. Between 1883 and 1892 Max Nordau wrote three popular books, *The Conventional Lies of Our Civilization* (1883), *The Sickness of the Century* (1887) and, most famously, *Degeneration* (1892). Among the intellectuals whom Brahms admired most was Jacob Burckhardt, a devoted music lover and author of *Der Cicerone*, a guide to the art of Italy, first published in the mid-1850s and revised in 1873, which Brahms cherished. Burckhardt was pessimistic about modernity, both its politics and its culture. His doubts, thinly veiled in his 1860 masterpiece *The Culture of the Renaissance in Italy*, became explicit in his lectures from the 1880s, published in English after his death as *Force and Freedom*.

The resemblances between Brahms's Second Symphony from 1877 and the *Eroica* suggest that Brahms shared Burckhardt's pessimism about the direction of history (as the late Reinhold Brinkmann brilliantly argued).[35] Brahms does not merely evoke the *Eroica* in the material in his symphony's first movement, but also recalls its rhythmic elaborations and orchestration. The similarities are intentional reference points for listeners, alerting them to differences between the era of the *Eroica* and the late nineteenth century. Brahms understood that Beethoven articulated a sense of newness and optimism characteristic of the historical moment, particularly through a dynamic use of musical time. Brahms sought to highlight, through allusions to the *Eroica*, a 'change in the historical situation'. In a manner resembling Webern's reading of Segantini's landscapes, Brahms explicitly introduces calm and repose in musical space and time, qualities evident in Segantini's vision of nature. The explicit references to the *Eroica* expressed 'a skeptical reaction against the optimistic and utopian promise of that forward-looking, perspectivist idea of history which Beethoven's formal process implies'; Brahms would repeat this use of the *Eroica* in the opening chords of his Third Symphony from 1883 and in the variation from the finale of the Fourth from 1885.[36]

The utopian impulse that inspired Beethoven to break with past models of symphonic form (including his own first two forays into the genre) led to his deployment of novel compositional procedures in the *Eroica*, suggestive of vectors of progress. Among these novel features, of which Brahms was keenly aware, was rhythmic unpredictability. Beethoven's breaking of regularity and his relentless use of syncopation defied established expectations of continuity. The predictable and the asymmetrical are juxtaposed in the third movement of the *Eroica* from the very start, giving the contrasting and varied uses of rhythmic elements a leading role in establishing the dynamism of the musical structure.[37]

Wagner emulated this path towards an extended musical drama and monumentality, not with rhythm but with the extension of harmony,

augmenting the possibilities of repetition and avoiding closure. Brahms, with a melancholy sensibility, countered this approach. Although he made use of complex rhythmic asymmetry and syncopation, the dominant character of the music of the Second Symphony suggests isolation and solitude. Brahms took refuge in nature, highlighting beauty of a static kind. Brahms's allusions to Beethoven's driving energy in the *Eroica* functioned as signals of twilight and not a new dawn in history.

In Richard Strauss's *Metamorphosen* can be found the most arresting use of a musical reference to the *Eroica* to mark the decline and end of a great era of art and culture. Strauss achieved a brilliant synthesis of the opposing trends in nineteenth-century music. He started out in the orbit of Brahms under the patronage of Hans von Bülow in Meiningen. He then embarked on a spectacular career using the tone poem format developed by Liszt. Strauss utilised explicit programmes but retained an idiosyncratic allegiance to classical models of thematic development, variation and form. He admired and emulated Wagner, but in the end, his ideal remained Mozart, as it would for Brahms. Nevertheless, between the late 1880s and the outbreak of World War I, Strauss earned a reputation as a modernist in the Wagnerian mould.

After 1918 Strauss struggled to retain his place in music as more than a holdover from the past. He collaborated with the Nazi regime after more than a decade of fierce opposition to post-1918 modernism. In 1944, faced with the impending defeat of Nazi Germany and the ongoing physical destruction of the major German cities, Strauss composed his *Metamorphosen* for twenty-three string instruments, which premiered in March 1945. A quote from the second movement of the *Eroica* appears at the opening. At the end of this extended essay, which is marked by an uncanny virtuosity in thematic elaboration, extended tonality and counterpoint, Strauss inserts a quote from the funeral march of the *Eroica*. Under this quotation, Strauss wrote in the manuscript, 'In Memoriam!'

The *Eroica* became an epitaph for the art and culture of modern European history. *Metamorphosen* foregrounds lyric intensity but eschews the dynamic energy of the *Eroica*. In this respect Strauss emulated Brahms, and assumed the image of the artist in solitude, as expressed by Webern via Segantini. He articulated the endpoint of Brahms's scepticism and pessimism regarding modernity and progress. Yet he did not evoke what Brinkmann termed a 'sentimental' idyll. Brahms's symphonic commentary on the *Eroica* was a musical representation of loss in history, of having come late in history, after a golden age. But beauty and joy manage to break through the melancholy. The perspective of the painter, in Segantini, was one of intense interior reflection as a consequence of the embrace of

nature. In Strauss, however, hope is extinguished and the illusion of refuge or rebirth shattered. No scherzo follows.

Performing and Listening to the *Eroica* in the Twentieth Century

In the twentieth century, the late nineteenth-century tradition of seeing the *Eroica* as a harbinger of the future, emancipated from its specific history, waned. Theodor W. Adorno's account of the history of music, which revolved around Beethoven, is a case in point. For Adorno, music of historical and aesthetic greatness had to reveal the 'structure of society' through the composer, either consciously or sub-consciously, with a 'substantial, objective like-mindedness'. The *Eroica* showed that 'Beethoven did not accommodate himself to the ideology of the oft-cited rising bourgeoisie of the era of 1789 or 1800; he partook of its spirit.' Hence his 'unsurpassed achievement' revealed 'an inner coincidence with society'.[38] The *Eroica* was rooted, for Adorno, in its time and place. The evidence for this belief was that the work was not built up from themes and motives, although 'it seems as though everything develops out of the motive power of the individual elements'. On the contrary, Beethoven's music was 'in fact identical with the structure of Hegelian logic'. The 'conception of a whole dynamically conceived, in itself defines its elements'; the elements, already conceived (as within a prepared piano, Adorno argued) 'adapt themselves to become part of the pervading idea of the whole'.[39] The overarching structure of the *Eroica* (in Bekker's sense) determined the constituent musical materials.

The conception of the *Eroica* as defining a historical context has dominated twentieth-century reception and performance. Webern's 1930 performance mirrored a belief in an overarching compositional logic governing the entire work. This rendered illegitimate the Wagnerian and post-Wagnerian approach to performance that invited adaptations to the expressive rhetoric of later nineteenth-century Romanticism. The stress on the structural totality of the symphony's design rendered the implications of Beethoven's narrative intentions and even the changed title page irrelevant. The historical content in the work derived from its totalising musical logic. A translation seeking to articulate musical meaning as history in ordinary language could not rely on biographical claims regarding intentions but on the work's distinctive musical structure and procedures.

Furthermore, during the twentieth century, research in historical performance practices and instruments was inspired by this approach. The

Eroica was reconnected to its historical context by replicating the expressive devices and performance habits of Beethoven's lifetime. The fast tempo indications were honoured. The sound lost its lush and rich post-Wagnerian quality. Doublings of wind instruments were discontinued. The balances among wind, brass and strings shifted away from the strings, and timpani sonorities assumed a hard-edged prominence that rendered the antique novel.

Nonetheless the alliance between formal analysis, historical scholarship and period performance practice grew out of late nineteenth-century patterns of reception among musicians and critics, including efforts to emancipate the *Eroica* from the limitations implied by the biographical circumstances of its composition. But the broader public has remained fascinated by inherited and long-unanswered questions. Was the 'heroic' aspect generic or tied to Bonaparte? Was the argument of the *Eroica* located in the ideals of the French Revolution? Did Beethoven prefigure the end of absolutism, and democracy? Does the *Eroica* point to a cosmopolitan utopia in which the end of history, as the last movement, culminates in a joyous and universal affirmation? Was the interpretive shift away from history by Wagner and Berlioz justified? Do the symphony's revolutionary elements – from the extended form of the first movement, including the unprecedented Coda, to the transfer of emphasis to the last movement and its variation form – sound significant to the modern audience in terms of politics and society?

By presuming to return the *Eroica* back to history in analysis and performance, has the twentieth century not only modernised the work but also unintentionally rendered it irrelevant and without the power to inspire the awe and ambition it retained throughout the nineteenth century? Not entirely. It was given a riveting performance by Adam Fischer (a vocal opponent of Viktor Orban's government and the assault on liberal democracy in Hungary) in Düsseldorf in 2018, at a ceremony where a prize was given to George Soros for the Open Society Foundation's advocacy for the rights of the Roma. This performance, of astonishing speed and intensity, sought to command the attention of the audience and vindicate the popular image of Beethoven as rebel, critic of convention, and advocate of political freedom and the moral obligation to act against injustice.

The Düsseldorf audience's reaction confirmed the resilience of the nineteenth-century discourse about the *Eroica* as expressed in innumerable books on music history and guides to the repertoire. A representative sample will be discussed below. The writers of concert guides treated listeners as if they were tourists embarked on a journey to foreign lands, dependent on Baedeckers. The claims, conclusions and clichés circulated by the authors of these musical tour guides continue to dwarf serious attempts at theoretical or historical revisionism. The habits of reading

about music before and after playing or listening that flourished in the nineteenth and early twentieth centuries still persist among the audience.

The prevailing view of the *Eroica* as formulated and disseminated in one of the first popular guides from the 1850s reveals the centrality of Wagner's reading of the work. Ernst von Elterlein (actually Ernst Gottschald), a state functionary and musical amateur born in 1826, wrote two famous guides, one to the Beethoven piano sonatas, and the other, published in 1858, to the Beethoven symphonies. For Elterlein, the *Eroica* marked the beginning of Beethoven's 'emancipation' from the past. He came into his own with one 'gigantic onward stride'. The *Eroica* ushered in a new era of musical aesthetics. Its 'poetic idea' and formal 'embodiment' represented an indivisible unity.[40]

Elterlein credited Wagner with discovering this unity and resolving the seeming disconnect between the first two movements and the last two. The *Eroica* was revealed as representing the full range of human emotions, reconciling disparate human attributes by distilling the 'inmost nature' of human individuality. The reconciliation of contradictions in human nature – therefore the journey and its triumphant conclusion – defines Beethoven's realisation of the 'heroic' in music.[41]

A starker contrast to Elterlein than Hermann Kretzschmar would be hard to imagine. Kretzschmar was among the most admired and influential historians of music in German-speaking Europe. In 1887, the 40-year-old Kretzschmar published his *Führer durch den Konzertsaal*. It became the most widely distributed and respected German guide to the concert repertoire. Kretzschmar flattered his reader by foregrounding the incomprehension with which the *Eroica* had been initially greeted. Its 'exotic' grandeur both delighted and offended its contemporaries, in part because what sounded new had appeared 'overnight' without warning. The *Eroica* defined Beethoven's genius and secured his reputation as an innovator. It was therefore no surprise that the composer considered it his finest symphony (before the publication of the Ninth).[42]

Kretzschmar pioneered in asserting the authority of historical scholarship and the objective validity of descriptive analysis couched in the technical language of music theory. He provided a detailed sequential account of the events of the symphony, including themes, key changes and instrumentation. His descriptive analysis of events is limited to events the audience can easily identify. He alerts them as to what to listen for. Kretzschmar's ambition was to guide the audience through the unfolding musical fabric. The 'plot' of the music, in his summary, in turn becomes the basis for an eloquent appraisal of the greatness and novelty of the *Eroica*.

Kretzschmar is therefore dismissive of efforts to read into the music the story of the work's dedication to Napoleon and its withdrawal. Likewise, he

discourages speculation on the meaning of the heroic. He rejects Wagner's attempt to assign a unifying meaning to each movement. Imputing a coherent programme to the outer movements seems 'petty'. Kretzschmar assimilated from Wagner and Berlioz the idea that the symphony is distinguished by contradictory qualities, each potentially suggestive of the heroic. Power and action are implied by the music, as are pathos and the elegiac. Kretzschmar seeks to guide the reader to appreciate Beethoven's ingenuity. He explains in detail why the horn entrance before the recapitulation in the opening movement was not a mistake even though it unsettled expert listeners. For Kretzschmar, by focusing on Beethoven's originality as a composer, one can sense how idiosyncratic and personal the composer's understanding of the heroic was.

Kretzschmar's concert guide went through many editions. The *Eroica* entry in the 1919 edition is essentially unchanged, augmented only by references to new historical scholarship.[43] What was added included Bekker's insight into the last movement, the link to the figure of Prometheus, the thematic resemblance to Mozart's overture to *Bastien und Bastienne*, and an echo from a work by Beethoven's teacher in Bonn, Neefe. Kretzschmar's guide was expanded and revised posthumously; he died in 1924. Friedrich Noack, who took over, chose not to tamper with the original text.[44] Kretzschmar's overriding goal was to counter the Wagnerian disposition to infer implicit or explicit philosophical, historical or political meanings in the *Eroica*, despite his evident sympathy for Wagner's brilliant appropriation of Beethoven in his music.

In the year Kretzschmar's guide appeared, Wilhelm Langhans (an orchestral musician before turning to music history in the 1870s) undertook a two-volume expansion of August Wilhelm Ambros's classic history of music. In contrast to Kretzschmar, Langhans accepted Wagner's reading of the *Eroica*. Langhans interpreted the poor reception of the symphony in its time as proof that it was a harbinger of the triumph of the Wagnerian aesthetic.[45] This allegiance to the Wagnerian account dominated the *Eroica* entry in Max Chop's popular book on the Beethoven symphonies, published in the first decade of the twentieth century. Reclam, a pioneer in the production and distribution of inexpensive pocket-size books, was its publisher, insuring success for Chop, a music journalist, composer and ardent advocate of Wagner. Chop quoted extensively from Wagner.

What distinguished Chop's account of the *Eroica* was his expansive biographical account of Beethoven's rejection of the dedication to Napoleon. Chop took pains to describe Beethoven's distaste for Bonaparte after 1804, his awareness of the hypocrisy and superficiality of Napoleon's character, and the bankruptcy of any claim that Napoleon

merited the status of a hero. Although Chop's book resembled Kretzschmar's guide in its presentation of musical examples, it deviated by engaging explicitly in politics. Chop sought to reinterpret Beethoven as a modern German patriot. He exploited the context of Wilhelmine nationalism, which had been profoundly influenced by Wagner. An anti-French bias flourished in Imperial Germany, particularly in the two decades before World War I. Chop appropriated Beethoven to the Wagnerian and nationalist cause. The volume remained in print after Chop's death in 1929.[46]

Perhaps the most popular German-language guide to the concert repertoire after Kretzschmar was a multi-volume series issued in 1912 by the Viennese publisher Schlesinger. The first volume was on the Beethoven symphonies, edited by Adolf Pochhammer (born in 1864, and the head of the Musikhochschule in Aaachen), with the *Eroica* entry written by Ernst Radecke (1866–1920) who came from a long line of musicians and trained as a music historian. Radecke, obviously influenced by Bekker, emphasised the significance of the final movement. Beethoven transcended the limits of variation form and achieved a seemingly effortless triumph of inspiration and spirit over convention.[47]

Radecke compared Beethoven's genius to that of a painter, rather than a poet. He was clearly no Wagnerian and identified Schumann as the heir to Beethoven's innovative use of rhythm in the third movement of the *Eroica*. Radecke assured his readers that they need not worry if the final two movements did not fit easily into a construct of the heroic or a narrative. The music in those movements managed to reverse the mourning and gravity of the first two. The *Eroica* ended, in Radecke's account, with music suggestive of a visual image of an idealised reality characterised by 'the Good, the True and the Beautiful'.[48]

Radecke's remarkable reliance on the visual dimension led him to stress the second movement's imagery as a public event. The coffin, surrounded by 'the entire community', inspires mourning for their 'leader, their supporter, their defender and friend'. The heroic is crystallised as political within a quotidian setting. The mythic, poetic and philosophical construct of the heroic articulated by Wagner is circumvented. For Radecke the first movement is cinematic, a sequence of images created by sound. The listener becomes a witness to the hero's development, growth, ambition, striving and victory. At the movement's end, the hero is seen standing before his people, in illuminated splendour, as the supporter and benefactor of humanity.

Radecke sought to persuade the listener to set aside exaggerated programmatic speculation. If, however, one wished to ruminate on the nature of the hero Beethoven might have had in mind, then the music held the key. The hero of the *Eroica* emerges as a 'great man' worthy of praise, whether in 'politics, war, science or art' on account of the 'breakthrough' of

his original formal achievements. The heroic in the *Eroica* breaks free, in Radecke's reading, from the realm of power and violence, and is redefined as creativity in science and art.[49]

Radecke's account pointed to the possibility of locating a new utopian vision in the *Eroica*: a new age defined not by war and politics but by the life of the mind and the imagination. Nietzsche, not Wagner, set the terms of Radecke's hero as artist and thinker. Radecke's version of the *Eroica*'s utopian vision mirrored values from the work's historical context. Beethoven, like Goethe and Kant, linked the heroic to the triumph in history of reason, truth, the good and the beautiful. Perhaps Radecke's vision will have the last word.

Notes

1. P. H. Goepp, *Symphonies and Their Meaning* (Philadelphia and London: Lippincott, 1925), pp. 104, 108, 97.
2. Ibid., pp. 97–8, 107.
3. Ibid., p. 97.
4. H. Moldenhauer and R. Moldenhauer, *Anton von Webern: A Chronicle of His Life and Work* (New York, NY: Knopf, 1979), p. 76.
5. See E. F. Jensen, 'Webern and Giovanni Segantini's Trittico della natura', *The Musical Times*, 130 (1989), pp. 11–15.
6. L. Hevesi, *Acht Jahre Sezession: Kritik, Polemik, Chronik*, ed. and intro. O. Breicha (Vienna: Konegen, 1906; repr. 1984), pp. 187–8.
7. Ibid., pp. 185–6.
8. L. Hevesi, *Oesterreichische Kunst 1848–1900* (Leipzig: E. A. Seeman, 1903), part 2, pp. 320–2.
9. Hevesi, *Acht Jahre Sezession*, pp. 185–6.
10. F. Weingartner, 'Wo bleibt die moderne Eroika' ['Where is the Modern Eroika?'] (1918), in *Unwirkliches und Wirkliches* (Vienna: Saturn, n.d.), pp. 64–72.
11. Ibid., p. 64.
12. Ibid., p. 65.
13. Ibid., p. 68.
14. Ibid., p. 71. See also *Im Mass der Moderne: Felix Weingartner – Dirigent, Komponist, Autor, Reisender*, ed. S. Obert and M. Schmidt (Basel: Schwabe, 2009).
15. Weingartner, 'Wo bleibt die moderne Eroika?', p. 67.
16. A. B. Marx, 'Beethoven', in *Encyclopädie der gesammten musikalischen Wissenschaft, oder Universal-Lexikon der Tonkunst*, ed. G. Schilling (Stuttgart: Köhler, 1835), pp. 513–20, especially p. 519.
17. H. Berlioz, *A Critical Study of Beethoven's Nine Symphonies*, trans. E. Evans (London: Reeves, n. d.), p. 41.
18. Ibid., pp. 46, 44.
19. R. Wagner, 'Beethoven's "Heroic Symphony"', in *Richard Wagner's Prose Works*, vol. 3: *The Theater*, trans. W. Ashton Ellis (New York, NY: Broude, 1966), pp. 221–4.
20. C. Wagner, *Diaries. Vol. 1: 1869–1877*, ed. M. Gregor-Dellin and D. Mack, trans. G. Skelton (New York, NY and London: Harcourt Brace Jovanovich, 1978), p. 183.
21. In Romain Rolland's *Jean Christophe*, completed in 1915 and the culmination of the nineteenth-century French image of Beethoven, the composer would emerge as a hero in his own right, as the Napoleon of the arts, a genius dedicated to French revolutionary ideals.
22. Goepp, *Symphonies and Their Meaning*.
23. Wagner, 'Beethoven's "Heroic" Symphony', pp. 221–2.
24. A. Schoenberg, 'How I Came to Compose the *Ode to Napoleon*' (1944), in *Stile herrschen, Gedanken siegen: Ausgewählte Schriften*, ed. A. M. Morazzoni (Mainz: Schott, 2017), p. 468.
25. P. Bekker, *Beethoven* (Berlin: Schuster & Loeffler, 1912), pp. 209–27.

26. Ibid.

27. M. Broyles, *Beethoven in America* (Bloomington, IN: Indiana University Press, 2011), p. 295.

28. Bekker, *Beethoven*, p. 211.

29. Ibid., p. 219.

30. Ibid., pp. 209–11 and 224–5.

31. F. Weingartner, *On the Performance of Beethoven Symphonies*, trans. J. Crosland (New York, NY: Kalmus, n.d.), pp. 30, 41.

32. Stein, quoted in Moldenhauer and Moldenhauer, *Anton von Webern*, p. 345.

33. D. F. Tovey, 'Symphony in E♭ major *(Sinfonia Eroica)*, No. 3, Op. 55', in *Symphonies and Other Orchestral Works* (New York, NY: Oxford University Press, 1989), p. 47.

34. F. Weingartner, 'Eine Begegnung mit einer Zeitgenossin Beethovens', in *Akkorde* (Leipzig: Breitkopf & Härtel, 1912), p. 4, and 'Zurück zu Mozart?' in ibid., pp. 108–11.

35. R. Brinkmann, *Late Idyll: The Second Symphony of Johannes Brahms*, trans. P. Palmer (Cambridge, MA: Harvard University Press, 1995), p. 55.

36. Ibid., pp. 59–60.

37. See J. Yust, *Organized Time: Rhythm, Tonality and Form* (Oxford: Oxford University Press, 2018), pp. 191–5.

38. T. W. Adorno, 'On the Problem of Musical Analysis' (1969), in *Essays on Music*, ed. R. Leppert, trans. S. Gillespie (Berkeley, CA: University of California Press, 2002), p. 176.

39. Ibid.

40. E. von Elterlein, *Beethoven's Symphonies in Their Ideal Significance* (London: Reeves, n.d.), pp. 33–43.

41. Ibid., pp. 36–7.

42. H. Kretzschmar, *Führer durch den Konzertsaal*, Part 1: *Sinfonie und Suite* (Leipzig: Liebeskind, 1887), pp. 77–8.

43. H. Kretzschmar, *Führer durch den Konzertsaal*, Part 1: *Sinfonie und Suite* (Leipzig: Breitkopf & Härtel, 1919), pp. 199–207.

44. H. Kretzschmar, *Führer durch den Konzertsaal: Sinfonie und Suite: Von Gabrieli bis Schumann*, ed. F. Noack (Leipzig: Breitkopf & Härtel, 1924), pp. 206–14.

45. W. Langhans, *Die Geschichte der Musik des 17., 18., und 19. Jahrhunderts* (Leipzig: Leuckart, 1887), pp. 219–22.

46. M. Chop, *Ludwig van Beethovens Symphonien* (Leipzig: Reclam, n.d.), pp. 77–81.

47. E. Radecke, 'Symphonie in Es-dur (Eroica), op. 55', in *Beethoven's Symphonien, erläutert mit Notenbeispielen, nebst einer Einleitung von A. Pochhammer* (Berlin: Schlesinger'sche Buch- und Musikhandlung [c.1913–14), pp. 62–87.

48. Ibid., pp. 78 and 74.

49. Ibid., pp. 66–7.

11 Performing, Arranging and Rearranging the *Eroica*: Then and Now

NANCY NOVEMBER

If this symphony is not by some means abridged, it will soon fall into disuse.[1]

A reviewer for the London *Harmonicon* in 1829 expressed dismay at the *Eroica* Symphony's difficulty and length, a reaction typical for the time. To modern-day readers, though, such opinions might be puzzling. Whose standards are reflected here? Could the work still be considered to *be* Beethoven's *Eroica* Symphony if it were abridged? And if performing the symphony entails 'use', then by whom and for what purpose? Such questions about the work's ontological status reflect latter-day ideas and assumptions about the nature of Western classical musical works, which did not necessarily apply in the period in question. This chapter explores performances of the *Eroica*, from the time of its premiere to the present day, considering how performance history changed with changing conceptions of the symphony as a musical work.

Performance is thus treated as an important aspect of reception history in this chapter. And abridged versions, arrangements and rearrangements are a significant part of this history: they were one of the main ways people came to experience and know symphonic music in the nineteenth century. As the nineteenth century progressed, factors such as new venues, playing techniques, instruments, orchestral sizes and conductors all led to fresh interpretations of the work. Reinvention of the work through performance continues into the present day, perhaps most notably in the form of the BBC's film *Eroica*, which dramatises the first performance, and makes much of the work's touted 'turning point' status. Thus performance is also considered to be a process of canon formation.

William Weber discusses the 'performance canon' as one central way in which canons of musical works are created – the most obvious and 'public' mechanism of canon formation.[2] However, the numerous nineteenth-century arrangements of symphonic music, which were largely for private use, still played a vital role in canon formation, and in the emerging idea of the symphony as a canonic genre.[3] Owing to the large number of arrangements of the *Eroica* for various ensembles in the nineteenth century, the

work never fell out of the repertory of actively performed music. This long-standing culture of varied performance, combined with appealing narrative and biographical aspects of the work, have made the *Eroica* one of the most popular of Beethoven's nine symphonies in terms of performance, second only to the Fifth.

The Premiere and Early Performances

The earliest rehearsals and performances of the Third Symphony were semi-private, taking place in the palace of Prince Lobkowitz, one of Beethoven's Viennese patrons. An account record dated 9 June 1804, submitted by Anton Wranitzky, Kapellmeister to the prince, shows that Lobkowitz hired twenty-two extra musicians (including the third horn required for the *Eroica*) for two rehearsals of the work, which might seem very few by today's standards but was then rather generous. A typical orchestra at this time had around forty musicians. The fee paid to Beethoven by Prince Lobkowitz would also have secured further private performances of the symphony that summer on his Bohemian estates, Eisenberg (Jezeří) and Raudnitz (Roudnice). The first public performance was on 7 April 1805, at the Theater an der Wien. In these senses – few rehearsals, small scale, and private performance before the debut – the performance history of this work began in a fashion fairly typical for a symphonic work for the time. In fact, Beethoven was comparatively lucky, especially with the extra musicians: high inflation and political unrest took a toll on court orchestras, and the Viennese, in particular, struggled to perform symphonic works at this time. Lobkowitz's unusual and extravagant expenditure on music led to financial strain in the early 1800s.[4]

New with the *Eroica* was the degree to which performers and listeners struggled with the work – in terms of both its length and its complexity. Early reviewers were often ambivalent, and the ambivalence often turned on difficulties of performance (see also Chapter 9). To be sure, early reviewers did not immediately consider Beethoven's earlier symphonies much easier to listen to or play. But especially with and after the *Eroica*, the earlier works came to be considered less demanding by comparison. Writers looked back longingly to the First and Second Symphonies, wishing Beethoven would stay within the more traditional (known, comprehensible) models of symphonic writing. In the following review, for example, from the Viennese correspondent for the *Allgemeine musikalische Zeitung*, from 1805, the *Eroica* is compared unfavourably to the First Symphony with regard to difficulty of performance:

> At the residence of Mr. von Würth, the Beethoven Symphony in C Major was performed with precision and ease. A magnificent artistic creation. All instruments are used exquisitely, and an uncommon wealth of beautiful ideas is magnificently and charmingly displayed in it. Nevertheless, cohesion, order and light dominate everywhere. A completely new symphony by Beethoven [the *Eroica*] . . . is written in a completely different style . . . [The *Eroica* is] exceedingly difficult to perform . . . very often seems to lose itself in irregularities.[5]

Such opinions of the work were partly a function of the standards of those who were now attempting to perform it: ad hoc amateur groups were starting to take the place of court orchestras, and many of the amateur groups were probably not up to the difficulties imposed by the *Eroica*.[6] The semi-public concerts that took place in the residence of the Viennese banker Joseph Würth are a case in point.

The reviews suggest that the difficulties of understanding that began with the *Eroica* were largely related to its being addressed to the connoisseur. Comparing the work unfavourably to the Second Symphony, an early reviewer observed:

> Two years ago Beethoven wrote a third great symphony, approximately in the same style as the second, but *yet* richer in ideas and artistic development, and certainly even broader, deeper, and more drawn out, so that it takes an hour to perform. Now this is certainly overdone, since everything must have its limits. If a true great genius may demand that criticism not set these limits for him according to caprice or custom, he must also respect those limits that are not dictated to him by this or that public, but by the ability of people in general to comprehend and enjoy.[7]

Citing Schiller's trilogy of dramas, *Wallenstein*, the writer went on to argue that a concession to the limits of the comprehension of 'everyman' is all the more important with instrumental music, where there is no text to aid understanding.

Many other early reviewers suggest difficulties for the early performers. In 1805, the above-cited writer for the *Allgemeine musikalische Zeitung* used the idea of the 'wild fantasia' to hammer home his complaint, the fantasia being a private genre for the connoisseur, so not well suited for large-scale concerted music:

> This long composition, exceedingly difficult to perform, is actually a very broadly expanded, bold, and wild fantasia.[8]

The Mannheim correspondent for the *Allgemeine musikalische Zeitung* remarked of a performance of the *Eroica* Symphony in 1807: 'Trying to perform such a colossal work was a great gamble, and only through the support of several members of the court orchestra could it be brought about.'[9] In this context, the 'colossal' nature of the work can be understood

in terms of its length and style, rather than the number of instruments that it required, which, as mentioned, was not particularly large.

The growing culture of rehearsal, and of treating a symphonic work as something that would need to be performed repeatedly in order to be properly understood, was emerging with particular force with this work. Another reviewer of the *Eroica* from 1807 could report admirable fidelity to the composer's intentions. This was just three months after the report cited immediately above, but now in Leipzig rather than Mannheim, where a skilled orchestra was available. This successful performance depended on a degree of preparation that was exceptional for the time, as is clear from the length at which the writer describes the rehearsals:

> Such a work as this requires some special preparation on the part of the orchestra, as well as several precautions with regard to a mixed public, if it is to be given its due in terms of performance and reception . . . The orchestra had voluntarily gathered for extra rehearsals without recompense, except for the honour and special enjoyment of the work itself. At these rehearsals the symphony was available in score, so that even the slightest triviality would not escape observation, and overall the players would penetrate the meaning and purpose of the composer with greater certainty. And so this most difficult of all symphonies (if, that is, one does not wish simply to play the notes correctly) was performed not only with the greatest accuracy and precision, but also everywhere with congruence and consistency, with grace, neatness and delicacy, and with an accommodation of the specially combined instruments to each other. In short, it was performed just as anyone could wish who had studied the score, even the ingenious composer himself.[10]

According to this reviewer, performers must not only follow the composer's notation to the letter, but also study the score in minute detail to try to penetrate the spirit of the work.

Performances of Beethoven's *Eroica* soon became more widespread and more professional. The symphony was performed in Prague as early as 1807, for example. But English listeners were still having difficulty with Beethoven's complex and multi-layered symphonies into the third decade of the nineteenth century. Reviewers repeatedly noted that the *Eroica* was considered too long and complex to sustain concentration. So, for example, one *Harmonicon* writer of 1829 observed: 'The Heroic Symphony contains much to admire, but it is difficult to keep up admiration of this kind during three long quarters of an hour. It is infinitely too lengthy.'[11] The Viennese correspondent for the Leipzig *Allgemeine musikalische Zeitung* had reported in 1805 that 'it lasted an entire hour'. The writer was probably talking about psychological time, rather than actual elapsed performance time. Even with exposition repeats, the *Eroica* symphony is only approximately 50 minutes long.[12] But at the time of

the symphony's premiere it was the longest symphony that had ever been written.

Beethoven went some way towards ameliorating the listeners' discomfort with the symphony's length, without actually abridging the work. He appended a note to the original edition of the performing parts to suggest that, on account of its length and difficulty, the symphony ought to be programmed first. But this advice was not necessarily followed. As Weber notes, the order in which genres followed each other on concert programmes was a matter of custom at this time, and depended on how works were perceived and valued. Overtures and symphonies usually served to open or close a concert – thus functioning as lesser-valued bookends that either settled the audience or accompanied their often early departure. But in the 1807 Gewandhaus Orchestra concert, for example, the *Eroica* was programmed just after intermission, a break with tradition that helped to elevate the work to canonic status.[13]

Nineteenth-Century Arrangements

Arrangements, for domestic settings and for various chamber ensembles, helped listeners and performers to come to terms with the new level of complexity presented by Beethoven's symphonies. Indeed they provided opportunities for repeated and hands-on experiences of large-scale works in general in an era before professional orchestras became common. So, for example, an early reviewer of an arrangement for piano trio of Beethoven's Second Symphony complained about the *Eroica*'s difficulty, but saw arrangements as a possible compensating aid, commenting that 'one receives a not unworthy picture of the entire piece that is as complete as possible'.[14] Arrangements of Beethoven's symphonies allowed repeated performance and close study of the music in a convenient 'take home' form, which might still retain some of the benefits of the original version. A reviewer of August Eberhard Müller's four-hand version of the *Eroica* in 1807 first praised the Leipzig Gewandhaus orchestra for programming the symphony twice in its entirety, then moved on to compliment Müller's arrangement for in effect allowing listeners more of the same:

> This grand, rich composition was recently performed twice as an orchestral symphony in Leipzig with extraordinary effect and has already aroused astonishment in other great cities. It belongs among those few symphonies that, with their spirited energy, set the listener's imagination into a sublime flight and sweep his heart away to powerful emotions. But the connoisseur will only enjoy it as a complete work (and a repeated hearing doubles his spiritual enjoyment) the deeper he penetrates into the technical and aesthetic content of the original

work . . . Since there are so few orchestras complete and accomplished enough to perform such a difficult work suitably, and since even when one has heard it so performed, it is still very interesting to repeat this music to oneself on a good fortepiano, we will be grateful to the publisher and to Music Director Müller for having provided such a complete keyboard reduction so well suited to the instrument, as one could expect from the insights and talents of Mr. M. on the basis of other similar works. The list of distinguished compositions for four hands is not extensive, and accomplished keyboard players will find rewarding work here.[15]

The emphasis on 'completeness' in this review can be understood simply in terms of the two orchestral performances, which apparently included all the movements, and a full and able orchestra. But it also relates to the listening experience. The phrase used to describe the experience of the listener is striking: 'the listener's imagination' (die Phantasie des Zuhörers) is set in 'sublime flight' (erhabene Schwung). The idea of the sublime was drawn upon at this time to help reviewers to describe music that yields an experience that is overpowering, incomprehensible and awe-inspiring, but it also indicated an experience of the work in which the (connoisseur) listener plays a major role: here, feelings of the sublime arise within the listener and by means of the listener's imagination. The reviewer implies that with this composition, and a few other symphonies, the listener in an important sense 'completes' the work.

A review of an 1828 reprint of an anonymous 1807 piano quartet arrangement of the *Eroica* suggests how arrangements could work to inspire orchestral effects in the absence of an orchestra. This reviewer piles up visual metaphors that suggest that the onus lay on the listener in 'performing' the work, where performance is a matter of imaginative reconstruction:

> The copy of a giant tableau; a colossal statue on a reduced scale; Caesar's portrait shrunk by the pantograph; an antique bust of Carraran marble made over as a plaster cast. – One is readily satisfied, however, with a half-accurate silhouette when one cannot have the original. Then fantasy begins its sweet play, and all the world certainly knows the beneficial effect of the powers of imagination and recollection.[16]

In each case, the visual metaphors suggest a massive original reduced down greatly in one or more dimensions. The pantograph, for example, is a jointed-frame instrument that allows an image to be traced and simultaneously scaled down. In the case of the marble bust cast in plaster, the original is scaled down in terms of both weight and size. And with the silhouette, only the essential outline is retained. For each visual metaphor, the effect described is essentially the same: a play of imagination and

recollection ensues as the viewer carries out the requisite completion to re-imagine the original work. Ultimately, the listener 'performs' the *Eroica*.

Even if the listener were prepared to make an imaginative 'completion' of the *Eroica* symphony, it was still the role of the arranger to make the arrangement suggestive, and in the right kinds of ways, so that the listener is inspired to take on the role of co-creator or performer. Reviews from Beethoven's time indicate that the best arrangements bore in mind the instrumentation of their originals, and attempted to capture something of its character in translation. This feat was attempted in the earliest (anonymous) arrangement of the *Eroica*, for piano quartet, which was published in Vienna in 1807 and reviewed in the *Allgemeine musikalische Zeitung* in 1808. Arrangements were not necessarily simplifications of the originals to cater to amateur performers. In the case of the 1807 *Eroica* arrangement for piano quartet, the reviewer praised the extent to which the arranger captured the original contrast between wind and string instruments, and noted that the arrangement required experienced performers to render this contrast effective:

> This work, well known to all, and thoroughly reviewed in these pages, is here conscientiously arranged, and creates in this guise as great and good an effect as it possibly could in pieces that are carefully calculated to bring out the contrast between winds and strings. All four players must certainly be well practiced, in order to bring off this quartet.[17]

Thus the best arrangements were seen to be able to capture something of the original works' texture and timbre, even when no wind instruments were involved.[18]

Hummel's arrangement of the *Eroica* symphony, published by Schott around 1830, but completed in the 1820s, can be compared with two other early nineteenth-century versions with respect to the treatment of texture. Ries's piano quartet arrangement of Beethoven's *Eroica* Symphony (published posthumously by Simrock in 1857 but completed in the early nineteenth century), makes a useful point of comparison, as does the earliest arrangement (anonymous) for the same forces, which was published by Bureau des Arts et d'Industrie in 1807 and reviewed in the *Allgemeine musikalische Zeitung* (1808), cited above. Ries's arrangement of the *Eroica* clearly aims to translate the timbral contrasts for the new performing forces, giving all the parts important material and testing amateur performers' skills.

One can consider the third movement, Marcia funebre, for example. As in the 1807 piano quartet arrangement, the piano presents the strings' opening theme, leaving the violin to present the oboe version of the theme in bar 8 (Example 11.1a). The comparative difficulty of Ries's version is apparent in the thick texture of the piano part (four-note

Example 11.1 a) Anonymous arrangement of Beethoven's *Eroica* Symphony for piano quartet (Vienna: Bureau des Arts et d'Industrie, 1807), movement two, bars 1–5; b) Ferdinand Ries's piano quartet arrangement (Bonn: Simrock, 1857), movement two, bars 1–5; c) Johann Nepomuk Hummel's flute quartet arrangement (Mainz: Schott, *c.*1830), movement two, bars 1–5

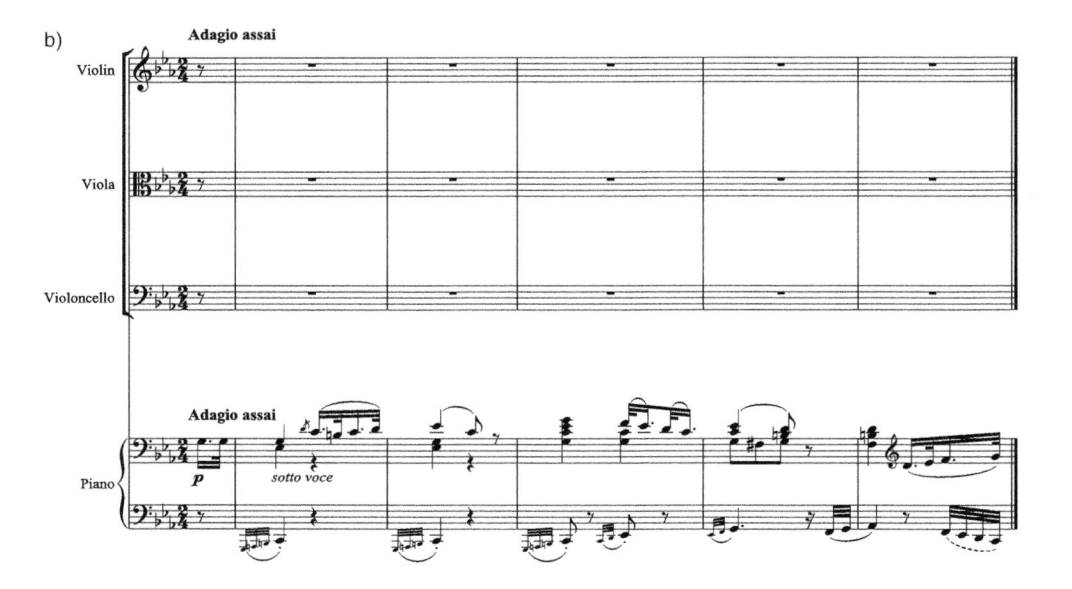

chords in the right hand, and octaves in the left, for example), which must still be performed *sotto voce* (Example 11.1b). There is also more attention to Beethoven's dynamic markings than in the 1807 arrangement. In both versions, the piano takes over with the strings' theme in bar 16, and in bar 36 the violin presents the oboe's theme. Here, and more generally

Example 11.1 (cont.)

in Ries's arrangement, he achieves more idiomatic string writing than the
1807 arranger by avoiding double stops in melodic passages. Meanwhile,
cello and viola are hardly just accompanying in their respective roles: the
viola's material derives from lower winds and brass, and Ries transposes
down the material from bar 41 so that the viola does not have to reach high
into the upper register in order to represent the clarinet and oboe; the viola
also takes the oboe solo at the lower octave at the beginning of the Maggiore.
The cello part is both higher and more active than that in the 1807 version,
and has a larger role in presenting thematic material – chiefly the wind and
brass lines. Also of note in Ries's version is the greater use of register to
represent the original score. In this opening, for example, Ries represents the
double bass's register; the 1807 version does not.

Hummel is less literal with his transcription than either of the above-
mentioned arrangers, but uses the means at his disposal to suggest to the
listener certain details of the instrumentation of the original that the other
versions do not capture. His is a more imaginative recreation, which
prompts listeners to do more work. The difficulty for the performers is
correspondingly greater. Consider the piano part at the opening of the
Marcia funebre. One sees details such as the metronome marking (quaver
= 80), which accurately represents Beethoven's metronome marking of
1817; the original dynamic marking (*pp sotto voce*, whereas Ries has *p sotto
voce*); and even an attempt to capture the original cello part in the left hand
in bars 3–4, giving a sense of space and depth that is not found in either of
the other two versions (Example 11.1c). Hummel's use of thicker chords in

both hands helps to preserve the original harmonies and give a sense of textural massivity despite the low dynamic range, as in the original orchestral opening.

However, Hummel's respect for the original does not necessarily mean that his version literally includes more material from the original than the other two versions. He clearly prioritises melodic over rhythmic content, for instance, apparently considering some quite prominent rhythmic material to be secondary or dispensable. One gets a sense of his priorities from the fact that the piano part has been designed to be played alone, and the other instruments function as an optional accompaniment. In bars 6–11 of the Marcia funebre, Hummel reverses what Ries does, giving the strings the repeated triplet motif (which is also found in the strings in the original), while piano and flute play the legato wind lines. Thus in Hummel's version for piano solo this otherwise pervasive rhythmic triplet figure will actually be omitted.

Negative reactions to the *Eroica* are scarce after 1805. This probably correlates with the numerous nineteenth-century arrangements of the work, which can be considered an index of a work's popularity as well as a means of helping with its perceived difficulties. It was one of the most popular of Beethoven's symphonies for arrangement. During Beethoven's lifetime, large-scale chamber arrangements of large-scale works were in favour. Before 1817, the First, Second, Third, Seventh and Eighth Symphonies of Beethoven had appeared in early arrangements for nonet. Of Beethoven's symphonies, only the first three were published in arrangements for string quartet in his lifetime: these are Carl Zulehner's arrangements of the First and Second Symphonies (1828); and an anonymous arrangement of the *Eroica* Symphony, which was issued by Bureau des Arts et d'Industrie (1807). Some of the more popular arrangements were for other kinds of quartet groupings: the Hummel arrangement of Beethoven's Fifth Symphony, for a piano quartet comprising flute, violin, cello and piano (or piano alone), is part of an extensive collection of arrangements he made for that grouping. The Hummel flute quartet arrangement of the *Eroica* Symphony is another example of the popularity of 'mixed' chamber groupings in general, and quartets involving strings and wind instruments in particular.

There were several grounds for preferring larger chamber ensembles for arrangements, especially for arrangements of orchestral works: to give a fairer representation of Beethoven's symphonic texture, and to help represent the different orchestral timbres. It was for these compositionally based reasons – the ability to represent texture and timbre – that a reviewer of an 1806 arrangement of Beethoven's *Eroica* Symphony for piano trio found the medium almost unfit for the task:

The Reviewer, who has heard the entire symphony often, but who certainly did not consider it in terms of an arrangement, would hardly have believed that, in regard to the major point, one so satisfactory and yet so well suited to all three instrument could be made from it as is actually given here. In fact, one received a not unworthy picture of the entire piece that is as complete as possible. In some parts, however, this was impossible. The beautiful Andante, for example, loses very much, since the masterful division among the various instruments, in particular the opposition of string and wind instruments, is missing. Also, several passages where the composer intended a beautiful effect based directly upon the charm or the distinctive characteristics of specific instrument here must leave us rather indifferent.[19]

Transcriptions and Reinterpretations

As the century wore on, the work became widely performed in symphonic form – which is not necessarily to say in its original guise. When the work was performed at the Philharmonic concert in 1827, it was thought fitting that it should end with the funeral march. When it was performed later that year in one of the Royal Academic Concerts, it was listed 'To end with the Marcia Funebre', as a tribute to Beethoven and omitting the other parts which are thought to be inconsistent with it. As will be seen, this emphasis on the Marcia funebre as the expressive 'heart' of the work persisted into the twentieth century. Indeed this movement would later sometimes be taken to stand for the entire work.

As orchestral concerts were becoming increasingly common, and were increasingly professionalised, emphasising fidelity to the score, so too arrangements were becoming more score-like and helping to instil a certain kind of concert-hall listening and performance. A prime example is the work of Liszt, who transcribed the entire cycle of Beethoven's symphonies for solo piano in the period 1837–65. He carefully marked in instrumentation, and wrote passages that were almost impossible to play (for anyone except himself) in an effort to preserve a sense of the original.[20] Arrangements were now more clearly becoming derivatives of 'complete' (original) works, intended to act as an *aide-mémoire*, or as stand-alone concert repertoire for public display. In the hands of Liszt especially, such arrangements aspired to the condition of scores, which now took over for the study of music. These arrangements, like the original *Beethoven-Gesamtausgabe* (Complete Critical Edition) deified Beethoven and made his symphonies seem untouchable.

On the other hand, some four-hand piano transcriptions gave rise to new embodied and social meanings for the symphonies. An example from Czerny's four-hand transcription of Beethoven's *Eroica*

Symphony demonstrates the intertwinement of the performers' hands and arms, which is typical of these more complex transcriptions, although the sharing of registral space is uncommon in Czerny's transcriptions. In bars 186–91 of the second movement, the Primo player's left hand must move to play notes that are lower than those played by the Secondo player's right hand. Achieving this requires the two pianists to adjust their hand positions simultaneously, to allow the other musician to occupy keyboard space that was his or hers only seconds before. This juggling act will inevitably result in physical contact between the two players. Such an arrangement moves far beyond mere presentation or replication of the original in miniature; rather, the arrangement gives rise to a challenging, entertaining and physically involved experience.

Liszt, who had the full (88-key) piano of more than seven octaves for at least the last twenty years of his life, spoke of the capability of the piano to replicate an orchestra in terms of use of register, and its ability to reproduce dense harmonies:

> Within the span of its seven octaves it encompasses the audible range of an orchestra, and the ten fingers of a single person are enough to render the harmonies produced by the union of over a hundred concerted instruments.[21]

But the idea of the symphony as numerically massive was more germane to Liszt's generation than it was to Beethoven's. In fact, the power and vastness produced by a hundred or so instruments playing together was only reached by Beethoven in the premiere of his Ninth Symphony in 1824. For the *Eroica* Symphony's first performances, the ensemble was very likely less than half the size Liszt had in mind.

With each new generation, and each new personality, new readings of the work arose, which are reflected in the performances. So, for example, Wagner connected the music abstractly with 'a Titan wrestling with the Gods'. Wagner's interpretations were written as a playbill for a performance of the *Eroica* in Zurich, which he himself conducted. They differed markedly from mainstream interpretations up to that point in that they connected the symphony to his own life and works, especially *Die Walküre* and *Siegfried*, rather than to Napoleon. There followed a shift towards psychological interpretations: the idea that Beethoven expressed his 'inner being' in the work took firm hold in the later nineteenth century. What remains common to many of the various interpretations of *Eroica* is a sense of heightened theatricality and penetrating dramatic power, prompting analogies with the work of Shakespeare, and with Greek drama – and the desire to see Beethoven himself as the hero depicted in the work.

Twentieth- and Twenty-First-Century Performance

Aspects of nineteenth-century *Eroica* interpretations persist. In a trend lasting from the mid-nineteenth century, the second movement, Adagio assai, has become a recurrent and at times almost automatic choice for music to be played at high-profile funerals, memorial services and commemorations. In 1847, the symphony's second movement was played at the funeral of the German composer Felix Mendelssohn. The choice was hardly surprising given Mendelssohn's connections to both Beethoven and the genre of the Funeral March. In our own time, the musical genre connections are no longer needed: the slow movement, in particular, has become linked with the act of public mourning. The deaths of two US presidents have been commemorated with this movement: Franklin D. Roosevelt in 1945 and John F. Kennedy in 1963; the latter occasion was an impromptu concert by the Boston Symphony Orchestra. And in 1957, the entire symphony was performed under Bruno Walter as a memorial concert for the conductor Arturo Toscanini. The movement was played in another high-profile, public memorial in 1972: the Munich Philharmonic under Rudolf Kempe played it at the funeral of the eleven Israeli athletes killed in a terrorist attack at the 1972 Summer Olympics in Munich.

One can regard these public performances as a new interpretational trend: the work, or rather the slow movement, which is now more frequently taken to represent the whole than it was in the nineteenth century, helps to create a sense of community understanding and empathy at a time of loss of national heroes. The *Eroica* is performed as a means of working through or coming to terms with the loss, in a public setting. This performance tradition arguably started with the early nineteenth-century 'abridged' *Eroica* performances in which the work ended with the funeral march, first in commemoration of Beethoven's death. The use of the *Eroica* slow movement to help mediate, understand and direct public grief is especially clear in the case of Kennedy, where the performance of the work is included as part of biographer Susan Bennett's moment-by-moment account of 'the four days that changed America'.[22] Performing the 'watershed' work became a way of thinking through this event as a turning point in US history.

In these contexts, the work is reinterpreted and used to new social and political ends. Accordingly, the work is performed in a manner that suits these particular ends. The large-scale commemorative performances of the twentieth and twenty-first century are prime examples of mainstream Beethoven symphony performance, differing from nineteenth-century performance practice in several principal ways. One of the most noticeable is tempo. Compared to the earliest performances – or at least those that

followed Beethoven's metronome markings – most mainstream orchestras take the *Eroica* at much faster tempi. Beethoven's tempo indications are as follows: movement 1, dotted crotchet = 60; movement 2, minim = 80; movement 3, dotted crotchet = 116; movement 4, minim = 76. In the case of Beethoven's Fifth, Peter Johnson finds that performances have generally slowed down over the twentieth century, at least among mainstream conductors and recordings. Johnson correlates this with a trend towards interpretations that emphasise pomp and solemnity.[23] In the case of the *Eroica*, the reverse is true. One of the slowest recordings is that of Wilhelm Furtwängler conducting the Vienna Philharmonic in 1948, although there are also some fairly slow recordings from the 1970s, notably Karl Böhm with the Vienna Philharmonic in 1972, and Leonard Bernstein with the same orchestra in 1978.

On the other hand, from the later twentieth century onwards, historically informed performance ensembles have tried to follow Beethoven's expectations to the letter. One of the fastest performances on record is David Zinman, with the Tonhalle Orchestra Zurich (1998), who take the third movement and the Presto of the finale even faster than Beethoven's notated tempi. Roger Norrington and the RSO Stuttgart likewise follow Beethoven's notated tempi in a 2002 recording, but only in slow movements and slow sections of the *Eroica*. These groups have experimented with considerably reduced performance forces, some even mirroring those that Beethoven would have had available to him at Lobkowitz's. An example is the 'Resonance' initiative of the Akademie Orchester in Vienna, led by Martin Haselböck, which includes a performance of the *Eroica* on original instruments in the Eroica-Saal of the Palais Lobkowitz, where the symphony was first rehearsed in 1804.[24] Such performances are contentious: this is hardly surprising given what has come to be invested in large-scale performances of this work in particular (national understanding, shared grief for national heroes, turning points in world political history). For example, one modern-day reviewer questions whether the work would really have been performed with such small forces, although this is a historically undeniable fact:

> Care has been taken to use the number of players appropriate to the setting. A letter by Beethoven from 1813 to Archduke Rudolph is quoted, 'I want at least four violins – four seconds, four firsts – two double basses and two cellos'. But this is a minimum number. And does it take into account the quite reverberant acoustic of the Hall which gives a pleasing glow to the wind instruments but allows the timpani to be booming?[25]

The case seems not dissimilar to the extensive arguments over 'Bach's chorus'. The B minor Mass has come to be one of the pillars of the High

Baroque. It is perceived as a pre-eminent representative of the massive corpus of Bach's vocal music and of Bach as the cultural figurehead of the North German Baroque. The so-called 'B minor madrigal' with one player per part does not do justice to this image any more than the 'Chamber *Eroica*' would seem to do justice to the 'watershed' symphony.[26] But the fact remains that Beethoven was prepared to live with an ensemble of just twelve strings as a minimum.

Modest performance forces (by modern standards) and faster tempi are just two aspects of historically informed performance today – and they are not necessarily the primary determinants of how we hear and interpret the music. The above-cited reviewer suggests that the slightly more sprightly performance of Le concert des nations under Jordi Savall is more in keeping with the work. Savall's *Eroica* is more 'incisive, dynamic', with 'more vital momentum and continuity of argument'; whereas Haselböck's is 'more smoothly melodious' and has a 'pleasing fluency'. Could it be that this reviewer mistakes hallmarks of modern-day historically informed performance in general – incision and dynamism – for imperatives of the *Eroica*'s performance in particular? Other defining features of historically informed performances of Beethoven's music include the ornamental use of vibrato and portamenti, and the more articulate manner of bowing and blowing. Each generation, including the HIP (historically informed performance) generation, arguably turns the work into something that accords with its own sensibilities. Today we can hear not only 'massive' *Eroica* performances that fit with the image of *Eroica* as watershed work, perhaps expressive of publicly experienced grief, but we also now have the smaller performances that fit with a new taste for things historically informed. As Taruskin would say, both instantiations represent a Beethoven wholly ours.[27]

The latest instance of an '*Eroica* wholly ours' is the BBC's 2003 period drama *Eroica*, directed by Simon Cellan Jones, which dramatises the first performance of the Third Symphony after the fashion of today's popular 'upstairs-downstairs' historical dramas. The music is played by Orchestre Révolutionaire et Romantique, conducted by Sir John Eliot Gardiner, so by a reasonably small orchestra compared with the mainstream, and in the original location, using original instruments. This film is on the one hand myth-debunking – in its choice of soundtrack – although Gardiner's forces are larger than Haselböck's and the orchestral sound is more lush. But in this film the first performance of the work is dramatised in a way that perpetuates and uses *Eroica* mythology on various levels.

The film is unique in taking a first performance of a musical work as its main subject. But on closer inspection, the performance is less the main subject than the occasion for rehearsing the main points of

Beethoven biography in connection with this work. Naturally the film does more than simply document an event: it interprets it thoroughly and interleaves the first performance with a completely new narrative of the film producers' own making (if partly based on historical record). The music itself, which one would think would be a main part of the diegesis, not infrequently becomes background music: lengthy shots of the first performance are intercut with other biographical anecdotes, while the symphony plays on. Ultimately, the Third Symphony provides a dramatic sonic backdrop against which the producers rehearse well-worn narratives about Beethoven's fiery temperament, his difficult love relationships, his creative process and his genius in general. To be sure, the producers go well beyond the 'performative' mode typical of documentaries of musical performance, showing close-up views of performers that might allow us to experience what it would be like to perform the music; in this way they try to 'take us there', to the time of the premiere. But more often than not in this film, the performance becomes an essentially non-diegetic soundtrack against which the producers' plot (a romance/clash of the classes) unfolds.

In the film, the performance difficulties of the work are thematised, and the overcoming of them is a part of the plot. Beethoven is portrayed as a firebrand, erecting difficult hurdles for the players. Prince Lobkowitz offers flattering praise to Haydn, while admonishing Beethoven who is within earshot: 'Unlike your own words [Beethoven's Third Symphony] does not strive for perfection of form . . . it's all roaring and grunting.' But the performers prevail: the film falls back on the teleological narratives of triumph and overcoming, which are recurrent in Beethoven biography and particularly in connection with this work. Asked how the work's performance is coming along, Ries reports glowingly that 'They've taken the symphony to new heights.' Most prominently, the film dramatises the traditional idea of *Eroica* as a watershed. Indeed, it carries the tagline 'The day that changed music forever.' Towards the end of the film, Haydn offers that the work is 'Quite new . . . everything is different from today.' Thus the film helps to further the conflation of history and work (here a work that 'does' weighty historical work) that has been typical in narratives of the *Eroica* since the nineteenth century.

Performances of the *Eroica* Symphony chart an important line of evidence in the work's reception history. First versions of the work, in the form of varied arrangements, were aids to understanding in a time in which orchestral performance was rare and Beethoven's symphonies represented a considerable cognitive challenge for listeners – not to mention an unprecedented challenge for orchestral performers, who were largely amateurs. But the numerous arrangements of the *Eroica* from the

nineteenth century are also a testament to the work's almost immediate and then continued popularity. Early nineteenth-century arrangements were unique in the performance history of the work in that they allowed hands-on experience of the work, by amateur performers in the home. From then on, the work would take on increasingly 'public' meanings, and move firmly into the domain of professional performance: the work's reception mirrors the increasing distance between listeners/audiences and performers in the realm of orchestral music, which emerged during the nineteenth century. Later nineteenth-century arrangements can be understood less as a substitute for the work and more as parallel means of performing, which would also help with the reception of the work in the concert hall setting.

The increasingly professional and large-scale performance of the *Eroica* went hand-in-hand with interpretations of Beethoven's career that would place a great emphasis on the turn to the middle ('heroic') period, and see this work as a watershed. *Eroica* has become not just a turning point for Beethoven, in the wake of his 'Heiligenstadt testament' and 'der neue Weg' (the much-touted 'new path'), but a massive turning point in the history of the symphony. In terms of performance, the understanding of *Eroica* as weighty, monumental and thus musically untouchable as is evident today in HIP performances, which, even in some radical instances, seem to remain within the fairly tight parameters associated with such performances. The 'weighty and monumental' reading of the work that still holds sway is perhaps most evident in *Eroica* the film, in which every turn in the work 'plays out' fresh suspense and revelation on 'the day that changed music forever'.

Notes

1. *The Harmonicon*, 5 (1827), p. 146.
2. W. Weber, 'The History of Musical Canon', in *Rethinking Music*, ed. N. Cook and M. Everist (Oxford: Oxford University Press, 1999), pp. 343–9.
3. On this subject see J. Parakilas, 'The Power of Domestication in the Lives of Musical Canon', *Repercussions*, 4 (1995), pp. 5–25.
4. D. W. Jones, *The Symphony in Beethoven's Vienna* (Cambridge: Cambridge University Press, 2006), p. 45.
5. *Allgemeine musikalische Zeitung*, 7 (1805), col. 321. Translations are the author's own unless otherwise noted.
6. See W. Senner, R. Wallace and W. Meredith (eds.), *The Critical Reception of Beethoven's Compositions by His German Contemporaries*, 2 vols. (Lincoln: University of Nebraska, 1999 and 2001), vol. 1 (1999), 168, n. 1. On Würth's concerts, including their fate during the Napoleonic Wars, see M. S. Morrow, *Concert Life in Haydn's Vienna: Aspects of a Developing Musical and Social Institution* (Stuyvesant, NY: Pendragon, 1989), pp. 121–5.
7. *Allgemeine musikalische Zeitung*, 9 (1806), col. 8; trans. in Senner et al., *The Critical Reception of Beethoven's Compositions*, vol. 1, p. 201 (emphasis original).
8. *Allgemeine musikalische Zeitung*, 7 (1805), col. 322; trans. in ibid., p. 168.
9. *Allgemeine musikalische Zeitung*, 9 (1807), cols. 285–6.

10. *Allgemeine musikalische Zeitung*, 9 (1807), cols. 497–8; trans. in Senner et al., *The Critical Reception of Beethoven's Compositions*, vol. 2, p. 53.
11. *The Harmonicon*, 7 (1829), p. 92.
12. For comparison: the Second, Fourth and Fifth Symphonies take 30 to 35 minutes to perform, the Sixth 40 minutes, the Seventh around 37 minutes, the First and Eighth 25 to 28 minutes, the Ninth 70 minutes.
13. Weber, 'The History of Musical Canon', pp. 348–9.
14. See n. 7.
15. *Zeitung für die elegante Welt*, 8 (1807), pp. 276–7 (emphasis added); trans. in Senner et al., *The Critical Reception of Beethoven's Compositions*, vol. 2, p. 35.
16. *Allgemeiner musikalischer Anzeiger*, 1 (1829), p. 199; trans. in Senner et al., *The Critical Reception of Beethoven's Compositions*, vol. 2, p. 41.
17. *Allgemeine musikalische Zeitung*, 10 (1808), col. 320.
18. Ibid.
19. *Allegmeine musikalische Zeitung*, 9 (1806), col. 9.
20. Z. Domokos, '"Orchestration des Pianofortes": Beethovens Symphonien in Transkriptionen von Franz Liszt und seinen Vorgängern', *Studia Musicologica Academiae Scientiarum Hungaricae*, 37 (1996), pp. 227–318; see also M. Kroll, 'On a Pedestal and Under the Microscope: The Arrangements of Beethoven Symphonies by Liszt and Hummel', in *Franz Liszt und seine Bedeutung in der europäischen Musikkultur*, ed. M. Štefková (Bratislava: Ustav hudobnej vedy SAV, 2012), pp. 123–44.
21. F. Liszt, *An Artist's Journey: Letters d'un bachelier ès musique, 1835–1841*, trans. C. Suttoni (Chicago, IL: Chicago University Press, 1989), p. 45.
22. S. Bennett, *President Kennedy Has Been Shot: Experience the Moment-to-Moment Account of the Four Days that Changed America* (Naperville, IL: Sourcebooks Mediafusion, 2003).
23. P. Johnson, 'The Legacy of Recordings', in *Collected Work: Musical Performance: A Guide to Understanding* (Cambridge: Cambridge University Press, 2002), pp. 197–212.
24. See www.wienerakademie.at/en/resound (accessed 3 July, 2019).
25. See M. Greenhalgh, 'Review: Resound Beethoven Volume 4 [*Eroica* Symphony]', www .musicweb-international.com/classrev/2017/Apr/Beethoven_sy3_474.htm (accessed 3 July 2019).
26. The term was coined in response to 'B Minor Madrigal', see J. Rifkin, 'Bach's Chorus: A Preliminary Report', *The Musical Times*, 123 (1982), pp. 747–51 and 753–4; and his 1981 recording of the B Minor Mass (Nonesuch 3/38 – nla).
27. See R. Taruskin, *Text and Act: Essays on Music and Performance* (Oxford: Oxford University Press, 1995).

12 The *Eroica* Endures: Beethoven's Third Symphony in the Twenty-First Century

MELANIE LOWE

Perennial Popularity

During the 2011–12 concert season, Beethoven's Third Symphony was the work most frequently performed by American orchestras. Only twice this century was the *Eroica* not among the top twenty programmed works in the United States. More often, it was in the top ten, as all of the 'tier one' orchestras in North America have programmed the symphony at least once since 2000.[1] Europe's leading orchestras remain equally committed to the *Eroica*. The Berlin Philharmonic, the London Symphony Orchestra and the Dresden Staatskapelle each already programmed the work several times in the twenty-first century, while the Royal Concertgebouw Orchestra and the Vienna Philharmonic racked up twenty-six and fifty-one performances respectively, the latter choosing the *Eroica* to close the 'Vienna Philharmonic Week in New York' concert in March 2019. The piece is no less favoured in Asia and Australia, where the Hong Kong Philharmonic, the KBS Symphony Orchestra, the Tokyo Philharmonic, the Melbourne Symphony Orchestra and the Sydney Symphony Orchestra (to name only five leading orchestras) continue to play Beethoven's Third Symphony every few years both at home and on tour.

More evidence of the *Eroica*'s enduring popularity is its reliable top-100 spot on Classic FM's Hall of Fame list, a survey conducted each year by the United Kingdom's on-air home for 'The World's Greatest Music'. Although consistently bested by Beethoven's Fifth, Sixth, Seventh and Ninth Symphonies in this contest, the *Eroica*'s popularity endures. Only once this century did the symphony slip on the 'world's biggest poll of classical musical tastes', plunging to number 123 in 2002 but rebounding, undaunted, to number 80 the next year. But conductors, it would seem, fly the *Eroica* banner highest, as Beethoven's Third Symphony was voted the number one 'greatest symphony of all time' in the BBC Music Magazine's 2016 survey of 151 of the world's current top conductors.[2]

Enduring Emblem: Heroism and Revolution in Contemporary Classical Musical Culture

Like its perennial popularity, the *Eroica*'s 'branding' in twenty-first-century mainstream classical musical culture has hardly deviated from its nineteenth-century construction as the pre-eminent musical emblem of heroism and revolution, both political and aesthetic. Scott Burnham's words provide the now classic late twentieth-century scholarly encapsulation of the symphony's critical reception: 'with the *Eroica* Symphony, Beethoven becomes the hero of Western music, "The Man Who Freed Music". With this one work, Beethoven is said to liberate music from the stays of eighteenth-century convention, singlehandedly bringing music into a new age by giving it a transcendent voice equal to Western man's most cherished values'.[3] Classic FM's *Eroica* blurb distils nearly two centuries of critics and commentators, declaring beneath images of Beethoven and Napoleon that 'of all the works in the history of classical music, this is the one that definitively closed the door on the Classical period and ushered in fully the Romantic era'.[4] Orchestras' marketing materials similarly parrot permutations of this axiom of *Eroica* reception. For their November 2017 concerts under the baton of a new music director, for instance, the National Symphony Orchestra advertised the *Eroica* as 'Beethoven's revolutionary tribute to the heroic ideal', the music with which Beethoven 'swept away all previous notions of what a symphony could be or ought to be'.[5] In a sentiment no less sweeping, to promote the opening concert of the 2018–19 season, the Baltimore Symphony Orchestra billed the *Eroica* as 'a work that changed the course of music history'.[6] And in copy both tortured and trite, for three April 2019 concerts the Toronto Symphony Orchestra credited the symphony itself with the act of stylistic insurrection: 'Beethoven's "Eroica" broke every rule in the book of composing a symphony'.[7]

At least Beethoven the human retains his composerly agency in the 2003 television film *Eroica*, the British Broadcasting Corporation's historical re-enactment of 'the day that changed music forever'.[8] 'Didn't obey the rules?' Beethoven snaps sarcastically at his pupil Ferdinand Ries for shouting 'Fool! Wrong!' to stop the orchestra after the 'early' horn-call entrance 'didn't sound right'. In this entertaining if improbable dramatisation of the first reading of Beethoven's new symphony in Vienna on 9 June 1804, musicians, servants and Austrian aristocrats mill about the music room at Prince Lobkowitz's palace, tossing political popcorn at the viewer expecting credible conversation. Near the beginning of the film, for instance, when the horn player hastily stumbles through the door, Beethoven quips 'You're late for the Revolution,

Otto.' And answering an unmannerly query – 'And what rank? Landowner?' – from the surprisingly mature Count Dietrichstein,[9] Beethoven replies in kind, 'No, I'm a brain-owner', a clever if ahistorical recontextualisation of actual Beethoven snark.[10] Ries and Princess Marie Lobkowitz most clearly articulate for Beethoven his personal and revolutionary estimation of his status. In response to copyist Wenzel Sukowaty's concern that Beethoven 'can't talk to the nobility of Austria and Hungary as if they were equals', Ries defends his teacher: 'He believes he is noble by virtue of his talent. He doesn't accept the inequality.' And Marie sheepishly apologises to Dietrichstein for the 'brain-owner' crack by explaining: 'Our friend thinks his talent exempts him from everyday customs of deference.' 'It does, it does. Well, here it does, anyway', remarks the Prince, offering Beethoven reassurance, however tempered.

But the BBC's *Eroica* delivers its best brain candy in response to the revolutionary aspects of the music of the symphony rather than the political backdrop of its first read-through. When asked by his patron the Prince if those gathered will find the music original, Beethoven prophetically delivers his own critical reception: 'It's original from beginning to end.' On the opening chords, he directs the orchestra: 'This is a summons, an imperative.' A surprisingly astute servant whispers to Ries just at the moment the first movement drops into the coda, 'A Haydn would be over by now, sir, wouldn't it? He's buggered about with the whole thing, hasn't he?' And after the slow movement, Dietrichstein, representing an alignment of political conservatism and the critical mainstream, complains to Beethoven directly: 'This is a formless mass. A mere arrangement of noise. A great piling up of colossal ideas. It's very moving. In parts it has elements of the sublime. But it is also full of discord. And it lacks rounding out. It is not what *we* call a symphony.'[11] As to the music's subject: 'Heroism', Beethoven states plainly to Haydn (yes, Haydn, who in the film arrives on the scene as the Scherzo comes to a close), just to clear up any confusion left by the title of either the symphony or the film. The final revolutionary proclamation, however, is reserved for the wise and aged Haydn who, presciently channelling Wagner, profoundly voices the anecdote informed viewers have been waiting to hear: 'He's done something no other composer has attempted. He's placed himself at the centre of his work. He gives us a glimpse into his soul. I expect that's why it's so noisy. But it is quite, quite new – the artist as hero. Quite new. Everything is different from today.' As Haydn exits the scene, the last heroic variation of the finale swells to the foreground in the soundtrack, providing the requisite musical gravitas to the film's heavy-handed historical exegesis. All that remains is for Beethoven to violently tear the title page bearing the dedication to Bonaparte from his score, which he does, of course, cut

perfectly to the last cadence in G minor just before the Presto surges to the finale's triumphant end.[12]

Count Dietrichstein's complaints about Beethoven's 'arrangement of noise' in the BBC's *Eroica* would seem more fair and fitting were he describing a more recent self-proclaimed revolutionary symphony titled *Eroica*: Tan Dun's Internet Symphony No. 1, *Eroica*, composed in 2009 to fulfil a commission for the YouTube Symphony Orchestra's debut concert in Carnegie Hall. According to Tan himself, the intention of his brash pastiche of quotations from Beethoven's Third Symphony and other war-horses was to reflect this new orchestra's 'revolutionary idea' to 'bridge music's past and the present'.[13] Lofty though this *Eroica* composer's aim was, *New York Times* critic Anthony Tommasini punctured the soaring ambition of the inaugural internet symphony with the first classic line of its reception: 'This five-minute crowd-pleaser takes riffs from Beethoven's "Eroica" and folds them into a score teeming with clanking percussion, corny brass chorales, and perky passages that sounded as if *Crouching Tiger and Hidden Dragon* had somehow encountered the Lone Ranger.'[14]

Smart Heroes, Sophisticated Revolutionaries and Superior Status in Popular Culture

Beethoven's Third Symphony collides more gently with the visual media of twenty-first-century popular culture when it is deployed more conventionally: to convey long-established extra-musical meanings in film and television soundtracks. The tired use of classical music as a sign of wealth and elite status in American movies persists in the new century, as two quick examples of the *Eroica*'s Scherzo used diegetically will confirm. In the opening scene of the 2014 coming-of-age independent film *Beach Pillows*, two twenty-somethings break into what they believe is a wealthy friend's posh apartment. The flat is beautiful, spacious and impeccably decorated in 'MoMA-esque' style. Large oil paintings adorn the walls, art and architecture books fill the bookshelves, and a presumably expensive bottle of scotch sits on the kitchen counter. Just after one of the intruders comments that 'this place must have cost a fortune', he moves the stylus to the vinyl sitting on the turntable. The Scherzo of Beethoven's *Eroica* sounds while the two uninvited guests drink beer, smoke a joint and talk about the failures that are their lives. Just as the Scherzo hits the coda (the cue started at the reprise), the duo's foolery is interrupted when the apartment's actual inhabitants – a mum, dad, two kids and a dog – arrive home, the shock on each face cut to the beats of the movement's final cadence. To be sure, the bounciness of the Scherzo is compatible with the

playful if irreverent energy of the scene, but the primary function of Beethoven's music in this scene in *Beach Pillows* is to reinforce the sophistication of the residence and convey its incongruity with the two uninvited visitors. Ironically, however, at least for the astute viewer, even this conventional cinematic meaning of classical music risks failure here: the vinyl on the platter, plainly visible, is actually Handel's *Water Music Suite* from the 1959 *Reader's Digest* box set *Music of the World's Greatest Composers*.[15]

The diegetic use of Beethoven's *Eroica* in the 2014 romantic comedy-drama *Obvious Child* depends on a related cliché of musical signification in American visual media: the association of classical music with intelligence and highbrow culture. When the scene cuts to the inside of an independent bookseller in New York City, the Scherzo is heard under the dialogue as if on the store's sound system, immediately establishing the learned atmosphere of the shop. Although the selection of Beethoven's music for this scene may have been largely arbitrary, one could be tempted to read a touch more sophistication in this particular use of an *Eroica* excerpt. 'Unoppressive Non-Imperialist Bargain Books' is the name of the store, and Beethoven's revolutionary symphony may be a clever, if subtle, nod to the progressive politics of the shop, its owner, employee, and customers within the story, the social commentary of the film (it's boldly pro-choice) and even of the filmmaker Gillian Robespierre herself (the name echo also helps). Perhaps a step too far, but certainly a possible, if serendipitous, reading.

The non-diegetic use of Beethoven's *Eroica* in the 2015 blockbuster film *Mission Impossible – Rogue Nation*, the fifth instalment of the *Mission Impossible* action spy series, likewise taps into the well-worn filmic association between classical music and elite culture, but the choice of soundtrack music in this instance seems to imply more than just the clichéd signification. While classical musical enthusiasts were quite delighted by the film's smart action sequence choreographed and cut to a performance of Puccini's *Turandot* at the Vienna State Opera (Alex Ross, for one, notes a possible 'deep-inside joke' in the resemblance between the opera's first three notes and Lalo Schifrin's *Mission Impossible* theme song),[16] the placement of the excerpt from the coda of the *Eroica*'s first movement would likewise bring a knowing smile to the initiated viewer. Benjamin 'Benji' Dunn, the British technician-turned-field-agent team-member of the Impossible Mission Force, has 'won' tickets to see Puccini's opera, and Beethoven's symphony fades in as he picks up the brochure, grunts indignantly and absconds from his CIA office. The *Eroica* supplies a lengthy sound bridge for the scene change to Vienna: the final iteration of the first movement's heroic first theme is heard at full volume as the viewer glides towards the Stephansdom spire in an aerial shot. The *Eroica* continues as

Benji, now in Vienna, exits the U-Bahn, strutting victoriously in his tux en route to the opera. The winning smile is knocked off his face, however, when a stranger aggressively plants an envelope in his stomach, cutting the music off mid-passage (but on a downbeat, at least) to interrupt the final surge to a triumphant conclusion.

No less secure are the heroic associations of the *Eroica*'s first movement when it sounds non-diegetically in the operating theatre of the American Broadcasting Company's primetime television medical drama *Grey's Anatomy*. In 'This Magic Moment' (Season 8, Episode 11), which first aired on 12 January 2012, the operating room is prepared – the scene set – to the first movement 'Alla rustica' of Vivaldi's Concerto for Strings in G major, RV 151, classical music once again tracking superior intelligence coupled with high occupational status. But the *Eroica*'s opening chords punch up the assertive command that follows: 'Team leaders, let's get in place.' The heroic first theme follows as the surgical teams move into position, Dr Owen Hunt's measured pep talk reminding his army of doctors (and informing the television viewers) of the high stakes of the epic campaign ahead – the separation of conjoined twins: 'Be sharp, be present, be focused. Dr. Robbins has been caring for these children since the day they were born. They will each get a new life today. Our actions will determine what kind of lives they will be.' Slick splicing provides the musical suture, and the movement's final cadence sounds as sterile drapes are pulled back from the table to reveal two conjoined – dolls. It may be just a practice run, but Dr Hunt's last command of the scene – 'Let's begin', inserted between Beethoven's penultimate and final chords – leaves no doubt about the heroic surgical struggle ahead.

But the very first episode of the Netflix award-winning original documentary series *Chef's Table*, now in its fifth season, takes the signification cake in its tracking of the fusion of sophistication, revolution, heroism and triumph over adversity with Beethoven's *Eroica* Symphony. The episode profiles Massimo Bottura, chef patron of Modena's three-Michelin-star restaurant Osteria Francescana, first at the time of writing in The World's 50 Best Restaurants.[17] The soundtrack is chock-full of classical music alongside original cues, all of which sound non-diegetically. The first movement of 'Winter' from Vivaldi's *Four Seasons*, the reliable pick for communicating refinement in a single bar, tracks the opening credits, as the visuals alternate between time-lapse photography of the frenetic activity in the Osteria Francescana kitchen and appreciative, slow-motion close-ups of individual dishes. But composer Max Richter has altered the metre in places, rendering Vivaldi's concerto as surprising as it is familiar, a clever nod to Chef Bottura's reimagining of traditional Emilian cooking. Chopin's Etude in C minor, Op. 10, No. 12 cleverly tracks the introduction

of the first intentionally 'provocative' (Bottura's word) plate served at Osteria Francescana, the 'revolutionary' (my word) dish 'Tortellini Walking Into Broth'. The reaction to Bottura's culinary insurrection? 'They want me dead', he recalls.

The next several years were difficult: Bottura's recipes were truly threatening to the Modenese. 'We were struggling, were really struggling', he explains in the documentary. 'I was ready to close the restaurant because it was totally empty.' Lara, Bottura's wife, elaborates, 'It wasn't like closing that restaurant was going to close down his desire to bring the Italian kitchen into the twenty-first century. If he left at that moment he would be surrendering, and surrendering a battle that would continue within him.' Fast forward to 2001, when the most important food critic in Italy wrote an article for *Espresso* in which he lamented that the Modenese didn't understand Bottura's cuisine. More gastronomic reviews followed, and as Lara explains, 'They started seeing in Massimo something that they hadn't seen for a while in Italy, which was someone who was willing to take risks.' Chef Bottura again: 'In November, we got the prize [from *Espresso Guide*] . . . as Best Chef, Young Chef in Italy, and the first star Michelin.' Cue Beethoven. As the *Eroica*'s opening chords sound, Bottura strides triumphantly through the front door of his restaurant, enters the kitchen and embraces his staff, the whole scene filmed in slow motion to amplify the momentousness. The Allegro con brio tracks a lengthy montage of service in a fully booked Osteria Francescana, with close-ups of the revolutionary culinary creations that secured Bottura's victory. A slick musical elision allows the final cadence to sound just as the last plate is served up for the viewing pleasure of esurient Netflix watchers.

Alongside predictable placements in film and television soundtracks, the *Eroica* also makes an appearance in Sid Meier's *Civilization IV*, the award-winning turn-based strategy computer game released in 2005. Widely celebrated for its multiple distinct playlists in the soundtrack, most of which make heavy use of Western classical music, *Civilization IV* proposes music as the most important cultural 'technology' in the game. Once discovered, music allows cathedrals to be built in a city, the construction of which increases culture which in turn boosts happiness.[18] Less inspired, however, is the particular use of the *Eroica*'s Marcia funebre as the diplomacy theme for Otto von Bismark.[19] Without too much effort, it is of course possible to hear the *Eroica* excerpt as memorialising the great hero who vanquished all enemies, unified Germany, and governed the German Empire for nearly twenty years as its first Imperial Chancellor. But Napoleon Bonaparte is also a named leader in *Civilization IV*, and his diplomacy theme is 'La Marseillaise', a choice which suggests not only missed opportunity but a certain lack of music-historical knowledge

among the game's designers and composers. True, legend has it that 'Bismark considered Beethoven's art a source of strength for his political achievements',[20] and Hans von Bülow did 'appallingly' rededicate the *Eroica* to Bismark in 1892.[21] But when one recalls that it was during Napoleon I's reign as Emperor of the French that 'La Marseillaise' was withdrawn as the French national anthem and, moreover, that Bismark requested that he be spared 'the monkey show' of a state funeral (a request that was honoured) while Bonaparte's remains were exhumed and carried through Paris in a grand funeral procession nearly two decades after he died, the *Eroica*'s *Marcia funebre* would seem the obvious choice for Bonaparte's diplomacy theme rather than Bismark's. There is also, of course, Beethoven's original dedication of the *Eroica* to Bonaparte.[22] Then again, by lead designer Soren Johnson's own admission, the *Civilization IV* musical selections were largely a result of his preference for the music of Bach, Mozart and Beethoven.[23] At the risk of undermining a central argument of this chapter, perhaps the lesson in this brief consideration of the *Civilization IV* soundtrack is not to read too much into such things.

Just as the hero mythology and stylistic revolutionary associations of the *Eroica* are reinforced in visual entertainments during the past two decades, the twenty-first-century's first English-language biography of Beethoven also subscribes to *Eroica* reception orthodoxy. Written not by a music historian but by the popular biographer and Pulitzer Prize-winner Edmund Morris for the Eminent Lives series, *Beethoven: The Universal Composer* (2005) has been knocked by critics for its hyperbole, reductive triumphal narrative and uncritical assertions of Beethoven's unparalleled greatness, even as this short book is appreciated for its readability and engaging rendering of character.[24] In the few pages devoted to the *Eroica*, Morris hears the symphony's two opening *fortissimo* chords as the 'cannon shot of a new symphonic language'[25] and the last movement as 'cast in a form never before to be attempted – part Classical variation, part an imperious exercise of will on intractable materials: godly fire applied to clay, the Code Napoléon transforming old laws'.[26]

Alternative Readings: Pastoral, Politics and Freedom in Musical Scholarship

In mainstream classical musical culture, visual media and popular biography, the homogeneity of twenty-first-century connotations of Beethoven's Third Symphony is quite striking. Such harmony among recent uses, associations and meanings of the *Eroica* extends the long-established

heroic-revolutionary trope further into the popular-cultural imagination while faithfully reflecting two centuries of the *Eroica*'s reception. Indeed, most contemporary engagements with the symphony do not challenge Burnham's assessment of the *Eroica*'s power: 'the conjunction of Beethoven's music with the ethical and mythical implications of the hero and his journey holds the entire reception history of this symphony in its sway'.[27] But alternative readings of the *Eroica* are emerging in musical scholarship alongside this basic heroic trope, as new critical theories engage with the work's traditional interpretations.

The pastoral is the linchpin in the first two new *Eroica* exegeses of the twenty-first century, both of which provide pivotal examples in the authors' respective book-length explorations of much broader issues and repertory. As the central work in the concluding chapter of *The Characteristic Symphony in the Age of Haydn and Beethoven* (2002), a groundbreaking study of eighteenth- and early nineteenth-century instrumental works in which a subject is specified by a text, Richard Will's reading of the *Eroica* shares much with those that situate the symphony within the art of the Napoleonic era: the first movement suggests conflict, battle, the constant threat of war and military deeds, and its heroic opening theme references the character of the *grand Uomo*. But when the famous chromatic C♯ of the opening phrase ascends to D, Will hears familiar pastoral references: the 'middle-register murmuring' of slurred figures in the second violins, the 'smoothing out of the first-violin syncopations into long tones', and the 'leisurely progress' of the violins and cellos towards tonic closure at the end of the phrase; in the restatement of the theme that immediately follows, solo woodwinds and horn 'prolong an idyllic atmosphere'.[28] In short, the hero of Will's reading is predisposed to digression from the outset. As forward motion in the exposition keeps 'giving way to a sensuousness that wafts out of the woodwinds, out of the pulsing rhythms and the *messe di voce* spanning each phrase, and out of the passing chromaticisms ... the *grand Uomo* would appear to have strayed into one of those erotic idylls where the heroes of epic are forever losing their way, the palace of Armida or the island of Calypso'.[29] More digressions follow in the movement, until the heroic theme finds its final form in the coda when the orchestration migrates from the pastoral to the military, culminating in a 'full-blown trumpet fanfare'. Because the military topic grows seamlessly out of the pastoral topic in Will's interpretation, 'the foil to the heroic identity has become its foundation, the conscience on which its endeavors build'. The character of the heroic theme in Will's reading is thus an amalgam, and just as the hero is transformed by the pastoral, so too are the meanings of idyllic stillness: 'If at first pastoral topics stand for distraction, for sensual or illusory retreats from duty, by the end [of the

first movement] they have become a landscape that inspires, like the Swiss mountains whose embedded history of freedom and justice motivate Schiller's Wilhelm Tell to his struggle against tyranny.'[30]

In *Beethoven after Napoleon* (2004), an exploration of political romanticism in Beethoven's late works, Stephen Rumph's reading of the pastoral element in the *Eroica*'s opening phrase is the converse of Will's. Where Will hears the pastoral topic surfacing at bar 9, when C♯ ascends to D, Rumph is 'drowsing in the idyllic countryside of the *Pastoral*' until the chromatic slip to C♯ in bar 7. With the addition of the jarring syncopations, off-beat violin 'shrieks', and diminished seventh harmony, the opening bars of the *Eroica* become 'a perfect musical symbol of an alienated nature'. This reading of the *Eroica*, in Rumph's own estimation, 'flies in the face of a long tradition ... of describing the symphony as a heroic military epic', as Rumph jettisons reception history to hear the work as drawing its 'chief sustenance from the naive realm of nature'.[31] Support for his argument comes from Beethoven's choice of key, the permeation of lower dance topics, the 'haunting' of Beethoven's work on *Prometheus* by Haydn's *Creation*, and even the pastoral literary references in the Heiligenstadt Testament.[32]

While the primary aim of Rumph's book may be to challenge traditional political interpretations of Beethoven's late works, he employs the same hermeneutic strategy when engaging the heroic style: hearing resonance of contemporary philosophical, aesthetic and political constructs in Beethoven's music. For the *Eroica*, the illuminating concept is the Enlightenment's narrative paradigm of the *Universalgeschichte*, which, in Rumph's elucidation, 'traces the education of humanity from an instinctual harmony with nature to a state of rational freedom'.[33] The *Universalgeschichte* allows Rumph to link Beethoven's ballet *Prometheus* to the Third Symphony philosophically and politically as well as musically and compositionally, a discursive connection that propels several sweeping interpretations: that the natural state, from which humanity was alienated in the seventh bar of the *Eroica*'s first movement, is finally regained in the periodicity of the finale's contredanse; that the individual is welcomed into the collective 'as the fragments of natural harmony reunite in the mirror patterns of choreography'; and that the dialectic of nature and culture is ultimately synthesised in the contredanse variations. Rumph's hermeneutics even link his *Eroica* to Beethoven's own heroic but alienated self: 'Out of the lonely depths of the Heiligenstadt Testament springs this festive, communal vision – the *Geschöpfe des Beethovens* become human simply by dancing together.'[34]

The repertory focus of Nicholas Mathew's book *Political Beethoven* (2013) may be Beethoven's much maligned occasional and overtly political

works, especially *Wellingtons Sieg*, *Der glorreiche Augenblick*, the Ninth Symphony and the *Missa solemnis*, but his task is much broader: 'to explore the ideological, musical and psycho-social mechanisms that have allowed Beethoven's music to collaborate with a succession of new historical actors'.[35] Mathew's 'network of collaborators' ultimately includes us, but he begins with Beethoven's 'collaborative politics' in Napoleonic Vienna and the critical history of the heroic style. No new exegesis of the *Eroica* per se is offered here, but Mathew's exploration of the critical reception that sets the intrinsic musical narrative of the *Eroica* in opposition to the extrinsic historical narrative of *Wellingtons Sieg* leads to a dialectical conception of the autonomy aesthetic, the philosophical construct at the heart of *Eroica* reception history. After tracing the history and historiography of the heroic style, especially criticism in which the ideal of the *Eroica* is placed in direct opposition to the real of *Wellingtons Sieg*, Mathew concludes that 'the autonomy of a work such as the *Eroica* can consequently only be measured by a disavowal of anything that it might be said to represent'. Or, put more generally, compositions that are granted 'independence from worldly matters' seem to 'have something to say about the world'.[36]

Daniel Chua's Adornian reading of the *Eroica* in his book *Beethoven & Freedom* (2017), however, rests on the notion that music's aesthetic autonomy is actually displaced political autonomy, as 'the eradication of reality on the surface allows music to retreat into an independent realm where it can reformulate the possibility of a freedom that has yet to be realised'.[37] Chua's rehearsals of German Idealist assertions of aesthetic autonomy and Adolf Bernhard Marx's claims for the self-determination of musical form certify the *Eroica*'s analogy with freedom as defined by Kant, leading to an essential point in his *Eroica* argument: in representing the unrepresentable, 'the *Eroica* is the embodiment of freedom, not just as a hero, but as a noumenal concept'.[38] This reading depends on the Third Symphony's articulations of Adorno's five states of nothingness, which, taken together, form the *Augenblick* – the aesthetic premise or, in Adorno's own words the 'very core', of his theory of the symphony: 'every artwork is an instant, a momentary suspension of its process'.[39] For example, Chua explains how, for Adorno, the opening of the *Eroica* is 'redeemed by nothing':

> what saves the motivic material from its nullity is its negation by the movement of the whole; the elements transcend the particular to become the totality. In fact, such is the process of perpetual negation that the hero's motif does not reach thematic selfhood until the very end of the movement, after 630 bars, where the 'insignificant' elements actually form themselves into a theme. But even here, with the hero's apotheosis in the coda, his victorious theme sounds almost *nichtig*. On its own, the theme is trivial, despite being trumpeted on the horns like a fanfare . . . The meaning of the particular 'is rescued though its nothingness'.

The theme does not close but is woven into the totality where its significance is affirmed ... So in the *Eroica*, the particular, through a process of perpetual cancellation, has its meaning deferred until the last cadence, where the 'totality of nothing' is confirmed as the 'totality of being'.[40]

In positing the *Eroica* as an 'eternal moment of freedom', Chua takes Adorno's *Augenblick* quite literally. To gauge the first movement as a blink in time, Chua measures

1. Time over distance to determine how fast the *Eroica* goes, and
2. Volume over distance to gauge how far sound travels in the *Eroica*.[41]

If this sounds gimmicky, well, it is. But overwrought metric cleverness notwithstanding, Chua links the *Eroica* to the *Zeitgeist* of the Napoleonic wars, the industrial revolution and notions of modern progress to argue that the first movement presents a 'radical reconception of speed'. As an act of will, speed in the *Eroica* is a 'potential energy'.[42] To demonstrate this reconception, Chua reads the first fourteen bars of the symphony as a thematic complex whose substance 'disperses and regroups at different points', yielding 'not a thematic timeline but a complex of multiple times that can rotate at different speeds and can be deployed at any given moment'. The hermeneutic upshot is that the heroic *Augenblick* 'proposes a different space-time dimension where speed is not a tempo but a decision that turns time into a subjective force'.[43] Because Beethoven's music can therefore cover vast distances in no time, Chua concludes that 'freedom, in the *Eroica*, is a moment'.[44]

Chua's final move is to analyse the 'early' horn-call and its super-imposition of a tonic triad over the dominant harmony as time out of joint:

somehow the hero's motif has misaligned itself, as if deflected at an odd angle within the form. Instead of articulating the point of thematic return, the echo's time-lag recycles the past to pre-empt the reprise, so that it literally becomes what Adorno pinpoints as the temporal structure of the Beethovenian symphony: 'a force retroacting in time' ... Originating from some undisclosed source in the exposition, the hero's motif ricochets back and forth, travelling almost 400 bars through the cataclysmic silence at the apex of the development section.[45]

Rather than some supernatural voice, as others have heard Beethoven's famous anticipation, the Adornian reading, transmitted through Chua, hears a collapse of distance: 'In effect, within the space of four bars, the speed of sound has become the speed of light.'[46]

Heroic Narrative and Disability: Overcoming

Turning now to a welcome grounding in the physical, the first movement of the *Eroica* is a central example in Joseph Straus's seminal article

on disability in music and music theory. By linking the primary tropes in the critical reception of the *Eroica* to the construction of disability, Straus shows how in most narrative readings Beethoven's music is 'metaphorically conflated with the body of a fleshly human being'.[47] Whether interpreted as a threat to mobility in the hero's journey or symbolic of Beethoven's deafness, the C♯ in bar 7 is the disabling obstacle to be heroically overcome in the drama of the movement. While such associations are deeply rooted in *Eroica* reception history, the relationship Straus reveals between these familiar readings and the history of disability is truly momentous. By pointing out that in 1802 it was a new idea that disability could be overcome and noting the founding of institutions for educating blind and deaf people in European capitals, particularly Vienna's *Taubstummeninstitut* for 'deaf-mutes', Straus establishes Beethoven's *Eroica* Symphony as an emblem in this new conception of disability: 'The narrative in the "Eroica" of disability overcome thus forms part of the history of disability, and that history in turn provides an essential context for the interpretation of Beethoven's life and work.'[48]

Human Narratives and Disability: Adaptation

Disability *not* overcome, however, may emerge as another new narrative thread in *Eroica* reception as disability studies are increasingly embraced in music scholarship. Robin Wallace's deeply personal book *Hearing Beethoven* does much to challenge the enduring 'triumph over adversity' mythology launched by the Heiligenstadt Testament and subsequently cemented in *Eroica* reception by the psychological approaches of Romain Rolland, Philip Downs and Maynard Solomon.[49] Part love letter to his late wife Barbara, who lost her hearing at the age of forty-seven, part examination of Beethoven's adaptations to his deafness, and part exploration of how Beethoven's diminishing hearing may have shaped his compositions, Wallace's book reveals Beethoven as human, not hero – a man who did not overcome his deafness but rather one who adapted. As Beethoven's hearing loss progressed, his compositional processes became more visual and physical, Wallace argues, and Landsberg 6, the *Eroica* sketchbook that immediately followed the Heiligenstadt crisis, provides key evidence. The opening melodic motive of the *Eroica*, which fills two bars in 3/4 time, Beethoven wrote with three quick penstrokes, and as Lewis Lockwood and Alan Gosman have noted, these three penstrokes are used over and over in the drafts for the first movement, sometimes even standing in for thematic material not yet written. Wallace sees

Beethoven using a simple visual cue in the *Eroica* sketches, one that was
'grounded in his physical sense of time', to stand for an important
musical event. Beethoven 'let his eyes take the lead ... The movement's
audible complexity was based on something he could see: something that
is still visible to anyone who cares to follow his path through the pages of
Landsberg 6'.[50] The truths Beethoven reveals through his adaptations
Wallace reminds us were true already: 'that music engages sight and
touch as well as hearing; that it originates in the body; that it is definitively shaped by the physical materials of its creation'.[51]

The *Eroica* is likewise denied the triumph of its heroic mythology in Joe
Wright's 2009 film *The Soloist*. The trope of Beethoven overcoming disability, not just his deafness but also his ostensible mental illness, haunts
the plot of the film for any viewer familiar with Beethoven's biography and
music. The presumed hero of *The Soloist*, Nathaniel Ayers, is homeless and
mentally ill, but he was once a promising young cellist studying at Juilliard.
Los Angeles Times columnist Steve Lopez tries to help Nathaniel get
treatment for schizophrenia and regain something of his previous life as
a musician. Lopez fails, but he does at least secure a place for Nathaniel to
sleep indoors.

Beethoven's heroic narrative, though unacknowledged in any of the
film's dialogue, literally sounds through *The Soloist*. In the first flashback to
Cleveland in the 1970s, the young Nathaniel hums the *Eroica*'s opening
heroic theme while walking to meet a potential music teacher; once in the
studio, Nathaniel plays the *Eroica*'s cello part from the beginning. When
the scene cuts back to present-day Los Angeles, young Nathaniel's cello
line continues, supplying a sound bridge from past to present. On the
phone with Lopez, Harry Barnoff, the music teacher, speaks over the now
non-diegetic *Eroica* melody, proclaiming Nathaniel as 'the most gifted kid
I ever met. I said that if he made a full commitment to music, if he really,
really gave it all he had, the whole world would open up to him'. Synced
perfectly with the dialogue, the cello part reaches the return to the heroic
theme just before Barnoff finishes his recollection: 'And he did, he really
did.' The disabling obstacle enters Nathaniel's narrative when the *Eroica*
hits the jarring syncopations of the development.[52] Nathaniel tunes out the
world around him while playing the cello part in his bedroom, the orchestra fading higher in the soundtrack to accompany him. At bar 279 in the
development, just four bars before the new theme, Nathaniel abruptly
stops playing and starts sobbing, the first hint of his impending psychological breakdown. When his mother comforts him later that night, assuring
him that 'you got something special here, baby ... a way out', the *Eroica*'s
heroic trajectory is clearly launched: Nathaniel is not fully formed but full
of potential; he will venture out into complexity and encounter adversity.

But, as we already know, he will not return renewed and completed. Nathaniel will not triumph.[53]

Nathaniel reaches his particular *ne plus ultra* in the *Eroica*'s Marcia funebre. During an orchestra rehearsal at Juilliard, Nathaniel, distracted by voices inside his head, plays out of time and flees from the rehearsal and ultimately his life as a student at the conservatory. The scene immediately cuts back to Nathaniel in the present, making music outside a shelter for homeless people with mental illness. He's playing the cello part of the Marcia funebre.

Especially significant in the soundtrack of *The Soloist* is the absence of the final form of the *Eroica*'s opening heroic theme, the trumpet fanfare that emerges in the theme only in the movement's coda. This crucial transformation is heard neither diegetically nor non-diegetically in the film. The moment of opportunity does present itself, however, when Lopez takes Nathaniel to the Los Angeles Philharmonic's rehearsal of the *Eroica*. As the opening chords strike, Nathaniel blinks;[54] when the heroic theme commences, with Nathaniel's heartbeat superimposed over the music, Nathaniel closes his eyes. The camera, up extremely close on his eyes, begins to zoom out and the scene eventually fades to black so as to allow the viewer to experience what Nathaniel sees (presumably) while listening: synesthetic flares of colour, like a psychedelic light show, cut to the music. Seamless audio editing jumps to the recapitulation, and the music abruptly stops at the end of the climactic passage of syncopated diminished seventh chords (bar 534), leaving the listener hanging with Nathaniel's words, uttered *sotto voce*, to fill the void: 'He's in the room.' 'Who is?' Lopez asks. Nathaniel: 'Beethoven.'

Nathaniel's *Eroica* never reaches the coda; its heroic theme never finds its triumphant blaze. In this way both the story and the soundtrack of *The Soloist* stay faithful to Steve Lopez's original narrative (at least on the course of Nathaniel's life), published in his 2008 book of the same title: Nathaniel is not cured of his mental illness, cannot recover his musical talents in full and does not emerge triumphant in the end. As Hollywood is denied its tired cliché of victory through art,[55] so too is the *Eroica* denied its customary heroic trajectory.

It remains to be seen how readings of the *Eroica* that have emerged in the first two decades of the twenty-first century might filter into broader cultural understandings or symbolic uses of the symphony, particularly in mainstream classical musical culture or visual entertainments. But at present, the *Eroica* remains the pre-eminent musical emblem of heroism in both critical reception and popular imagination, even when the heroic victory, however constructed, may elude.

Notes

1. League of American Orchestras, 'Orchestra Repertoire Report', americanorchestras.org, https://americanorchestras.org/knowledge-research-innovation/orr-survey/orr-archive.html (accessed 6 July 2019). Data available up to the 2012–13 season.
2. M. Brown, 'Beethoven's Eroica voted greatest symphony of all time', https://www.theguardian.com/music/2016/aug/04/beethoven-eroica-greatest-symphony-vote-bbc-mozart-mahler (accessed 24 January 2020).
3. S. Burnham, *Beethoven Hero* (Princeton: Princeton University Press, 1995), p. xvi.
4. Classic FM, 'Hall of Fame', classicfm.com, https://halloffame.classicfm.com/2018/#234 (accessed 9 July 2019).
5. The Kennedy Center, 'National Symphony Orchestra: Noseda conducts Beethoven's "Eroica"', kennedy-center.org, www.kennedy-center.org/calendar/Event/NSCSD#tickets (accessed 6 July 2019; website no longer active).
6. Baltimore Symphony Orchestra, '2018–2019 Events', https://www.bsomusic.org/calendar/events/2018–2019-events/beethoven-eroica-symphony/ (accessed 6 July 2019).
7. Toronto Symphony Orchestra, 'Beethoven Eroica Symphony', https://www.roythomsonhall.com/tickets/tso-beethoven-eroica-symphony-3/ (accessed 25 January 2020).
8. Tagline, *Eroica* [BBC film], directed by Simon Cellan Jones (London: Opus Arte, 2005).
9. Count Maurice Dietrichstein (Moritz Joseph von Dietrichstein) would have been 29 years old at the time of the first *Eroica* read-through at Prince Lobkowitz's palace, five years Beethoven's junior. In the film, however, Deitrichstein seems much older in both appearance and manner. He is portrayed by Tim Pigott-Smith who was his late fifties at the time of filming.
10. Beethoven's brother Johann had acquired an estate in 1819 and henceforth signed himself as 'Landowner'. Beethoven signed himself 'brain-owner' in a sarcastic reply. See A. Tyson, 'Ferdinand Ries (1784–1838): The History of his Contribution to Beethoven Biography', *19th-Century Music*, 7 (1984), pp. 209–21.
11. In essence, Dietrichstein's comments echo contemporary reviews of the *Eroica* (emphasis added). See also Chapters 9 and 11.
12. On the film's inaccurate portrayal of this event, along with its other factual inaccuracies, see N. Cook, 'Representing Beethoven: Romance and Sonata Form in Simon Cellan Jones's *Eroica*', in *Beyond the Soundtrack: Representing Music in Cinema*, ed. D. Goldmark, L. Kramer and R. Leppert (Berkeley, CA: University of California Press, 2007), pp. 27–47.
13. D. J. Wakin, 'Getting to Carnegie via YouTube', *New York Times*, 158 (4 December 2008), https://archive.nytimes.com/www.nytimes.com/learning/teachers/featured_articles/20081204thursday.html (accessed 6 July 2019).
14. A. Tommasini, 'YouTube Orchestra Melds Music Live and Online', *New York Times*, 158 (16 April 2009), https://www.nytimes.com/2009/04/17/arts/music/17symphony.html (accessed 6 July 2019).
15. On the ironic failure of classical musical signification in American media, see M. Lowe, *Pleasure and Meaning in the Classical Symphony* (Bloomington, IN: Indiana University Press, 2007), pp. 169–76.
16. A. Ross, 'Finally, A Non-Embarrassing Classical-Music Scene in a Blockbuster Movie', *The New Yorker* (11 August 2015), https://www.newyorker.com/culture/cultural-comment/finally-a-non-embarrassing-classical-music-scene-in-a-blockbuster-movie (accessed 6 July 2019).
17. O. Francescana, 'The World's 50 Best Restaurants,' https://www.theworlds50best.com/list/1-50 (accessed 6 July 2019).
18. K. M. Cook, 'Music, History, and Progress in Sid Meier's *Civilization IV*', in *Music in Video Games: Studying Play*, ed. K. J. Donnelly, W. Gibbons and N. Lerner (New York, NY: Routledge, 2014), p. 170.
19. The 'Bismark' theme's three stages of progress in *Civilization IV* can be heard here: https://www.youtube.com/watch?v=OZjHo3MqRY8 (accessed 6 July 2019).
20. D. B. Dennis, *Beethoven in German Politics, 1870–1989* (New Haven: Yale University Press, 1996), p. 37.
21. J. Oestreich, 'Beethoven as Idealist, Militarist, Rebel, Whatever', *New York Times*, 145 (6 March 1996), p. 17. Oestreich corrects Dennis's factual error concerning the tune to which Hans von Bülow fitted a heroic text. See Dennis, *Beethoven in German Politics*, pp. 45–7.
22. F. P. Stearns, The Life of Prince Otto Von Bismarck (London: J. B. Lippincott, 1899), p. 415.

23. Cook, 'Music, History, and Progress in Sid Meier's *Civilization IV*', p. 179.

24. See, for instance, R. Coles, 'Hooked on a Triumphal Groove', *The Times Literary Supplement*, 5430 (2007), p. 20; G. Sandow, 'The Concise Beethoven', *The New York Times Book Review* (6 November 2005), p. 37; and J. Raab, 'Beethoven: The Universal Composer (Review)', *Opera News*, 70 (2006), p. 65.

25. E. Morris, *Beethoven: The Universal Composer* (New York, NY: HarperCollins Publishers, 2005), p. 108.

26. Ibid., p. 100.

27. Burnham, *Beethoven Hero*, p. 27.

28. R. Will, *The Characteristic Symphony in the Age of Haydn and Beethoven* (Cambridge: Cambridge University Press, 2002), p. 210.

29. Ibid., p. 211.

30. Ibid., pp. 212–13.

31. S. Rumph, *Beethoven after Napoleon: Political Romanticism in the Late Works* (Berkeley, CA: University of California Press, 2004), p. 73.

32. Ibid., pp. 71–4.

33. Ibid., p. 66.

34. Ibid., p. 77.

35. N. Mathew, *Political Beethoven* (Cambridge: Cambridge University Press, 2013), p. 13.

36. Ibid., pp. 17–58.

37. D. Chua, *Beethoven & Freedom* (Oxford: Oxford University Press, 2017), p. 32.

38. Ibid., p. 37.

39. Quoted and trans. in B. Hoeckner, *Programming the Absolute: Nineteenth-Century German Music and the Hermeneutics of the Moment* (Princeton, NJ: Princeton University Press, 2002), p. 15.

40. Chua, *Beethoven & Freedom*, pp. 63–4.

41. Ibid., p. 71.

42. Ibid., p. 75.

43. Ibid., p. 79.

44. Ibid., pp. 73–84.

45. Ibid., pp. 85–6.

46. Ibid., p. 848.

47. J. N. Straus, 'Disability in Music and Music Theory', *Journal of the American Musicological Society*, 59 (2006), p. 155.

48. Ibid., 160.

49. R. Rolland, *Beethoven the Creator*, trans. E. Newman (New York, NY: Harper and Brothers, 1929), pp. 61–101; P. G. Downs, 'Beethoven's "New Way" and the Eroica', *Musical Quarterly*, 56 (1970), pp. 603–4; M. Solomon, *Beethoven*, 2nd edn (New York, NY: Schirmer Books, 1998), pp. 157–8.

50. R. Wallace, *Hearing Beethoven: A Story of Musical Loss and Discovery* (Chicago: University of Chicago Press, 2018), pp. 101–4.

51. Ibid., p. 222.

52. In this context, the C♯ in bar 7 is of course too subtle and sounds too soon to track the disabling obstacle.

53. This language is Burnham's: 'something (someone) not fully formed but full of potential ventures out into complexity and ramification (adversity), reaches a ne plus ultra (a crisis), and then returns renewed and completed (triumphant)'. Burnham, *Beethoven Hero*, p. 3.

54. Chua reads the imagery of Nathaniel's blinking as drawing from 'tacit knowledge of the Beethovenian *Augenblick*'. See Chua, *Beethoven & Freedom*, pp. 67–9.

55. Lopez's story, however, is every bit the Hollywood cliché: through his challenging experiences with Nathaniel, at the end of the film it is Lopez who is transformed, renewed and perhaps completed.

Further Reading

Chapter 1

Goethe, Johann Wolfgang von, *Egmont: A Tragedy in Five Acts*, trans. C. E. Passage (New York, NY: Frederick Ungar, 1980).

'Egmont', in H. Kurz (ed.), *Goethes Werke, Dritter Band* (Leipzig and Vienna: Bibliographisches Institut, no date, *c.*1870), pp. 97–170.

'Götz von Berlichingen', in H. Kurz (ed.), *Goethes Werke, Dritter Band* (Leipzig and Vienna, Bibliographisches Institut, no date, *c.*1870), pp. 5–96.

Head, Matthew, 'Beethoven Heroine: A Female Allegory of Music and Authorship in Egmont', *19th-Century Music*, 30 (2006), pp. 97–132.

Lockwood, Lewis, 'Beethoven, Florestan, and the Varieties of Heroism', in S. Burnham and M. P. Steinberg (eds.), *Beethoven and His World* (Princeton: Princeton University Press, 2000), pp. 27–47.

Schiller, Friedrich, *Schillers Werke: Nationalausgabe, Band 3: Die Räuber*, ed. Herbert Stubenrauch (Weimar: Hermann Bohlaus Nachfolger, 1953).

Schillers Werke: Nationalausgabe, Band 6: Don Karlos. Erstausgabe 1787. Thalia-Fragmente 1785–1787, ed. Paul Böckmann und Gerhard Kluge (Weimar: Hermann Bohlaus Nachfolger, 1973).

Schillers Werke: Nationalausgabe, Band 7, 1. Theil: Don Karlos. Hamburger Bühnenfassung 1787. Rigaer Bühnenfassung 1787. Letzte Ausgabe 1805, ed. Paul Böckmann und Gerhard Kluge (Weimar: Hermann Bohlaus Nachfolger, 1974).

'Was kann eine gute stehende Schaubühne eigentlich wirken?', in Benno von Wiese (ed.), *Schillers Werke: Nationalausgabe, Band 20: Philosophische Schriften, 1. Teil* (Weimar: Hermann Bohlaus Nachfolger, 1962), pp. 89–100.

Selfridge-Field, Elaine, 'Beethoven and Greek Classicism', *Journal of the History of Ideas*, 33 (1972), pp. 577–96.

Solomon, Maynard, *Beethoven Essays* (Cambridge, MA: Harvard University Press, 1988).

Chapter 2

Bent, Ian (ed.), *Music Analysis in the Nineteenth Century: Volume 1, Fugue, Form and Style* (Cambridge: Cambridge University Press, 1994).

Broyles, Michael, *Beethoven: The Emergence and Evolution of Beethoven's Heroic Style* (New York, NY: Excelsior, 1987).

Cook, Nicholas, 'The Other Beethoven: Heroism, the Canon, and the Works of 1813–14', *19th-Century Music*, 27 (2003), 3–24.

Dahlhaus, Carl, *Nineteenth-Century Music* (Berkeley, CA: University of California Press, 1989).

DeNora, Tia, *Beethoven and the Construction of Genius: Musical Politics in Vienna, 1792–1803* (Berkeley, CA: University of California Press, 1995).

'Deconstructing Periodization: Sociological Methods and Historical Ethnography in Late Eighteenth-Century Vienna', *Beethoven Forum*, 4 (1995), pp. 1–15.

Eggebrecht, Hans, *Zur Geschichte der Beethoven-Rezeption: Beethoven 1970* (Laaber: Laaber-Verlag, 1994).

Ferraguto, Mark. *Beethoven 1806, AMS Studies in Music* (New York, NY: Oxford University Press, 2019).

Goehr, Lydia, *The Imaginary Museum of Musical Works: An Essay in the Philosophy of Music* (Oxford: Oxford University Press, 1992).

Johnson, Douglas, Burnham, Scott G., Drabkin, William, Kerman, Joseph and Tyson, Alan, 'Beethoven, Ludwig van', *Grove Music Online*, https://doi.org/10.1093/gmo/9781561592630.article.40026 (accessed 18 July 2019).

Knittel, Krista Marta, 'The Construction of Beethoven', in J. Samson (ed.), *The Cambridge History of Nineteenth-Century Music* (Cambridge: Cambridge University Press, 2001), pp. 118–50.

'Imitation, Individuality, and Illness: Behind Beethoven's Three Styles', *Beethoven Forum*, 4 (1995), pp. 17–36.

'"Late", Last, and Least: On Being Beethoven's Quartet in F Major, Op. 135', *Music and Letters*, 87 (2006), pp. 16–51.

'Wagner, Deafness, and the Reception of Beethoven's Late Style', *Journal of the American Musicological Society*, 51 (1998), pp. 49–82.

Mathew, Nicholas, 'Beethoven and His Others: Criticism, Difference, and the Composer's Many Voices', *Beethoven Forum*, 13 (2006), pp. 148–87.

'Heroic Haydn, the Occasional Work and "Modern" Political Music', *Eighteenth-Century Music*, 4 (2007), pp. 7–25.

November, Nancy, *Beethoven's Theatrical Quartets: Opp. 59, 74, and 95* (Cambridge: Cambridge University Press, 2013).

Pestelli, Giorgio, *The Age of Mozart and Beethoven*, trans. Eric Cross (Cambridge: Cambridge University Press, 1984).

Sisman, Elaine, '"The Spirit of Mozart from Haydn's Hands": Beethoven's Musical Inheritance', in G. Stanley (ed.) *The Cambridge Companion to Beethoven* (Cambridge: Cambridge University Press, 2000), pp. 45–63.

Solomon, Maynard, *Beethoven* (New York, NY: Schirmer, 1998; orig pub. 1977).

Tyson, Alan, 'Beethoven's Heroic Phase', *Musical Times*, 110 (1969), pp. 139–41.

Webster, James, 'Between Enlightenment and Romanticism in Music History: "First Viennese Modernism" and the Delayed Nineteenth Century', *19th-Century Music*, 25 (2001–2), pp. 108–26.

'The Concept of Beethoven's "Early Period" in the Context of Periodization in General', *Beethoven Forum* 3 (1994), pp. 1–27.

'The Eighteenth Century as a Music-Historical Period?', *Eighteenth-Century Music*, 1 (2003), pp. 47–60.

Haydn's 'Farewell' Symphony and the Idea of Classical Style, Cambridge Studies in Music Theory and Analysis (Cambridge: Cambridge University Press, 1991).

Wilson, John David, 'Of Hunting, Horns, and Heroes: A Brief History of E♭ Major before the *Eroica*', *Journal of Musicological Research*, 32 (2013), pp. 163–82.

Chapter 3

Biba, Otto, 'Concert Life in Beethoven's Vienna', in R. Winter and B. Carr (eds.), *Beethoven, Performers, and Critics* (Detroit, MI: Wayne State University Press, 1980), pp. 77–93.

Irving, John, 'The Viennese Symphony 1750 to 1827', in J. Horton (ed.), *The Cambridge Companion to the Symphony* (Cambridge: Cambridge University Press, 2013), pp. 15–28.

Jones, David Wyn, *Music in Vienna: 1700, 1800, 1900* (Woodbridge: Boydell & Brewer, 2016).

Morrow, Mary Sue, *Concert Life in Haydn's Vienna* (Stuyvesant, NY: Pendragon, 1989).

Weber, William, *The Great Transformation of Musical Taste: Concert Programming from Haydn to Brahms* (Cambridge: Cambridge University Press, 2008).

The Symphony in Beethoven's Vienna (Cambridge: Cambridge University Press, 2009).

Zaslaw, Neal, *Mozart's Symphonies: Context, Performance Practice, Reception* (Oxford: Clarendon, 1989).

Chapter 4

Appel, Bernhard R., 'Zum Textstatus von Kompositions-Skizzen und -Entwürfen', in *Jahrbuch des Staatlichen Instituts für Musikforschung-Preußischer Kulturbesitz* (1999), pp. 177–210.

Brandenburg, Sieghard, 'Beethovens Skizzen. Probleme der Edition', *Die Musikforschung*, 44 (1991), pp. 346–55.

Cooper, Barry, *Beethoven and the Creative Process* (Oxford: Clarendon Press, 1990).

'L. Lockwood and A. Gosman, eds. Beethoven's "Eroica" Sketchbook' (review article), *Nineteenth-Century Music*, 12 (2015), pp. 1–5.

Fishman, Natan L., 'Das Skizzenbuch Beethovens aus den Jahren 1802–1803 aus dem Familienarchiv Wielhorski und die ersten Skizzen zur "Eroica"', in C. Dahlhaus (ed.), *Bericht über den internationalen musikwissenschaftlichen Kongreß Bonn 1970* (Kassel: Bärenreiter, 1971), pp. 104–7.

Kinderman, William, *The Creative Process in Music from Mozart to Kurtág* (Urbana, Chicago and Springfield: University of Illinois Press, 2012).

Konrad, Ulrich, *Werkstattblicke. Haydn, Beethoven und Wagner beim Komponieren beobachtet* (Mainz: Franz Steiner, 2014).

Lockwood, Lewis, *Beethoven: Studies in the Creative Process* (Cambridge, MA: Harvard University Press, 1992), pp. 167–80.

'The Compositional Genesis of the *Eroica* Finale', in William Kinderman (ed.), *Beethoven's Compositional Process* (Lincoln, NE: University of Nebraska Press, 1991), pp. 82–101.

Mikulicz, Karl L., 'Skizzen zur III. und V. Symphonie und über die Notwendigkeit einer Gesamtausgabe der Skizzen Beethovens' in *Beethoven-Zentenarfeier*.

Internationaler musikhistorischer Kongress (Vienna: Universal Edition, 1927), pp. 95–6.

Wade, Rachel, 'Beethoven's Eroica Sketchbook', *Fontes Artis Musicae*, 24 (1997), 254–89.

Chapter 5

Dahlhaus, Carl, *Ludwig van Beethoven: Approaches to his Music* (Oxford: Clarendon Press, 1991).

Epstein, David, *Beyond Orpheus: Studies in Musical Structure* (Cambridge, MA: MIT Press, 1979).

Halm, August, 'Über den Wert musikalischer Analysen, I: Der Fremdkörper im ersten Satz der Eroika', *Die Musik*, 21 (1929), pp. 481–4.

Lockwood, Lewis, '"Eroica" Perspectives: Strategy and Design in the First Movement', in A. Tyson (ed.), *Beethoven Studies 3* (Cambridge: Cambridge University Press, 1982), pp. 85–105.

Lockwood, Lewis and Gosman, Alan (eds.), *Beethoven's 'Eroica' Sketchbook: A Critical Edition*, 2 vols. (Urbana, Chicago and Springfield, IL: University of Illinois Press, 2013).

Nottebohm, Gustav, *Two Beethoven Sketchbooks: A Description with Musical Extracts*, trans. Jonathan Katz (London: Gollancz, 1979).

Riezler, Walter, *Beethoven*, trans. G. D. H. Pidcock (London: Forrester, 1938).

Schenker, Heinrich, 'Beethoven's Third Symphony: Its True Content Described for the First Time', trans. Derrick Puffett and Alfred Clayton, in W. Drabkin (ed.), *The Masterwork in Music*, vol. 3 (Cambridge: Cambridge University Press, 1997), pp. 10–68.

Tovey, Donald, *Musical Articles from the Encyclopaedia Britannica* (London: Oxford University Press, 1944).

Chapter 6

Byros, Vasili, 'Meyer's Anvil: Revisiting the Schema Concept', *Music Analysis*, 31 (2012), pp. 273–346.

'Topics and Harmonic Schemata: A Case from Beethoven', in D. Mirka (ed.), *The Oxford Handbook of Topic Theory* (New York, NY: Oxford University Press, 2014).

Cooper, Barry, 'Beethoven's Oratorio and the Heiligenstadt Testament', *The Beethoven Journal*, 10 (1995), pp. 19–24.

Hatten, Robert, *Musical Meaning in Beethoven: Markedness, Correlation, and Interpretation* (Bloomington, IN: Indiana University Press, 1994).

McClelland, Clive, *Ombra: Supernatural Music in the Eighteenth Century* (Lanham, MD: Lexington, 2012).

Mirka, Danuta (ed.), *The Oxford Handbook of Topic Theory* (New York, NY: Oxford University Press, 2014).

Sullivan, John William Navin, *Beethoven: His Spiritual Development* (New York, NY: Vintage Books, 1960).

Thayer, Alexander Wheelock, *Thayer's Life of Beethoven*, ed. Eliot Forbes (Princeton, NJ: Princeton University Press, 1980).

Chapter 7

Agawu, Kofi, 'Structural "Highpoints" in Schumann's "Dichterliebe"', *Music Analysis*, 3 (1984), pp. 159–80.

Fink, Robert, 'Going Flat: Post-Hierarchical Music Theory and the Musical Surface', in N. Cook and M. Everist (eds.), *Rethinking Music* (Oxford: Oxford University Press, 1999), pp. 102–37.

Lockwood, Lewis, 'Beethoven, Florestan, and the Varieties of Heroism', in S. Burnham and M. P. Steinberg (eds.), *Beethoven and His World* (Princeton, NJ: Princeton University Press, 2000), pp. 27–47.

Miller, Malcolm, 'Peak Experience: High Register and Structure in the "Razumovsky" Quartets, Op. 59', in William Kinderman (ed.), *The String Quartets of Beethoven* (Chicago, IL: University of Illinois Press, 2006), pp. 60–88.

Oster, Ernst, 'Register and the Large-Scale Connection', *Journal of Music Theory*, 5 (1961), pp. 54–71. Reprinted in M. Yeston (ed.), *Readings in Schenker* Analysis *and Other Approaches* (New Haven, CT: Yale University Press, 1977), pp. 54–71.

Chapter 8

Allanbrook, Wye J., *Rhythmic Gesture in Mozart: Le Nozze di Figaro and Don Giovanni* (Chicago, IL: University of Chicago Press, 1983).

Bertagnolli, Paul, *Prometheus in Music: Representations of the Myth in the Romantic Era* (Abingdon: Routledge, 2007).

Buurman, Erica, 'Beethoven's Compositional Approach to Multi-Movement Structures in His Instrumental Works', (unpublished PhD diss., University of Manchester, 2013).

Lockwood, Lewis, 'Beethoven's Earliest Sketches for the *Eroica* Symphony', *Musical Quarterly*, 67 (1981), 457–78.

McKee, Eric, 'Ballroom Dances of the Late Eighteenth Century', in D. Mirka (ed.) *The Oxford Handbook of Topic Theory* (New York, NY: Oxford University Press, 2014), pp. 164–93.

Rice, John A., *Empress Marie Therese and Music at the Viennese Court, 1792–1807* (Cambridge: Cambridge University Press, 2003).

Rosati, Gianpiero, 'Form in Motion: Weaving the Text in the *Metamorphosis*', in P. Knox (ed.), *Oxford Readings in Ovid* (Oxford: Oxford University Press, 2006), pp. 334–50.

Sisman, Elaine, *Haydn and the Classical Variation* (Cambridge, MA: Harvard University Press, 1993).

'Six of One: The Opus-Concept in the Eighteenth Century', in S. Gallagher and T. F. Kelly (eds.), *The Century of Bach and Mozart* (Cambridge, MA: Harvard University Press, 2008), pp. 79–107.

'Tradition and Transformation in the Alternating Variations of Haydn and Beethoven', *Acta musicologica*, 62 (1990), pp. 152–82.

'Variations', in Stanley Sadie (ed.) *The New Grove Dictionary of Music and Musicians*, rev. edn (Oxford: Oxford University Press, 2000), vol. 26, pp. 284–326.

Smart, Mary Ann, 'Beethoven Dances: Prometheus and His Creatures in Vienna and Milan', in N. Mathew and B. Walton (eds.), *The Invention of Beethoven and Rossini: Historiography, Analysis, Criticism* (Cambridge: Cambridge University Press, 2013), pp. 210–35.

Chapter 9

Brinkmann, Reinhold (trans. Irene Zedlacher). 'In the Times of the "Eroica"', in S. Burnham and M. P. Steinberg (eds.), *Beethoven and his World* (Princeton, NJ and Oxford: Princeton University Press, 2000), pp. 1–26.

Burnham, Scott, *Beethoven Hero* (Princeton, NJ: Princeton University Press, 1995).

Clubbe, John, 'The Eroica in its Revolutionary Context: Seume's Spaziergang nach Syrakus', *The Beethoven Journal*, 29 (2014), pp. 52–65.

Della Seta, Fabrizio, *Beethoven: Sinfonia Eroica. Una guida* (Rome: Carocci, 2004).

Floros, Constantin, *Beethovens Eroica und Prometheus-Musik. Sujet-Studien*, 2nd exp. edn (Wilhelmshaven: Florian Noetzel, 2008).

    Beethoven's Eroica. Thematic Studies, trans. Ernest Bernhardt-Kabisch (Frankfurt am Main: Peter Lang, 2013).

Geck, Martin and Schleuning, Peter, *'Geschrieben auf Bonaparte'. Beethovens 'Eroica': Revolution, Reaktion, Rezeption* (Reinbek: Rowohlt, 1989).

Kraus, Beate Angelika, *Beethoven-Rezeption in Frankreich. Von ihren Anfängen bis zum Unergang des Second Empire* (Bonn: Beethoven-Haus, 2001).

Rehding, Alexander, 'Heldentaten der Musik: Sinfonie Nr. 3 Eroica und Die Geschöpfe des Prometheus', in O. Korte and A. Riethmüller (eds.), *Beethovens Orchestermusik und Konzerte, Das Handbuch*, vol. 1 (Laaber: Laaber, 2013), pp. 71–94.

Sipe, Thomas, *Beethoven: Eroica Symphony* (Cambridge: Cambridge University Press, 1998).

    'Interpreting Beethoven: History, Aesthetics, and Critical Reception' (published PhD diss. University of Pennsylvania, 1992).

Chapter 10

Adorno, Theodor W., 'On the Problem of Musical Analysis' (1969), trans. S. Gillespie, in R. Leppert (ed.), *Essays on Music: Theodor W. Adorno* (Berkeley, CA: University of California Press, 2002), pp. 162–80.

Berlioz, Hector, *A Critical Study of Beethoven's Nine Symphonies*, trans. E. Evans (London: Reeves, n.d.).

Brinkmann, Reinhold, *Late Idyll: The Second Sympony of Johannes Brahms*, trans. Peter Palmer (Cambridge, MA: Harvard University Press, 1995).

Broyles, Michael, *Beethoven in America* (Bloomington, IN: Indiana University Press, 2011).

Goepp, Philip H., *Symphonies and Their Meaning* (Philadelphia, PA and London: Lippincott, 1925).

Jensen, Eric Frederick, 'Webern and Giovanni Segantini's Trittico della natura', *The Musical Times*, 130 (1989), pp. 11–15.

Marx, Adolph Bernhard, 'Beethoven', in G. Schilling (ed.), *Encyclopädie der gesammten musikalischen Wissenschaft, oder Universal-Lexikon der Tonkunst* (Stuttgart: Köhler, 1835), pp. 513–20.

Moldenhauer, Hans and Moldenhauer, Rosaleen, *Anton von Webern: A Chronicle of His Life and Work* (New York, NY: Knopf, 1979).

Schoenberg, Arnold. 'How I Came to Compose the *Ode to Napoleon*' (1944), in *'Stile herrschen, Gedanken siegen': Ausgewählte Schriften*, ed. A. M. Morazzoni (Mainz: Schott, 2017), pp. 467–73.

Tovey, Donald Francis, 'Symphony in E♭ major (*Sinfonia Eroica*), No. 3, Op. 55', in *Symphonies and Other Orchestral Works* (New York, NY: Oxford University Press, 1989), pp. 44–49.

Wagner, Richard, 'Beethoven's "Heroic Symphony"', trans. W. Ashton Ellis, in *Richard Wagner's Prose Works. Vol. 3: The Theater* (New York, NY: Broude, 1966), pp. 221–4.

Weingartner, Felix, 'Wo bleibt die moderne Eroika' (1918), in *Unwirkliches und Wirkliches* (Vienna: Saturn, n.d.), pp. 64–72.

Yust, Jason, *Organized Time: Rhythm, Tonality and Form* (Oxford: Oxford University Press, 2018).

Chapter 11

Bennett, Susan, *President Kennedy Has Been Shot: Experience the Moment-to-Moment Account of the Four Days that Changed America* (Naperville, IL: Sourcebooks Mediafusion, 2003).

Domokos, Zsuzsanna, '"Orchestration des Pianofortes": Beethovens Symphonien in Transkriptionen von Franz Liszt und seinen Vorgängern', *Studia Musicologica Academiae Scientiarum Hungaricae*, 37 (1996), pp. 227–318.

Johnson, Peter, 'The Legacy of Recordings', in J. Rink (ed.), *Musical Performance: A Guide to Understanding* (Cambridge: Cambridge University Press, 2002), pp. 197–212.

Jones, David W., *The Symphony in Beethoven's Vienna* (Cambridge: Cambridge University Press, 2006).

Kroll, Mark, 'On a Pedestal and Under the Microscope: The Arrangements of Beethoven Symphonies by Liszt and Hummel', in M. Štefková (ed.), *Franz Liszt und seine Bedeutung in der europäischen Musikkultur* (Bratislava: Ustav hudobnej vedy SAV, 2012), pp. 123–44.

Liszt, Franz, *An Artist's Journey: Letters d'un bachelier ès musique, 1835–1841*, trans. Charles Suttoni (Chicago, IL: Chicago University Press, 1989).

Parakilas, James, 'The Power of Domestication in the Lives of Musical Canon', *Repercussions*, 4 (1995), pp. 5–25.

Senner, Wayne, Wallace, Robin, and Meredith, William (eds.), *The Critical Reception of Beethoven's Compositions by His German Contemporaries*, 2 vols. (Lincoln, NB: University of Nebraska Press, 2001).

Taruskin, Richard, *Text and Act: Essays on Music and Performance* (Oxford: Oxford University Press, 1995).

Weber, William, 'The History of Musical Canon', in N. Cook and M. Everist (eds.), *Rethinking Music* (Oxford: Oxford University Press, 1999), pp. 343–49.

Chapter 12

Chua, Daniel, *Beethoven & Freedom* (Oxford: Oxford University Press, 2017).

Cook, Karen M., 'Music, History, and Progress in Sid Meier's *Civilization IV*', in K. J. Donnelly, W. Gibbons and N. Lerner (eds.), *Music in Video Games: Studying Play* (New York, NY: Routledge, 2014).

Cook, Nicholas, 'Representing Beethoven: Romance and Sonata Form in Simon Cellan Jones's *Eroica*', in D. Goldmark, L. Kramer and R. Leppert (eds.), *Beyond the Soundtrack: Representing Music in Cinema* (Berkeley, CA: University of California Press, 2007), pp. 27–47.

Jones, Simon Cellan (dir.), *Eroica* [DVD] (London: Opus Arte, 2005).

Mathew, Nicholas, *Political Beethoven* (Cambridge: Cambridge University Press, 2013).

Morris, Edmund, *Beethoven: The Universal Composer* (New York, NY: Harper Collins, 2005).

Rumph, Stephen, *Beethoven after Napoleon: Political Romanticism in the Late Works* (Berkeley, CA: University of California Press, 2004).

Straus, Joseph N., 'Disability in Music and Music Theory', *Journal of the American Musicological Society*, 59 (2006), pp. 113–84.

Wallace, Robin, *Hearing Beethoven: A Story of Musical Loss and Discovery* (Chicago, IL: University of Chicago Press, 2018).

Will, Richard, *The Characteristic Symphony in the Age of Haydn and Beethoven*, (Cambridge: Cambridge University Press, 2002).

Wright, Joe (dir.), *The Soloist* [DVD] (Universal City, CA: DreamWorks Pictures, 2009).

General Index

Abercromby, Ralph, 195, 209
Abert, Hermann, 117
Adams, Louis, 108
Adorno, Theodor W., 154, 214, 249–50
Allegro con brio. *see* first movement
Ambros, August Wilhelm, 35
Amenda, Karl Friedrich, 56, 106
analysis, music, 110–12
André, Johann (publisher), 53
Aristotle, 19
arrangements, 58, 225–31, 236–7 *see also*
    transcriptions
Artaria & Co (publishers), 50, 51, 53
Artaria 153 sketchbook-miscellany, 63
audiences, demands on, 130–2, 183–4, 185–6,
    222–3
autograph score, reconstruction of, 65–7

Bach, Johann Sebastian
    Goldberg Variations, 164
    Jesus nahm zu sich die Zwölfe, BWV 22, *113*,
        123
BBC television film *Eroica*, 130, 235–6, 240–2
Beach Pillows (film), 242–3
Beethoven, Kaspar Karl van, 61–2, 69, 74, 161,
    162
Beethoven, Ludwig van
    correspondence with Amenda, 56, 106
    creative development, 35–40, 111–12, 130–4
    deafness, 81, 105, 251–2
    and Fate, 10, 111, 133
    Goethe's deference to nobility, dismay at, 13
    Heiligenstadt Testament, 13, 33–5, 105–6,
        117, 119, 120, 124, 134, 248
    as hero, 32–5, 193
    and Homer, 9, 10
    and Napoleon, 8, 68–9, 108–9, 187–9, 204,
        206, 217–18, 241–2
    and *ombra* style, 118–19
    his politics, 188–9, 206–7
    portrayal in BBC *Eroica* film, 235–6, 240–2
    resignation to suffering, 105–8, 130, 132–4
    Schiller's *Don Carlos* admiration for, 18
    symphony-writing context in Bonn and
        Vienna, 54–9
    Tagebuch, 111, 125, 133
    use of titles, 109
    on variations and their numbering, 161–3
    Wegeler, correspondence with, 56, 81, 106,
        132

Beethoven, Ludwig van (works)
    *Christus am Ölberge (Christ on the Mount of
        Olives)*, Op. 85, 56, 105–7, 111–12, 118,
        120, 132
    Contredanses, WoO 14, 158–60
    Die Geschöpfe des Prometheus (The Creatures
        of Prometheus), Op. 43, 30, 157–61, *159*,
        208–9, 248
    Egmont, Op. 84, 17–18, *73*, 155
    Fidelio, Op. 72, 10, 18–20
    Fünfzehn Variationen mit einer Fuge, Op. 35.
        see Variations and Fugue in E♭ major
    'German Dance', WoO 8 No. 3, 120
    Mass in C Major, Op. 86, 132
    Missa Solemnis, Op. 123, 132
    Piano Sonata in A♭ major, Op. 26, 190
    Piano Sonata in C major, Op. 53
        ('Waldstein'), 86–7, 97
    Piano Sonata in F minor, Op. 57
        ('Appassionata'), 86–7
    Piano Sonatas, Op. 14, 57
    Piano Variations, Op. 35. *see* Variations and
        Fugue in E♭ major
    String Quartets, Op. 59 ('Razumovsky'), 86–7
    String Quartet in F minor, Op. 95 ('Serioso'),
        130–1
    String Quartet in C♯ minor, Op. 131, 37
    String Quartet in F major, Op. 135, 36
    First Symphony, Op. 21, 53, 58, 74, 170,
        222–3, 230
    Second Symphony, Op. 36, 53, 58, 170, 230
    Third Symphony, Op. 55. *see Eroica*
        Symphony, Op. 55
    Fourth Symphony, Op. 60, 36, 37
    Fifth Symphony, Op. 67, 37, 38, 111, 230, 234
    Sixth Symphony, Op. 68 ('Pastoral'), 117
    Seventh Symphony, Op. 92, 53–4, 230
    Eighth Symphony, Op. 93, 36, 53–4, 74, 230
    Ninth Symphony, Op. 125, 37, 39, 57, 74, 154
    Variations and Fugue in E♭ major, Op. 35
        ('Eroica Variations'), 63, 143–4, 147, 157,
        160–6, *163*, *165*, *171*, 171
    Six Variations in F major, Op. 34, 161–4, 165
    Violin Sonata in A minor, Op. 47, 108
    Wellingtons Sieg, Op. 91, 56, 249
Bekker, Paul, 208–9, 211
Berger, Karol, 7
Berlioz, Hector, 190, 191–2, 204
Bernadotte, Jean-Baptiste, 188, 189
Berstein, Leonard, 234

Bertolini, Joseph, 194–5
Biba, Otto, 71, 75
Bismark, Otto von, 245–6
Bodmer, Johann, 8
Böhm, Karl, 234
Bonds, Mark Evan, 24, 25, 130–1
Bonn, 54–5, 118
Bottura, Massimo, 244–5
Brahms, Johannes, 211, 212–13
Braun, Baron Peter von, 48, 57
Brauneis, Walther, 194
Breitinger, Johann, 8
Breitkopf & Härtel, 62–3, 69, 74, 161–2
British reception of the *Eroica*, 195, 224–5
Broyles, Michael, 39
Bülow, Hans von, 246
Burckhardt, Jacob, 212
Burnham, Scott, 27–8, 110–11, 155, 240, 247

Cassirer, Fritz, 94
chamber ensembles, 44–5, 46, 52–4
chamber music concerts, 49
Chef's Table (television series), 244–5
Chop, Max, 217–18
Christ, as heroic model, 105–7, 128, 132
Chua, Daniel, 249–50
church music, 122–4, 128
Churgin, Bathia, 72, 75
Cianchettini & Sperati (publishers), 75, 186
Civilization IV (computer game), 245–6
coherence, musical, 29, 91–5, 97–103
composition process. *see* genesis of the *Eroica*
concert guides, 215–19
concerts
    private, 43–6, 54–5
    public, 46, 47–50, 55–6, 57–8
contredanse style, 157–61
Cooper, Barry, 164
copyists and copying, 50, 51, 68–74
court musicians, 43–6, 222, 223
cues (*Stichnoten*), 74
Czerny, Carl, 194–5, 231–2

d'Ortigue, Joseph, 190
Dahlhaus, Carl, 25–6
Darcy, Warren, 85, 116
death, theme of, 119–30, 155
dedication of the *Eroica*, 8, 34–5, 62, 68–9,
    108–9, 110, 187–9, 194, 204, 241–2
Del Mar, Jonathan, 67, 75
DeNora, Tia, 24
Dessauer, Joseph, 68
destiny. *see* Fate
disability studies, 250–3

Eberl, Anton, 27
Eggebrecht, Hans Heinrich, 35
Elterlein, Ernst von, 216

Epstein, David, 94–5
Erdödy, Countess Anna Marie, 130, 133
Eroica (BBC television film), 130, 235–6, 240–2
Eroica sketchbook. *see* Landsberg 6 sketchbook
Eroica Symphony, Op. 55.
    dedication of, 8, 34–5, 62, 68–9, 108–9, 110,
        187–9, 194, 204, 241–2
    overarching structure, 208–10, 214
    in popular culture, 235–6, 240–6
    popularity of, 222, 230, 237, 239–40
    publication of, 61–3, 74–5, 186–7
    use in soundtracks, 242–6, 252–3
    title of, 109, 186–9
    see also first movement; fourth movement;
        genesis of the *Eroica*; heroism;
        performance practice; reception; second
        movement; third movement; watershed
        work, *Eroica* as
ethical, music as, 28–30

failure, narrative of, 154–5
Fate, 10, 17, 111, 133
Fétis, François-Joseph, 38–9, 190–1
film and television soundtracks, 242–5, 252–3
Finale. *see* fourth movement
finance, symphonies and, 56–7, 58
first movement, 82–103, 139–43
    Berlioz on, 192
    as a blink in time, 250
    and *Christus am Ölberge*, 106–7, 112
    coda, 96–7, 141, 142, 143, 243–4, 247–8
    development section 'new theme', 86–9
    horn, 'early' entrance of, 89–90, 217, 240,
        250
    introductory chords, 95–6, 110–11, 241, 244,
        246
    length of, 81
    le-sol-fi-sol idiom, 112–19, *113*
    musical form as process, 26
    and the Op. 35 variations, 166
    opening bars, 110–11, 112–20, *113*, 139–40,
        141, 142–3, 247, 248, 249–50, 251
    overall structure, 97–103
    pastoral features, 119–20, 247–8
    Radecke on, 218
    recapitulation, 89–91, 140, 141–2
    register, 139–43
    repeat signs, 69
    repetition of bars 150–51, 75
    second subject, 82–6
    as soundtrack for films, etc., 244, 245
    thematic development and relationships,
        91–5
First World War, 201–2
Fischer, Adam, 215
Foucault, Michel, 33
fourth movement, 81, *124*, 124–30, *127*, *146*,
    150, *151*, 157–77, *173*, *175*

fourth movement (cont.)
  Die Geschöpfe des Prometheus, 157–61, 208–9
  joy through suffering, 124–30
  movement plan in Landsberg 6 sketchbook,
    166–71, *167*
  Mozart's *Le Nozze di Figaro*, 30
  orchestral parts, 71
  register, 143–55
  significance of, 208–10, 218, 246
  variations, 171–7
  and the Variations in E♭ major, Op. 35,
    161–6, 175
freedom, 207, 209, 215, 249–50
French reception of the *Eroica*, 190–3
French Revolution, 7–8, 28–9, 30–1, 39,
  44, 211
French Revolutionary Wars, 55
funeral marches, 27, 190 *see also* second
  movement
Furtwängler, Wilhelm, 99, 234

Gardiner, Sir John Eliot, 235
Gebauer, Benjamin, 68, 69, 72
genesis of the *Eroica*, 61–75
  autograph score, 65–7
  copying the full score, 68–9
  earliest evidence, 61–2
  first printed edition, 74–5
  orchestral parts, 71–5
  sketches and folded leaves, 63–6, 82, 88–9,
    158, 166–71, *167*, 251–2
German *Klassik* dramas, 15–18
Gjerdingen, Robert, 123
Goepp, Philip H., 198–9, 205
Goethe, Johann Wolfgang von, 8–9, 10, 11–13,
  17–18
Gosman, Alan, 64, 89
Gottsched, Johann Christoph, 11–12
Greek classical literature, 7, 8–10, 19–20, 191,
  192, 204
Grey's Anatomy (television series), 244
Griesinger, Georg August, 48

Habeneck, François-Antoine, 190
Halm, August, 88
Harmonie ensembles, 44–5
Haselböck, Martin, 234, 235
Hatten, Robert, 111–12, 121
Haydn, Joseph, 26–7, 28, 29–30, 31, 46, 84–5, 86,
  92–3, 164
  'London' Symphonies, 46
  Mass in B♭ major, Hob. XXII:12
    ('Theresienmesse'), 128, *129*
  Mass in B♭ major, Hob. XXII:14
    ('Harmoniemesse'), 128
  'Paris' Symphonies, 46
  String Quartet in B minor, Op. 33, No. 1,
    Hob. III:37, 27, 162

String Quartet in D major, Op. 50, No. 6,
  Hob. III:49 ('The Frog'), *113*
Symphony No. 45 in F♯ minor, Hob. I:45
  ('Farewell'), 26
Symphony No. 101 in D major, hob. I:101
  ('The Clock'), *113*
The Creation, Hob. XXI:2, 29–30, 248
Heiligenstadt Testament, 13, 33–5, 105–6, 117,
  119, 120, 124, 134, 248
Hepokoski, James, 85, 116
heroic style, 27–8, 30–2, 34–5, 39, 97, 155, 216
heroism, 7–21
  Beethoven as the hero, 32–5, 193
  desire for a hero, 202–3, 206
  and the *Eroica*, 21, 34–5, 105–12, 202–7,
    208–9, 218–19, 240–2, 244–5
  in German *Klassik* dramas, 15–18
  in Greek classical literature, 7, 8–10, 19–20,
    191, 192, 204
  heroines, 18–20
  identifying the hero, 186–9, 191–6
  resignation as heroic practice, 105–8, 111–12,
    120–4, 130, 132–4
  in *Sturm und Drang* dramas, 10–15 *see also*
    heroic style
Hevesi, Ludwig, 200, 201, 211
Hinderer, Walter, 14
historically informed performance, 234–5
history, art and the progress of, 210–14
Hoffmann, Ernst Theodor Amadeus, 37
Hoffmeister, Franz Anton (publisher), 51
Homer, 8–10, 19, 192, 204
Hummel, Johann Nepomuk, 227–30, *228*
Hyer, Brian, 155

instrumental parts, 71–5

Jahn, Otto, 194
Joan of Arc, as heroic model, 20
Johnson, Peter, 234
Jones, David Wyn, 58
Joseph II, Emperor, 43, 44

Kapellen, 43–4, 54–5
Kennedy, John F., 233
Kerman, Joseph, 24, 26, 28, 97
Knittel, K. M., 32–3, 36
Koch, Heinrich Christoph, 116
Kretzschmar, Hermann, 217
Kreutzer, Rodolphe, 108
Kuffner, Christoph, 111
Kunst- und Industrie-Comptoir (publishers),
  58, 75

Landsberg 6 sketchbook, 64–5, 82, 166–71, *167*,
  251–2
Landsberg 7 sketchbook, 63, 158
Langhans, Wilhelm, 217

Lausch, Lorenz, 45, 51, 52
Lawson, Colin, 139
Leipzig, 109, 184, 224, 225–6
Lenz, Wilhelm von, 38
le–sol–fi–sol schema-topic, 112–19, 120, 121,
    123, 128, 129
Lessing, Gotthold, 8
Lichnowsky, Prince, 57–8
Liechtenstein, Prince Alois, 44
Listenius, Nicolaus, 164
Liszt, Franz, 37, 231, 232
Lobkowitz, Prince Franz Joseph Maximilian
    von, 45–6, 49, 62, 68, 188, 189, 194, 222
Lockwood, Lewis, 21, 66, 89, 157, 166, 168, 169
London, 46
Louis Ferdinand, Prince of Prussia, 193–4

Marcia Funebre. *see* second movement
Maria Theresa, Empress, 158
Martin, Philipp Jakob, 48
Marx, Adolf Bernhard, 37, 204
Mathew, Nicholas, 30–1, 248–9
Matthews, W. S. B., 117–18
Maximilian Franz, Elector of Cologne, 54–5
McClelland, Clive, 117
Mendelssohn, Felix, 233
metronome markings, 210, 215, 233–4
Meyer, Leonard, 125–6
Michaelis, Christian Friedrich, 31–2
Mirka, Danuta, 117
Mission Impossible – Rogue Nation (film), 243–4
money, symphonies and, 56–7, 58
Morris, Edmund, 246
Moscheles, Ignaz, 134
Mozart, Leopold, 169
Mozart, Wolfgang Amadeus, 31, 47–8, 84–5, 86,
    93, 164
    Bastien und Bastienne, K. 50, 119
    Die Zauberflöte, K. 620, 29
    Don Giovanni, K. 527, 118
    Grabmusik, K. 42, *113*, 118
    Le Nozze di Figaro, K. 492, 30, 158
    Mass in C major, K. 317 ('Coronation'), 128
    Mass in C minor, K. 139, *113*
    Requiem in D minor, K. 626, *113*, 118
    Symphony No. 41 in C K. 551 ('Jupiter'), 27
Müller, August Eberhard, 225–6
Munich Olympics terrorist attack, 233
music analysis, 110–12
music dealers, 45, 51–2
music publishing, 50–4, 58, 61–3, 74–5, 186–7,
    253 *see also* Breitkopf & Härtel,
musicians. *see* court musicians

Napoleon Bonaparte, 8, 34–5, 68–9, 109, 110,
    187–9, 193, 203, 205, 206–7, 217–18,
    241–2, 245–6
Nelson, Horatio, 1st Viscount Nelson, 194

Nettl, Bruno, 32
Norrington, Roger, 234
Nottebohm, Gustav, 88–9
November, Nancy, 40

Obvious Child (film), 243
ombra style, 117–19, 121, 123–4, 126–30
opus, defining an, 161–4
orchestral parts, 71–5
orchestral scores, 74
orchestras, 43–5, 222, 223, 224, 234–5, 240
Ovid, 169

Paris, 46
pastoral style, 117, 119–20, 123–4, 129, 247–8
performance practice, 221–37
    arrangements, 225–31
    premiere and early perfomances, 222–5
    reception changes, influence of, 196
    transcriptions and reinterpretations, 231–2
    twentieth- and twenty-first-century, 214–15,
        233–7, 239–53
Pergolesi, Giovanni Battista, 123
Pestelli, Giorgio, 39–40
philosophy, music as, 130–4
Plutarch, 132
political context, 194–5, 202–3, 204–7, 211, 215,
    218, 248–9
popular culture, *Eroica* in, 1, 235–6, 240–6
popularity of the *Eroica*, 222, 230, 237, 239–40
presence, sense of, 27–8
private concerts, 43–6, 54–5
programmatic interpretation, 109–11
programming of symphonies, 43–6, 50, 225
Prometheus, 12–13, 33–4, 125, 126, 209
public concerts, 46, 47–50, 55–6, 57–8
publication of the *Eroica*, 61–3, 74–5, 186–7
publishers and publishing, 50–4, 58, 61–3, 74–5,
    186–7 *see also* Breitkopf & Härtel
Puffett, Derrick, 144–5

Radecke, Ernst, 218–19
Ratner, Leonard, 117
rebirth, theme of, 124–30
reception of the *Eroica*, 183–96
    in Britain, 195, 224–5
    challenging nature of the *Eroica*, 185–6,
        222–5
    disability studies, 250–3
    early reviews, 183–6, 222–5
    in France, 190–3, 205
    history, relation to, 210–14
    identifying the hero, 193–6
    nineteenth-century, 198–214, 232
    programmatic interpretation, 108–10
    reclaiming the idealism of the *Eroica*, 207–10
    twentieth-century, 214–19
    twenty-first-century, 239–53

register
  first movement, 139–43
  fourth movement, 143–55
  in transcriptions and arrangements, 229, 232
Reicha, Anton, 162, 169
resignation, as heroic practice, 105–8, 111–12,
    120–4, 130, 132–4
resurrection, theme of, 124–30
reviews, 36–7, 109, 124–5, 130, 158, 160–1, 176,
    183–6, 187, 190–1, 221, 222–6, 227, 230–1
revolution, 240–2, 244–5
Reynolds, Christopher, 164
rhythmic features, 212, 218, 230
Rice, John A., 158
Ries, Ferdinand, 62, 68–9, 71, 72, 89–90, 108,
    187–8, 189, 227–9, *228*
Riezler, Walter, 84–5, 88, 93–4, 95, 103
Rochlitz, Friedrich, 112–13, *113*, 116, 123, 125,
    127, 131
Roosevelt, Franklin D., 233
Rosati, Gianpiero, 169
Rumph, Stephen, 40, 116–17, 120, 124, 125, 126,
    248

Savall, Jordi, 235
Schenker, Heinrich, 85–6, 88, 92, 95, 98–103,
    140–3, 144–7, 148, 149, 151, 154
Schenker, Jeanette, 99
Scherzo. *see* third movement
Schiller, Friedrich von, 9, 10, 11, 13–17, 20, 112
Schindler, Anton, 188–9
Schlemmer, Wenzel, 72
Schlesinger (publisher), 218
Schleuning, Peter, 123
Schlosser, Johann Aloys, 38
Schoenberg, Arnold, 206
Schönfeld, Johann Ferdinand von, 43–4
Schuppanzigh, Ignaz, 49
scores. *see* genesis of the *Eroica*; Vienna score
    copy
second movement
  allusions in the finale, 125, 126–8, 129
  analysis, 120–4, 184
  Berlioz on, 190–1
  and death of the hero, 109, 120–4, *121*, 190–1
  as 'heart' of the work, 190–1, 231
  performance at times of mourning, 208, 233
  in quartet arrangements, 227–30, *228*
  Radecke on, 218
  reception, 184, 187, 190–1, 218
  referenced in Strauss's *Metamorphosen*,
    213–14
  as soundtrack, 245–6
  and the Wielhorsky sketchbook, 63
Segantini, Giovanni, 199–201, 209–10, 212, 213
Selfridge-Field, Eleanor, 20
self-sacrifice, 10, 15–17, 123
Shakespeare, William, 8, 10–11, 13

sheet music, 50–4, 58
Simrock, Fritz (publisher), 62, 75
Sinfonia pastorella, 43
Sipe, Thomas, 64, 109
sketchbooks, 61, 63–6, 166–71
  Artaria 153 sketchbook-miscellany, 63
  Landsberg 6 (*Eroica* sketchbook), 61, 64–5,
    82, 88–9, *167*, 251–2
  Landsberg 7, 63, 158
  Wielhorsky, 105, 124
The Soloist (film), 252–3
Solomon, Maynard, 28–9, 34–5, 36, 81, 108, 119
sonata form, 82–6
soundtracks, *Eroica* used in, 242–6, 252–3
Steblin, Rita, 109
Stein, Erwin, 210
S. A. Steiner & Comp. (publishers), 54
Stichnoten (cues), 74
Straus, Joseph, 250–1
Strauss, Richard, 213–14
Sturm und Drang ('Storm and Stress'), 10–15
Sturm, Christoph Christian, 132–3
subscription series concerts, 48–9
Sullivan, J. W. N., 33–4, 108, 130, 134
Sulzer, Johann Georg, 123, 169
Swafford, Jan, 24
Syer, Katherine R., 64
symphonic ideal, 26–7, 28
symphonies, 43–59
  as heroic genre, 31–2
  performance contexts, 43–6, 50
  as sheet music, 50–4, 58

Tan Dun, 242
television film *Eroica*, 130, 235–6, 240–2
television soundtracks, 244–5
tempo markings, 210, 215, 233–4
Thayer, Alexander, 133
theatres, as concert venues, 47, 48, 57–8
theatrical influences, 40
thematic development, 27–8, 91–5
themes, thematic material, 25–6, 31
third movement, 63, 69, 72–4, 81, 123–4, 192,
    212, 242–3
Thomas à Kempis, 132
Thompson, George (publisher), 63
time, first movement as a blink in, 250
title page, 68–9, 188, 189, 206, 241–2
title *Sinfonia eroica*, 109, 186–9
Tommasini, Anthony, 242
topic theory, 117–19, 121–2
Toscanini, Arturo, 210, 233
Tovey, Donald, 83–4, 92, 98, 210
Traeg, Johann, 45, 51–2, 53
transcriptions, 52–4, 231–2 *see also*
    arrangements
triumph over adversity, 32–5, 244–5, 250–3 *see
    also* resignation as heroic practice

Tusa, M. C., 72–4
Tyson, Alan, 71, 72

Valetta, Ippolito, 191
variations, numbering of, 161–6, 176–7
Vienna
    Beethoven in, 54–9
    concert life, 47–50, 55–6
    Die Geschöpfe des Prometheus premiere,
        157–60
    music publishing, 50–4, 58
    professional musical life, 43–6, 222
Vienna score copy, 68–9, 74
Viganò, Salvatore, 157–8
Virgil, 19, 191, 204
Vocke, Theodora Johanna, 18
Voss, Johann Heinrich, 9–10

Wagner, Richard, 21, 27, 37, 38–9, 193, 204–7,
        211, 212–13, 216, 217, 232
Wallace, Robin, 251–2
watershed work, *Eroica* as, 24–40, 81–2
    in Beethoven's career, 32–5, 81
    in Beethoven's creative development, 35–40
    in musical development, 25–32, 81–2, 236,
        237, 240–2

Weber, Carl Maria von, 185
Weber, William, 221–2
Webern, Anton von, 199–201, 209–10, 211, 212,
        214
Webster, James, 26–7, 28, 29, 37
Wegeler, Franz G., 56, 71, 81, 106, 132,
        187
Weingartner, Felix, 202–3, 210,
        211
Weisse, Hans, 99
Werner, Zacharias, *Die Söhne des Thales*
        (The Sons of the Valley), 111, 125
Wielhorsky sketchbook, 63, 105, 124
Will, Richard, 247–8
William Weber, 225
Wilson, John David, 31
Winn, James, 7
work, as both labour and result,
        163–4
Wranitzky, Paul, 27
Wright, Joe, 252–3
writing process. *see* genesis of the *Eroica*
Würth, Joseph, 45, 223

Zedler, Johann Heinrich, 164
Zinman, David, 234